The Founders and the Classics

The Founders and the Classics

GREECE, ROME, AND THE
AMERICAN ENLIGHTENMENT

Carl J. Richard

Harvard University Press
Cambridge, Massachusetts
London, England

SECOND PRINTING, 1994

This book is printed on acid-free paper, and its binding materials
have been chosen for strength and durability.

Library of Congress Cataloging-in-Publication Data

Richard, Carl J.
The founders and the classics : Greece, Rome, and the American
enlightenment / Carl J. Richard.
p. cm.
Includes bibliographical references (p.   ) and index.
ISBN 0–674–31425–5 (acid-free paper)
1. Politial science—United States—History—18th century.
2. Political science—Greece—History. 3. Political science—Rome—
History. I. Title.
JA84.U5R48   1994
320—dc20
93–28468
CIP

For my parents, to whom I owe everything

Preface

In this work the "founders" are defined as prominent late eighteenth- and early nineteenth-century American leaders, excluding loyalists. By such a definition the term includes Antifederalist leaders. The "classics" are defined as Greek and Roman writings (both in their original languages and in translation) and art, excluding Christian artifacts. The classical tradition and the Christian heritage are treated as distinct, though overlapping, legacies which the founders interwove to form a unique cosmology.

No accomplishment of any worth is ever made by a single person alone. In the words of the Greek maxim, "One man is no man." I must begin by thanking Richard Cusimano, my undergraduate Greek teacher. Although I subsequently specialized in American intellectual history, the classics became my favorite pastime. Richard M. Gummere, Meyer Reinhold, and the other pioneering scholars of the classical influence lighted my path. Without them, I would have stumbled in the darkness. Samuel T. McSeveney and Joyce Chaplin reviewed an early draft of this book. Jack P. Greene and Meyer Reinhold critiqued a paper, extracted from the work, concerning the classics and the U.S. Constitution. Forrest McDonald, Jennifer Tolbert Roberts, and James Broussard commented insightfully on a paper containing my principal conclusions. Lance Banning, James H. Dormon, and Jim Williams contributed helpful advice during the later stages of this work. Thomas McGinn was frequently willing to drop his own work in order to substantially improve mine. Ann Hawthorne contributed her considerable editorial skills to the book's improvement. Ramona Abshire provided valuable aid in proofreading. Carl Brasseaux's computer assistance proved essential. I thank the *Journal of the Early Republic* for permission to use the substance of a

1989 article, "A Dialogue with the Ancients: Thomas Jefferson and Classical Philosophy and History," in Chapter VI and throughout this volume.

I owe the greatest debt of gratitude to my Vanderbilt mentors in American intellectual history and the classics, Paul K. Conkin and Susan Ford Wiltshire, who embody all that is good in their respective disciplines. It was incredible good fortune (the Fates?) which brought me to their tutelage. They have given me what the founders valued most in the classics, models of excellence.

Contents

The Founders and the Classics

Introduction

It is a surprising fact that this is the first book-length study of the founders' classical reading. Although historians of the founders have often alluded to the influence of "classical republicanism," they have seldom focused much attention upon individual ancients and their relationship to the founders' thought. Carl Becker's "Jeremiah Wynkoop," his composite of the Revolutionary American, exulted in the classics. Merle Curti described the classics as both "a practical tool and a badge of gentility," providing the founders with "lessons of patriotism and statesmanship, models of pure taste in writing, and personal solace and inspiration." C. Dewitt Hardy and Richard Hofstadter noted the privileged position of the classics in eighteenth-century education. Howard Mumford Jones considered the classics a formative influence on American culture. Henry Steele Commager credited the classics with helping Revolutionary Virginia produce George Washington, Thomas Jefferson, James Madison, George Mason, George Wythe, John Marshall, and other great men. Commager claimed: "Intellectually, the founding fathers knew the ancient world better perhaps than they knew the European or even the British world, better, in all likelihood, than they knew the American outside their own section." Yet despite their enthusiasm for the idea of classical influence, these historians provided little detail concerning its origin and nature. Other historians addressed some of these questions in pioneering articles and essays, many of which were thoughtful, provocative, and original. But, however elegant and essential, these works remained isolated pieces of a larger puzzle, scattered strands capable of being woven into a larger fabric.[1]

Only Clinton Rossiter and Bernard Bailyn dissented from the view that the classics had exerted a formative influence upon the founders. In

Seedtime of the Republic (1953) Rossiter argued: "Most authors used the ancient Greeks for window dressing . . . The Americans would have believed just as vigorously in public morality had Cato and the Gracchi never lived." In the pathbreaking *Ideological Origins of the American Revolution* (1967) Bailyn agreed that eighteenth-century American leaders had used the classics as mere "window dressing." He concluded that the classics were "illustrative, not determinative, of thought." Bailyn cited Charles F. Mullett for the term "window dressing," neglecting to note that Mullett had applied it only to a few isolated instances. Mullett had emphasized the numerous cases in which the classics had exerted real influence.[2]

While the source of Rossiter's judgment is obscure, Bailyn's conclusion can be traced to two faulty assumptions. One was that the founders were entirely dependent upon seventeenth- and early eighteenth-century British Whigs for their interpretation of ancient history, because their own classical learning was "superficial." But there is abounding evidence that Thomas Jefferson, John Adams, James Madison, James Wilson, John Dickinson, Patrick Henry, and numerous other founders read and interpreted classical works for themselves. Second, Bailyn assumed that the Whig interpretation of ancient history was entirely their own creation. But in fact this interpretation was largely (though not entirely) the creation of Greek and Roman historians, nostalgic aristocrats disgruntled by monarchical and democratic encroachments upon the power of their class. Fixtures in the classical canon which had dominated the western world since the Middle Ages, these classical historians were virtually the sole source of knowledge concerning ancient history available in the eighteenth century. Although Bailyn was correct to recognize the founders' intellectual debt to the Whigs, who had influenced American perceptions of classical thought through the emphasis of certain themes and the transformation of others, he failed to recognize the Whigs' vast intellectual debt to the ancients. The founders knew well the fountainhead where the Whigs drew their water, having spent most of their childhood filling their own buckets there. But, constrained by the presupposition that the founders could approach the ancients only through the Whigs, Bailyn had no reason to examine the founders' classical reading. The thoroughness and originality which characterized his treatment of the British Whig tradition were absent from his analysis of the role of the classics in the founders' intellectual lives.

Gordon S. Wood and Joyce O. Appleby have since established a new paradigm, which has restored the significance of classical influence to the Revolutionary era. But Wood and Appleby add that the early national period witnessed a shift from "classical republicanism," which emphasized civic duty and social cohesion, to "liberalism" (or "modern republicanism"), which stressed individual rights and the self-regulating marketplace. In *The Creation of the American Republic* (1969) Wood claims that Revolutionary classicism "was not only a scholarly ornament of educated Americans; it helped to shape their values and their ideals of behavior." But in the same work Wood concludes that the ratification of the Constitution marked the "end of classical politics." Similarly, in *Capitalism and a New Social Order* (1984) and *Liberalism and Republicanism in the Historical Imagination* (1992), Appleby argues that American ideology during the Revolutionary and Constitutional eras combined classical and liberal elements. During the early national period, however, the economic opportunities which the Napoleonic Wars afforded American farmers provided the material basis for the triumph of liberalism. The tremendous demand for grain in war-torn Europe lured American farmers even farther into the marketplace, prompting a new confidence in the ability of nature to regulate human behavior without government interference. Jeffersonian Republicans were not romantics, wedded to the pastoral tradition, but rationalists, confident of progress through individual effort. They looked forward, not backward. Appleby writes concerning this shift from classical republicanism to liberalism: "Necessity was the mother of this intellectual invention in part because classical republicanism offered only a language for lamenting, as opposed to understanding, commerce." Again, these historians' scant treatment of the founders' classical reading contrasts sharply with the boldness of their statements concerning classical republicanism and with the true brilliance with which both deal with other matters.[3]

Not until classicists entered the field, contributing provocative articles and essay collections, was there any attempt at a comprehensive analysis of the founders' classical reading. The most thorough of these works is Meyer Reinhold's *Classica Americana* (1984), a survey of the classical tradition throughout American history. Reinhold's chapters on the eighteenth century represent the best attempt yet at an exploration of the founders' relationship with the classics. Yet even he is too inclined to accept the new paradigm. He contrasts the Revolutionary and Constitutional eras, which he terms the "golden age" of the classics in America, with the early national period, which he dubs the "silver age." Reinhold concludes: "Belief in a morally better society after the classical pattern, which had no deep roots in America, began to wither rapidly after 1789. The classical models and classical political theory had served useful purposes in the crisis of the independence movement and the forging of the Constitution. They were now to be jettisoned. The retreat from antiquity and disenchantment with the ancient guidelines were in full swing in the early national period. The ancient world was losing its bloom as an absolute standard for testing modern political innovations." Reinhold's only evidence for this conclusion consists of some reformers' unsuccessful efforts to remove the Greek and Latin requirements from the schools and a few ambiguous statements made by Thomas Jefferson. Oddly, much of Reinhold's own research concerning the continued vibrancy of the classics during the early national period refutes his conclusion. It is conceivable that Reinhold, who is acutely aware of some American historians' skepticism concerning the classical influence, has overreacted against the tendency of his predecessor, classicist Richard M. Gummere, to overemphasize such influences. Though justly acclaimed for its pioneering efforts, Gummere's collection of essays, *The American Colonial Mind and the Classical Tradition* (1963), had tended to ascribe direct influence to every classical allusion. While expressing admiration for Gummere's contributions, Reinhold adds that Gummere went too far. But, in my opinion, Reinhold's determination to avoid overstating classical influence has led him to understate it.[4]

J. G. A. Pocock, Lance Banning, and Drew R. McCoy have led an assault against the new paradigm, extending classical republicanism into the early national period. In *The Machiavellian Moment* (1975) Pocock reasserts the primacy of classical republican ideology in the founders' intellectual lives. The founders derived their political thought from the British Whigs, who had inherited it from the Florentines. Indeed, in an article published three years earlier, Pocock had characterized the American Revolution less as the first great act of liberalism than as "the last great act of the Renaissance." In the same article he had drawn a parallel between the "Country-Court" struggles of seventeenth-century Britain, which had pitted the classically oriented Whig opposition against the supporters of the monarchy, and the Republican-Federalist disputes of the 1790s. In *The Jeffersonian Persuasion* (1978) Banning makes even greater efforts to demonstrate the influence of classical republicanism on the polemics of the 1790s. Banning believes that classical politics continued until the end of the First Party System in 1815. In *The Elusive Repub-*

lic (1980) McCoy ascribes Thomas Jefferson's determination to expand the nation to classical pastoralism, which maintained that only an agricultural lifestyle could produce the virtue necessary to societal happiness. By forestalling landlessness among an exploding population, Jefferson believed, geographical expansion could prevent the otherwise inevitable degeneration and corruption of society predicted by classical texts. But like Bailyn, these historians continue to subordinate direct classical influence to that of the Whig mediators. Consequently, they devote as little attention to the founders' classical reading as their predecessors.[5]

The strict dichotomy between classical republicanism and liberalism which has dominated Revolutionary and early republican historiography for the past generation undervalues the complexity of the relationship between the two intellectual constructs, underestimates the human propensity for inconsistency, and ignores the contribution of Christianity to the founders' thought. Although classical republicanism and liberalism are two distinct constructs, the former ideology provided the latter's intellectual foundation. The Stoic theory of natural law and the optimistic view of human nature from which it derived gave birth to the modern doctrines of natural rights and social progress which undergird liberalism. Bolstered by the Scientific and Commercial Revolutions, modern republicans drew radical social implications from the theory of natural law— implications which would have astounded the theory's creators. Furthermore, the classical pastoral tradition was partially responsible for the growth of that laissez-faire economics which so distinguished liberalism from classical republicanism. Economists like the French Physiocrats and Adam Smith sought free trade partly as a means of neutralizing mercantilist threats to an agricultural lifestyle to which they were emotionally attached. However rational their arguments concerning the greater productivity of agriculture, laissez-faire economists often exhibited a strong devotion to classical authors who preached that agriculture was essential to the creation of societal virtue. In addition, since one of the chief elements of "classical virtue" was an independent cast of mind, it sometimes served as the inspiration for anticlassical ideas. The founders knew that intellectual independence had been a defining characteristic of their Greek and Roman heroes, who had formulated the revolutionary theories of popular sovereignty, natural law, and mixed government and had defended them against the rampant absolutism of the ancient world. Ironically, emulating the intellectual independence of such heroes sometimes involved rejecting their theories for more liberal doctrines. Classical republicanism was, in many ways, the parent of liberalism. The birth of liberalism was messy, painful, and debilitating to the parent. Liberalism has since reached a hardy old age and seems destined to outlive even its own prodigal son, Marxism. Whether it will serve as parent to yet another ideology remains to be seen.

The neat dichotomy between classical republicanism and liberalism also masks the notorious inconsistency of humans, who have always proven quite capable of holding contradictory views simultaneously. The founders wandered the unmarked borderlands between classical republicanism and liberalism, scavenging for building materials. The specific materials selected on each foray depended upon the nature of the problem at hand and upon the mood of the scavenger, which helped determine the scavenger's perception of the nature of the problem. While humans are attracted to intellectual systems, because they bring meaning to the puzzling complexity of the world, static concepts cannot reflect their many moods. Hence, even the wariest and most systematic philosophers will occasionally be captured off the grounds of their favorite systems. This principle holds especially true for educated laymen, like the founders, whose knowledge gave them the building materials for many different intellectual constructs, but who were not as obedient to the rules of geometric construction as formal philosophers.

The founders' susceptibility to inconsistency was further enhanced by the tremendous turmoil their generation experienced. During their lifetime, American society was transformed by the effects of the Scientific Revolution, the Enlightenment, the Financial Revolution, the Commercial Revolution, the two Great Awakenings, the American Revolution, the spate of state and federal constitutions, the Industrial Revolution, and the transition to representative democracy. Since the concepts embodied in each of the founders' ideologies were necessarily abstract and static, like those of all cosmologies, none could explain a world in rapid transition to the complete satisfaction of these multifaceted individuals. Hence, the intellectual scavenging endemic to humans reached a fever pitch in the founders' age. Historians distort the past when they dismiss either the founders' classical republican dicta or their liberal pronouncements, which may be cited in equal abundance, for the sake of maintaining inviolate categories. Categories are important tools for reducing the vast and varied totality of experience to some meaning, but since they do so by eliminating contradictory information, they should not be considered a photograph of reality. To insist that the founders were always hopeful or always fearful, that they were always rational or always romantic, that they always looked forward or always backward— or to deny the significance of one or the other of these moods and tendencies and its corresponding ideology—is unrealistic.

Finally, the classical republican–liberal dichotomy ignores the contribution of Christianity to the founders' thought. Although many of the founders held unorthodox religious views, they sometimes interpreted classical virtue in a Christian light. They also retained purely Christian beliefs in positive benevolence and the afterlife.

Indeed, historians of the founders are beginning to demonstrate a greater appreciation for the complexity of their thought. As early as 1986 Lance Banning concluded: "It should be evident that Appleby and her opponents have all grasped portions of important truths, that all have been incautious, and that insights from both camps must be combined for further progress. As things now stand, the literature appears to force a choice between mutually exclusive interpretations of Jeffersonian ideology—a choice we do not really have to make, and one that would impede a better understanding." Similarly, in *New Order of the Ages* (1988) Michael Lienesch contends: "The truth lies somewhere in between. That is, in the late eighteenth century, American political thought was in transition, moving from classical republicanism to modern liberalism. Yet the transition was inconclusive, neither clear nor complete, and the result was a hybrid mixture that combined republican and liberal themes in a creative but uneasy collaboration." While Gordon Wood continues to emphasize the emergence of liberalism in post-Revolutionary American society in *The Radicalism of the American Revolution* (1992), he also demonstrates the persistence of classical republican values, particularly among the founders' generation and aristocratic class. Likewise, while Paul A. Rahe's magisterial *Republics, Ancient and Modern* (1992) stresses the liberal character of the founders' thought, he recognizes the classical elements in their ideology as well: "Where American historians debate whether the regime produced by the American Revolution was republican or liberal, ancient or modern, or simply confused, I argue that it was a deliberately contrived mixture of sorts—liberal and modern, first of all, but in its insistence that to vindicate human dignity one must demonstrate man's capacity for self-government, republican and classical as well."[6]

It is my contention that the classics exerted a formative influence upon the founders, both directly and through the mediation of Whig and

American perspectives. The classics supplied mixed government theory, the principal basis for the U.S. Constitution. The classics contributed a great deal to the founders' conception of human nature, their understanding of the nature and purpose of virtue, and their appreciation of society's essential role in its production. The classics offered the founders companionship and solace, emotional resources necessary for coping with the deaths and disasters so common in their era. The classics provided the founders with a sense of identity and purpose, assuring them that their exertions were part of a grand universal scheme. The struggles of the Revolutionary and Constitutional periods gave the founders a sense of kinship with the ancients, a thrill of excitement at the opportunity to match their classical heroes' struggles against tyranny and their sage construction of durable republics.

In short, the classics supplied a large portion of the founders' intellectual tools. It is true that, when confronted with unprecedented dilemmas, the founders hammered the old tools into a variety of new shapes, often without fully appreciating the extent of their modifications. But just as minds constantly reshape intellectual tools, such tools leave an indelible imprint upon the minds accustomed to using them. The founders' very interpretations of the new dilemmas they faced were often quintessentially classical. Steeped in a literature whose perpetual theme was the steady encroachment of tyranny upon liberty, they became virtually obsessed with spotting the early warning signs of impending tyranny, so that they might avoid the fate of their classical heroes. They learned from the political horror stories of the ancient historians that liberty was as precarious as it was precious—precarious because cunning individuals were constantly conspiring against it, precious because virtue could not survive its demise. Tyranny was the worst fate not so much because it deprived one of liberty, as because it deprived one of virtue. The corrupting effects of living in tyranny—the dehumanizing sycophancy and the degrading collaboration necessary to avoid the tyrant's bad graces—were more abhorrent and disgusting than the oppression itself. While the obsessive fear of conspiracies which the founders derived from the classics served them well in the struggle against George III, it poisoned their postwar relations with one another. The theory that there were always talented and ambitious people plotting against liberty was an intellectual tool that could cut both ways.

The founders' thought never lost the imprint of their classical tools. Indeed, most never stopped reading the classics, relishing the gift of time granted by retirement to reacquaint themselves with their ancient friends. Far from presaging an end to classical republicanism, the very obsolescence of certain tools, like mixed government theory, required a return to the tool kit. While Federalists remained attached to mixed government, Republicans reached for the equally worn and revered tool of classical pastoralism. Republicans comforted themselves with the idea that the United States could safely adopt a democracy, however vilified by classical political theorists, since the abundance of land allowed for a citizenry of Virgilian farmers. The fact that the ideals of mixed government and classical pastoralism were myths which had originated in the prejudices of ancient aristocrats was lost on the founders. Whatever their origin, these ideals had taken on a life of their own. The existence of one classical tool made possible the relinquishment of another. Old myths became the essential catalysts for the production of new realities. People will rarely brave the cold uncertainty of new realities without the warm comfort of old myths.

It is true that the founders used "classical tools" of a more modern origin as well. But they did not segregate their Greco-Roman, Whig, and colonial American tools in separately marked boxes, as modern historians are inclined to do. In viewing these traditions as one, the "tradition of liberty," the founders were partly correct. The classics had provided the British Whigs with most of their ideas and many of their supporting examples. Even the Whig concept of natural rights, which served as the principal bridge between classical republicanism and modern liberalism, was not entirely unknown to, though rarely pursued by, the ancients themselves. Although the Greeks and Romans had emphasized civic duties over individual rights, they had also acknowledged the right of society to be free from arbitrary government, an idea revolutionary for its day and fraught with (then unpursued) implications for the individual. The founders viewed the American experience (including their own experiences) through the same classically based prism. Free from the stain of feudalism and possessed of abundant land, American society was uniquely capable of translating classical ideals into reality. The ancients, the Whigs, and the founders were bound together by the strong fibers of a common tradition, though each clung to a different strand of it.

The principal means by which the classical heritage was transmitted from one generation to the next was the educational system, a standardized system which had originated in the Middle Ages. The classical canon established in the schools remained virtually unchanged from era to era and nation to nation throughout the western world. Standardization possessed two advantages. First, it provided a stable basis for awarding status. Classical knowledge, including a facility with classical symbols, was a badge denoting class, taste, wisdom, and virtue. Ironically, as American wealth and social mobility increased, the aristocratic classics became a means by which the rising middle class could acquire social status. By appropriating what had previously been purely aristocratic symbols, middle-class figures like John Adams gained social acceptance, and through it, political power. In the process, however, the middle class imbibed the aristocratic fears of democracy common in classical texts, as well as the religious rationalism of the classical philosophers. The canon's ancient lineage inhibited the founders' critical instincts. They accepted the accuracy of these select sources as an article of faith and remained largely oblivious to the literature's aristocratic and other biases. The existence of a canon also discouraged the publication of classical works outside the canon, making it difficult for the founders to escape its confines. Since modern archaeology was still in its infancy, there was no source of information regarding the ancient world other than these meager volumes and a few modern histories similarly lacking in skepticism. Yet the founders possessed a firm command of, and a zealous devotion to, those works fortunate enough to be included in the western canon.

Second, by supplying a common set of symbols, knowledge, and ideas, the classical canon facilitated discourse. Eighteenth-century authors and orators who referred to Helvidius Priscus could be as confident of creating a certain image in the minds of their audience as the modern American writer or speaker who refers to George Washington. The canon exerted as great a homogenizing influence as that often ascribed to television today. Even those who fell outside the realm of formal education could not escape this form of social conditioning. Indeed, men who lacked formal education frequently proved even more eager to demonstrate their classical knowledge in order to secure status. Social conditioning left many unable to imagine the teaching of virtue independent of the teaching of the classics and, hence, made the transmission of the classical heritage an urgent concern.

To reassert the founders' direct connection to the works of antiquity, as this book seeks to do, is neither to deny the influence of their Whig intermediaries nor to question the impact of liberal and Christian doctrines upon their thought. It is, rather, to attempt to uncover the means by which the founders mediated between these diverse perspectives. If the attempt reveals founders who were sometimes inconsistent, opportunistic, confused, or inaccurate, it will merely demonstrate their shared humanity with our own generation. Indeed, it is a great comfort to know that humans who were often as confused as ourselves, and who faced problems of equal complexity and terror as our own, built a record of achievement so stunning that they long commanded a degree of awe and reverence usually reserved for the divine.

The organization of this book is designed to elucidate the origins and nature of the various classical influences. The work begins by examining classical conditioning in the eighteenth century, particularly through the educational system. It then explores the founders' various uses of the classics, including their utilization of classical symbolism, models, "anti-models," mixed government theory, pastoralism, and philosophy. It concludes by examining the evidence which Meyer Reinhold has presented for the decline of classical influence in the early national period, demonstrating that Benjamin Franklin, Benjamin Rush, Thomas Paine, and other reputed critics of the classics were, at worst, ambivalent toward the classics and that fierce resistance blocked even their most modest attempts at educational reform.

I

The Classical Conditioning of the Founders

The eighteenth-century educational system was the institution most responsible for the classical conditioning of the founders. It was mostly in the schools that the founders learned to venerate the classics. The socialization process was so complete, and the classics themselves so attractive, that even bad teachers, employing the most brutal and unimaginative pedagogical techniques, often instilled a love of the literature in their students. The founders' classical conditioning was so successful that most learned to relish the classics as a form of entertainment and to consider the ancients wise old friends. The founders loved and respected the classics for the same reason that other people love and respect other traditions: because the classical heritage gave them a sense of identity and purpose, binding them with one another and with their ancestors in a common struggle; and because it supplied them with the intellectual tools necessary to face a violent and uncertain world with some degree of confidence. Even when these tools failed to reflect reality, they proved essential to the self-assurance and enthusiasm necessary for many of the founders' achievements. Throughout their lives, the founders continued to believe that the classics provided an indispensable training in virtue which society could abandon only at its own peril. Hence, most of the founders argued passionately that the educational system must maintain the classical emphasis.

The founders' classical training frequently began at age eight, whether under the direction of public grammar schoolmasters or private tutors. As Robert Middlekauff has noted: "Since grammar masters knew that colonial colleges required young scholars to display their knowledge of Latin and Greek, they exercised their charges in the classics—and little else." Teachers concentrated on the works from which candidates for college admission were expected to recite, a list which changed little throughout the seventeenth and eighteenth centuries. Such works included the writings of the first-century B.C. Roman philosopher and statesman Cicero and the poet Virgil, the fourth-century B.C. Athenian statesman Isocrates or historian Xenophon, the eighth-century B.C. Greek epic poet Homer, and the Greek New Testament. As Noah Webster put it: "The minds of youth are perpetually led to the history of Greece and Rome or to Great Britain; boys are constantly repeating the declamations of Demosthenes and Cicero or debates upon some political question in the British Parliament." Only the poorest areas lacked grammar schools. Massachusetts law required every town to maintain one, though some poor frontier towns failed to comply.[1]

Grammar school students commonly studied the classics every morning from eight to eleven and every afternoon from one until dark. The learning process generally began with the memorization of the grammatical rules contained in Ezekiel Cheever's *Short Introduction to the Latin Tongue*. The pupil then translated the Latin dialogues in Marthurius Corderius' *Colloquies,* which contained both Latin and English columns. At more advanced stages he translated Cicero's *Epistles* or *Orations,* followed by Virgil's *Aeneid.* The first day the pupil translated a given passage aloud, the second he wrote out his translation, and the third he converted his own English translation back into Latin in a different tense. He then took up Greek, memorizing the grammatical rules in William Cambden's *Instituto Graecae Grammatices Compendiaria,* before translating the New Testament, Isocrates or Xenophon, and Homer. Finally, the grammar student had to convert Greek passages into both Latin and English. He also encountered Aristotle in his rhetorical and logical training and Euclid in his mathematical studies. Neither the classical curriculum nor the routine employed in teaching the languages changed much from colonial times through the days of the early republic. Not until after the Revolution did students begin to study their mother tongue. Even then, some educators and laymen considered the study of English grammar a mere matter for the home, unworthy of formal academic attention.[2]

Society's veneration for the classics was so complete, and the classics themselves so attractive, that the founders' love and respect for the literature survived even eighteenth-century pedagogy. British master John Clarke's caustic criticisms of contemporary teachers and methods in 1730 were as applicable to America as to Great Britain. Clarke complained that many schoolmasters possessed only a superficial knowledge of the classics and viewed their poorly paid positions as mere stepping-stones to more lucrative jobs. (In fact many masters were the nineteen- or twenty-year-old recent recipients of bachelor's degrees, teaching only until they earned enough funds to obtain the requisite master's degree in divinity. The resulting turnover of teachers inevitably harmed some students' education.) Clarke denounced the most common pedagogical methods of his day. He contended that pupils would learn grammatical rules much faster, and understand them much better, by reading literature than by memorizing the rules (which, Clarke noted, were sometimes themselves written in Latin!). He argued that most school days were needlessly wasted by the widespread prohibitions against the use of English translations. Since students did not know which dictionary definition was appropriate for a given word in an assigned passage, and could not use a translation to learn, they continually harassed each other and the master for the correct answer. Clarke maintained, contrary to the common practice, that pupils should read historians before poets, since the former strove to be conventional in terminology and syntax, while the latter endeavored to be unconventional and, hence, were much more difficult for beginners. Clarke ridiculed the customary policy of having students read numerous authors at the same time, a practice which merely confused them. What sane individual would order his own studies in such a fashion, Clarke demanded, adding heatedly: "I am clearly of Opinion that such a Man deserves to be whipt for his Folly [more] than any Boy he teaches." This last remark was a pointed assault on corporal punishment. Students would love the classics as much as sports or their other diversions, Clarke contended, if they were not always being beaten with rods for the minor mistakes which resulted from their masters' poor teaching methods. He might have added that masters were sometimes so overloaded with pupils and other duties (such as building maintenance and chapel duty) that even the aid of teaching assistants (called "ushers") was insufficient to enable them to teach effectively.[3]

Although Clarke's book was widely read on both sides of the Atlantic, it had little effect on pedagogical techniques. Whipping continued to be a common practice. In *Spectator* No. 157 Richard Steele testified: "No one who has gone through what they call a great school, but must remember to have seen children of excellent and ingenuous natures (as has afterwards appeared in their manhood); I say no man has passed through this way of education, but must have seen an ingenuous creature expiring with shame, with pale looks beseeching sorrow, and silent tears, throw up its honest eyes, and kneel on its tender knees to an inexorable block-head, to be forgiven the false quantity of a word in making Latin verse. The child is punished, and the next day he commits a like crime, and so a third with the same consequence." Samuel Johnson remembered that his own schoolmaster "used . . . to beat us unmercifully; and he did not distinguish between ignorance and negligence; for he would beat a boy equally for not knowing a thing, as for neglecting to know it. He would ask a boy a question, and if he did not answer it, he would beat him, without considering whether he had an opportunity of knowing how to answer it. For instance, he would call up a boy and ask him [the] Latin [word] for a candlestick, which the boy could not expect to be asked." Edward Gibbon recalled: "By the common methods of discipline, at the expense of many tears and some blood, I purchased the knowledge of the Latin syntax." Bitterness against such methods of classical training found its way into popular English literature. In the novel *Tom Jones* one finds the lines: "'D——n Homer with all my heart,' says Northerton. 'I have the marks of him in my a——e yet . . . And there's Corderius, another d——ed son of a whore, that has got me many a flogging.'"[4]

American masters were no more impressed by Clarke's arguments against whipping than their British counterparts. As late as 1811, the Boston Latin School employed a master named Sawney, whose brutal sense of humor Rufus Dawes vividly recalled:

"Well!" continues Sawney, switching the air with his cane, "well, mutton-head, what does an active verb express?"

After a little delay—"I'll tell you what it expresses," he resumes, bringing the stick down upon the boy's haunches with decided emphasis, "it expresses an action and necessarily supposes an agent (flourishing the cane, which descends again as before) and an object acted upon, as [in] *castigo te,* I chastise thee; do you understand?"

'Yes, sir! Yes, sir!' replies the boy, doing his best to get out of the way of the rattan. But Sawney is not disposed to let him off so.

"Now tell me when an active verb is called transitive."

"I don't know, sir," drawls Bangs doggedly.

"Don't you?" follows Sawney. "Then I'll inform you. An active verb is called transitive when the action passeth over (whack, whack) to the object. You (whack) are the object. I am (whack) the agent. Now take care how you go home and say that I never taught you anything. Do you hear?" (whack)

Granted, Sawney was unusually sadistic. More typical was Samuel Hunt, another Boston Latin schoolmaster who utilized corporal punishment but did not relish it. One of his students, Charles Winston Green, recalled a whipping:

I could not help crying bitterly. He called me up and seemed willing to console me. He said: "You know one Christopher Gore?" (afterwards Governor Gore) "Yes, sir." "He's a great man, isn't he?" "Yes, Sir." "Do you know one Harrison Gray Otis?" "Yes, sir." "He is a great man, is he not?" "Oh yes, Sir," said I. "I whipped it into them both!" said Master Hunt. I replied, "Guess you mean to make a plaguey great man of me!" I was in a roaring passion, but the boys in the school laughed outright, and the old man smiled, patted me on the head, and said, "Go to your seat, you rogue; I will not touch you again." And he never did.

Boys were accustomed to being whipped at home and generally took it in stride. Only the rare sadism of a Sawney brought down the condemnation of parents and the dismissal of the offending master. The better teachers, such as Ezekiel Cheever, rarely required the rod. But rare was a John Davis, instructor of the Petersburg (Virginia) Academy, who advertised that no corporal punishment would ever be employed in his school, "because beating the body debases the mind."[5]

It is remarkable that the association of Greek and Latin with physical punishment so rarely left a lasting distaste for the classics. The case of the distinguished patriot Josiah Quincy testifies to the emotional power of classical literature. Late in life, Quincy vividly recalled his terror upon entering Phillips Academy at the age of six. Quincy wrote:

The discipline of the Academy was severe, and to a child, as I was, disheartening. The Preceptor was distant and haughty in his manners. I have no recollection of his ever having shown any consideration for my childhood. Fear was the only impression I received from his treatment of myself and others. I was put at once into the first book of Cheever's Accidence and obliged, with the rest of my classmates, to get by heart passages of a book which I could not, from my years, possibly understand . . . I cannot imagine a more discouraging course of education than that to which I was subjected . . . I needed and loved perpetual activity of body, and with these dispositions I was compelled to sit with four other boys on the same hard bench, daily, four hours in the morning and four in the afternoon, and study lessons which I could not understand . . . I was kept in Cheever's Accidence I know not how long. All I know is, I must have gone over it twenty times before mastering it. I had been about four years tormented with studies not suited to my years before my interest in them commenced.

Yet such was the persistence of the master, the power of society's equation of the classics with learning, and the eloquence of the authors themselves that what began as a terror for Quincy ended as a passion. Quincy continued: "But when I began upon Nepos, Caesar, and Virgil, my repugnance to my classics ceased, and the Preceptor gradually relaxed in the severity of his discipline, and, I have no doubt, congratulated himself on its success as seen in the improvement he was compelled to acknowledge. During the latter part of my life in the Academy he was as indulgent as a temperament naturally intolerant and authoritative would permit." Quincy may have grown to love the classics, but never the teacher.[6]

This is not to deny that poor teaching methods took some toll. In 1780 John Witherspoon, the influential president of the College of New Jersey (now Princeton), complained: "Nothing is more common than to meet boys who say they have read Virgil or Horace who cannot speak three sentences in Latin upon the most common subjects." As late as 1832, over a century after Clarke wrote, William Hooper of the University of North Carolina sniffed that too many schoolmasters, "if they have diplomas in their hands, must be confessed to have more Latin in their hands than in their heads." He added that a visitor to a typical grammar school was likely to "hear a class of little marble-players recite a lesson in Caesar, giving poor Julius, alas!, more stabs than he received from the daggers of all the conspirators in the Senate-house, and avenging the Gauls upon him for all his murders."[7]

The limits of students' classical knowledge occasionally revealed themselves in embarrassing ways. School administrators, generally accompanied by an entourage of as many as fifty dignitaries, visited the grammar school classes periodically. Because these "visitations" were scheduled in advance, the schoolmaster had plenty of time to coach his students in the simulation of learning. Even so, occasional accidents marred the visitations. As Pauline Holmes related: "One Latin School boy, having been drilled in the declining of *duo*, was inadvertently called upon to decline *tres*. He faltered, looked towards Master Biglow, and then in utter despair cried out, 'That's not my word, Sir!' The mistake was instantly corrected, and the boy declined *duo* to perfection." Holmes did not describe the reaction of the gallery.[8]

But many of the criticisms concerning the classical ignorance of students were exaggerated, representing the enduring lament of classics professors that the rest of society failed to meet their rigorous standards. The Reverend James Maury, Donald Robertson, Nathan Tisdale, Samuel Moody, and many others may be cited as schoolmasters of great skill and inspirational ability. In the late 1750s the Reverend Maury convinced his pupils, including Thomas Jefferson, that "an Acquaintance with the Languages antiently spoken in Greece & Italy, is necessary, absolutely necessary, for those who wish to make any reputable Figure in Divinity, Medicine, or Law." By 1760 Jefferson was uncommonly well prepared for the College of William and Mary. In the 1760s Robertson's boarding school near Dunkirk, Virginia, provided James Madison, John Taylor of Caroline, John Tyler (father of the later president), and George Rogers Clark with a rigorous classical training. He taught them Greek, Latin, and French, albeit with a Scottish brogue. Having read selections from Virgil, Horace, Justinian, Cornelius Nepos, Julius Caesar, Tacitus, Lucretius, Eutropius, Phaedrus, Herodotus, Thucydides, and Plato at the boarding school, Madison then returned home in 1767 for two years of study under the Reverend Thomas Martin. Madison's early training was so thorough that although he arrived at the College of New Jersey in 1769 only two weeks before final examinations in Greek, Latin, the New Testament, English, and mathematics, he passed them all. Madison later testified regarding Robertson: "All that I have been in life I owe to that man."[9]

Northern schoolmasters Nathan Tisdale and Samuel Moody were no less capable than their southern counterparts. An instructor in Lebanon, Connecticut, for most of the second half of the eighteenth century, Tisdale attracted children from every North American colony and the British West Indies, instructing some seventy to eighty students per year. Although some of his pupils, such as the painter John Trumbull, were already well advanced (Trumbull had begun Greek and Latin before he commanded English and was prepared to enter Harvard at age twelve), others, like Jeremiah Mason, fondly recalled how Tisdale had transformed their complete ignorance of the classics into competence within two years. Tisdale's students mastered Eutropius, Cornelius Nepos,

Virgil, Cicero, Horace, Juvenal, the New Testament, and the *Iliad*. All praised his kindness. Similarly, pupils remembered Moody, who presided over the Dummer Academy from 1763 to 1790, as "a superior teacher of Latin and Greek who managed to inspire affection in his boys at the same time that he nurtured competence." Moody contributed more than a quarter of Harvard's entering students, along with entrants to numerous other colleges, without ever using the rod. He taught a future president of Harvard, a future governor of Massachusetts, and scores of future teachers, lawyers, politicians, merchants, and ministers.[10]

College entrance requirements, which remained remarkably stable for almost two hundred years, mandated a basic knowledge of the classical languages. When John Winthrop's nephew, George Downing, applied to Harvard in the mid-seventeenth century, he was required to "understand Tully [Cicero], Virgil, or any such classical authors, and readily to speak or write true Latin in prose and have skill in making Latin verse, and be completely grounded in the Greek language." When John Adams entered Harvard a century later, in the 1750s, Harvard demanded that he be able "extempore to read, construe, and parse Tully, Virgil, or such like common classical authors, and to write Latin in prose, and to be skilled in making Latin verse, or at least in the rules of the Prosodia, and to read, construe, and parse ordinary Greek, as in the New Testament, Isocrates, or such like, and decline the paradigms of Greek nouns and verbs." In 1760, when John Jay entered King's College (now Columbia), he was obliged to give a "rational account of the Greek and Latin grammars, read three orations of Cicero and three books of Virgil's *Aeneid*, and translate the first ten chapters of John into Latin." In 1774, when Alexander Hamilton chose King's College over the College of New Jersey because Witherspoon refused to allow the impatient West Indian to move through his program at an accelerated pace, the Princeton entrance examination required "the ability to write Latin prose, translate Virgil, Cicero, and the Greek gospels, and a commensurate knowledge of Latin and Greek grammar." Finally, in 1816, when Horace Mann applied for entrance to Brown University, he faced requirements with which Downing would have been completely comfortable: the ability "to read accurately, construe, and parse Tully and the Greek Testament and Virgil . . . to write true Latin in prose, and [to know] the rules of Prosody." Colleges were interested in a candidate's ability to read Latin and Greek and little else.[11]

The college curricula were as standardized and classically based as the grammar school curricula and the college entrance examinations. Reflecting a much greater consensus concerning the nature of "useful learning," colleges offered far fewer electives than universities today. Typical were the curricula of King's College and the College of New Jersey. King's College emphasized the classical languages the freshman, sophomore, and junior years, while the College of New Jersey stressed them the freshman, sophomore, and senior years. In his first commencement address Witherspoon declared: "The remains of the ancients are the standard of taste." He corresponded with his son David in Latin and wrote an essay under the pseudonym "Epaminondas," in which he pointed out: "A man is not, even at this time, called or considered a scholar unless he is acquainted in some degree with the ancient languages, particularly the Greek and Latin." He added that the classics were also necessary "to fit young men for serving their country in public stations." Indeed, his graduates included ten cabinet officers, thirty-nine congressmen, twenty-one senators, twelve governors, thirty judges (including three Supreme Court justices), and fifty state legislators. The curriculum of the College of William and Mary was even more rigorous, requiring four years of Latin and two of Greek. Few challenged such requirements. As Middlekauff put it: "Prone as they were to controversy, men in colonial New England rarely questioned the value of this curriculum . . . Whether or not they knew Latin and Greek themselves, most New Englanders respected the intellectual excellence the classics upheld . . . Even the poorest country parson could testify that a college degree raised a man's status, and all recognized that the path to the professions lay through a liberal education."[12]

Americans derived their curricula and pedagogical methods from the English educational system, which, like the other European systems, had originated in the Middle Ages. The medieval "trivium" (rhetoric, logic, and grammar) and "quadrivium" (arithmetic, music, geometry, and astronomy) continued to dominate western curricula well into the nineteenth century. Jesuit schoolmasters thoroughly grounded their students in theology, philosophy, Latin, Greek, and the ancient historians Herodotus, Xenophon, Plutarch, Livy, Sallust, Quintus Curtius, and Cornelius Nepos. Their method emphasized the usual rote memorization. The Jansenists, rivals of the Jesuits, offered a similar program. The Protestant nations of Germany, England, and especially Scotland equaled the Jesuits in the rigors of their classical training. The same ancient Romans—Cicero, Horace, Virgil, and Ovid—held sway throughout Europe. Far from abolishing the standard classical studies, the Protestant Reformation had only added programs designed to promote literacy in the vernacular languages. Roughly the same hours, strict discipline, declamations, and competitions existed in each nation. The only noteworthy difference between British and American grammar schools was that some American grammar schools were publicly supported (especially in New England), though public school students received the same blend of classical and Christian training as those attending denominational schools. As Howard Mumford Jones noted: "If Latin was no longer a universal tongue, it was a tongue universally studied . . . Most of the philosophes seemed to know more about ancient Greece and Rome than they did about St. Louis or the Hundred Years War."[13]

As in grammar schools, the quality of instruction in American colleges varied greatly. In 1761 a board of inquiry found that Harvard's instructors were demanding neither that their students translate English into Latin nor the converse. Until 1763 classical reading at the college was confined almost exclusively to Cicero, Virgil, and the New Testament. While admitting his own laziness as a student, John Adams later complained bitterly about his classical instruction at Harvard. In 1760, only five years after graduating from the college, Adams confided in his diary: "By constant dissipation among amusements in my childhood, and by the ignorance of my instructors in the more advanced years of my youth, my mind has laid uncultivated; so that, at twenty-five, I am obliged to study Horace and Homer—proh dolor [with painful difficulty]!" In an 1802 autobiography Adams bemoaned his early concentration upon mathematics and science, since he had been "destined to a Course of Life in which these Sciences have been of little Use, and the Classicks would have been of great Importance." Nevertheless, Adams' complaints regarding his own indolence and the incompetence of his Harvard instructors were somewhat exaggerated. It was at Harvard that Adams began his lifelong acquaintance with Sallust and Cicero and at Harvard that he was selected, as one of five graduates, to give a "Syllogistic Disputation" in Latin at the college's commencement ceremony in 1755. Apparently, Adams' Latin was good enough to impress a minister from Worcester, who was scouting for a Latin master for the town's grammar school. Adams occupied this position for a few miserable months before studying law and starting his own practice at Braintree in 1758.[14]

As late as the 1820s Julian Sturtevant protested similarly against his Yale instructors. Sturtevant recalled bitterly: "Professor James Kingsley seldom lectured, but often instructed his classes in certain favorite authors. He once taught our class, and at the end of the lesson, as he closed his book, he said, 'Young gentlemen, you read Latin horribly and translate it worse.' In another instance, he astonished us while closing a series of readings on Tacitus's Agricola, by saying, 'Young gentlemen, you have been reading one of the noblest productions of the human mind without knowing it.' We might justly have retorted to these severe and perhaps deserved remarks, 'Whose fault is it?'"[15]

But such was both the practical need and the positive passion for classical knowledge that good students were generally able to overcome bad colleges. When Thomas Jefferson entered the College of William and Mary in 1760, the college had a reputation for chaos and incompetence. The chair of moral philosophy, the Reverend Goronwy Owen, had just been forced to resign after leading his pupils in brawls with the townsmen of Williamsburg. Key positions were left unoccupied for years. Critics charged that classical instruction at the college went little beyond that of a typical grammar school. But Jefferson found an oasis of calm and of learning in the company of Professors William Small and George Wythe, whose fondness for Greek bound him to Jefferson. Jefferson's fellow student John Page marveled at his self-discipline, writing: "I was too sociable, and fond of the conversation of my friends, to study as Mr. Jefferson did, who could tear himself away from his dearest friends and fly to his studies." Other schoolmates of Jefferson remembered that he studied fifteen hours per day and carried his Greek grammar with him wherever he went.[16]

The quality of classical texts varied as greatly as the quality of instructors and students. In 1815 Robert Finley, a trustee of the College of New Jersey, complained bitterly:

> The Latin and Greek authors printed in this country abound so exceedingly with typographical errors that very great injury is sustained from the use of them in schools. When inaccuracies frequently occur, the teacher is incessantly harassed and the business of the school interrupted, by [students'] applications to have the classical text examined, and the existing errors exposed and corrected. In this manner much time is lost and the school is injured; and, besides, the student, always ready to impute difficulty to inaccuracy and to suspend his efforts till doubt is removed, finds his diligence in application and independent exercise of thought much impaired. These disadvantages have been experienced so seriously that it has been judged expedient in some instances to keep a European

edition, of the principal authors read, as a standard to refer to—a fact disgraceful and humiliating to American scholars!

Finley's solution to this problem, as well as to the immorality bred in youth by their reading polytheistic or lewd classical passages, was the publication of technically accurate but sanitized American texts.[17]

College students' secret societies served as an equally essential conduit of classical conditioning, reinforcing students' sense of kinship with classical heroes. The Linonian Society and the Brothers in Unity were founded at Yale in the 1750s, the American Whig and Cliosophic societies at the College of New Jersey in the 1760s, and the Speaking Club at Harvard in the 1770s. Colleges within a college, the societies formulated and taught their own curricula, awarded their own diplomas, operated their own libraries, established and enforced their own codes of conduct (through elected "censors," who often punished through shame), and set the ideological tone for the student body. Members expanded the classical curriculum by reading unassigned works (often in translation) from the libraries. Each initiate was given the name of a historical figure. A surviving list of initiates of the Cliosophic Society from 1770 to 1777 reveals that almost half of their pseudonyms (thirty-one of sixty-eight) were classical. Henry Lee, the Revolutionary cavalry hero and father of Robert E. Lee, was dubbed "Hannibal," after the second-century B.C. Carthaginian general. John Davenport, son of the famous preacher, was called "Cicero." Aaron Burr was named "Cyrus," after either the founder of the Persian empire (sixth century B.C.) or the fourth-century B.C. Persian general who employed Xenophon. After 1799 the American Whig Society's seal featured Minerva (Athena), the goddess of wisdom, guiding a youth up a mountain to the Temple of Virtue.[18]

If the correspondence between Brown students in the year 1789–90 is any indication, students discussed the classics even during breaks. One pupil wrote a colleague asking, "What progress do you make in my Lord Euclid?" Another complained that he had managed to read only six books of the *Aeneid* and one oration of Cicero during a break, while yet another confided his embarrassment at having read only seven books of Virgil and having "looked at Greek grammer, mind, looked at it." One student informed his roommate, "Your chum studies Latin like a Trojan," a reference to Virgil's myth that the sons of the Trojan Aeneas had formed the Roman people by intermarrying with the local Latins.[19]

Commencement ceremonies presented students with the opportunity to demonstrate their classical prowess to an admiring public. On such occasions, colleges sometimes held exhibitions in which students competed for prizes by reading Greek and Latin or by speaking Latin extemporaneously. The bachelor's and master's theses, oral defenses of a proposition against all comers, also tended to reflect the classical learning of the students. After the Stamp Act of 1765, many theses applied the political principles of Aristotle, Cicero, and Polybius to the debates concerning independence and the Constitution. Samuel Adams had anticipated these issues in his own master's thesis, delivered in flawless Latin in 1743. In answer to the title question "Whether It Be Lawful to Resist the Supreme Magistrate, if the Commonwealth Cannot Be Otherwise Preserved," Adams resoundingly asserted: absolutely![20]

As a reward for his effort, a graduate could generally look forward to the praise of relatives and teachers. Typical was the commendation which graduate Abijah Whiting received from his father: "I have felt happy to hear that during the course of your Colledg Studies you have made so close an application and depoarted yourselfe so well as to require some degree of Classical Merit." Dr. Robert Saunders informed graduates of the College of William and Mary upon the completion of their classical education: "You have separated yourselves from the throng who grope in the night of ignorance, scarcely conscious of the possession of intellect." He added that, by virtue of having completed this rite of passage, the young scholars were "entitled to that homage which the awakened intellect universally commands."[21]

A few possessed the wealth or good fortune to obtain a classical education in Europe. South Carolina patriot Christopher Gadsden studied Greek, Latin, and French at a grammar school near Bristol. His colleague Charles Pinckney was a star pupil at the rigorous Westminster School, where the only subjects were classics and religion. Having immersed himself in Ovid, Homer, and Virgil there, Pinckney went on to Oxford University. Born in Scotland, James Wilson received a thorough grounding in the classics at Cupar Grammar School and at the University of St. Andrews. While at the university he attended the optional, as well as the required, classes on ancient history. Wilson's linguistic training must have been equal to his historical training, since he later became an instructor of Latin and law at the College of Philadelphia (now the University of Pennsylvania) before launching his political career.[22]

While students, and frequently afterward, the founders kept "commonplace books," in which they copied the literary passages which most interested them. John Adams transferred sizable excerpts from Sallust's *Catiline's War* into his Harvard commonplace book. Thereafter, he maintained a great respect for the first-century B.C. Roman historian. In 1778, when Benjamin Franklin told the author of a Russian history that he had surpassed Sallust, Adams declared: "I thought this as good a french Compliment as the best of the Company could have made." In 1782 Adams wrote to a friend: "My boy should translate Sallust and write to his papa." In 1812, when some New Englanders, opposed to Republican war measures, spoke of secession, Adams quoted Sallust: "Small communities grow great through harmony; great ones fall to pieces through discord."[23]

Similarly, Madison kept a commonplace book from age eight in 1759 until his graduation from the College of New Jersey in 1772. Although the book consisted largely of passages gleaned from popular British and French works, Madison peppered it with Latin quotations adding to, or detracting from, the modern authors' sentiments. Whenever the modern writers quoted Roman authors and provided an English translation, Madison ignored the translation and transcribed the Latin directly into his commonplace book. The excerpts ranged widely from the philosophical to the literary to the political. Madison quoted Plato on slander and Aristotle on bashfulness: "Plato, being slandered, said, I shall behave as Nobody shall believe it . . . Bashfulness, says Aristotle, is an Orniment to Youth, but a reproach to old Age." As a marginal note to a poem from the *American Magazine,* which described a field, Madison added a line from Virgil's *Eclogues* (1.69), meaning: "And marvel as I gaze at the ears of corn, my realm of old."[24]

Madison's political excerpts suggest that classical conditioning instilled in youths a fear of both monarchs and demagogues. He cited second-century Roman historian Tacitus on the vice of the Roman emperors and followed it with a line from Horace's *Odes* (3.24.31–32): "Though living virtue we despise, / We follow her when dead with envious eyes." Conscious of the masses' susceptibility to demagogic rhetoric, Madison also wrote: "It should seem that Caesar excell'd Cicero in the Art of Persuasion."[25]

During the same period, Plato and Aristotle influenced Madison's essay "A Brief System of Logick." He appropriated Aristotle's ten categories of ideas, and his conversation between the "Theist" and the "Atheist" was modeled on the Socratic dialogues, as recounted by Plato. Nevertheless, Madison claimed that the Socratic method was both insidious and provocative, and appropriate for use only by masters against pupils. He concluded that in political debates, "Honour and Justice should carry it against Utility, and a greater Utility should carry against a lesser." As an example of the application of this principle, he contended that Scipio Nasica's argument against the injustice of attacking Carthage without provocation in the Third Punic War (146–144 B.C.) should have prevailed over Cato the Elder's argument regarding the utility of destroying a financial rival.[26]

Alexander Hamilton and Thomas Jefferson kept commonplace books even after leaving college. Although Hamilton's education at King's College was cut short by the outbreak of the Revolution, which drew him into the Continental Army in January 1776, he converted his military pay book into a commonplace book. In 1777 he copied into his pay book a few lines from Demosthenes' orations, including this significant sentence: "As a general marches at the head of his troops, so ought wise politicians, if I dare to use the expression, to march at the head of affairs; insomuch that they ought not to [a]wait the event, to know what measures to take; but the measures which they have taken ought to produce the event." Hamilton certainly lived by this maxim, if the events of the 1790s are any indication. He also copied large extracts from Plutarch's lives of Theseus, Romulus, Lycurgus, and Numa Pompilius, all founders of republics. Indeed, Hamilton's son John later testified that Plutarch and Alexander Pope were Hamilton's favorite authors.[27]

Jefferson maintained two commonplace books. His literary commonplace book contains excerpts from his favorite poets, dramatists, and prose writers. Forty percent of its passages, compiled between 1758 and 1773, were copied from classical works. Even the British authors Jefferson quoted almost invariably dealt with classical subjects. Examples of the latter phenomenon include passages from Shakespeare's *Julius Caesar* and *Troilus and Cressida,* Buckingham's *Julius Caesar* and *Death of Marcus Brutus,* Jonson's *Catiline's Conspiracy,* and a Bolingbroke essay on the "heathen moralists." By contrast, Jefferson's legal and political commonplace book, compiled while he was a law student from 1765 to 1767, contains no Greek or Latin excerpts, though the British and French writers he quoted consistently cited classical works, and though Jefferson himself occasionally added quotations of Roman authors as marginal notes.[28]

A good measure of the educational system's success at classical conditioning was the lifelong friendship most of the founders maintained with the classical heroes of their childhood. Between 1770, when a fire destroyed Jefferson's library at Shadwell, and 1815, when he sold to Congress for less than half its cost the new library he had so tirelessly and meticulously collected, Jefferson bought thousands of books, many of which were classical works. In 1788, no doubt pressed for time, he requested a list of Greek authors whose works consisted of a mere 8 volumes or less. In 1791 he bargained over the purchase of 223 volumes, almost all classical. While it is doubtful that Jefferson actually read all these works (which included a Latin cookbook), his grandchildren later attested to his love of the classics. They paraphrased him in this manner: "If he had to decide between the pleasure derived from the classical education which his father had given him, and the estate left him, he would decide in favor of the former." One granddaughter added: "I saw him more frequently with a volume of the classics in hand than with any other book." But perhaps Jefferson himself wrote most tellingly on the matter, when, in the midst of his sale of "eighteen or twenty" wagonloads of books, he begged leave to keep a few books "to amuse the time I have yet to pass," these books "being chiefly classical and mathematical." A few years later he reiterated the importance of these delights: "My business is to beguile the wearisomeness of declining life, as I endeavor to do, by the delights of classical reading and mathematical truths, and by the consolation of a sound philosophy, equally indifferent to hope and fear." As we shall see, the philosophy to which Jefferson referred was also classical.[29]

In his later years Jefferson's correspondence was filled with classical allusions. He was so fond of quoting Greek passages in his letters that John Adams finally protested, "Lord! Lord! What can I do with so much Greek?" Jefferson stated in 1810: "I read one or two newspapers a week, but with reluctance give even that time from Tacitus and Homer and so much agreeable reading." In 1819 he added: "I feel a much greater interest in knowing what has happened two or three thousand years ago than in what is now passing." In the same year Jefferson emphasized the value of the classics as "models of pure taste in writing," as entertainment, and as "stores of real science," "science" being a derivative of the Latin word for "knowledge." He contended regarding Greek and Latin: "To these we are certainly indebted for the rational and chaste style of modern composition which so much distinguishes the nations to whom these languages are familiar." Having expressed gratitude that his father had bequeathed him a classical education, Jefferson added: "When the decays of age have enfeebled the useful energies of the mind, the classick pages fill up the vacuum of ennui, and become sweet composers to that rest of the grave into which we are all sooner or later to descend." Jefferson lectured Adams and others on changes in Greek pronunciation, the fine points of Greek grammar, and the legitimacy of the Latin word "gloriola." He decried the evils of "Connecticut Latin" ("which renders doubtful whether we are listening to a reader of Cherokee, Shawnee, Iroquois, or what") and wrote a dissertation comparing English and classical prosody.[30]

Jefferson's favorite language was Greek, and his favorite poet was Homer, who was universally acclaimed as the "Father of Western Literature" and the ideal according to which all writers were measured. In 1819 Jefferson termed Greek "the finest of human languages." He complained that, since the educational system favored Latin over Greek, Americans wanted only "as much Greek as will pass a candidate for ordination." Jefferson quoted either Homer or Alexander Pope's famous translation of the *Iliad* twenty-nine times in his literary commonplace book. In 1787 he showed uncharacteristic zeal in attempting to refute a Paris journal article which claimed that it was an English farmer who had, after reading Homer, reinvented the process of making the circumference of a wheel from a single piece. Contending that the honor belonged to a New Jersey farmer, Jefferson boasted: "Ours are the only farmers who can read Homer." In 1800, after expressing a preference for the original *Iliad* over Pope's translation, Jefferson acknowledged the debt he owed to his father for his classical training. He wrote regarding the epic poem: "I thank on my knees Him who directed my early education, for having put into my possession this rich source of delight; and I would not exchange it for anything which I could then have acquired, and have not since acquired." In 1813 Jefferson responded to the anxieties of "the Edinburgh Reviewers" that the Americans would "disfigure" the English language by asking: "Did the Athenians consider the Doric, the Ionian, the Aeolic, and other dialects as disfiguring or as beautifying their language? . . . They were sensible that the variety of dialects, still infinitely varied by poetic license, constituted the riches of their language, and made the Grecian Homer the first of poets, as he must ever remain, until a language equally ductile and copious shall again be spoken." In the 1820s, in his "Thoughts on Prosody," Jefferson noted: "When young any composition pleases which unites a little sense, some imagination, and some rhythm, in doses however small. But as we advance in life these things fall off one by one, and I suspect that we are left at last with only Homer and Virgil, and perhaps with Homer alone."[31]

Jefferson was so immersed in the classics that they profoundly influenced his writing style, helping to produce the clarity and concision which stand as his trademark. Jefferson used the Roman historians Livy, Sallust, and Tacitus as models for oratorical writing. Well aware that nearly all the ancient historians had crafted fictitious speeches for their subjects, Jefferson took care, after declaring that the best speeches were those of Scipio Africanus, Cato, and Caesar, to identify the historians (Livy and Sallust) who had drafted them. On another occasion he contended that the finest model for "senatorial eloquence," which required logic, was Demosthenes, the fourth-century B.C. Athenian whose *Philippics* warned against the growing Macedonian power. By contrast, the finest model for the bar, which demanded imagination, was Cicero. This last statement was a barb aimed at the legal profession, since Jefferson not only detested the Ciceronian rhetoric popular in the House of Representatives, but warned that it would undermine the Constitution by exciting such disgust in the people that they would transfer their allegiance from the legislative to the executive branch. Jefferson seemed to say that such disgusting rhetoric was useful only to lawyers.[32]

From classical rhetoric Jefferson learned the three qualities which he deemed essential to good republican oratory. These were simplicity, brevity, and rationality. In his literary commonplace book Jefferson copied from the fifth-century B.C. Athenian dramatist Euripides this passage on the virtue of simplicity in rhetoric: "The words of truth are simple, and justice needs no subtle interpretations, for it has a fitness in itself; but the words of injustice, being rotten in themselves, require clever treatment." Jefferson's criticism of the Ciceronian rhetoric practiced in the House of Representatives focused upon the length of the speeches. In 1824, after applauding the speeches of Livy, Sallust, and Tacitus for "that sententious brevity which, using not a word to spare, leaves not a moment for the inattention of the hearer," Jefferson preached: "Amplification is the vice of modern oratory. It is an insult to an assembly of reasonable men, disgusting and revolting instead of persuading. Speeches measured by the hour die with the hour." Jefferson ended his sermon by criticizing "the disposition of the age to sermonize." Jefferson insisted that republican speeches be rational. He explained in 1824 that "in a republican nation, whose citizens are to be led by reason and persuasion, and not by force, the art of reasoning becomes of the first importance." He claimed that Livy, Sallust, and Tacitus were the models for rationality as well. Indeed, though Jefferson was not an impressive speaker, his speeches, like his other writings, were graced with the three qualities he so admired in classical oratory. As Gilbert Chinard put it (paradoxically employing a simile): "His speech, in which metaphors and similes are rarely found, has the trim, stripped beauty of a Greek athlete." Other founders also viewed Roman oratory as a model.[33]

Although John Adams struggled against the classics in early childhood, forgot his Greek, and never gained an elegant writing style from the classical languages, he acquired as great a passion for the classics as Jefferson. Considering classical prowess a path to social mobility, Adams' middle-class father responded to his young son's announcement that he would no longer study Latin by sending him out to dig ditches instead. After two days of backbreaking labor, the boy surrendered his shovel and returned reluctantly to his lexicon. John Adams never forgot the lesson: knowledge of the classics produced a glorious life of upward mobility, their neglect a wretched life of manual labor. He soon became proficient enough to pass the Harvard entrance examination and to distinguish himself in Latin there. By 1758, only three years after his graduation, Adams had become a true lover of the classics, translating numerous classical authors during his leisure time. In a letter of that year he asked rhetorically of the "young Spark whose Attention is dissipated among Horses and Ladies, fiddles, and frolicks, Cards and Romances": "[Is there] No Pleasure in studying the Eloquence of Greece and Rome in these stupendous Monuments of it which have been the Wonder and Delight of every Age, to the present day?" Adams' resounding reply: "Far otherwise!" In 1759 Adams confided to his diary that he was attracted to "thinking women," whom he defined as women who asked such questions as, "What do you think of Helen? What do you think of Hector and c.?" Abigail Smith was just such a woman. Two years later, when Adams heard James Otis' famous speech against the British writs of assistance, what most impressed him was Otis' "promptitude of classical allusions." Considering classical literature superior to modern works, Adams claimed that even Milton's *Paradise Lost* fell short of Homer's *Iliad* or Virgil's *Aeneid*. He added: "The Aeneid is a well ordered Garden, where it is impossible to find any Part unadorned, or to cast our Eyes upon a single Spot that does not produce some beautiful Plant or Flower." In 1812 Adams again judged the ancient bards superior to a modern author. He responded indignantly to an account of Frederick the Great's dream, in which Homer and Virgil returned to Earth to burn their works in frustration at the superiority of Voltaire's writings. Adams grumbled: "His adulation of Voltaire is babyish. He knew nothing of Homer or Virgil. He was totally ignorant of the languages of both."[34]

Adams was even more apt than Jefferson to quote a Roman author. In a 1758 diary entry he quoted a line from Virgil, which he himself translated as, "He nurses a Wound in his Veins and is consumed by a blind, hidden fire." Adams followed this line with the names of five young men who were in love. Writing for the Boston Sons of Liberty in 1768, he embedded a line from Virgil's *Eclogues* (1.46) in a statement addressed to the British Whig John Wilkes: "'Tis from your endeavors we hope for a Royal 'Pascite, ut ante, boves.'" The Latin, meaning "put your cows out to pasture as you did before," no doubt confused Wilkes, who was not known for his classical prowess. In 1774, believing that rebellion and war with Great Britain might soon be necessary, Adams quoted from Horace's *Odes* (3.2.13): "It is sweet and becoming to die for one's country." In 1807 he quoted from Juvenal's *Satires* (10.365) regarding Aaron Burr: "All Divinities are absent if Prudence is absent." By then Adams' library contained the complete works of Herodotus, Thucydides, Xenophon, Tacitus, Sallust, Livy, Homer, Plato, Aristotle, Horace, Ovid, Lucretius, Cicero, Epictetus, and Marcus Aurelius. In fact by the end of his life Adams had come to love the classics so much that he concluded: "If I have gained any distinction, it has been owing to the two days' labor in that abominable ditch."[35]

Other founders loved the classics as well. Like Jefferson and Adams, George Mason, the author of the influential Virginia Bill of Rights, spent most of his (albeit few) retirement years rereading the classics. He often quoted Virgil for family members. Alexander Hamilton adored John Dryden's translation of Plutarch's *Lives*. Having read Livy in the original Latin at age fifteen, Patrick Henry made it a rule to read a translation of the historian through every year. During the Revolution, Henry conversed in Latin with a foreign visitor. Even after beginning his law practice in 1757, John Dickinson found he could not confine himself to law books. He ordered Homer's *Odyssey,* Callimachus' Hymn to Jupiter, and the works of Plato and Tacitus. Dickinson often recited lines from Roman histories. He was particularly fond of Memmius' declaration in Sallust's *Jugurtha:* "I shall certainly aim at the freedom handed down from my forebears; whether I am successful or not in doing so is in your control, my fellow countrymen." He used the line to begin a 1764 speech and to end his famous and influential *Letters from a Pennsylvania Farmer* (1768), which rallied the patriots against the Townshend Acts. Dickinson was also fond of Sallust's more famous statement regarding the corruption of late republican Rome. He first used it in 1754, while a law student in London. Shocked by the electoral corruption he saw there, Dickinson instantly connected London with republican Rome in its decline, writing in Latin, "Easy to be bought, if there were but a purchaser." In later years, when away from his wife, he assured her that the ancients kept him company. In 1760 James Otis, the first patriot leader of New England, put aside his legal and political duties to publish *The Rudiments of Classical Prosody*. He also penned a treatise on Greek verse, though a shortage of Greek type prevented its publication in America. Even James Madison, who seems to have strayed farther from the classics in retirement than most of his contemporaries, became suddenly and unaccountably disturbed by "the alleged minuteness of the Roman farms & the impossibility of accounting for their support of a family," and speculated at length on the matter.[36]

If one includes translations in the definition of "classics" (since some founders had difficulty maintaining their proficiency in the classical languages), one can truly say that the classics were a source of entertainment for the founders. The classics filled their days and nights, providing comfort for the distressed, adventure for the bored, and lessons, both moral and political, for the student of life.

The founders' passion for the classical heritage produced an intense desire to ensure that future generations were not deprived of it. Steeped in the classics, the founders were determined that their children should be, too.

When John Adams went to Paris in 1778 to help Benjamin Franklin secure the French alliance necessary for the defeat of the British in the Revolution, he brought his sons, John Quincy and Charles, with him. Critical of his own classical training at Harvard, the elder Adams resolved that his sons must study the ancients in Europe. Immediately upon landing in France, he enrolled them in a Latin grammar school at Passy. In the following year, while the Adams trio waited at Lorient to sail back to America aboard the aptly named *Alliance,* John acquired a copy of the Latin text John Quincy had been using, so that his eldest son would not have to miss a day of translation. Aboard the ship Adams assisted his boy in translating Cicero's first oration against Catiline, no doubt a nostalgic treat for the statesman. A good measure of Adams's enjoyment of this activity was the Puritan defensiveness he displayed in the diary entry concerning it: "Are these classical amusements becoming my situation? Are not courts, camps, politics, and war more proper for me? No; certainly, classical amusements are the best I can obtain on board ship, and here I cannot do any thing or contrive any thing for the public."[37]

When the three Adamses returned to Europe in 1780, Adams engaged a tutor for his boys. He wrote to John Quincy: "My Wish at present is that your principal Attention should be directed to the Latin and Greek tongues . . . I hope soon to hear that you are in Virgil and Tully's orations, or Ovid, or Horace, or all of them." Mathematics and geography, said the old lover of these subjects, could wait. To ensure that his directive was not ignored, Adams instructed the boys' tutor: "I would not have them put by any longer to the Master of Fencing or Dancing—let them attend the Drawing and Writing Masters, and bend all the rest of their Time and attention to Latin and Greek, and French, which will be more useful and necessary for them in their own Country, where they are to spend their Lives." Such directives continued to flow from Adams even after he enrolled his sons in a Latin school on the Singel in Holland. Although the boys' stay there was short, owing to John Quincy's inability to master Dutch, the elder brother went off to the University of Leyden, the younger to Harvard.[38]

Adams continued to scrutinize his elder son's education. In 1781 he revealed intense anxiety regarding the state of his son's classical education. Convulsed by the inexplicable fear that John Quincy might be falling behind in his studies at the University of Leyden, he berated the youth for dawdling on simple works. He concluded his tirade: "I want to have you upon Demosthenes. The plainer Authors you may learn yourself at any time. I absolutely insist upon it, that you begin upon Demosthenes and Cicero. I will not be put by. You may learn Greek from Demosthenes and Homer as well as from Isocrates and Lucian—and Latin from Virgil and Cicero as well as from Phaedrus and Nepos. What should be the Cause of the Aversion to Demosthenes in the World I know not, unless it is because his sentiments are wise and grand, and he teaches no frivolities. If there is no other Way, I will take you home and teach you Demosthenes and Homer myself." He did not make John Quincy dig any ditches, however.[39]

The parental heckling must have achieved its purpose, for in 1785, when John Quincy entered Harvard, his father could boast of him: "It is rare to find a youth possessed of so much knowledge. He has translated Virgil's Aeneid, Suetonius, the whole of Sallust, and Tacitus's Agricola, his Germany, and several books of his Annals, a great part of Horace, some of Ovid, some of Caesar's commentaries, in writing, besides a number of Tully's orations . . . In Greek his progress has not been equal; yet he has studied morsels in Aristotle's Poetics, in Plutarch's Lives, and

Lucian's Dialogues, the choice of Hercules in Xenophon, and lately he has gone through several books in Homer's Iliad." In fact the energetic John Quincy held the chair of rhetoric and oratory at Harvard while serving as a U.S. senator in 1806, though his father feared for his health. John Adams noted anxiously: "Aristotle, Dionysius Halicarnassensis, Longinus, Quintilian, Demosthenes, and Cicero, with twenty others, are not easily read and studied by a man of the world and a senator of the United States."[40]

Adams' interest in the classical training of his progeny did not end with his sons. He was determined that his grandsons learn virtue from the classics as well. In 1813 he gave a copy of Philippe Brunck's *Ethike Poiesis,* a collection of Greek ethical maxims, to grandson George Washington Adams, then preparing for Harvard. In 1816, at the age of eighty-one, he read Terence's six extant plays and excerpted approximately 140 passages from them for his grandchildren. In 1823 he expressed delight at his grandson Thomas Boylston Adams' progress in Virgil, perhaps remembering his own youthful resistance to the classics. These lessons in Roman virtue evidently impressed the grandchildren, for whenever one of them, also called John, became too passionate, he reminded himself: "Sobrius esto John"—"Be sober, John." The elder Adams spent his final years trying to secure the construction of a Greek and Latin academy in his home town of Quincy.[41]

Thomas Jefferson was another passionate advocate of classical education. In 1782 he wrote: "The learning [of] Greek and Latin, I am told, is going into disuse in Europe. I know not what their manners and occupations call for: but it would be very ill-judged in us to follow their example in this instance." In 1816, when fixing requirements for the University of Virginia, he wrote that the classical languages were the "foundation preparatory for all the sciences" and "the portico of entry to the university." Two years later he termed them "the foundation common to all the sciences." In 1819 Jefferson worried that if the entrance requirements for his beloved university were not made rigorous enough, it would become a mere grammar school, reduced to teaching the rudiments of the classical languages. As a result, he approved Thomas Cooper's proposal to exclude from the university any student who could not read classical authors "with facility, convert a page of English into Latin at sight, and demonstrate a thorough knowledge of Euclid." Such was Jefferson's zealousness in demanding classical knowledge of entering students that a university board member protested, with some exaggeration, that "the student should be a better scholar than most of our teachers before he shall enjoy the benefit of classical instruction in the university." Although Jefferson had no sons of his own, he rebuked his daughter Martha for not keeping up with her Livy, though her gender entitled her to read the Roman historian in Italian translation.[42]

Patrick Henry's father, John, considered his son's classical education so vital that he refused to surrender him to a tutor, teaching the boy himself. Known as "a man more familiar with his Horace than with his Bible," though also quite familiar with the latter, John Henry sent Patrick to an English school until he was ten and then personally taught his son Latin and some Greek. Constantly concerned with such questions as whether "the Greek word Aiwvios is always taken for a limited duration," John instilled in Patrick a reverence for the classics. Patrick studied Livy, Virgil, Horace, Juvenal, Ovid, Homer, and a translation of Demosthenes as a model of oratory. He then carried on the Henry tradition of demanding detailed classical knowledge of progeny. Patrick Henry's grandson claimed that he dreaded his grandfather's quizzes far more than any recitation before a professor.[43]

Christopher Gadsden was equally insistent on the importance of the classics. In 1764 he chaired the committee of the Charleston Library Society whose task was to prepare a list of the best classical authors and the most prominent modern philologists. When the society refused to expand its classical collections, Gadsden threatened to resign. Initially demanding that the organization spend seventy pounds sterling annually on the purchase of classics, he consented, with great reluctance, to a compromise of thirty pounds annually.[44]

Other founders were equally concerned that their children receive a good classical education. In 1791 Alexander Hamilton urged his nine-year-old son Philip, then entering boarding school, to study his Latin diligently. George Mason left instructions in his will for the rigorous classical training of his nephews. Perhaps recalling his own prize-winning Latin essay at the College of New Jersey, Henry Lee advised his son Carter, away at Harvard, to "dwell on the virtues & imitate, so far as lies in your power, the great & good men whom history presents to your view—Lycurgus, Solon, Numa, [and] Hannibal."[45]

Even George Washington, who lacked formal classical training, saw to it that his stepson, Jack Custis, was not similarly deprived. In 1761 Washington purchased copies of Phaedrus, Eutropius, Sallust, Horace, Terence, and Cornelius Nepos and several Latin grammars and dictionaries for his eight-year-old stepson. Eight years later he bought dozens of classical works for the boy. Reflecting the typical preference for Latin over Greek, Washington suggested that French and mathematics (for surveying) were more important subjects than Greek. But he added that the latter was "no bad acquisition" and lamented Jack's deficiencies in that area. He boasted of Jack's command of Latin, based on his having begun study of the language "as soon as he could speak."[46]

Aaron Burr even made certain that his daughter, the classically named Theodosia, learned the classical languages, an unusual acquisition for an eighteenth-century woman. He insisted that his daughter's tutor demand much of her. Burr even scribbled for Theodosia a mock journal entry of the type he desired to see from her in the future: "Learned 230 lines which finished Horace. Heigh ho. for Terence & the Greek Grammar Tomorrow . . . Began Gibbon this evening—I find he requires as much study as Horace."[47]

Even those founders who lacked formal education were not immune from this social conditioning. George Wythe, a signer of the Declaration of Independence and a member of the Second Continental Congress, the Virginia Ratifying Convention, the Virginia House of Burgesses, and the Virginia High Court of Chancery, never attended college. Yet he learned the classical languages from his mother, an exceedingly intelligent woman who had somehow become fluent in them. She instilled such a love and knowledge of the classics in Wythe that he was revered by his law students, including Thomas Jefferson, James Monroe, John Marshall, and Henry Clay, for his classical prowess. Jefferson later referred to Wythe as "the best Latin and Greek scholar in the State" of Virginia. Despite his mother's horrified pleas, young John Rutledge refused to learn the classical languages. But at twelve he became enchanted by Joseph Addison's *Cato* (1713) and saw the play numerous times during his life. John Marshall's entire formal education consisted of only six weeks at the College of William and Mary, and he once stated from the bench: "These seem . . . the conclusions to which we are led by reason and the spirit of the law. Bro. [Joseph] Story will furnish the authorities." Nevertheless, he read Horace and Livy, patterned his portrayal of George Washington, in his famous five-volume biography of the general, after Cicero, and told his grandsons that Cicero's *De officiis* was "among the most valuable treatises in the Latin language, a salutary discourse on the duties and qualities proper to a republican gentleman." George Washington's father's death, when Washington was eleven, prevented his planned college education in Europe, and he never learned Greek or Latin. Yet through the use of Roman analogies, William Fairfax, Washington's mentor and surrogate father, impressed upon him "that the greatest of all achievements was, through honorable deeds, to win the applause of one's countrymen." Decades later, during the French and Indian War, when Fairfax sought to cheer a troubled Washington, he reassured the young man that he was reaching his goal: "Your good health and fortune is the toast at every table. Among the Romans such general acclamation and public regard shown to any of their chieftains was always esteemed a high honor and gratefully accepted." It was customary for guests at Belvoir, the Fairfax estate, to sign their names in a register, followed by a favorite Latin quotation.[48]

Although the founders always endorsed classical education on utilitarian grounds, they defined "utility" in the broadest possible manner. In addition to the writing models, knowledge, and ideas which the classics furnished, the founders contended that they were an indispensable training in virtue. John Adams lectured John Quincy: "I wish to hear of your beginning Sallust, who is one of the most polished and perfect of the Roman Historians, every Period of whom, and I had almost said every Syllable and every Letter, is worth Studying. In company with Sallust, Cicero, Tacitus, and Livy, you will learn Wisdom and Virtue. You will see them represented with all the Charms which Language and Imagination can exhibit, and Vice and Folly painted in all their Deformity and Horror. You will ever remember that all the End of study is to make you a good Man and a useful Citizen." The connection between the classics and virtue was deeply ingrained and implicitly understood. In 1778 Adams wrote regarding Arthur Lee's sons (including Richard Henry Lee): "Their father had given them all excellent classical educations, and they were all virtuous men." To Adams, the causal relationship between the first fact and the second was too obvious to require explanation. Such a relationship could be assumed, since the stated purpose of most classical literature, including works of history, had always been to inculcate morality. Since the inculcation of a fixed moral code is not the expressed purpose of most modern literature (perhaps because there is no longer a consensus concerning morality), modern people would be perplexed by the statement, "They all study American history, and they are all virtuous people." But to the founders, the connection between classical training and virtue was clear.[49]

Nevertheless, however important, these factors alone cannot explain the high esteem in which the founders held the classics. As we moderns know well, other forms of literature can furnish writing models, knowledge, and moral lessons. There is another reason for the founders' passionate support for the classics, a reason which eighteenth-century rationalists were either unable or unwilling to recognize: that they themselves had been conditioned by their society as a whole, and by their educational system in particular, to venerate the classics. The founders were conditioned as children to associate the works of certain ancient republican authors with personal and societal virtue. This social conditioning was so successful that it left many of the founders unable to imagine the teaching of virtue independent of the teaching of the classics and, consequently, made the transmission of the classical heritage an urgent concern. Even in the "Age of Reason" tradition triumphed.

II

Symbolism

The founders used classical symbols and allusions to communicate, to impress, and to persuade. The existence of a classical canon, transmitted principally through the educational system, facilitated communication among the educated men of the western world. With a single classical pseudonym, statue, or allusion, a gentleman could be certain of generating a chain of associations in the minds of his audience. These symbols also served a powerful legitimating function. To appropriate such emblems was to claim social status for oneself and the support of venerable authorities for one's cause. Classical symbols provided badges of class, taste, wisdom, and virtue. To use them aptly was also to claim the endorsement of ancient sages, the very longevity of whose reputations attested to their greatness. Hence, the founders frequently enveloped themselves and their causes in classical symbols, much as modern politicians wrap themselves and their policies in the flag.

The most common classical symbol was the pseudonym. During the Revolutionary era, classical pseudonyms were exceedingly popular. In a 1769 essay signed "Americus Britannicus" Christopher Gadsden urged greater unity between the eastern and western portions of South Carolina in the common fight again parliamentary tyranny. Meanwhile, Samuel Adams penned essays under the names "Clericus Americanus," "Candidus," and "Sincerus." He signed one essay protesting the British maintenance of a standing army "Cedant Armae Togae" (Let weapons yield to the toga), a slogan popular with Roman republicans like Cicero who had insisted upon tight civilian control of the army. Even medical reformers used pseudonyms. Joseph Warren signed an essay against bloodletting "Philo Physic" (a lover of nature).[1]

During the constitutional debates of 1787–88, both Federalists and

Antifederalists rifled the classics for ancient republican pseudonyms. Eager to cast the Constitution and its supporters as monarchical and oligarchic, Antifederalists often adopted the names of such tyrant-slayers as Brutus and Cassius, the leading assassins of Julius Caesar. Some Antifederalists dubbed themselves "Cato," after Cato the Younger, one of Julius Caesar's principal political opponents; and "Helvidius Priscus," after a Stoic and republican martyr killed by the Roman emperor Nero in the first century A.D. Still others named themselves "Cincinnatus," after the mythical Roman hero who, having reluctantly accepted a dictatorship and having defeated Rome's enemies, retired to the plow. Finally, some Antifederalists claimed the appellations "Philanthropos" (a lover of man), "Veritas Politica" (political truth), "Vox Populi" (the voice of the people), "Candidus," "Poplicola" (one who heeds the people), "Honorius" (an honorable man), and "A Plebeian," implying that their opponents were the opposite of these things.[2]

The Federalists rushed to appropriate the names of ancient republicans as well. Alexander Contee Hanson dubbed himself "Aristides," after the fifth-century B.C. Athenian whose reputation for justice was legendary. According to Plutarch, "Aristides the Just" once even went so far as to aid an illiterate man in writing Aristides' own name on a potsherd (*ostrakon,* whence comes "ostracism") which was to be counted in the annual vote for banishment. John Dickinson took the name "Fabius," after the second-century B.C. Roman general whose guerrilla tactics helped defeat Hannibal and the Carthaginians in the Second Punic War, thereby preserving the republic. Another Federalist, seeking to escape the aristocratic stigma, called himself "Civis Rusticus" (a rustic citizen).[3]

The popularity of classical pseudonyms continued into the early national period. In 1790 the ironically named "Philanthropos" penned an article against female participation in politics. In 1791 Robert R. Livingston wrote essays against Hamilton's fiscal program under the name "Aristides." In 1795 he appropriated "Cato," "Decius," and "Cinna" for sixteen essays against the Jay Treaty. Decius had sacrificed his life in battle for the Roman republic; Cinna had been another of Caesar's assassins.[4]

Alexander Hamilton proved one of the most adept users of pseudonyms. Indicative of the care with which he selected them was his choice of "Phocion" for a 1784 open letter to the citizens of New York opposing a state law which would confiscate more loyalist property. According to Plutarch (*Phocion,* 36.3), Phocion was a fourth-century B.C. Athenian general who was so magnanimous that he befriended his own personal enemies, even to the extent of telling his son not to resent the Athenian people for sentencing Phocion to death. More important, Phocion always sought decent treatment for prisoners of war. Hamilton was suggesting that his fellow New Yorkers emulate Phocion's wise magnanimity.[5]

It was probably Hamilton's idea to use "Publius" as the pseudonym for the *Federalist* essays in 1787–88, since he had already written essays under that name in 1778. According to Plutarch (*Publius,* 1–3), Publius Valerius established republican government in Rome in 509 B.C., after he and Lucius Brutus expelled Tarquin, the last Roman king. Similarly, in the days after Washington had expelled George III's armies from the United States, Hamilton, Madison, and Jay sought to establish a new republican government there.[6]

In 1792, when engaged in a heated dispute with the Republicans concerning his fiscal policies, Hamilton used "Metellus" and "Catullus" as pseudonyms for essays attacking Thomas Jefferson. According to Plutarch (*Tiberius Gracchus,* 14.3), Quintus Metellus was a second-century B.C. Roman senator who rebuked Tiberius Gracchus, the leading proponent of land redistribution, for currying favor with the masses by ignoring his duties as censor. Similarly, in the "Metellus" essay, Hamilton upbraided Jefferson for holding demagogic positions. According to Plutarch (*Caesar,* 8.1), Catulus Lutatius was a first-century B.C. Roman senator who joined Cato the Younger in opposing Julius Caesar's efforts to prevent the execution of the co-conspirators of Catiline, the Roman aristocrat who had attempted to overthrow the republic in 63 B.C. Similarly, in the (misspelled) "Catullus" essays, Hamilton presented himself as opposing the Virginia Caesar's antirepublican aspirations.[7]

In 1794 Hamilton selected "Tully" (a diminutive of Marcus Tullius Cicero) for a series of essays denouncing the Whiskey Rebellion. Hamilton's attack on the Whiskey rebels paralleled Cicero's famous orations against Catiline. Hamilton considered the rebel leaders demagogues who emulated Catiline in their attempt to foment popular unrest in order to seize power. But Hamilton, the American Cicero, would foil the plan of these latter-day Catilines and save the republic by reaffirming the duly elected government's constitutional power to make and enforce laws, free from intimidation.[8]

In the next year Hamilton employed the names of two Roman heroes, "Horatius" and "Camillus," for essays defending the Jay Treaty, an accord whose concessions to Great Britain infuriated the Republicans. According to Plutarch (*Publicola*, 16.4–7; also Livy 2.10), Horatius Cocles was a sixth-century B.C. Roman soldier who saved the Roman republic by single-handedly holding off the Etruscans at a bridge outside Rome. According to Plutarch (*Camillus*, 42.3), Camillus was a general who, having been recalled from exile, united the Romans and drove the Gauls from Rome in 386 B.C., thereby saving the republic. He then constructed a temple to Concordia. Hamilton was attempting to establish the same concord with his fellow Americans by uniting them in a common struggle against the real threat to their liberties, the modern Gauls. (Historians now know that the Gauls left Rome not because of Camillus, but because of a senate bribe and because of threats to their territory in the north.)[9]

In 1798, when Hamilton sought a war against France, in the wake of the XYZ affair, he adopted the name "Titus Manlius" for a series of essays called "The Stand." According to Livy, Titus Manlius was a Roman senator who urged total war against Carthage, particularly advocating an attack on Carthage's ally, Sardinia. The name suited Hamilton's argument perfectly. Prophesying that the United States would be unable to avoid taking sides in the total war between Great Britain and France, Hamilton urged an attack on France's ally, Spanish Louisiana.[10]

Finally, in 1803, when Hamilton was again advocating an attack on the Isle of Orleans, in the aftermath of Napoleon's acquisition of Louisiana from Spain, he used the pseudonym "Pericles." Hamilton's central argument in these essays paralleled Pericles' contention when addressing the Athenian assembly at the outbreak of the Peloponnesian War in 431 B.C. Just as Pericles, when advocating aid to Corcyra in opposition to Sparta's Corinthian ally, argued that war with Sparta was inevitable (*Pericles*, 29.1), so Hamilton, when advocating the attack on the Isle of Orleans, argued that war with France was inevitable, now that French territory bordered the United States.[11]

As Douglass Adair noted, Hamilton selected these pseudonyms because all were wise aristocrats famous for their pursuit of justice and their unwillingness to "flatter the follies of the people." (Even Pericles met with popular disfavor, near the end of his life, for urging the wise strategy of avoiding land battles with the Spartans.) Though the wisdom and integrity of these aristocrats had been the cause of their unpopularity and, in many cases, their deaths, all were vindicated by posterity. According to Plutarch (*Camillus*, 1.1–2), "the most singular and surprising" fact about Camillus was that, despite his numerous military triumphs and his justly awarded title, "Second Founder of Rome," the people never elected him consul. Hamilton sounded like these aristocrats in 1802, when he borrowed Virgil's description of the Cyclops (*Aeneid*, 3.659), "shapeless, huge, [and] blind" to describe the masses.[12]

Since Hamilton selected his pseudonyms from one of the most widely read classical works, he could be fairly certain that all but the most casual readers would grasp his meaning. Even in the rare instances in which a reader would not immediately comprehend the significance of the pseudonym, he would probably have a copy of Plutarch's *Lives* at hand. Hamilton understood that the use of such simple and convenient republican names as "Brutus" and "Cassius" would leave the extent of his classical knowledge in doubt. Just as today's nouveau riche might betray their inexperience with wealth through gaudy excess, so some eighteenth-century gentlemen betrayed their classical ignorance by choosing pseudonyms which could easily be obtained from William Shakespeare or some other popular modern author. Hamilton would not make such an error. Through the literary equivalent of a knowing nod or smile, he would make it subtly, but unmistakably, clear to his audience that he was a cultured gentleman.

But Hamilton's appropriation of classical pseudonyms was not merely a tactic to win public approval for his causes. He used such pseudonyms in private discourse as well. In 1792 he proposed a cipher for secret correspondence with Gouverneur Morris. All but three of Hamilton's twenty-six suggested code names were classical. Half were taken from Plutarch.[13]

By contrast, Thomas Jefferson's leadership of the classical revival movement in American architecture represented his principal use of classical symbols. Even so committed a rationalist as Jefferson endorsed neoclassical architecture not only because its "simplicity" paralleled that of nature, but also because, having received the approval of millennia, it would confer legitimacy upon the United States within the western world.

Although Jefferson drafted a plan for the Virginia governor's mansion in the 1770s, a plan he may have derived from the Parthenon, his first major public project was the Virginia Capitol at Richmond. His revolutionary proposal, which involved the construction of three separate buildings, one for each branch of government, was rejected as too expensive. In the 1790s Jefferson recalled that he had based the Capitol, designed with the help of Charles Louis Clerisseau in 1785, upon the temple of Erectheus at Athens (fifth century B.C.) and upon the Maison Carrée at Nîmes (16 B.C.). But the latter was more clearly represented in the building. While in Nîmes, Jefferson had gazed at the Maison Carrée for so many hours ("like a lover at his mistress") that he claimed: "The stocking-weavers and silk spinners around it consider me an hypochondriac Englishman, about to write with a pistol the last chapter of his history." Jefferson repeatedly defended his choice of the Maison Carrée as the model for the Capitol, summarizing his reasoning in 1785: "It has obtained the approbation of fifteen or sixteen centuries, and is therefore preferable to any design which might be newly contrived . . . It is very simple." A few days later he explained: "You see I am an enthusiast on the subject of the arts. But it is an enthusiasm of which I am not ashamed, as its object is to improve the taste of my countrymen, to increase their reputation, to reconcile to them the respect of the world, and to procure them its praise."[14]

But Jefferson did not merely reproduce the Maison Carrée in Richmond. Though rigorously maintaining the proportions of the Roman structure, he changed the columns from Doric to Ionic and agreed to Clerisseau's suggestion that the depth of the portico be reduced from three to two columns, in order to admit more light. True, Jefferson grumbled, "What is good is often spoiled by trying to make it better." But it was Jefferson himself who made the greatest innovation: he replaced the side pilasters with windows, producing a pleasing marriage of classical and modern styles. Jefferson's approach was one of respectful adaptation, not slavish imitation.[15]

By the early 1790s Jefferson was making recommendations for both the President's House and the Capitol. For the President's House, he first suggested as models such modern buildings as the Louvre and the Hôtel de Salm in Paris, but finally settled on the Villa Rotunda. The Villa Rotunda was the creation of sixteenth-century Italian architect Andrea Palladio, whose *Four Books of Architecture* were considered the most authoritative works on classical architecture. For the U.S. Capitol, Jefferson first recommended vaguely "the adoption of some one of the models of antiquity which have had the approbation of thousands of years." He urged that brick be used in its construction, noting, "The remains of antiquity in Europe prove brick more durable than stone." When Jefferson received William Thornton's plan in 1793, he was charmed by the "grandeur, simplicity, and beauty" of his neoclassical design. Thornton's plan set a dome, modeled on a copy of the Pantheon in Paris, at the center and balanced it with two wings. But it was Jefferson and Benjamin H. Latrobe who designed the central building, Jefferson suggesting a portico based on that of a structure built during the reign of the Roman emperor Diocletian (284–305 A.D.). Furthermore, Jefferson insisted on the more ornate Corinthian column for the south wing against Latrobe's preference for the simple Doric column. When the Capitol was finally completed in 1812, having survived the countless feuds of its architects, Jefferson praised it as "the first temple dedicated to the sovereignty of the people, embellishing with Athenian taste the course of a nation looking far beyond the range of Athenian destinies." Burned by the British in 1814, the Capitol was rebuilt with only minor modifications. In its final form, it was a compromise between Jefferson's pro-Roman, Latrobe's pro-Greek, and Thornton's unorthodox views.[16]

Jefferson spent his twilight years planning the University of Virginia campus. He modeled the university's library, its temple of learning, on the Pantheon, which he considered the finest example of spherical architecture. His plan even restored the Pantheon's podium or foundation, obscured, at the original site, by the debris of millennia. Here, too, Jefferson avoided slavishness. Believing he could improve upon a masterpiece, he increased the building's symmetry by reducing the depth of the porch to equal its height, extended the porch around the rotunda so as to avoid the abrupt transition from the columned porch to the dome, and admitted more light. The result was a building which equals the Pantheon in beauty, if not in grandeur (being only half its size). For other campus buildings he adapted the designs of the Temple of Nerva Trajan and the Theatre of Marcellus, both found in Palladio. He retained the general proportions of the buildings while reducing their ornamentation. Although Jefferson arranged the campus with symmetry in mind, radiating the other buildings from the library much as the buildings of a Roman villa radiate from the main house, he introduced variety as well by alternating the column types and facings of adjacent buildings. Jefferson wanted students at the University of Virginia to return home to the Deep South and the West as missionaries, carrying with them as deep an enthusiasm for Roman architecture as for Roman republicans.[17]

From 1770 until his death in 1826, Jefferson planned and remodeled his home at Monticello. With each remodeling, the influence of Palladio grew stronger. Shortly before his death the Virginia architect himself acknowledged Palladio's influence, declaring: "The Hall is in the Ionic, the dining room is in the Doric, the parlor is in the Corinthian, and [the] dome in the Attic . . . In the other rooms are introduced several different forms of these orders, all in the truest proportions according to Palladio." Jefferson's idea of having white columns relieve the red brickwork of his walls, the moldings with which he accented, and the detail with which he sparingly enriched plain surfaces all derived from Palladio. In fact most of Jefferson's house plans featured Palladian-style structures set on high basements, with one story in the front and, if possible, two on the garden side. Jefferson's use of four porticoes, one on each side, and his inclusion of mezzanine levels were also characteristic of Palladio. Jefferson's practice, unusual for his day, of living atop a hill seems also to have proceeded from Palladio's second volume, in which the Italian noted that the Villa Rotunda stood on a "monticello." (*Monticello* means "little hill" in Italian, a language Jefferson called "a living dialect of Latin.") Cato the Elder, Varro, and Pliny the Younger had all recommended such a position.[18]

Indeed, Jefferson turned directly to the ancients for some of his plans for Monticello. The style of the garden, the interconnection of the outlying buildings with one another and with the main house through porticoes, and the plans for underground passageways, for a large birdhouse, and for a weather vane on the porch (to be manipulated from inside the house) were all features which Pliny had described in detail. His brick-lined fish pond, an ellipse five yards wide and ten yards long, was inspired by Varro's *piscina*. Jefferson's plans for his burial ground, though never executed, included a Greek temple, a pedestal with urns, a reclining nymph, and an Aeolian harp. Perhaps his most grandiose neoclassical proposal, however, was his plan, drafted shortly before his marriage, to build a triumphal column larger than Trajan's, no doubt in celebration of his conquest of Martha Skelton.[19]

Yet, as always, Jefferson placed his own distinctive stamp upon the building. He selected an octagonal shape, a form unorthodox in both classical and modern architecture, because it provided twenty percent more interior space than a square and admitted twice as much sunlight. Furthermore, although the central portico featuring two orders of columns, the attic story over the wings, the basement, and the broad flight of steps are all found in Palladio, they correspond to no single prototype. Jefferson's neoclassical architecture typified the founders' thought: it interwove classical, modern European, and American fabrics into a unique tapestry.[20]

Fiske Kimball, Karl Lehmann, and Merrill D. Peterson have theorized that Jefferson was attracted to classical architecture because he found the same simplicity, regularity, and rationality in its precise symmetry that he saw in nature. Certainly, Jefferson referred often to the simplicity of his favorite structures. He also expressed a preference for regularity and rationality when he informed James Madison of the architectural "law" regarding porticoes: "A Portico may be five to ten diameters of the column deep, or projected from the building. If of more than five diameters there must be a column in the middle of each flank, since it must never be more than five diameters from centre to centre of columns." But one should not slight the importance of tradition ("the past approbation of fifteen or sixteen centuries") or the desire for legitimacy ("to increase their reputation, to reconcile to them the respect of the world") in Jefferson's neoclassicism.[21]

Less plausible is Garry Wills's theory that Jefferson used the simple Doric column in his dining hall because it housed his collection of Jean-Antoine Houdon busts of Revolutionary figures. According to Wills, Jefferson was saying, as he had during his administration, that republicanism demanded frugality, a message he reinforced by making the house's exterior columns Doric. The problem with this theory is that Jefferson favored Ionic and Corinthian columns on other "republican buildings," both early and late in life. Yet, Wills's principal point, that Jefferson equated the simplicity of classical architecture with republican virtue, is certainly valid.[22]

Lehmann suggested that Jefferson favored Roman architecture over Greek because of the scarcity of books on Greek architecture; because of the greater variety found in Roman architecture, which combined spherical and cubic forms (the Greeks employed only cubic forms); and because of Jefferson's tour of Roman sites in the 1780s. Jefferson transmitted wide-eyed accounts of Roman structures while in France. In one letter he expressed outrage at the replacement of the Corinthian columns of the Praetorian Palace at Vienne with Gothic windows and at the razing of the circular wall at Arenas to pave a road. In another he provided detailed measurements of the Praetorian Palace, as well as measurements of the amphitheater at Arles.[23]

Jefferson played a leading role in the classical revival movement in American architecture. The Virginia Capitol and the U.S. Capitol rank as some of the earliest and best monuments of classical revivalism in America.

By contrast, Jefferson regarded painting and sculpture with ambivalence. In 1788, in making notes for Americans planning a European tour, Jefferson counted architecture "among the most important arts," but added that painting and sculpture were "too expensive for the state of wealth among us. It would be useless, therefore, and preposterous, for us to make ourselves connoisseurs in those arts. They are worth seeing, but not studying." Yet in 1771 he himself had compiled two lists of classical statues and late Renaissance paintings he wished to secure for Monticello. In its expanded form in 1782, the list included such paintings as *The Sacrifice of Iphigenia, Cocles Defending the Bridge,* and *Seleucus Giving His Wife Stratonice to His Son;* and such statues as "Venus of Medicis, Florence; Hercules of Farnese, Rome; Apollo of Belvedere, Rome; Antoninus, Florence; Dancing Faunus; Messenger pulling out a thorn; Roman slave whetting his knife; The Gladiator at Montalto; Myrmillo expiring; The Gladiator reposing himself after the engagement (companion to the former); Hercules and Antaeus; The two wrestlers; The Rape of the Sabines (3 figures)." In 1784 he purchased the painting "Democritus and Heraclitus, called the laughing and weeping philosophers." In acquiring the *Democritus and Heraclitus* Jefferson also contradicted his expressed opposition to modern depictions of ancient historical figures based on speculation. In retirement he compiled a list of fifty-eight paintings he desired; one-third of them featured classical themes. He possessed the paintings "Diogenes in the Market at Athens . . . copied from Rubens" and *Diogenes Visited by Alexander.* As late as 1816 Monticello's hallway contained a full-length statue of *Ariadne Reclining on the Rocks at Naxos,* next to a model of the Pyramid of Cheops; and its parlor featured a smaller statue of the sleeping Venus. Jefferson was also inconsistent concerning the representation of moderns in ancient dress. In a 1787 letter to George Washington he praised Houdon's statue of Washington in modern dress, declaring: "I think a modern in an antique dress as just an object of ridicule as a Hercules or Marius with a periwig or chapeau bras." But in 1816 he remarked concerning Canova's projected statue of Washington: "As to style or costume, I am sure the artist and every person of taste in Europe would be for the Roman, the effect of which is undoubtedly of a different order. Our boots and regimentals have a very puny effect." He also proudly displayed Ceracchi's marble bust of himself in Roman costume (facing Ceracchi's bust of Hamilton: "opposed in death as in life," Jefferson joked).[24]

Jefferson used other classical symbols as well. He named his horses Tarquin, Diomede, Castor, Celer, and Arcturus. He called one of his farms "Pantops" (view all around). He recommended the stave and ax (the Roman symbol of executive authority, the *fascii,* which Benito Mussolini later employed) as the Virginia symbol. He suggested that the American colonies adopt a classical motif, a father presenting the Aesopic bundle of rods to his sons (the thirteen colonies), and the Latin motto "Insuperabiles si Inseparabiles." He recommended "Polypotamia" (land of many rivers) as the territorial name for the land in the Ohio River Valley which he hoped Virginia would cede to the federal government.[25]

More significant was Jefferson's selection of a classical passage as an epitaph for his deceased wife. When Martha died, the grieving Jefferson used as her epitaph two of Achilles' lines in the *Iliad:* "If in Hades the dying forget, / Yet even there I will remember my dear companion." (Martha is the intended speaker.)[26]

John Adams loved paintings with classical themes. Above all, he was enamored of the *Judgment of Hercules,* the 1713 engraving by Simon Gribelin (based on the 1712 painting by Paulo de Matthaeis), which graced the title page of the Earl of Shaftesbury's *Characteristics of Men, Manners, Opinions, Times.* The engraving depicted a fable related by Socrates in Xenophon's *Memorabilia.* Adams described the work: "The Hero resting on his Clubb. Virtue pointing to her rugged Mountain, on one Hand, and persuading him to ascend. Sloth, glancing at her flowery Paths of Pleasure, wantonly reclining on the Ground, displaying the Charms both of her Eloquence and Person, to seduce him into Vice." As early as 1759 Adams wrote in his diary that "the Choice of Hercules came into my mind and left impressions which I hope will never be effaced nor long unheeded." He declared: "Let Virtue address me—'Which, dear Youth, will you prefer? A Life of Effeminacy, Indolence, and obscurity, or a Life of Industry, Temperance, and Honor? . . . Then return to your Study, and bend your whole soul to the Institutes of the Law and the Reports of Cases.'" Two days later, Adams confessed to minor diversions, leading him to moan that he had allowed himself to be "seduced into the Course of unmanly Pleasures that Vice describes to Hercules." Adams was so smitten with this engraving that he proposed it as the great seal for the United States in 1776, although after it was rejected he reluctantly admitted that it was "too complicated" for that purpose. In 1780 he wrote to his wife from Paris: "There are few who make the Choice of Hercules. That my Children may follow his Example is my earnest Prayer: but I sometimes tremble, when I hear the syren songs of sloth, least [lest] they should be captivated with her bewitching Charms and her soft, insinuating Musick." While in Paris in 1778, Adams was also moved by the *Adieus of Hector and Andromache,* a painting depicting the famous parting of the *Iliad*'s Trojan hero from his wife and child. Adams wrote: "With Feelings too exquisite to produce tears or Words, I gazed in silence at every Line, at every light and shade of this Picture, and could scarcely forgive Homer for introducing the Gleam of the Helmet and its Effect upon Astyanax [Hector's infant son], or any circumstance which could excite a Smile and diminish the Pathetic of the Interview."[27]

Other founders utilized classical symbols as well. James Madison placed the busts of Homer and Socrates beside those of Jefferson, himself, and his wife. John Witherspoon named his country home "Tusculum," after Cicero's villa. John Randolph named his horses Plutarch, Gracchus, Diomed, Mark Antony, and Regulus. John Rutledge named his horse Caesar. Henry Laurens named his slaves Tully, Valerius, and Claudius. George Washington purchased paintings called *Cupid's Pastime* and *Diana Deceived by Venus* and ordered busts of Sallust, Terence, and Horace. On July 6, 1756, during the French and Indian War, Washington chose "Xanthippe," the name of Socrates' wife, for the countersign at Fort Cumberland. Benedict Arnold's drugstore signboard ironically featured a Latin line: "Deeming himself born, not for his own, but for the world's service." While head of the Virginia High Court of Chancery, George Wythe chose for the seal of the Chancellor's Office a depiction of Herodotus' story (5.25) of a corrupt Persian judge whose flayed skin served as the covering for the judgment seat of his replacement, as an effective warning to the latter. The founders attached the word "Capitol" to their congressional building and "Senate" to the upper branch of their legislature, adopted the Roman eagle as the national bird, and freighted their seals and currency with Latin mottoes. They even named the tiny stream running through Washington, D.C., "the Tiber," prompting the Irish satirist Thomas Moore to intone: "Where tribunes rule, where dusky Davi bow, And what was Goose-Creek once is Tiber now."[28]

The founders used classical symbols and allusions to claim social status. In colonial, Revolutionary, and early national America, classical education, at least at the college level, was confined to the middle and upper classes. The apt use of classical symbols identifed one as a "gentleman," a man of some means and, hence, leisure—a "scholar" in the original Greek sense, "one possessing leisure." Most of the founders—including

John and Samuel Adams, Elbridge Gerry, Thomas Jefferson, James Madison, John Marshall, James Otis, Benjamin Rush, and James Wilson—were the first in their families to attend college. Of the ninety-nine men who signed the Declaration of Independence or were members of the Constitutional Convention, only eight are known to have had fathers who attended college. George Washington and Benjamin Franklin did not attend college at all. Although most of the founders were wealthy by the 1760s, the snobbish courtiers who surrounded the royal governors treated these "upstarts" with disdain. This fact explains the passion with which patriot leaders attacked royal "patronage." Revolutionary leaders sought to replace a society dominated by an aristocracy of birth with a society led by an aristocracy of merit. In the eighteenth century "merit" meant "learning"—and learning meant classical knowledge. The persistence of the equation of merit with classical knowledge explains why Americans continued to brandish classical symbols long after other aristocratic emblems, like the powdered wig, had been consigned to the nation's attics. Ironically, the classics represented a far more formidable opponent of radical egalitarianism than the socially proscribed wig. Many radical democrats failed to note that what went into American heads was much more important than what went on them.[29]

Having employed classical symbols and allusions to secure social status for themselves, the founders also used them to secure European respect for the United States. The American plethora of classical allusions betrayed a hint of defensiveness. Living on the frontiers of western civilization, American aristocrats were anxious to prove to haughty Europeans that theirs was a cultured nation. Hence Jefferson's insistence upon neoclassical architecture as a means of increasing European respect for the United States. Jefferson feared that republicanism itself might be stigmatized, and prospects for world happiness thus destroyed, if Europeans considered the United States a society of ignorant barbarians. Europeans must not be allowed to view republicanism as a system of government suited only to a primitive society. In 1785 Jefferson was deeply embarrassed by the "rude, misshapen piles" of Georgian brick which passed as public buildings in his native state and worried that if the new Virginia Capitol continued in that line, it would constitute "a monument of our barbarism which will be loaded with execrations as long as it shall endure."[30] Yet republican art and architecture must also represent republican simplicity, not monarchical opulence. The republican way was

Aristotle's "middle way." Jefferson's ambivalence concerning paintings and statues reflected this anxiety concerning the proper republican balance.

The founders suspected that the United States occupied the same position in western society that they themselves had occupied in pre-Revolutionary America: that of the self-made gentleman who must prove his worth to his social superiors by surpassing them in classical knowledge. Even while repudiating European corruption, American leaders longed for European respect. Like the Puritan ministers before them, these leaders defined America in European terms, emphasizing the national mission to save the mother continent by acting as a political "city on a hill." This mission, which provided the nation with a sense of identity and purpose, could not be achieved if America's European audience dismissed the great drama unfolding on American shores as a low-brow comedy.

III

Models

While the founders used classical symbols to create implicit analogies, identifying themselves and their causes with the ancients, they also formulated explicit analogies and contrasts between ancient and contemporary individuals, societies, and governments. Decades after some of the founders lost their facility with the classical languages, they retained a thorough knowledge of ancient history. Ancient history provided the founders with important, if imprecise, models of personal behavior, social practice, and government form. Such models gave the founders a sense of identity and purpose during the struggles of the Revolutionary and Constitutional periods.

The founders' models of personal behavior included mythological figures, Athenians, and Romans. The founders met their mythological heroes in the works of Homer, Hesiod, Virgil, and Ovid. They found their Athenian heroes in Herodotus, Thucydides, Xenophon, and especially Plutarch. Even as a teenager James Madison typified the founders' regard for the second century Greek historian when he copied into his commonplace book Cardinal de Retz's statement: "The E. of Montrose was the only Man in the World that recalled in me the Ideas of some Heroes who are now to be found only [in] Plutarch's Lives." Similarly, in 1782 Charles Lee declared: "I have ever from the first time I read Plutarch been an Enthusiastick for liberty . . . and for liberty in a republican garb." When John Taylor of Caroline wished to insult the Federalist commercial elite, he stated that few would make good "subjects for a Plutarch."[1]

The founders encountered their Roman heroes in the works of Polybius, Livy, Sallust, Plutarch, and Tacitus. Thomas Jefferson particularly admired Tacitus, whose moralistic *Annals* heaped scorn on the emperors and glorified the republic. In 1808 Jefferson wrote: "Tacitus I consider the first writer in the world without a single exception. His book is a compound of history and morality of which we have no other example." In 1823 Jefferson reiterated his claim that Tacitus was "the strongest writer in the world." By that time he had quoted Tacitus on the role of the historian: "This I hold to be the chief duty and office of the historian, to judge the actions of men, to the end that the good and the worthy may meet with the rewards due to eminent virtue, and that pernicious citizens may be deterred by the condemnation that waits on evil deeds at the tribunal of posterity." "History" was the ultimate judge, dispensing fame to the virtuous, infamy to the vicious. Reading Tacitus as a young man in 1756, John Adams was filled with horror at the violence of the Roman emperors. John Dickinson praised Tacitus as "that excellent historian and statesman . . . whose political reflections are so justly and universally admired." In his 1774 will Josiah Quincy left his son the works of Tacitus, Francis Bacon, Algernon Sidney, and John Locke, books he considered most apt to instill "the spirit of liberty" in a boy. He described Tacitus' work as "masterly," "elegant," and "instructive." Charles Lee noted regarding the tremendous influence of the ancient historians on the youth of his age: "It is natural to a young person whose chief companions are the Greek and Roman Historians and Orators to be dazzled with the splendid picture."[2]

The founders also encountered classical models of every variety in popular modern histories of the ancient world, such as Charles Rollin's *Ancient History* (1731–1750). When deprived of the rectorship of the University of Paris for his Jansenist views while still in his thirties, Rollin had begun writing ancient history. A predestinarian with a bleak view of human nature, Rollin's chief message was the same as that of the ancient Roman historians he cited: defeat lurks within victory, since the wealth and power which result from success lead to corruption and, hence, to ultimate ruin. Rollin contended: "Asia [the eastern empire], vanquished by Roman arms, in its turn vanquished Rome by its vices." John Adams reflected this cyclical view of history when he asked Thomas Jefferson in 1819: "Will you tell me how to prevent riches from becoming the effects of temperance and industry? Will you tell me how to prevent riches from producing luxury? Will you tell me how to prevent luxury from producing effeminacy, intoxication, extravagance, vice, and folly?" Rollin's classical conception of history as training in morality no doubt also enhanced his popularity in eighteenth-century America. Rollin declared that "history may properly be called the common school of mankind, equally open and useful to great and small . . . History, when it is well taught, becomes a school of morality." Hoping to instill a love of virtue in her son, Abigail Adams passed her days, while John Adams was away at the First Continental Congress, by having John Quincy read passages from the *Ancient History* to her. She wrote to John: "I have taken very great fondness for reading Rollin's ancient History since you left me. I am determined to go thro with it if possible in these days of solitude. I find great pleasure and entertainment from it, and I have perswaided Johnny to read me a page or two every day, and hope he will from his desire to oblige me entertain a fondness for it." Similarly, John Randolph repeatedly recommended the *Ancient History* to a young relative. Members of Princeton's American Whig Society read Rollin's history more frequently than any other modern history of the ancients.[3]

Many of the founders' heroes originated in Greek and Roman mythology. Thomas Jefferson dubbed Samuel Adams "the Palinurus of the American Revolution," after Virgil's mythical hero, who, having piloted the Trojan ships to Italy past many dangers, fell overboard and drowned. While preparing to replace the Federalist John Adams as president, a relieved Jefferson compared the republican experiment in the United States with the famed *Argos,* the ship which bore Jason's courageous band to the Golden Fleece. Jefferson wrote: "The storm through which we have passed has been tremendous indeed. The tough sides of our Argosie have been thoroughly tried. Her strength has stood the waves into which she was steered, with a view to sink her. We shall put her on a republican tack, & she will now show by the beauty of her motion the skill of her builders." Jefferson continued the analogy late in life, calling the leaders of the American Revolution "argonauts." Charles Thomson compared Patrick Henry with Aeneas, claiming that Congress listened to him with as rapt an attention as Aeneas's audience in Dido's palace.[4]

The most popular mythological model was the legendary Cincinnatus, though the founders considered him a real historical figure. In 1776 John Adams expressed his desire to emulate the Roman hero by resigning his worldly powers and cares. He wrote: "When a few mighty matters are accomplished here, I [will] retreat like Cincinnatus . . . and farewell Politicks." In 1780 Samuel Adams emphasized the need for Americans to elect capable and selfless men like Cincinnatus, noting: "How different was Pisistratus from that Roman Hero and Patriot Lucius Quinctius Cincinnatus, who, tho vested with the Authority of Dictator, was so moderate in his Desires of a Continuance of Power, that, having in six weeks fulfill'd the Purposes of his Appointment, he resign'd the dangerous office, which he might have held till the expiration of six Months. When we formerly had weak and wicked Governors & Magistrates, it was our Misfortune; but for the future, while we enjoy and exercise the inestimable right of chusing them ourselves, it will be our Disgrace." John Adams probably had Cincinnatus in mind again in 1794, when he wrote to Jefferson, who had resigned as secretary of state a year earlier and had left Philadelphia, then the national capital. Adams declared: "If I had your Plantation and your Labourers I should be tempted to follow your Example and get out of the Fumum et Opes Strepitumque Romae [the smoke, the wealth, and the din of Rome], which I abominate."⁵

Not surprisingly, many of the founders' Athenian heroes were aristocrats who had attempted, unsuccessfully, to rein in the mobs. Indeed, most of the founders admired the sixth-century B.C. reformer Solon for his moderation. In opposing the creation of a national judiciary at the Constitutional Convention Pierce Butler contended: "The States will revolt at such encroachments. Supposing such an establishment to be useful, we must not venture on it. We must follow the example of Solon, who gave the Athenians not the best Government he could devise; but the best they would receive." Similarly, in 1816 Jefferson congratulated Du Pont de Nemours on following Solon's example in suggesting moderate reforms for Latin America, reforms which would give the people "not the best possible government, but the best they can bear." Jefferson later explained: "The institutions of Lycurgus, for example, would not have suited Athens, nor those of Solon, Lacedaemon [Sparta]." In 1790 James Wilson praised Solon for his "wisdom and moderation" and exaggerated his role in western history. Wilson claimed: "His institutions concerning marriage, succession, testaments, the rights of persons, and things, have been disseminated through the jurisprudence of every civilized nation in Europe. The trial by jury, therefore, as well as other establishments may, it is said, refer, with great propriety, its original to Athens."⁶

Themistocles, Xenophon, and Demosthenes also served as models. Thomas Jefferson likened John Adams, a staunch supporter of a strong American navy, to Themistocles, whose success in building an Athenian fleet had led the Greeks to an astonishing victory over the Persians in the fifth century B.C. Jefferson also compared France's universal acclaim with that of the Athenian. After noting that every Greek general had voted himself the best general in the Persian War, and Themistocles the second best, Jefferson wrote: "So ask the traveled inhabitant of any nation, In what country on earth would you rather live?—Certainly in my own, where all my friends, my relations, and the earliest & sweetest affections and recollections of my life [dwell]. Which would be your second choice? France." In 1775 Jefferson claimed that Benedict Arnold's daring march to Quebec through the dense woods of Maine was equal to Xenophon's famous fifteen-hundred-mile retreat from the heart of the Persian empire in 401 B.C. As a young man in 1763, John Adams likened himself to Xenophon. He claimed: "If engagements to a party are necessary to make a fortune, I had rather make none at all, and spend the remainder of my days like my favourite author, that ancient and immortal husbandman, philosopher, politician, and general, Xenophon, in his retreat." In 1774 Adams contrasted the First Continental Congress' economic response to Parliament's Coercive Acts with the bolder policies of Demosthenes and Cicero. He wrote: "Is it easy to believe they would propose Non Importation? Non Exportation? Non Consumption? If I mistake not, Something a little more Sublime, and mettlesome, would come from Such Kind of Spirits." He noted: "When Demosthenes (God forgive the Vanity of recollecting his Example) went [as] Ambassador from Athens to the other States of Greece, to excite a Confederacy against Philip [of Macedon], he did not go to propose a Non Importation or Non Consumption Agreement!"[7]

The founders' principal Roman heroes were Cato the Younger, Brutus, Cassius, and Cicero, statesmen who had sacrificed their lives in unsuccessful attempts to save the republic in its expiring moments. Typical was Abigail Adams' 1781 compliment to Elbridge Gerry, comparing him with Cato. Only Thomas Jefferson doubted Cato's perfection, calling his mentor, George Wythe, "Cato without the avarice of the Roman." Though self-conscious about his lack of formal education, George Washington modeled himself upon Cato to such an extent that his biographer James Thomas Flexner claimed: "Washington was Cato turned Virginia country gentleman."[8]

George Washington's favorite play was Joseph Addison's *Cato,* a tragedy based closely on Plutarch's lives of Cato and Caesar. The play, which ended with Cato's suicide following Caesar's occupation of Utica, was intensely classical. It contained so many declamations on virtue that Samuel Johnson characterized it as "a succession of just sentiments in elegant language, rather than a representation of natural affections, or of any state possible or probable in human life." Addison went so far out of his way to avoid alluding to contemporary British politics (even ignoring Queen Anne's hint that she would not be averse to having the play dedicated to her) that both Whigs and Tories praised it. At the play's debut in 1713 each party attempted to surpass the other in applause, in order to prove that theirs was the party of liberty. The Tory Lord Bolingbroke even collected money from friends to give to the actor who played Cato, in order to lay claim to the play. (Bolingbroke collected fifty-four guineas, but gave the actor only fifty—a flagrant violation of Cato's strict ethics.) Similarly, Tory Alexander Pope claimed that Cato called "forth Roman drops from British eyes." In America the play was perceived as a Whiggish work and hence was tremendously popular. It underwent nine American editions before 1800 and eight more in the nineteenth century.[9]

Washington associated himself with Cato. In 1775 he prevented the resignation of General John Thomas, who was angered by an unjust demotion, by paraphrasing Cato's line: "Surely every post ought to be deemed honorable in which a man can serve his country." Despite congressional resolutions in 1774 and 1778 prohibiting all public officials from attending plays, Washington ordered *Cato* performed at Valley Forge. He hoped to improve the soldiers' morale by inspiring them with the example of Cato's men, who had demonstrated extreme selflessness in the struggle for liberty. During these difficult times, Washington often repeated another line from Cato: "'Tis not in mortals to command success." Perhaps it was the memory of Cato's willingness to sacrifice his property on behalf of the republic that led Washington to reproach his overseer for placating British troops with grain. Washington declared that the overseer should allow Mount Vernon to be leveled before giving any aid to the enemy.[10]

In 1783 Washington turned to *Cato* when his officers, furious over Congress's perpetual inability to pay them, mutinied at Newburgh. The rebels planned to threaten the states with a coup d'état unless they yielded more power to Congress. Although Washington considered the strengthening of the weak Congress vital to national survival, his classical conditioning had taught him to perceive even the threat of a military coup as dangerous and dishonorable. In his speech to the officers he used the same three tactics Cato employed to face down his mutineers in Act III, Scene 5 of Addison's play. First, Washington rebuked the anonymous author of a circular letter which urged mutiny. Cato had also lambasted his rebels, though Washington was able to adopt a friendlier tone with his audience, since he was able to feign ignorance of the identity of the mutineers.[11]

Washington's second tactic was to appeal to his officers to maintain the republican honor they had won. He urged them not to "adopt measures which may cast a shade over that glory which has been so justly acquired; and tarnish the reputation of an Army which is celebrated thro' all Europe for its fortitude and Patriotism." Washington returned to the theme at the end of the speech: "You will give one more distinguished proof of unexampled patriotism and patient virtue, rising superior to the pressure of the most complicated sufferings; And you will, by the dignity of your Conduct, afford occasion for Posterity to say, when speaking of the glorious example you have exhibited to Mankind, 'Had this day been wanting, the World had never seen the last stage of perfection to which human nature is capable of attaining.'" This last line was similar to an earlier one (Act I, Scene 4) in *Cato:*

> To strike thee dumb, turn up thy eyes to Cato!
> There may'st thou see to what a godlike height
> The Roman virtues lift up mortal man.

Similarly, in Act III Cato asked:

> . . . And will you thus dishonor
> Your past exploits, and sully all your wars?
> Do you confess 'twas not a zeal for Rome,
> Nor love of liberty, nor thirst of honour,
> Drew you thus far; but hopes to share the spoil
> Of conquered towns and plunder'd provinces?
> Fired with such motives you do well to join
> With Cato's foes, and follow Caesar's banners.[12]

Washington's third tactic was to appeal to the sympathy and respect which his past service had earned him. Colonel David Cobb recalled that Washington preceded his speech with the statement: "Gentlemen, you will permit me to put on my spectacles, for I have not only grown gray, but almost blind, in the service of my country." Cato was even less subtle, reminding his troops of the hardships he had endured in the deserts of Libya, when he had seen to the needs of his soldiers before quenching his own thirst:

Behold my bosom naked to your swords,
And let the man that's injured strike the blow.
Which of you all suspects that he is wrong'd,
Or thinks he suffers greater ills than Cato?
Am I distinguished from you but by toils,
Superior toils, and heavy weight of cares!
. . .
Have you forgotten Libya's burning waste,
Its barren rocks, parch'd earth, and hills of sand,
Its tainted air, and all its broods of poison?
. . .
When on the banks of the unlook'd-for stream
You sunk the river with repeated draughts
Who was the last that thirsted?

The soldiers' response to both appeals was the same: tearful remorse.[13]

Even while president, Washington continued to recite lines from *Cato*. Lamenting the difficult decisions of his office, Washington declared: "The post of honor is a private station." Such quotations are all the more remarkable because Washington rarely quoted authors. Since Washington never owned a copy of the play, he must have remembered the lines by heart.[14]

Other founders admired Addison's *Cato* as well. The popular play was probably the source of the most famous statements of the American Revolution, those of Patrick Henry and Nathan Hale. In Act II, Scene 4 we find the lines: "It is not now a time to talk of aught / But chains or conquest, liberty or death." In Act IV, Scene 4 we discover: "What pity is it / That we can die but once for our country." Cato had made the latter statement when the corpse of his son Marcus was brought to him after a battle. Hale uttered a paraphrase before the British hanged him as a spy. In the third volume of his famous reader, the first in North America, Noah Webster included most of Act I, Scene 4 of Addison's play, a dialogue between Juba and Syphax on the Roman mission to bring civilization and law to the world. In the same book Webster portrayed Cato's daughter, Marcia, as a model of female modesty. Webster's popular reader underwent seventy-seven editions between 1785 and 1835.[15]

While Washington derived a sense of identity and purpose from his emulation of Cato, John Adams derived the same benefits from his lifelong identification with Cicero. In the autumn of 1758 Adams gloried in the fact that law, his chosen profession, was "A Field in which Demos-

thenes, Cicero, and others of immortal Fame have exulted before me!"
That winter he confessed to his diary the pleasure he derived from reading Cicero's orations aloud: "The Sweetness and Grandeur of his sounds,
and the Harmony of his Numbers give Pleasure enough to reward the
Reading if one understood none of his meaning. Besides, I find it a noble
Exercise. It exercises my Lungs, raises my Spirits, opens my Porrs, quick-
ens the Circulation, and so contributes much to [my] Health." Indeed,
after a family quarrel a few days later, Adams "quitted the Room, and
took up Tully to compose myself." In 1765 he joined several other Boston lawyers in forming "Sodalitas," a small club whose "main Object"
was to "read in Concert the Feudal Law and Tully's Orations." In 1774
Adams urged an aspiring politician to adopt Cicero as his model. He
wrote regarding Cicero's proconsulship at Lilybaeum in Sicily: "He did
not receive this office as Persons do now a days, as a Gift, or a Farm, but
as a public Trust, and considered it as a Theatre, in which the Eyes of the
World were upon him." When Rome was short of grain, Cicero managed to feed the city without treating his own province unfairly.[16]

When Adams, one of the greatest orators of his day, rose before the
Continental Congress on July 1, 1776, to rebut John Dickinson's contention that American independence would be premature, the New Englander thought of Cicero. He recorded in his diary: "I began by saying
that this was the first time of my Life that I had ever wished for the Talents and Eloquence of the ancient Orators of Greece and Rome, for I
was very sure that none of them ever had before him a question of more
importance to his Country and to the World."[17]

Adams' admiration for Cicero outlived the American Revolution. He
spent the summer of 1796, several months before assuming the presidency, reading the Roman statesman's essays. In 1803 Adams quoted
Cicero regarding the true public servant: "Such a man will devote himself entirely to the republic, nor will he covet power or riches . . . He
will adhere closely to justice and equity, that, provided he can preserve
these virtues, although he may give offence and create enemies by them,
he will set death itself at defiance, rather than abandon his principles." No
one followed this ethic better than Adams. In the 1760s he had refused
the lucrative and prestigious position of admiralty court judge because he
considered the juryless British courts unconstitutional. In 1770 he had
sacrificed his popularity to defend the British soldiers accused of murder
in the "Boston Massacre." As president, in 1799–1800 he had made peace
with Napoleonic France, leaving Jefferson the glory of the Louisiana

Purchase, at the expense of his own reelection. While no other founder yearned so much for popularity, none so continually sacrificed it to a strict code of ethics. It is not fanciful to suppose that, when making such painful decisions, Adams found consolation in contemplating the Roman statesman's sacrifices and the eternal glory they had earned him.[18]

Adams continued to express admiration for Cicero in the correspondence of his twilight years. In his own notes of 1804 in defense of Cicero against Lord Bolingbroke's charge of military ineptitude, Adams cited both Conyers Middleton and Julius Caesar on Cicero's skill. Adams retorted to Bolingbroke's accusation of vanity against the Roman, a charge which Bolingbroke based on Cicero's having "impudently" demanded a triumph: "He did no more than all imperators had done. His Lordship's impudence here is greater than Tully's." In 1805, after chiding Benjamin Rush for destroying documents regarding the American Revolution which Rush had collected, Adams wrote: "The period in the history of the world the best understood is that of Rome from the time of Marius to the death of Cicero [second to first century B.C.], and this distinction is entirely owing to Cicero's letters and orations. There we see the true character of the times and the passions of all the actors on the stage. Cicero, Cato, and Brutus were the only three in whom I can discern any real patriotism . . . Cicero had the most capacity and the most constant, as well as the wisest and most persevering attachment to the republic." Adams explained that he had first become familiar with Cicero through Conyers Middleton's *History of the Life of Marcus Tullius Cicero* (1741), though he had read the Roman statesman in the original Latin shortly thereafter. In an 1808 letter to Rush, Adams again defended Cicero against the frequent charge of vanity, arguing: "What other People call Vanity in Cicero, I denominate Naivete." Cicero was faced with "Jealousy and Envy" of his talents and was surrounded by libelers. Adams continued: "In this distressing Situation he poured out the feelings of his tortured heart with the utmost Naivete . . . He blazoned forth his own Virtues, Talents, and great Services in the Face of the Senate and the whole Roman People . . . It was Self Defense, Independence, Intrepidity, or in one Word, Naivete." Nevertheless, fearful of facing the same charge of vanity for this implicit analogy between Cicero and himself, Adams never dispatched the letter. Although he allowed his son, John Quincy, to read the missive, he told him to burn it afterward.[19]

But in the following year what little self-restraint Adams retained collapsed. In a letter to Rush which he did dispatch, Adams cried out:

Panegyrical romances will never be written, nor flattering orations spoken, to transmit me to posterity in brilliant colors. No, nor in true colors. All but the last I loathe. Yet, I will not die wholly unlamented. Cicero was libeled, slandered, insulted by all parties—by Caesar's party, Catiline's crew, Clodius's myrmidions, aye, and by Pompey and the Senate too. He was persecuted and tormented by turns by all parties and all factions, and that for his most virtuous and glorious actions. In his anguish at times and in the consciousness of his own merit and integrity, he was driven to those assertions of his own actions which have been denominated vanity. Instead of reproaching him with vanity, I think them the most infallible demonstration of his innocence and purity. He declares that all honors are indifferent to him because he knows that it is not in the power of his country to reward him in any proportion to his services.

Pushed and injured and provoked as I am, I blush not to imitate the Roman.

In 1811, when Adams wished to console Rush upon his son's departure to the national capital and government service, he recalled Cicero's patriotic axiom (De officiis, 1.7.22): "Not for ourselves, not for ourselves alone were we born." Finally, in 1812, Adams wrote: "Letters! What shall I say of letters? Pliny's are too studied and elegant. Cicero's are the only ones of perfect simplicity, confidence, and familiarity." Each year of his retirement Adams set aside time to reread Cicero's De Senectute, which extolled the virtues of rural life.[20]

Adams was all too successful in his lifelong attempt to emulate Cicero. Adams' integrity, which found its greatest expression in his unwillingness to endorse party favoritism, led to unpopularity in both parties; and his responses to critics were marked by the same petulance and vanity as the Roman's. The only difference between Cicero and Adams was that Cicero, uninfluenced by Christian notions of humility, had found nothing shameful in vanity. Not only would it have never occurred to Cicero to deny the charge of vanity; it would never have occurred to his contemporaries to make it. Classical heroes were hardly known for their modesty.

Adams merely clung more tenaciously to a theme which the other founders also embraced: the theme of the lone-wolf hero (Socrates, Demosthenes, and Cicero are all good examples) who sacrifices short-term popularity, which can be purchased only by vice, for long-term fame, which can be purchased only by virtue—the aristocrat who saves the ignorant masses, often at the cost of his own life, from themselves. The

classical hero treated the follies of the people and the bribes of monarchs
with equal disdain. Likewise, the founders were as disgusted by the fawn-
ing courtiers who crowded around George III and his colonial governors
in search of preferment as they were by demagogues who manipulated
popular passions to increase their own power. This equation of virtue
with independence of thought and action, when combined with a
concomitant equation of vice with "factionalism" (Roman historians
despised the *factio,* the favorite instrument of demagogues), contributed
greatly to the antiparty sentiment which dominated the early history of
the United States. According to the classical doctrine, membership in
a political party inevitably involved defending the indefensible vices of
one's allies and attempting to dominate one's fellow citizens in order to
satisfy a narrow self-interest. In the eighteenth century the greatest compliment one man could pay another was to call him "disinterested." To
be disinterested was to place justice above all other considerations, including one's own interest and those of one's family, friends, and political
allies. Both Federalist and Republican leaders decried "party spirit."
They considered their own parties temporary aberrations, necessary only
to block the antirepublican ambitions of their opponents, and looked
forward to the day when they could be safely eliminated. George Washington devoted most of his Farewell Address to an attack on political
parties, which he feared might produce civil war. Many Americans
breathed a sigh of relief when American politics reverted to a partyless
condition following the death of the Federalist Party in 1816. The "Era
of Good Feelings" seemed a return to the mythical days of patriot una-
nimity during the American Revolution. John Quincy Adams inherited
his father's determination to resist party favoritism. He refused to remove
hundreds of political opponents from federal office. As late as the antebellum period many members of the Whig Party, still tied to classical
theory, continued to perceive parties as an evil. They dubbed Andrew
Jackson "King Andrew," claiming that his wholesale replacement of opponents resembled the corrupt patronage policy of George III.[21]

In any case, Adams' admiration for Cicero was infectious. In 1780 Abigail Adams exhorted her son, John Quincy, to seize the opportunity
afforded by the Revolution to accomplish noble deeds. She wrote:
"These are the times in which a Genius would wish to live. It is not in
the still calm of life, or the repose of a pacific station, that great characters
are formed. Would Cicero have shone so distinguished an orator, if he
had not been roused, kindled, and enflamed by the Tyranny of Catiline?"[22]

James Wilson also idolized Cicero. Conceding vanity as the sole flaw in Cicero's character, Wilson cited the Roman statesman more often than any other author in his 1790 lectures to law students at the College of Philadelphia. Regarding education, Wilson asked: "What, I repeat it, can be intrinsically more dignified than to assist in forming a future Cicero, or Bacon?" Cicero himself had taught law, even after serving as consul and after representing kings. Wilson quoted Cicero on the importance of the rule of law: "Believe me, a more inestimable inheritance descends to you from the law than from those who have left, or may leave, you fortunes. A farm may be transmitted to me by the will of any one; but it is by the law alone that I can peacefully hold what is already my own. You ought, therefore, to retain the publick patrimony of the law, which you have received from your ancestors, with no less assiduity than you retain your private estates; not only because these are fenced and protected by the law; but for this further reason, because the loss of the law would be deeply detrimental to the whole commonwealth." Wilson exulted: "The jurisprudence of Rome was adorned and enriched by the exquisite genius of Cicero, which, like the touch of Midas, converts every object into gold." He cited Cicero on the Roman jury system. He called Cicero's *De officiis* "a work which does honour to human understanding and the human heart." He quoted the statesman against torture and in defense of property rights. Wilson declared: "'A publick theater,' says Cicero, with his usual luminous propriety, 'is common to all citizens, but the seat which each occupies may, during the entertainment, be denominated his own.'"[23]

The founders revered Caesar's assassins Brutus and Cassius. During the Stamp Act crisis in 1765 John Adams declared optimistically: "Let us take it for granted that the same great spirit which once gave Caesar so warm a reception . . . [and] which first seated the great grandfather of his present most gracious Majesty on the throne of Britain is still alive and active and warm in England; and that the same spirit in America, instead of provoking the inhabitants of that country, will endear us to them forever and secure their good will." In 1767 he quoted Shakespeare: "Cassius from Bondage shall deliver Cassius." Adams also admired Brutus' famous ancestor, Lucius Brutus, who had helped expel Tarquin. In 1777 Adams contrasted Lucius Brutus' sincere republicanism with John Hancock's secret ambition. Denouncing Hancock's well-publicized donation of 150 cords of wood to the poor of Boston, Adams wrote: "Did [Lucius] Brutus in the Infancy of the Commonwealth and before the Army of Tarquin was Subdued, acquire Fame and Popularity by Largesses? No!

These arts were reserved for Caesar in the Dotage and the last expiring Moments of the Republic." (Ironically, Hancock's generosity, so great that it eventually exhausted his vast fortune, was an attempt to prove himself a genuine classical republican, willing to sacrifice his wealth for the good of the republic.) Charles Lee credited the example of the younger Brutus with his love of liberty. In 1790 James Wilson quoted Cicero in praise of Brutus: "Even those against whom he made decisions he sent away unruffled and placated."[24]

As head of Congress' Board of War during the Revolution, John Adams found military models in the Roman generals Fabius, Scipio Africanus, and Julius Caesar. In 1775 he confessed that although Fabius' patient policy of attrition against the Carthaginians had been "wise and brave," Adams himself was too impatient for such a strategy. He declared: "Zeal and Fire and Activity and Enterprise Strike my Imagination too much. I am obliged to be constantly on my Guard. Yet the Heat within will burst forth at Times." This last statement was certainly true, for in 1776 and 1777 Adams repeatedly complained that American strategy was too cautious. In 1776 he concluded, in a letter to General Henry Knox: "The Policy of Rome in carrying their arms to Carthage, while Hannibal was at the Gates of their Capital, was wise and justified by the Event, and would deserve Imitation if We could march into the Country of our Enemies." Adams understood that British control of the seas prohibited a reenactment of Scipio Africanus' famous amphibious assault on Carthage, but still felt that some offensive action was in order. In this, he anticipated John Paul Jones's daring raids on British commerce. In 1777 Adams wrote to General Nathanael Greene: "It is high Time for Us to abandon this execrable and defensive Plan . . . We must have a fighting, enterprizing Spirit conjured up in our Army. The Army that Attacks has an infinite Advantage and ever has had from the Plains of Pharsalia to the Plains of Abraham." Pharsalia was the plain in Thessaly where Caesar's force defeated Pompey's. Abraham was the plain outside Quebec where James Wolfe defeated Louis Joseph de Montcalm in 1759, resulting in the British annexation of Canada.[25]

Adams bewailed the fact that the Continental Army possessed no Epaminondas, the fourth-century B.C. Theban general who, with the help of Pelopidas, ended Spartan domination of Greece. Adams wrote: "And perhaps there is not in all Antiquity, if there is in universal History, an Example more apposite to our Situation than that of Thebes, or a Character more deserving of imitation than Epaminondas." The ancient

Thebans, like the modern Americans, were a peace-loving people driven to war by foreign tyranny. Their troops were raw, untrained farmers, who loved liberty and fought hard for it. Thus, Adams related: "Greece saw, with Astonishment, the Spartans defeated by inferiour numbers of Men, who had been held in Contempt . . . Epaminondas, with six thousand Men only, by his admirable disposition of them and their bravery, engaged and defeated three times their number [at Leuctra in 371 B.C.] and soon afterwards marched to the Gates of Sparta and exhibited to that haughty people a Sight they had never before beheld." But the Continental Army, Adams concluded, lacked the Epaminondas who could teach the British the same lesson. Adams even criticized American generals' writing, claiming that their battle accounts lacked the vividness of Sallust's, Xenophon's, and Caesar's. But perhaps worst of all, he once unfairly accused American generals of cowardice. Upset by the American retreat from Canada in 1776, he said: "Flight was unknown to the Romans . . . I wish it was to Americans." This lack of discipline was the fault of the generals, not the troops, and American officers should emulate Polybius in recognizing this fact, rather than slandering their soldiers.[26]

Adams maintained his admiration for Roman military skill. In 1806 he contrasted President Jefferson's military leadership skills with those of the Romans. Claiming that Jefferson's policies were designed to distract the people from national problems through a war against either Britain or France, Adams wrote: "The Romans were obliged to practice this policy for seven hundred years. But Jefferson is not a Roman. If peace should be concluded between France and England, we shall be in a perilous situation."[27]

The founders were not merely the formulators of classical analogies and contrasts, but the objects of them as well. Though theoretically an opponent of classical education, Abigail Adams often compared various founders with classical heroes. In 1782 she wrote to her husband, then negotiating a Dutch alliance for his infant country: "Eight years have already past since you could call yourself an Inhabitant of this State. I shall assume the Signature of Penelope, for my dear Ulysses [Odysseus] has already been a wanderer from me near half the term of years that Hero was encountering Neptune, Calipso, the Circes and Sirens." Voltaire compared John Dickinson with Cicero. In 1774, after giving political advice to Samuel Adams, Joseph Warren added that this was "perhaps too much like the declaimer who delivered a lecture upon the art of war to the illustrious General Hannibal." In the South Patrick Henry and

Richard Henry Lee were dubbed "the Demosthenes and Cicero of the American Revolution." Lord Byron and George Mason agreed regarding Henry. Byron called Henry "the forest-born Demosthenes." In 1774 Mason wrote: "He is, in my opinion, the first man upon this continent, as well in abilities as public virtues, and had he lived in Rome about the time of the first Punic War, when the Roman people had arrived at their meridian of glory, and their virtue not yet tarnished, Mr. Henry's talents would have put him at the head of that glorious commonwealth." After the Revolution Brissot de Warville noted, on visiting John Adams' farm: "He has, finally, returned to his retreat, in the midst of the applauses of his fellow-citizens, occupied in the cultivation of his farm, and forgetting what he was [a lowly colonist] when he trampled on the pride of his king, who had put a price on his head and who was forced to receive him as the ambassador of a free country. Such were the generals and ambassadors of the best ages of Rome and Greece; such were Epaminondas, Cincinnatus, and Fabius."[28]

Benjamin Franklin was the object of numerous analogies. In 1756 Immanuel Kant called him "the modern Prometheus," after the Greek god who gave fire to humankind. Turgot later made the same comparison, adding a Latin statement, meaning, "He snatched lightning from the sky and the scepter from tyrants." Jean-Honoré Fragonard's painting *Eripuit Coelo* (1778) depicted Franklin as half Mars, defeating tyrants, and half Minerva, deflecting lightning from the Temple of Liberty. Georgiana Shipley told Franklin she read everything she could about Socrates, "for I fancy I can discover in each trait of that admirable Man's character a strong resemblance between him and my much-loved Friend, the same clearness of Judgment, the same uprightness of intention and the same superior understanding." A member of the Royal Academy of Sciences compared Franklin with Cato. Wishing the Americans success in their revolution, the Frenchman added, "But I hope that I shall never see the time of saying," and then quoted Lucan's *Pharsalia* (1.128): "If the victor had the gods on his side, the vanquished had Cato." In 1778 John Adams recorded in his diary the story of Franklin's meeting with Voltaire at the French Academy of Sciences. Both heroes being present, a "general Cry" arose that they be introduced to each other. Adams recalled:

> This was done, and they bowed and spoke to each other. This was no Satisfaction. There must be something more. Neither of our Philosophers seemed to divine what was wished or expected. They, however, took

each other by the hand . . . But this was not enough. The Clamour continued, until the explanation came out "Il faut s'embrasser, a la francoise." The two Aged Actors upon this great Theatre of Philosophy and frivolity then embraced each other by hugging one another in their Arms and kissing each others' cheeks, and then the tumult subsided. And the Cry immediately spread through the whole Kingdom and I suppose over all Europe. "Qu'il etoit charmant. Oh! Il etoit enchantant, de voir Solon et Sophocle embrassans! How charming it was! It was enchanting to see Solon and Sophocles embracing!"

Europeans considered Franklin the Solon, the premier statesman, and Voltaire the Sophocles, the literary giant, of the age.[29]

Perhaps the most apt analogy concerned the two colossi of the American Revolution, Thomas Jefferson and John Adams, who died on the same day, July 4, 1826, the fiftieth anniversary of the Declaration of Independence. A grandson of John Adams, Charles Francis Adams, laid the two patriots to rest with a classical analogy which both would have relished. He related the story, from Herodotus (1.30.1), of Solon's trip to the wealthy kingdom of Lydia in Asia Minor. Having shown Solon his vast treasury, Croesus, the Lydian monarch, asked the wise Athenian: "Who, of all men that you have seen, do you deem most fortunate?" The Lydian monarch expected, of course, that Solon would answer, "Croesus." But Solon "named two brothers, Cleobis and Bion, who once put themselves to the wagon and drew their mother to Juno's temple, and then, after sacrificing and feasting, went to rest and died together at the height of their reputation of filial piety." Charles Francis concluded regarding Jefferson and Adams: "How much more deserving to be called blessed is the life of these two, who drew their nursing-mother, against strong resistance, to the temple of liberty and who, after a long period of labors and services devoted to her welfare, went to the same rest under auspices a thousand-fold more sublime."[30]

George Washington was the most common subject of classical analogies. In calling him "the Father of the Country" Americans emulated Cato, who had given that title to Cicero. Alexander Hamilton called Washington the "American Fabius." Fisher Ames, disagreeing with John Adams' earlier assessment of Washington, compared him with Epaminondas, writing: "Some future Plutarch will search for a parallel to his character. Epaminondas is perhaps the highest name of antiquity. Our Washington resembled him in the purity and ardor of his patriotism; and, like him, he first exalted the glory of his country . . . There it is to be hoped the parallel ends; for Thebes fell with Epaminondas." In 1800, a year after Washington's death, David Ramsay wrote: "Enemies he had, but they were few, and chiefly of the same family with the man who could not bear to hear Aristides always called the just. Among them all I have never heard of one who charged him with any habitual vice, or even foible." In his (in)famous biography of Washington, Parson Weems set a record for the most classical analogies in two sentences, writing: "Washington was as pious as Numa, just as Aristides, temperate as Epictetus, and patriotic as Regulus. In giving public trusts, impartial as Severus; in victory, modest as Scipio—prudent as Fabius, rapid as Marcellus, undaunted as Hannibal, as Cincinnatus disinterested, to liberty firm as Cato, and respectful of the laws as Socrates." Lest any philologist consider this cavalcade of classical analogies insufficient, Weems added regarded Washington's father: "Never did the wise Ulysses take more pains with his beloved Telemachus than did Mr. Washington with George."[31]

Sometimes analogies became self-fulfilling. Garry Wills has suggested that George Washington not only took notice of the Cincinnatus analogy, but worked consciously to promote it. The comparison captured the imagination of numerous domestic and foreign artists. Horatio Greenough's twelve-ton statue of Washington for the Capitol Rotunda, based somewhat on Phidias' *Zeus* but altered to fit the Cincinnatus analogy, depicted the Virginian in classical dress. Washington's right arm was raised, index finger pointing heavenward, his left arm offering his sword, handle outward. Unfortunately, by the time it was delivered to the Capitol in 1847, its classical garb offended Victorian sensibilities. Philip Hose complained: "Washington was too careful of his health to expose himself thus in a climate so uncertain as ours." S. W. Wallis added: "The last time I saw Greenough's colossal *Washington* in the garden of the Capitol, some irreverent heathen had taken the pains to climb up and insert a large 'plantation' cigar between the lips of the pater patriae . . . I could not help thinking, at the time, that if Washington had looked less like the Olympian Jove and more like himself, not even the vagabond who perpetrated the trick of the cigar would have dared or dreamed of such desecration." Similarly, Antonio Canova's statue of Washington depicted him in Roman military garb, with his sword laid down and his left hand clutching the Farewell Address, symbols of his two great surrenders of power. Giuseppe Ceracchi's bust portrayed the Virginian with Roman curls. Both John Trumbull and Charles Willson Peale painted

Washington as Cincinnatus. John J. Barralet's engraving *George Washington's Resignation* depicted Washington surrendering power to Columbia, while in the background, oxen, a plow, and Mount Vernon awaited.[32]

Poets and laymen proved equally susceptible to the Cincinnatus analogy. Maryland poet Charles Henry Wharton's "A Poetical Epistle" to Washington (1779) exulted:

> Thus, when of old, from his paternal farm
> Rome bad her rigid Cincinnatus arm
> Th' illustrious peasant rushed to the field,
> Soon are the haughty Volsii taught to yield:
> His country sav'd, the solemn triumph o'er,
> He tills his native acres as before.

A Fourth of July toast, offered at Wilmington, Delaware, in 1788, declared: "Farmer Washington—may he, like a second Cincinnatus, be called from the plow to rule a great people." Lord Byron concurred wholeheartedly. His "Ode to Napoleon" contained these lines:

> Where may the wearied eye repose
> When gazing on the Great;
> Where neither guilty glory glows
> Nor despicable state?
> Yes—one—the first—the best:
> The Cincinnatus of the West
> Whom envy dared not hate,
> Bequeath'd the name of Washington
> To make men blush there was but one.

An astonished western world agreed with the judgment of George III. Unable to believe that any military leader would voluntarily surrender such power, the king scoffed that if Washington resigned his commission, "He will be the greatest man in the world." The king's confusion epitomized his inability, throughout the Revolutionary conflict, to comprehend the enormous emotional power which classical republican ideals wielded over American minds.[33]

Fully conscious of the Cincinnatus image and determined to nurture it, Washington recognized that his appeal lay not in military victories, of which he had precious few, but in the republican virtue revealed in his surrender of power. As Wills put it: "People did not admire a conquering Caesar in him, but a Cincinnatus resigning." Hence, Washington never offered to resign as commander of the Continental Army, even after the worst defeats, because he did not wish to spoil, by anticipation, the offer of resignation which he planned once he had, like Cincinnatus, defeated the enemy. Soon after that day arrived in 1783, Washington withdrew completely from public life, even going to the extreme of resigning from his local vestry. In his letters of 1784 Washington referred to Mount Vernon as his "villa," a term he had never before employed in allusion to his estate. Sounding like Horace, he referred to himself as "a private citizen of America, on the banks of the Patowmac . . . under my Vine and my own Fig-tree, free from the bustle of a camp and the intrigues of a court." Indeed, the Cincinnatus analogy benefited from a fact so obvious to every schoolboy it was rarely mentioned: "George" derives from the Greek *georgos,* meaning "farmer." Proud of his position as the first president of the Society of the Cincinnati, an association of Revolutionary War veterans, Washington demanded reforms when popular fears of the organization threatened to destroy the image associated with its name.[34]

Virtually obsessed with his reputation, Washington agonized over the decision to suspend his retirement and attend the Constitutional Convention. In the end, he served as president of the convention because he feared the accusation that he was neglecting his duty to the republic out of a vain desire to preserve his reputation. Two years later Washington accepted the presidency of the United States for the same reason.[35]

Washington's dilemma, shared by all the founders in varying degrees, illustrates the demanding nature of classical virtue. Although duty called the virtuous man to political office, he was supposed to prefer the quiet blessings of life on the farm to the wielding of power. Indeed, he must never cease expressing an intense desire to retire from the ordeal of public service to the simple joys of the homestead. Nothing is more ubiquitous in the founders' correspondence than this sentiment, a pretense which can rarely be taken entirely at face value.

Only James Wilson bothered to praise the women of antiquity. After all, the very word "virtue," like "virile," derived from the Latin *vir,* meaning "man." Classical authors equated virtue with the independence of thought and action peculiar to propertied males, vice with "effeminacy," and a servile dependence on luxury with the female dependence on the male. Nevertheless, Wilson noted that Cicero had benefited from hearing the declamations of Laelia, a woman of natural oratorical skill.

Wilson also praised Cornelia, the mother of the Gracchi, the second-century B.C. Roman land reformers. When a frivolous lady asked to see Cornelia's jewels, the virtuous Cornelia showed the lady her sons. Wilson quoted Cicero on the mother of these "demagogues": "I have read the letters of Cornelia, the mother of the Gracchi; and it appears that her sons were not so much nourished by the milk, as formed by the style, of their mother."[36]

The founders also encountered societal models among the ancients. When Samuel Adams prayed that Boston would become a "Christian Sparta," he referred to Spartan frugality, selflessness, valor, and patriotism. Similarly, in his *Letters from a Pennsylvania Farmer,* John Dickinson reserved his praise for Spartan calm and courage, writing: "To such a wonderful degree were the ancient Spartans, as brave and free a people as ever existed, inspired by this happy temperature of soul that rejecting even in their battles the use of trumpets and other instruments for exciting heat and rage, they marched up to scenes of havoc and horror, with the sound of flutes, to the tunes of which their steps kept pace—'exhibiting,' as Plutarch says, 'at once a terrible and delightful sight, and proceeding with a deliberate valor, full of hope and good assurance, as if some divinity had sensibly assisted them.'" Americans ought to imitate this calm firmness in resisting unconstitutional taxation. The Boston town meeting publicly thanked Dickinson for his "Spartan, Roman, British Virtue, and Christian spirit joined." In 1790 James Wilson applauded the Spartan emphasis on education: "In Sparta, one of the most respectable members of the state was placed at the head of all the children. Would not some similar institution be eligible with regard to such of them as are deprived of their parents?" In 1814 John Taylor contrasted the virtues of the landed aristocracy of Sparta with the vices of the British commercial elite. Thomas Jefferson celebrated the courage and patriotism of the Spartans under King Leonidas, who had volunteered to give their lives at Thermopylae in 480 B.C. He compared the inane question of which American contributed the most to the American Revolution with the question, "Who first of the three hundred Spartans offered his name to Leonidas?"[37]

But while the founders admired many of the traits which the Spartans' intense military training had instilled in them, few were prepared to advocate so complete a submersion of individuality. Thomas Jefferson referred to the Spartans as "military monks." In *Federalist* No. 6 Alexander Hamilton noted: "Sparta was little better than a well regulated camp." Federalist Party leader Fisher Ames repeated the criticism of the Athenian Alicibiades: "No wonder the Spartans cheerfully encounter death; it is a welcome relief to them from such a life as they are obliged to lead." John Adams agreed. He called Sparta's communal ownership of goods "stark mad." To the Abbé de Mably's statement "How right Lycurgus was in forbidding the Spartans to communicate with other Greeks!" Adams retorted: "Is it such a felicity to be confined in a cage, den, or cave? Is this a liberty?" The founders sought the Spartans' numerous admirable qualities without the brutal system of socialization which produced them.[38]

James Wilson applauded the openness of Athens and republican Rome, as well as the frugality and temperance of the latter city. Wilson wrote: "Machiavel, when he inquires concerning the causes to which Rome was indebted for her splendour and greatness, assigns none of stronger or more extensive operation than this—she easily compounded and incorporated with strangers." He also praised the Athenians of Solon's day for their "generous" and unusual policy of recruiting skilled foreigners and granting them citizenship. Regarding the frugality and temperance of the early Roman republic, Wilson contended: "They were the values which nursed and educated infant Rome and prepared her for all her greatness. But in the giddy hour of her prosperity, she spurned from her the obscure instruments by which it was procured; and, in their place, substituted luxury and dissipation. The consequence was such as might have been expected. She preserved, for a time, a gay and flourishing appearance; but the internal health and soundness of her constitution were gone. At last, she fell a victim to the poisonous draughts which were administered by perfidious favourites. The fate of Rome, both in her rising and in her falling state, will be the fate of every other nation that shall follow both parts of her example."[39]

The founders also turned to the ancients for their models of government, most notably the Greek republics of the fifth and fourth centuries B.C. and the Roman republic from the sixth to the first century B.C. In 1764 James Otis contrasted the corruption of modern European monarchies with "the grandeur of the ancient republics." John Adams expressed a common view in 1774 when he wrote: "The Grecian Commonwealths were the most heroic Confederacy that ever existed . . . The Period of their Glory was from the Defeat of Xerxes [king of Persia] to the Rise of Alexander. Let Us not be enslaved, my dear Friend, Either by Xerxes or Alexander." Thomas Jefferson expressed an equally common view in 1795. After speaking in glowing terms of the "experiment" being undertaken in the United States of basing government "on principles of honesty, not of mere force," he declared: "We have seen no instance of this since the days of the Roman republic." In 1790 James Wilson traced the doctrine of popular sovereignty to the Greeks and Romans. Wilson contended: "Let them be called covenants, or agreements, or bargains; or stipulations, or any thing similar to any of those, still I am satisfied; for still everything mentioned and everything similar to everything mentioned imports consent." He praised the Greeks' love of liberty. Of Athens, he wrote specifically: "At the mention of Athens, a thousand refined and endearing associations rush immediately into the memory of the scholar, the philosopher, the statesman, and the patriot." He added that when Homer listed the Greek forces that fought at Troy (*Iliad*, 2.5.547), he arranged them all under the names of their kings, but when he came to the Athenians, he distinguished them "by the peculiar appellation of 'the people' of Athens," suggesting a popular government as early as the eighth century B.C. Wilson repeated this entire series of statements a few years later, as an associate justice of the Supreme Court, when deciding a states' rights issue in the case of *Chisholm v. Georgia*. In 1814 John Taylor praised the popular governments of the ancients: "As rivals of Rome and Carthage, the contemporary monarchies are almost imperceptible; and above an hundred generations, almost forgetting what the rest of the world at that time [contributed], have transmitted to us an admiration of the little Athenian democracy, which we shall hand down to a fathomless posterity." He particularly lauded the freedom of expression allowed in these societies, remarking: "[Free] Expression is the respiration of the mind . . . It flourished in the climates of Greece and Italy whilst it could breathe freely."[40]

In the Revolutionary period the founders most fervently applauded the Greek and Roman republics' lenient treatment of their colonies. In his 1775 "Letters of Novanglus" John Adams drew a sharp contrast between the colonial policies of the ancients and the British mistreatment of the American colonies. He declared: "But let these 'best writers' say what they will, there is nothing in the law of nations, which is only the law of right reason applied to the conduct of nations, that requires that emigrants from a state should continue, or be made a part of the state. The practice of nations has been different. The Greeks planted colonies, and neither demanded nor pretended any authority over them, but they became distinct, independent commonwealths." Similarly, Adams argued that Romans of the republican era acknowledged the equal rights of their own colonies in Italy. Hence, when an envoy from a Roman colony threatened rebellion if the colony were not treated fairly, most of the senators coolly concluded: "That they had heard the voice of a man and a son of liberty; that it was not natural or credible that any people, or any man, would continue longer than necessity should compel him in a condition that grieved and displeased him. A faithful peace was to be expected only from men whose affections were conciliated—nor was any kind of fidelity to be expected from slaves . . . That they who regarded nothing so much as their liberty deserved to be Romans." Adams added pointedly: "The Senate and people of Rome did not interfere in making laws for their colonies, but left them to be ruled by their governors and senates. Can Massachusettensis [a prominent Tory essayist] produce from the whole history of Rome, or from the Digest, one example of a *Senatus consultum* or *Plebiscitum* laying taxes on a colony?" John Dickinson told the same story, taken from Livy, identifying the Roman colonists in question as the Privernates. He added that their love of liberty had so endeared them to the Romans that they were made citizens of Rome, "which at that Time could boast of the bravest and most virtuous Subjects of the Universe."[41]

Others were also aware of the difference between ancient Greek and British colonial policies. In *An Inquiry into the Rights of the British Colonies* (1766) Richard Bland cited Thucydides' discussion of Corcyra (1.2–3) to prove that Greek colonies had enjoyed independence. In the 1760s Thomas Jefferson copied into his legal and political commonplace book numerous quotations from Abraham Stanyan's *Greek History,* most of which concerned Greek colonization of the Mediterranean. Stanyan noted that each of the Greek colonies had been independent of its "metropolis" (mother city) from the time of its establishment.[42]

Most of the founders disagreed with Adams' and Dickinson's perception of the Roman republics' colonial policy, however. In 1764 James Otis wrote: "Greece was more generous and a better mother to her colonies than Rome. The conduct of Rome towards her colonies and the corruptions and oppressions tolerated in her provincial officers of all denominations was one great cause of the downfall of that proud republic." The following year Otis responded to Tory Martin Howard's use of the Roman model of colonization: "'Tis well known the Grecians were kind, humane, just, and generous toward their [colonies]. 'Tis as notorious that the Romans were severe, cruel, brutal, and barbarous toward theirs. I have ever pleased myself in thinking that Great Britain since the

[Glorious] Revolution might be justly compared to Greece in its care and protection of its colonies. I also imagined that the French and Spaniards followed the Roman example. But our Letter Writer tells quite a different story." In 1771 Samuel Adams (as "Valerius Poplicola") retorted to Thomas Hutchinson's use of the Roman model in *A History of Massachusetts Bay:* "Why the conduct of Rome towards her colonies should be recommended as an example to our parent state, rather than that of Greece, is difficult to conjecture, unless it was because, as had been observed, the latter was more generous and a better mother to her colonies than the former . . . We are willing to render to her [Great Britain] respect and certain expressions of honor and reverence, as the Grecian colonies did to the city from whence they deriv'd their origin . . . so long as the colonies were well treated."[43]

Other founders shared this perception of Roman colonial policy. In 1774 Alexander Hamilton wrote: "Rome was the nurse of freedom. She was celebrated for her justice and lenity; but in what manner did she govern her dependent provinces? They were made the continual scene of rapine and cruelty. From thence let us learn how little confidence is due to the wisdom and equity of the most exemplary nations." In the next year Hamilton did not dispute Tory Samuel Seabury's assertion that it was only late in the Roman republican period that Rome's Italian subjects were granted local self-government. Rather, he contended: "The mistress of the world was often unjust. And the treatment of her dependent provinces is one of the greatest blemishes in her history. Through the want of that civil liberty for which we are now so warmly contending, they groaned under every species of wanton oppression. If we are wise, we shall take warning from thence; and consider a like state of dependence as more to be dreaded than pestilence and famine." In 1778 George Mason claimed regarding the Revolution: "The truth is that we have been forced into it, as the only means of self-preservation, to guard our Country & posterity from the greatest of all Evils, such another infernal Government (if it deserves the Name of Government) as the Provinces groaned under, in the latter Ages of the Roman Commonwealth." Similarly, when William Grayson opposed an increase in federal power at the Virginia ratifying convention, he cited the Roman republics' "remarkable" brutality toward their provinces.[44]

But John Adams loved the early Roman republic so much that he frequently compared America with it. As early as 1755 he contended: "If we look into History we shall find some nations rising from contemptible beginnings, and spreading their influence, 'till the whole Globe is subjected to their sway. When they reach'd the summit of Grandeur, some minute and unsuspected Cause commonly effects their Ruin, and the Empire of the world is transferred to some other place. Immortal Rome was at first but an insignificant Village, inhabited only by a few abandoned Ruffians, but by beginnings it rose to a stupendous Height, and excell'd in Arts and Arms all the nations that preceded it." Similarly, America began as a few scattered settlements, but might soon become "the greatest seat of Empire." The idea that "empire" always moved westward (as, in the past, from the Middle East to Greece to Rome to France to Great Britain) had long been a popular European belief. By 1774 Adams could write: "In Short, as comprehensive [a] Knowledge of Arts and Sciences, and especially of Law and History, of Geography, Commerce, War, and Life, is necessary for an American Statesman, at this Time as was ever necessary for a British or a Roman Senator, or a British or Roman General." When the Chevalier de la Luzerne complimented American eloquence, Adams replied modestly that it was "the Time of Ennius with Us." Ennius was a third-century B.C. Roman epic poet, whose unpolished *Annals* was superseded by Virgil's *Aeneid*.[45]

John Dickinson and Joseph Warren joined Adams in presenting the government of early republican Rome as a model. In 1768, when urging merchants to adhere to the boycott of British goods, Dickinson said: "I would beg Leave to ask whether any People in any Age or Country ever defended and preserved their Liberty from the Encroachment of Power without suffering present Inconveniences. The Roman People suffered themselves to be defeated by their Enemies, rather than submit to the Tyranny of the Nobles." In his famous 1772 speech commemorating the Boston Massacre, Joseph Warren declared concerning the Roman love of liberty: "It was this noble attachment to a free constitution which raised ancient Rome from the smallest beginnings to the bright summit of happiness and glory to which she arrived; and it was the loss of this which plunged her from that summit into the black gulph of infamy and slavery."[46]

During the Constitutional debates of 1787–88, the Antifederalists expressed admiration for the ancient republics' short executive terms. At the Virginia ratifying convention William Grayson protested the president's four-year term, arguing: "The [Roman] consuls were in office only two years [actually, one year]. This quadrennial power cannot be justified by ancient history. There is hardly an instance where a republic trusted its executive so long with much power." "The Federal Farmer" agreed, noting that no limit had been placed on the number of terms the president might hold office. He explained: "The Roman consules and the Carthaginian suffetes possessed extensive powers while in office; but being annually appointed, they but seldom, if ever, abused them. The Roman dictators often possessed absolute powers while in office; but usually being elected for short periods of time, no one of them for ages usurped upon the rights of the people." Years later John Taylor praised the Roman practice of rotating consuls and bewailed the lack of a constitutional limit on the number of presidential terms. He noted: "The same period demonstrates the errour of the objection that rotation causes a loss of talents to the publick. It would have been most likely to produce this loss in military affairs. For seven centuries Rome applied the principle to her generals, and conquered; for five, she trusted to experience and was subdued. The rotary generals and statesmen of the little Athenian republick destined it to live for ever in the annals of fame, and most of its contemporary governments are for ever dead."[47]

The Antifederalists also admired the ancient republics' citizen–armies. They argued that the constitutional clause allowing Congress to maintain a federal army in peacetime was unnecessary. "The Impartial Examiner" contended that the best defense was a "well–regulated militia." He claimed: "By a policy somewhat similar to this, the Roman Empire rose to the highest pitch of grandeur and magnificence." "A Farmer" demanded of his readers: "Are we then to look up to a standing army for the defence of this soil from foreign invasion? Have we forgot that a few freemen of Sparta defended their country against a million of Persian slaves?" Even if we accept Herodotus' exaggerated Persian count, as "A Farmer" evidently did, we must note that the Spartan and Roman armies, though citizen–armies, were also professional armies. Spartan males were trained exclusively in the military life, leaving the foreign population of helots to till the soil. Likewise, a recent scholar has noted that the Romans experienced, at most, fourteen years of peace between 327 B.C. and 116 B.C., so that its army, in the centuries of expansion to which the Antifederalists referred, was also essentially professional. Nevertheless, as late as 1814, during the War of 1812, Thomas Jefferson wrote that the United States should emulate the Greeks and Romans in avoiding standing armies and relying on citizen–armies, like the state militias, whose republican spirit would make them "invincible."[48]

By contrast, some Federalists admired Roman and Persian centralization. At the Constitutional Convention James Wilson said that the states should be maintained only as "lesser jurisdictions," similar to the provinces of the Roman and Persian empires. Alexander Hamilton concurred. The states, he said, should be preserved as "subordinate jurisdictions," though the Roman and Persian analogies disturbed him, "the great powers delegated to the Satraps [Persian provincial governors] & proconsuls [Roman provincial governors] having frequently produced revolts and schemes of independence." But in *Federalist* No. 34 Hamilton abandoned this analogy for a far different (and more felicitous) one. He claimed that the Constitution gave the state legislatures "coordinate authority" with Congress, just as legislative authority in Rome had been divided, for a while, between the Comitia Centurata, controlled by the patricians, and the Comitia Tributa, controlled by the plebeians. Hamilton claimed that "these two legislatures coexisted for ages, and the Roman republic attained to the utmost height of human greatness."[49]

Some founders acquired another model from Tacitus, the primitive republicanism the Roman perceived among the Germanic tribes of the first century A.D. In the colonial period, when Jefferson sought to justify American opposition to British measures, the Germanic model was particularly important. Although British and French writers dominate Jefferson's legal and political commonplace book, the British authors invariably referred to Tacitus' *Germania* to prove that the Anglo-Saxon "constitution" had been republican, consisting of an elected king and parliament reinforced by "allodial" (nonfeudal) land ownership, until the Normans had overturned it. Lord Kames quoted Tacitus to show that the Germanic tribes had possessed free land tenure and that this system had promoted productivity. John Dalrymple cited Tacitus to show that the Germans had prohibited primogeniture, since they deemed illogical the concept that a dead man, who no longer possessed any rights, could alienate property from its rightful heirs. William Somner quoted both Tacitus and Julius Caesar to show that the Germanic tribes had not possessed these feudal trappings. In a marginal note Jefferson concluded regarding Tacitus and Caesar: "If these authors are so to be understood, the person taking the land from the chief does not appear to have owed him any services of a feudal nature; tho' doubtless he was ready to join in defending his country in general."[50]

Jefferson later had the original Latin text of *Germania* collated with his favorite English translation, that of Thomas Gordon (1728–1731). With the assistance of John Trenchard, Gordon had already published the two most influential Whiggish works of the eighteenth century, the *Independent Whig* and *Cato's Letters*. In the introduction to the *Germania* Gordon declared: "To vindicate the Deity from the impious charge of protecting Tyrants, to maintain the cause of Liberty, and shew its blessings, to assert the rights of men and of society, and to display the sad consequences of public corruption, with the beauty and benefit of public virtue, is the design of these discourses." Gordon interjected into the text his own moralistic "discourses," such as the one in which he explained that the Germans had lived "in a state of chastity well secured, corrupted by no seducing shews and public diversions, by no irritations from banqueting." His translation was more literal in passages denouncing the Roman emperors than in the few which noted their good qualities. Indeed, Tories like Alexander Pope ridiculed the translation. In the *Epilogue to the Satires* Pope wrote: "There's honest Tacitus once talked big / But he is now an Independent Whig."[51]

Jefferson's love of Tacitus, as seen through the prism of British Whiggery, manifested itself in his 1774 instructions to the Virginia delegates at the First Continental Congress. Published in pamphlet form as *A Summary View of the Rights of British America,* the essay earned Jefferson his first notoriety outside Virginia. In his most complete statement before the Declaration of Independence concerning American resistance to British measures, Jefferson argued that just as the Anglo-Saxons, after immigrating to Britain, owed no obedience to their mother country, American colonists owed no obedience to Britain. Jefferson then added to this natural law argument the force of tradition. Using phrases similar to Somner's, he argued: "In the earlier ages of the Saxon settlement feudal holdings were certainly altogether unknown." Feudalism, he contended, had been foisted upon the Anglo-Saxons by William the Conqueror and the "Norman lawyers" who followed him. Hence, Jefferson concluded that George III had no right to control the colonies' public lands, a happy conclusion, since the king had just doubled their price. Jefferson claimed that he merely desired to return to a golden age when governments had observed natural rights.[52]

Jefferson idealized ancient Anglo-Saxon society in this fashion throughout his life. When advocating the elimination of fees for public lands in 1776 he asked: "Are we not the better for what we have hitherto abolished of the feudal system? Has not every restitution of the antient Saxon laws had happy effects? Is it not better now that we return at once into that happy system of our ancestors, the wisest and most perfect ever yet devised by the wit of man?" As late as 1825 Jefferson wrote that the Whig historians of England always dated the origins of the British Constitution, correctly, from the Anglo-Saxon period, while the Tories dated it from the Norman Conquest. Having learned the ancient Anglo-Saxon language by that time, Jefferson was gladdened by the University of Virginia's inclusion of the language in its curriculum. He predicted that students of Anglo-Saxon would "imbibe with the language their free principles of government."[53]

Richard Bland and James Wilson joined Jefferson in celebration of the ancient Anglo-Saxons. In 1766 Bland cited Tacitus' *Germania* to prove that the Anglo-Saxons had enjoyed liberty. Wilson cited Tacitus regarding the "nearly indestructible" confederacy of Germanic tribes, arguing that they provided a good model for the American republic. He quoted the Roman historian concerning German republicanism: "On large matters all consult." He cited Tacitus on the Saxons' moderation in punishment, their public trials, their prohibition of infanticide, and their practice of having criminals compensate their victims. He called the *Germania* "a masterly account of the manners of that people." Indeed, so ardent was Wilson's love of both the classical and Anglo-Saxon societies that he inaccurately linked the two, arguing that the Germanic tribes must have received their laudable institutions from the Greeks via the Romans.[54]

The founders considered the histories of the classical world, England, and America (including their own experiences) their three most significant pasts. Inextricably intertwined in the founders' minds, these pasts were denied separate identities. The manner in which this occurred was complex. The founders often portrayed ancient republicans as early British Whigs. But the Whig writers the founders read were themselves classicists, who derived many of their ideas and most of their examples from Greek and Roman works. Such modern British authors as Joseph Addison and Thomas Gordon engrafted onto the themes of Plutarch, Tacitus, and the other ancient authors the English dialect essential to their vitality within the British empire. But the founders viewed America as the only land in which classical ideals could be translated into reality. John Adams considered it a matter of great importance that his Puritan ancestors had been classicists. Following the passage of the Stamp Act in 1765, Adams boasted of the early colonists: "To many of them, the historians, orators, poets, and philosophers of Greece and Rome were quite familiar: and some of them have left libraries that are still in being, consisting chiefly of volumes in which the wisdom of the most enlightened ages and nations is deposited." He concluded that his forefathers had detested all of the servile dependencies of the feudal system, since they "knew that no such unworthy dependencies took place in the ancient seats of liberty, the republics of Greece and Rome." America was the only land in which the classical tradition of liberty was pure, unsullied by the stain of feudalism.[55]

So skillfully were the classical, Whig, and American traditions interwoven that the founders considered them one and the same: "the tradition of liberty." No one thought it odd that the membership of Princeton's Cliosophic Society should be divided between classical and Whig pseudonyms—that "Burke" should debate "Pindar," or that "Wilkes" should confer with "Brutus." Nor did anyone sneer when James Warren donned a toga for his 1775 speech commemorating the Boston Massacre—or the following year, when Cliosophic initiate Robert Whorry took the name "Warren" to honor the patriot, who had, in the meantime, been killed in the Battle of Bunker Hill. *Bickerstaff's Almanac* of 1769 expressed a virtually unquestioned opinion when it asserted: "Locke and Sidney revived the spirit of the ancient republics." Similarly, John Adams later recalled: "Whig principles were the principles of Aristotle and Plato, of Livy and Cicero, and Sidney, Harrington, and Locke."[56]

Classical models gave the founders a sense of identity and purpose. In 1813 Jefferson wrote to Adams: "The same political parties which now agitate the U.S. have existed thro' all time. Whether the power of the people or that of 'the aristoi' should prevail were questions which kept the states of Greece and Rome in eternal convulsions, as they now schismatize every people whose minds and mouths are not shut up by the gag of a despot." This perception of ancient history gave Jefferson the satisfaction of believing that his own democratic exertions were part of a grand universal scheme. To the founders, the study of the past was not a mere antiquarian hobby. The past was alive with personal and societal meaning. Their perception of that living past shaped their own identities.[57]

The conflicts of the Revolutionary and Constitutional periods increased the founders' sense of kinship with the ancients. Proud of America's firm resistance to the Intolerable Acts, Samuel Adams declared in 1774: "I think our Countrymen discover the Spirit of Rome or Sparta." In a 1776 letter to George Wythe, John Adams exulted: "You and I, my dear Friend, have been sent into life at a time when the greatest lawgivers of antiquity would have wished to have lived." In the same year, shortly after the Declaration of Independence was signed, Charles Lee told Patrick Henry: "I us'd to regret not being thrown into the world in the glamorous third or fourth century [B.C.] of the Romans; but now I am thoroughly reconcil'd to my lot." Edmund Pendleton cherished the memory of the Virginia Constitutional Convention of 1776, recalling: "The young boasted that they were treading upon the Republican ground of Greece and Rome." In 1777 George Washington replied to British general John Burgoyne's peace offers: "The associated armies in America act from the noblest motives, liberty. The same principles actuated the arms of Rome in the days of her glory; and the same object was the reward of Roman valour." George Tucker later recalled the excitement of these days, writing regarding Henry's "Liberty or Death" speech: "Imagine to yourself this speech, delivered with the calm dignity of Cato of Utica; imagine to yourself the Roman Senate assembled in the Capital when it was entered by the profane Gauls. Imagine that you had heard Cato addressing such a Senate!" Never mind that to achieve the image he wished to convey Tucker had to join a Roman hero from one epoch with a Senate from another era. The image was real to Tucker. As late as 1805 John Adams declared concerning Middleton's *Life of Cicero:* "I seem to read the history of all ages and nations in every page, and especially the history of our country for forty years past. Change the names and every anecdote will be applicable to us."[58]

Imagine the founders' excitement at the opportunity to match their ancient heroes' struggles against tyranny and their sage construction of durable republics—to rival the noble deeds which had filled their youth. The founders were thrilled by the belief that they were beginning anew the work of the ancient republicans, only this time with an unprecedented chance of success. Cato and Cicero had lost the first round of combat against the tyranny of Caesar and Augustus, but the founders, starting afresh in a virgin country with limitless resources, could pack the punch that would win the second and decisive round. It is not surprising that the founders referred to their classical works as often during the Revolutionary and Constitutional periods as during the leisure of their retirement. They truly believed that ancient history was a source of knowledge which must be utilized in making decisions.

IV

Antimodels

The founders' classical "antimodels," those ancient individuals, societies, and government forms whose vices they wished to avoid, were as significant as their models. The antimodels the founders encountered everywhere in their classical reading left them obsessed with conspiracies against liberty, particularly when hatched by monarchs or demagogues. This fear accounts for the founders' overreaction to the modest taxes Parliament sought to impose on the American colonies in the 1760s. The horror and disgust which Roman historians' accounts of imperial corruption had instilled in the founders' minds in their youth accounts for much of their exaggeration of the brutality of the well-intentioned but inept George III. Similarly, the classical historians' ubiquitous depictions of mob violence and chaos explain much of the founders' fear of demagogues. Although the founders' most prevalent antimodels were the Roman emperors, even their scrutiny of the ancient republics frequently resembled autopsies. The purpose of these autopsies was to save the life of the American body politic by uncovering the cancerous growths which had caused the demise of its ideological ancestors.

The founders believed that the purpose of history was the prevention of tyranny. In his Bill for the More General Diffusion of Knowledge (1779) Thomas Jefferson wrote regarding tyranny: "The most effectual means of preventing this would be to illuminate, as far as practicable, the minds of the people at large, and more especially to give them knowledge of those facts which history exhibiteth, that possessed thereby of the experience of other ages and countries, they may be enabled to know ambition under all its shapes, and prompted to exert their natural powers to defeat its purposes." He then suggested that Greek, Roman, British, and American history were most apt to perform this function. Almost half a century later, when planning the University of Virginia curriculum, Jefferson retained this belief in the political purpose of history. Jefferson's outline placed "History, being interwoven with Politics and Law" as a subheading under "Government," and he urged that students be required to read the "usual suite" of ancient historians. To Jefferson, the establishment of American universities was particularly important, since the wholesome effect of reading republican history, ancient and modern, would be lost if the student did so in the corrupt environment of aristocratic and monarchical Europe.[1]

John Adams shared Jefferson's assumption that the purpose of history was the prevention of tyranny. As early as 1758 he ridiculed the idea of studying the "Dress, Entertainments, and Diversions" of the ancients. Such studies would be as irrelevant as learning the type of lamp Demosthenes used, the height of Cicero, or the number of hairs on his head. "History" always had been, and always should be, political history. Adams' defense of classical education against the assaults of Benjamin Rush focused on the assertion that the classics instilled a healthy hatred of tyranny in young minds. In 1810, after acknowledging to Rush that his wife opposed the classics on feminist grounds, Adams noted: "Hobbes calumniated the classics because they filled young men's heads with ideas of liberty and excited them to rebellion against Leviathan. Suppose we should agree to study the oriental languages, especially the Arabic, instead of the Greek and Latin. This would not please the ladies so well, but it would gratify Hobbes much better. According to many present appearances in the world, many useful lessons and deep maxims might be learned from the Asiatic writers. There are great models for the imitation of the emperors of Britain and France." Having cited Tamerlane, who had once declared that "as there is but one God, there ought to be but one King," as a typical hero in oriental literature, Adams asked facetiously: "Where can you find in any Greek or Roman writer a sentiment so sublime and edifying for George and Napoleon? There are some faint traces of it in the conduct of Alexander and Caesar, but far less frank and noble, and these have been imprudently branded with infamy by Greek and Roman orators and historians." Adams further claimed that what little classical learning Napoleon possessed had "damped his ardor and prevented his rising as yet to the lofty heights of the Asiatic emperors." When Rush blamed the "classical revival" in Europe on Napoleon, Adams disagreed, writing: "I cannot . . . do so much honor to him as to ascribe this . . . resurrection of learning to him; it is rather due to the

American Revolution. That great event turned the thoughts and studies of men of learning to the ancient Greeks, their language, their antiquities, their forms of government."[2]

Other founders agreed that the function of history was the prevention of tyranny. John Taylor lamented: "Caesar profited by the failure of Marius in the art of enslaving his country; will no nation ever profit by the failure of another in the art of preserving its liberty?" John Dickinson echoed the sentiment when he quoted the Latin epigram that translates: "Happy the people who grow wise by the misfortunes of others."[3]

The founders inherited their political conception of history from the ancients. Central to the lives of the aristocratic Greek and Roman historians, political and military affairs dominated their works. Even Herodotus, whose ingenious and hilarious digressions concerning other cultures constituted the first social history, felt compelled to justify such passages by their (often tenuous) relationship to his principal topic, the Persian War. Biographers like Plutarch selected statesmen and warriors as their subjects, presenting information concerning their private lives solely to illuminate their characters. Classical historians would have been astonished to hear their modern successors lament their silence concerning the trivial details of average citizens' private lives, much less those of women and slaves. Even most poets and playwrights focused upon political and military matters, and those who did not (such as the lyric poets of Ionia) were considered frivolous. The equation of virtue with political and military skill and vice with abuse of power robbed the powerless of all relevance to ancient historians. Although medieval Christianity temporarily shifted the focus of history from the worldly statesman–warrior to the otherworldly saint, modern republicans returned to the classical conception of history as politics and war, a conception which dominated historical scholarship until the 1960s.[4]

In order to extract meaningful lessons from ancient history, the founders had to believe that ancient and modern republics were exceedingly similar. Contrasts were as much premised on this assumption as analogies. One can draw lessons from contrasts between two individuals, societies, or governments, only if one believes they are similar in other respects. John Adams expressed this perception of similitude in 1812, when he wrote regarding Thucydides and Tacitus: "When I read them I seem to be only reading the History of my own Times and my own Life."[5]

The most prevalent personal antimodels, or villains, were the Roman emperors. The founders believed that the chaste Roman republic had been corrupted in the first century B.C., resulting in the rise of the emperors. Then, in a vicious circle, the practice of living under the thumb of these tyrants had corrupted Rome even further, so that soon even high officials lacked political courage. Jefferson noted that even those who had opposed imperial rule had chosen suicide over the "better remedy" of "a poignard in the breast of the tyrant." In 1821 Jefferson argued: "There are three epochs in history, signalized by the total extinction of national morality. The first was of the successors of Alexander, not omitting himself: The next, the successors of the first Caesar: The third, our own day." Nonetheless, as he had explained in 1813, Jefferson preferred to read even about Rome's corrupt periods than to read about his own era: "I turn from the contemplation with loathing, and take refuge in the histories of other times, where, if they also furnish their Tarquins, their Catilines, and Caligulas, their stories are handed to us under the brand of a Livy, a Sallust, and a Tacitus, and we are comforted with the reflection that the condemnation of all succeeding generations has confirmed the censures of the historian, and consigned their memories to everlasting infamy, a solace which we cannot have with the Georges and Napoleons but by anticipation."[6]

During the Revolutionary period, the founders compared the British Parliament and the Tories with the Roman emperors and their minions. In his *Letters from a Pennsylvania Farmer* John Dickinson wrote: "Indeed we ought firmly to believe, what is an undoubted truth, confirmed by the unhappy experience of many states heretofore free, that unless the most watchful attention be exerted, a new servitude may be slipped on us, under the sanction of usual and respectable terms. Thus, the Caesars ruined the Roman liberty, under the titles of tribunical and dictatorial authorities, old and venerable dignities, known in the most flourishing times of freedom." Similarly, under the Townshend Acts, Parliament was trying to hide "impositions for raising a revenue" under the venerable title of "regulations of trade." Samuel Adams compared a certain Tory with the multitude of informers whom Caligula and Nero had hired. Adams added: "The Stamp Act was like the sword that Nero wished for to have decollated the Roman People at a stroke." John Adams compared the Tories' slander of William Pitt the Elder and Benjamin Franklin with Nero's murder of the Stoic philosopher Seneca. Adams wrote: "Nero murdered Seneca that he might pull up virtue by the roots, and the same maxim governs the scribblers and speachifyers on the side of the minister." These improbable analogies were not mere rhetorical flourishes. They represented the genuine fear of tyranny inherent in nearly all classical texts. Tyranny was an inexorable cancer which must be destroyed in its early stages. Unconstitutional taxes, however small, violated sacred principles of liberty as surely as mass executions. Indeed, if unchecked, the former would likely eventuate in the latter. The "slippery slope" was a quintessentially classical idea.[7]

In a similarly serious vein during the constitutional debates the Antifederalists compared the Federalists with Roman emperors. Responding to the Federalist James Wilson's assurance that the federal government would not be able to dissolve the state legislatures under the new Constitution, since the legislatures would be needed to elect senators, "Centinel" argued that form might be maintained without substance: "Augustus, by the aid of a great army, assumed despotic power, and not withstanding this, we find even under Tiberius, Caligula, and Nero, princes who disgraced human nature by their excesses, the shadows of the constitution held up to amuse the people. The senate sat as formerly; consuls, tribunes of the people, censors, and other officers were annually chosen as before, and the forms of republican government continued." The Federalists were playing the same game, "Centinel" claimed. George Clinton applied the same argument to the constitutional clause guaranteeing republicanism to state governments. This was mere form, like the Roman emperors' use of republican symbols. The "Impartial Examiner" applied the analogy to the "Federalist" appropriation of that name. He compared their adoption of that title with the emperors' clever avoidance of the title "king." He contended: "That which in any particular form has once produced much evil and discontent generally stamps a lasting impression on the mind, and is not contemplated but with extreme detestation; although evils of the same nature, when inflicted under a different appearance, are frequently submitted to without repining." Although the last Roman king was expelled in 509 B.C., and "the name of King was ever odious to the Roman people" thereafter, the Romans at last concentrated even greater power in a single man named "emperor." In the same fashion the Federalists avoided revealing their true identity because they knew that the American people staunchly opposed the annihilation of state power.[8]

Other Antifederalists also expressed the common hatred of the Roman emperors. Rejecting the Federalist claim that Americans should support the new Constitution simply because George Washington and other respected leaders endorsed it, "A Republican Federalist" asked impatiently:

"If the plan is properly before the States, is good, and will secure to them [the people] 'peace, liberty, and safety,' should it not be adopted, were they even sure that every member who subscribed [to] it was in principle a Caligula or Nero? And if the plan is bad and will entail slavery on the land, ought it not to be rejected should every subscriber excel in wisdom and integrity Lycurgus or Solon?" "Philadelphiensis" was more melodramatic. He wailed: "Ah, my friends, the days of a cruel Nero approach fast." He added that "the language of a monster, of a Caligula, could not be more imperious" than that of the "lordlings" of the Constitutional Convention and concluded by reviling old patriot soldiers who supported the document ("Curse on the villain who protects virgin innocence only with a view that he may himself become the ravisher"). The near-hysterical nature of these unlikely comparisons was even more remarkable than those leveled against the British, since the Antifederalists had just fought beside the Federalists against British "tyranny." But anyone who dared introduce the cancer of tyranny into the vibrant American body politic, in however small a degree, must be regarded as a cunning enemy of the ilk of Caligula or Nero.[9]

Only occasionally and with great reluctance could the founders find any good qualities in the emperors. In a 1784 open letter to New Yorkers in which he opposed further confiscation of Tory property, Alexander Hamilton begged his fellow citizens to emulate the magnanimity of Augustus. Hamilton declared: "How wise was that policy of Augustus, who, after conquering his enemies, when the papers of Brutus were brought to him, which would have disclosed all his secret associates, immediately ordered them to be burnt. He would not even know his enemies, that they might cease to hate when they had nothing to fear." But Hamilton's favorable reference to Augustus probably only increased the suspicions of his opponents.[10]

The founders also detested leaders, like Sulla, Catiline, Marc Antony, and Julius Caesar, whose corruption of the Roman republic had resulted in the rise of the emperors. In 1777 John Adams compared British general William Howe's peace proposals with Sulla's favorite tactic of bribing his rivals' troops. In his *Vindication of the Conduct of the House of Representatives* (1762) James Otis quoted Cicero's rebuke of Catiline in denunciation of Martin Howard for advancing the doctrine of virtual representation: "Do you dare to show yourself in the light?" In 1766 John Dickinson insisted that opposition to oppression was not equivalent to disloyalty to the king. Dickinson wrote: "Should he complain, would it not be the complaint of Catiline, that the senator he attempted to assassinate was so disrespectful to him, he would not receive the sword in his body?" In 1779 Christopher Gadsden claimed: "Catiline's Gang was not more atrocious than such as are daily deluded over to the Enemy from our back [western] parts." In 1806, as the Aaron Burr conspiracy progressed, Thomas Jefferson compared Burr with Catiline. (Perhaps Jefferson was engaged in wishful thinking here: Catiline had been killed in his attempt to destroy the Roman republic.) Both Jefferson and John Adams accused the Hamiltonian Federalists of using public grief over George Washington's death for political purposes, as Marc Antony had utilized Julius Caesar's demise, though Jefferson believed that the publication of Washington's papers would prevent "the high priests of federalism" from using them to support their own views as Marc Antony had utilized Caesar's secret papers. In 1804 Adams copied this Bolingbroke statement: "The citizens of Rome placed the images of their ancestors in the vestibules in their houses; so that . . . these venerable bustoes met their eyes and recalled the glorious actions of the dead." Adams retorted: "But images of fools and knaves are as easily made as those of patriots and heroes. The images of the Gracchi were made as well as those of Scipio, and the images of Caesar, Antony, and Augustus as well as those of Cicero, Pompey, Brutus, and Cassius. Statues, paintings, panegyrics, in short all the fine arts, even music and dancing, promote virtue while virtue is in fashion. After that they produce luxury, effeminacy, corruption, prostitution, and every species of abandoned depravity."[11]

The founders' greatest villain was Julius Caesar. In 1764 James Otis called Caesar "the destroyer of the Roman glory and grandeur, at a time when but for him and his adherents both might have been rendered immortal." In a famous part of Patrick Henry's Stamp Act Speech of 1765, considered genuine by Henry's biographer Robert Douthat Meade, Henry even compared George III with Caesar, declaring: "Caesar had his Brutus, Charles the First his Cromwell, and George III [cries of 'Treason!'] may profit by their example." In 1771 John Adams compared Massachusetts' new royal governor, the pious Thomas Hutchinson, with Caesar: "Caesar, by destroying the Roman Republic, made himself a perpetual Dictator; Hutchinson, by countenancing and supporting a System of Corruption and Tyranny, has made himself Governor." Four years later, when a British army under General Thomas Gage occupied Boston, Abigail Adams compared him unfavorably with Caesar. Christopher Gadsden and Josiah Quincy summed up patriot sentiment when both claimed that Great Britain was to America "what Caesar was to Rome," a corrupting influence.[12]

Both John Adams and Thomas Jefferson compared Alexander Hamilton with Julius Caesar. Adams wrote: "When Burr shot Hamilton, it was not Brutus killing Caesar in the Senate-House, but it was killing him before he passed the Rubicon." Adams compared Caesar's and Augustus' exploitation of the First and Second Triumvirates with Hamilton's tactics, noting that "their intrigues and cabals have analogy enough with Hamilton's schemes to get rid of Washington, Adams, Jay, and Jefferson and monopolize all power to himself." In 1811 Jefferson told the story that at a party he had hosted while secretary of state in 1791, Hamilton had inquired into the identity of the three men portrayed in Jefferson's wall paintings. When Jefferson replied that they were "the three greatest men the world had ever produced," Isaac Newton, Francis Bacon, and John Locke, there had been a pause. Hamilton had then declared that "the greatest man that ever lived was Julius Caesar." Jefferson considered this story highly significant: while Jefferson, a true republican, modeled himself after men of learning, Hamilton, a secret monarchist, modeled himself after a military figure who had done more than anyone else to corrupt and overturn the illustrious Roman republic. The evidence indicates, however, that either Jefferson misunderstood Hamilton, or Hamilton was playing a joke on the humorless Virginian. Thomas P. Govan has shown that all of Hamilton's references to Caesar in his correspondence were negative, with the sole exception of a neutral reference to his military skill.[13]

Indeed, although Hamilton was well aware that detractors compared him with Caesar, he considered his opponents more deserving of the infamous name. As early as 1779, after remarking to his friend John Laurens that Henry Lee was "an officer of great capacity" but had "a little spice of the Julius Caesar or Cromwell in him," Hamilton declared in a postscript to the letter: "Apropos—Speaking of a Caesar & a Cromwell . . . the Cabal have reported that I declared in a public house in Philadelphia 'that it was high time for the people to rise, join General Washington, & turn Congress out of Doors' . . . But you who know my sentiments will know how to join me in despising these miserable detractors." In a 1792 letter to George Washington defending his plan for funding the national debt at face value Hamilton declared: "It has aptly been observed that Cato was the Tory—Caesar the whig of his day. The former frequently resisted—the latter always flattered the follies of the people.

Yet the former perished with the Republic, [while] the latter destroyed it. No popular Government was ever without its Catalines & its Caesars. These are its true enemies." In the next month Hamilton publicized the charge in the Philadelphia *Gazette of the United States,* calling the Republicans "the Catalines and the Caesars of the community (a description of men to be found in every republic) who, leading the dance to the tune of liberty without law, endeavor to intoxicate the people with delicious, but poisonous draughts, to render them the easier victims of their rapacious ambition."[14]

Hamilton left no doubt regarding the particular Republicans to whom he referred. In the same essay he concluded regarding Jefferson: "But there is always a first time, when characters studious of artful disguises are unveiled; when the vizor of stoicism is plucked from the brow of the Epicurean; when the plain garb of Quaker simplicity is stripped from the concealed voluptuary; when Caesar coyly refusing the proffered diadem is seen to be Caesar rejecting the trappings, but tenaciously grasping the substance of imperial domination." Three days earlier Hamilton had declared: "In a word, if we have an embryo-Caesar in the United States, 'tis [Aaron] Burr."[15]

Ironically, while a student at the College of New Jersey, Burr himself had written an essay ("On the Passions") in which he had stated: "A greater curse cannot befall a community than for princes and men in eminent departments to be under the influence of ill-directed passions. So Alexander and Caesar, the fabled heroes of antiquity, to what lengths did passion hurry them? Ambition with looks sublime bad[e] them on, bad[e] them grasp at universal disposition, and wade to empire through seas of blood." Since professors frequently assigned such essays to correct a perceived character flaw in a student, it may be that Burr was considered overly passionate and ambitious even as an adolescent.[16]

If the founders' chief Roman villain was Julius Caesar, their chief Greek villain was Alexander of Macedon, the fourth-century B.C. conqueror of the eastern Mediterranean and much of the Middle East. In 1767 John Adams rather improbably compared the dull royal governor of Massachusetts, Francis Bernard, with Alexander, as well as with Nero, Caligula, Attila the Hun, and Caesar. In 1810 Thomas Jefferson compared Napoleon with Alexander, as well as with Attila and the "parricide scoundrel" Augustus, perceiving the roots of Napoleon's aggression in the desire of an Italian to recreate the Roman empire. Adams was slightly more sympathetic to Napoleon. In 1814 he claimed that a thorough reading of Quintus Curtius indicated that Napoleon was "a saint" compared with Alexander. In an 1821 speech to West Point cadets, Adams contrasted George Washington, a military leader motivated "by the purest patriotism and philanthropy," with Alexander and Caesar, who had been actuated only by personal ambition.[17]

The reputations of Caesar and Alexander seem to have declined in Revolutionary America, as reverence for Cato and Cicero increased. It was after reading Caesar's *Commentaries* as a child that George Washington first developed dreams of military glory. In 1756, during the French and Indian War, William Fairfax encouraged Washington by writing: "I am sensible such a medley of undisciplined militia must create you various troubles, but, having Caesar's Commentaries, and perhaps Quintus Curtius, you have therein read of greater fatigues, murmuring, mutinies, and defections, than will probably come to your share; though, if any of those casualties should interrupt your quiet, I doubt not but you would bear them with a magnanimity those heroes remarkably did." As late as 1759 Washington ordered busts of Caesar, Alexander, and four other military geniuses. Yet by the time of the Revolution Washington had clearly abandoned such models. The complement of his embrace of the Cincinnatus image was his avoidance of the Caesar stigma. In 1796 Washington left Philadelphia for Mount Vernon before his Farewell Address was published, so that it would not appear that his real purpose was to be invited to remain, as with Caesar's false attempts to surrender power. During Washington's retirement years, he would not have dreamed of considering Caesar and Alexander heroes. James Thomas Flexner noted: "When an admirer sent him six huge engravings of Alexander's victory, Washington was no longer interested in that Greek general. He deposited the sumptuous masterpieces of the mezzotinter's art in a portfolio (where they still languish today)."[18]

Only James Wilson found anything good to say about Alexander and his father, Philip. Both had appreciated education. According to Wilson, Philip wrote to Aristotle after Alexander's birth: "We thank the gods, not so much for having bestowed him on us, as for bestowing him at a time when Aristotle lives. We assure ourselves that you will form him a prince worthy to be our successor, and a king worthy of Macedon." Wilson further claimed that Alexander had appreciated his own education, at least before he was driven mad by ambition.[19]

The founders derived from Plutarch and Thucydides as powerful a distaste for the "demagogues" of Athens as for the emperors of Rome. In

1766 George Mason compared British prime minister George Grenville, the leading advocate of the Stamp Act, with Pericles. According to Plutarch, Pericles had drawn Athens into the fatal Peloponnesian War in order to further his own financial interests. Mason wrote regarding the repeal of the Stamp Act: "No thanks to Mr. Grenville and his party, who without his genius or abilities, has dared to act the part that Pericles did, when he engaged his country in the Peloponnesian War, which, after a long and dreadful scene of blood, ended in the ruin of all Greece, and fitted it for the Macedonian yoke." The founders particularly detested Cleon, Pericles' successor, whose vices Thucydides vividly portrayed. In his *Letters from a Pennsylvania Farmer* John Dickinson warned that passions against Britain should not overwhelm reason to the point at which "the sway of the Cleons[,] . . . the designing and detestable flatterers of the prevailing passion[,] becomes confirmed."[20]

The ancients also provided the founders with societal antimodels. Alexander Hamilton equated the ambitions of modern France with those of ancient Rome. In 1798 Hamilton wrote: "France, swelled to gigantic size and aping Rome, except in her virtues, plainly meditates the controul of mankind." Five days later he added: "The conduct of France towards Great Britain is the copy of that of Rome towards Carthage. Its manifest aim is to destroy the principal obstacle to a domination over Europe. History proves that Great Britain has repeatedly upheld the balance of power there, in opposition to the grasping ambition of France." Furthermore, France, like Rome, had every chance of succeeding. Hamilton asked regarding this French scheme of world domination: "Has not a more rapid progress been made towards its execution than was ever made by Rome in an equal period? In their intercourse with foreign nations, do not the directory affect an ostentatious imitation of Roman pride and superiority? Is it not natural to conclude that the same spirit points to the same ends?" All that awaited execution of the plan was a Julius Caesar. But four years earlier Hamilton had prophesied that such a man would arise from the turmoil in France. In a 1797 essay John Dickinson agreed with the analogy, but still argued that the United States should aid France, the inevitable victor.[21]

Some founders perceived Greek and Roman slavery as an antimodel. As early as 1765 George Mason wrote regarding the Roman republic: "One of the first signs of the decay and perhaps the primary cause of the destruction of the most flourishing government that ever existed was the introduction of great numbers of slaves, an evil very pathetically de-

scribed by Roman historians." On August 22, 1787, during the important debate over the importation of slaves at the Constitutional Convention, Charles Pinckney responded to George Mason's charge that slavery
was an immoral and dangerous institution. James Madison recorded
Pinckney's rebuttal: "If slavery be wrong, it is justified by the example
of all the world. He cited the case of Greece, Rome, & other antient
States." But John Dickinson retorted: "Greece and Rome were made
unhappy by their slaves."[22]

Thomas Jefferson, who favored the emancipation and colonization of
slaves in Africa, also considered Roman slavery an antimodel. In a famous passage in his *Notes on the State of Virginia* Jefferson enumerated the
reasons why whites and blacks could never live in the same society as
equals: "Deep rooted prejudices entertained by the whites; ten thousand
recollections, by the blacks, of the injuries they have sustained; new
provocations; the real distinctions which nature has made; and many
other circumstances, will divide us into parties, and produce convulsions
which will probably never end but in the extermination of the one or the
other race."[23]

Recognizing that the most dubious of his reasons was the one involv-
ing "natural distinctions" between whites and blacks, Jefferson immediately launched into a disquisition on black inferiority. Claiming that
blacks were ugly, odorous, adventurous (from stupidity), lustful, griefless
(also from stupidity), and desirous of sleep while not working—qualities
Jefferson associated with animals—he found the chief evidence for the
innate inferiority of blacks in Roman slavery. Contending that Roman
slaves were treated more harshly than American slaves, Jefferson declared: "Yet, notwithstanding these and other discouraging circumstances among the Romans, their slaves were often their rarest artists.
They excelled too in science, insomuch as to be usefully employed as
tutors to their master's children . . . But they were of the race of whites.
It is not their [African slaves'] condition, then, but nature, which has
produced the distinction." Jefferson then offered Epictetus and Terence
as examples of Roman slaves who had overcome the hindrance of their
enslavement and had achieved prominence in philosophy and drama.
Taking care to criticize the poetry of Phillis Wheatley and the prose of
Ignatio Sancho, Jefferson argued that there was not a single black of intellectual distinction. He could not find any black "capable of tracing and
comprehending the investigations of Euclid," or one who "had uttered a
thought above the level of plain narration." Hence, the answer to the

racial problem was emancipation combined with colonization. Jefferson concluded: "Among the Romans emancipation required but one effort. The slave, when made free, might mix with, without staining, the blood of his master. But with us a second is necessary, unknown to history. When freed, he is to be removed beyond the reach of mixture."[24]

The lesson Jefferson drew from Roman slavery is dubious at best. First, it is highly doubtful that Roman slavery, particularly in its later stages, was harsher than American slavery. Second, while American slaves were often denied education by law, Epictetus and Terence, who were clearly atypical slaves, were well educated by their masters for the very reason that they were expected to tutor their masters' children. Third, though having recommended Edward Gibbon's *History of the Decline and Fall of the Roman Empire* as the best work of its kind, Jefferson seems to have ignored Gibbon's crucial statement regarding slavery: "Hope, the best comforter of our imperfect situation, was not denied to the Roman slave." Hope of social equality, either for themselves or for their children, was certainly denied to African-Americans.[25]

Indeed, recognizing the tension which existed between his racial views and his environmentalism, Jefferson expressed some ambivalence about black intellectual inferiority. Though adapting Aristotle's "natural slave" to the American context by making him black, Jefferson could not completely accept Aristotle's organic conception of society. He had preceded his discussion of slavery with an environmentalist defense of American Indians and whites against the charge of inferiority introduced by the Comte de Buffon. He had contended that the few deficiencies which the Indians possessed were the result of their nomadic lifestyle, comparing them with the European tribes before the Roman conquest, and had argued that American whites had produced no great poets because, having formed a new society, they were necessarily concerned with basic needs. Similarly, Jefferson used an environmentalist argument to claim *moral* equality for blacks. Rejecting the popular view that blacks were morally depraved thieves, Jefferson wrote: "The disposition to theft with which they have been branded must be ascribed to their situation, and not to any depravity of the moral sense. The man in whose favour no laws of property exist probably feels himself less bound to respect those made in favour of others." Thus, aware of the conspicuousness of his greatest departure from environmentalism, Jefferson remarked that since the question of black intellectual inferiority had never been empirically tested, "I advance it therefore as a suspicion only, that the blacks, whether originally a distinct race or made distinct by time and circumstances, are inferior to whites in the endowments of both body and mind"—before proceeding to argue again that blacks certainly were inferior.[26]

Jefferson feared that sectional disputes concerning slavery would lead to a civil war. In 1821, still agitated by the recent Missouri Crisis, he asked John Adams: "Are we then to see again Athenian and Lacedae-monian confederacies? To wage another Peloponnesian War to settle the ascendancy between them?" In this analogy the commercial North was Athens; the agricultural South was Sparta. The North and South spoke the same language and shared many of the same customs, as had the Athenians and Spartans; but, like Athens and Sparta also, they would wage war against each other. Later, southern "fire-eaters" could note, optimistically, that Sparta had won the Peloponnesian War.[27]

John Taylor perceived Roman militarism as an antimodel. In 1814 he argued that just as Roman aristocrats had aggrandized themselves through warfare, by monopolizing conquered territory, the English and American financial elites sought to increase their own power through wars, by raising the national debt and profiting from the interest. Taylor claimed: "The Roman aristocracy engaged the nation in war to aggrandize itself; but it entertained the people with shows, feasts, and triumphs and allowed them some small share of the booty. The English aristocracy of paper and patronage engages the nation in war for the same purpose, and entertains the people with heavy taxes, hard labour, penal laws, and Botany Bay." The same fate would befall the United States if it did not heed Taylor's warning against neomercantilist programs. Taylor claimed that both the Roman republic and the Roman empire had fallen as a result of the tremendous inequalities of wealth produced by conquest. He contended: "A gradual monopoly of lands and wealth overturned the Roman Republick. By assailing it in time, it might have been suppressed. The murder of the Gracchi is a proof that usurpation can only be corrected in its infancy and that fraudulent acquisitions will perpetuate any crime for self-defense." By providing the basis for vast inequalities of wealth, the Roman conquest of the Carthaginian empire had carried with it a "Punic Curse." The persistent inequalities produced civil war, absolute monarchy, and, finally, conquest by Germanic tribes. Taylor continued: "A nation is never conquered by an army or enslaved by a faction so long as it is willing to defend itself. The concentration of wealth in a few hands obliterates this disposition. The disciplined Romans were subdued by raw barbarians when the lands of Italy were held by less than three thousand proprietors." Ironically, when Taylor's book was published, it was a Republican president (James Madison) who was increasing the national debt by waging a war against Great Britain—though the party had since become, to Taylor's horror, "Federalized."[28]

James Wilson criticized the Greek and Roman treatment of women. In 1790 he wrote: "In the heroick [Homeric] ages of Greece, we are told, the rights of beauty and feminine weakness were highly respected and tenderly observed. The simplicity of those ages was equally remote from the cruel tyranny of savages, which condemns the fair sex to servitude, and the sordid selfishness of luxury which considers them solely as instruments of pleasure. Hence those affecting scenes so exquisitely described by Homer, which in the interviews of Hector and Andromache, exhibit the most striking image of nuptial felicity and love. But this beautiful picture of ancient manners was soon miserably defaced, and, in the degenerate periods of Greece, the fair sex were as much neglected and despised as they had been loved and admired in the heroick ages." Nevertheless, some of the specific evils which disturbed Wilson (lack of education, arranged marriages for wealth) were as much a staple of his own society as of classical societies.[29]

The ancients also provided the founders with governmental antimodels. The most important antimodel was the Roman empire. In 1771 Samuel Adams warned against the societal vices which had contributed to the rise of the Roman emperors. He asked:

Is it possible that millions could be enslaved by a few, which is a notorious fact, if all possessed the independent spirit of [Lucius] Brutus, who, to his immortal honor, expelled the proud Tarquin of Rome, and his 'royal and rebellious race'? If therefore a people will not be free; if they have not virtue enough to maintain their liberty against a presumptuous invader, they deserve no pity, and are to be treated with contempt and ignominy. Had not Caesar seen that Rome was ready to stoop, he would not have dared to make himself the master of that once brave people . . . By beguiling arts, hypocrisy, and flattery, which are even more fatal than the sword, he obtain'd that supreme power which his ambitious soul had long thirsted for: The people were finally prevail'd upon to consent to their own ruin . . . The will and pleasure of the Prince had the force of law . . . What difference is there between the present state of this province, which in course will be the deplorable state of all America, and that of Rome, under the law [giving Caesar the power to tax] before mention'd? The difference is only this, that they gave their formal consent to the change, which we have not yet done.

Seven years later Adams again underscored the opinion that liberty was as dead in Great Britain as in imperial Rome. Scoffing at the plan of reconciliation the British offered her former colonies after John Burgoyne's surrender at Saratoga, an offer which spoke of the benefits of British citizenship, Adams remarked: "A few of our wealthy citizens may hereafter visit England and Rome to see the ruins of those august temples in which the goddess of Liberty was once adored. Those will hardly claim naturalization in either of those places as a benefit." The goddess had emigrated to the United States. In 1775 John Adams twice compared British tyranny with that of the Roman empire. Adams noted that the term "the imperial crown of Great Britain . . . was introduced in allusion to the Roman Empire, and intended to insinuate that the prerogative of the imperial crown of England was like that of the Roman Empire." Now Parliament intended to employ this royal concept to increase its own power. Two months later he added: "Rome never introduced the term 'Roman empire' until the tragedy of her freedom was compleated. Before that, it was only the republic, or the city. In the same manner, the realm of the kingdom, or the dominions of the king, were the fashionable style in the age of the first [colonial] charter." But now Parliament was emulating the later Romans by using the term "British empire" as a tool of oppression.[30]

During the Constitutional debates the Antifederalists resurrected the specter of the Roman empire, suggesting that such a tyranny lay in store for Americans if the Constitution were ratified. Fearing that the president possessed too much power, "Poplicola" wrote: "For my part, I do not believe there is a man on earth to whom it would be safe for the people to entrust the powers of a despot . . . Nero was said to be blest with a kind and affectionate heart; but the powers of a despot intoxicated his mind." "A Friend to the Rights of the People" pursued the Nero analogy, writing: "Nero was one of the best among the Roman Emperors at his first entering the Imperial throne, [but] in a short time, he proved a monster of iniquity." Nathaniel Barrell concurred. He told the Massachusetts ratifying convention: "History tells us Rome was happy under Augustus, though wretched under Nero, who could have no greater power than Augustus; and yet this same Nero, when young in government, could shed tears on signing a death warrant, though afterwards he became [so] callous to the tender feelings of humanity as to behold, with pleasure, Rome in flames."[31]

Responding to the Federalist enticement that George Washington would be the first president, "A Farmer" argued that if the first president were a good one, he would only be opening the door wider for bad ones. The good administration of Augustus had "secured the power and gave full scope to the vices of Tiberious, Caligula, and Nero" in the first century A.D., and the "divine Marcus Aurelius," the philosopher-emperor, had paved the way for "that monster," Commodus, in the next century.[32]

Such emperors would corrupt the Congress and the American people, "A Farmer" claimed, as Caligula, Nero, and Domitian (81–96 A.D.) had corrupted the Senate and the people of Rome. Regarding Caligula's corruption of the Senate, he wrote: "A grave senate of Rome—that senate which twenty or indeed ten years before, had commanded the awe and veneration of mankind, solemnly proposed a law, as Suetonius informs us, to submit their wives and daughters to his embraces." Could not the United States Senate be corrupted by a powerful president, then? Regarding Nero's corruption of the Roman people, he added: "During the reign of Nero, fiddling—dancing—singing—burning cities—plundering States—perfidy and assassination were the manners of the age." Domitian's influence was equally baneful: "Tacitus informs us that during his life virtue became a death warrant—Philosophy fled—Pliny [the Younger] sat himself down quietly to compose a grammar—the only work then safe." He concluded: "But can these things happen to Americans? . . . America is in great measure peopled by emigrants from the old countries, now enthralled in slavery—Does crossing the Atlantic alter the nature of these people?—Let our countrymen reflect on this awful truth, that nothing creates that wide distinction between them and the white slaves of the old world, or indeed their black slaves here, but their government." Americans were as subject to corruption by a powerful executive as any other people.[33]

The Federalists retorted that it was absurd to compare the limited power and term of the president with the unlimited power and lifetime term of the Roman emperors. John Dickinson ("Fabius") explained that the president acted merely as a check on Congress. He contended: "As in the Roman armies, when the Principes and Hastati had failed, there were still the Triarii, who generally put things to rights, so we shall be supplied with another resource." This was a reference to the three types of heavy-armored troops in the Roman army of the early republican period. The *principes* were first in line, the *hastati* second, and the *triarii* third. (Note that Dickinson shrewdly gave Congress top billing.) Similarly, though Hamilton admitted at the Constitutional Convention that the president would be a monarch of sorts, he emphasized that he would be a limited one. Hamilton insisted that elective monarchies' reputation for tumultuousness was the product of an inappropriate Roman analogy. James Madison recorded: "He rather thought this character of Elective Monarchies had been taken from peculiar cases than from general principles. The election of Roman Emperors was made by the Army."[34]

Not surprisingly, the Antifederalists also utilized the late Roman republic and the Roman empire to assault the constitutional clause allowing the maintenance of a standing army. In doing so, they followed the colonial and Revolutionary traditions against standing armies. As early as 1764, alarmed at Britain's deployment of a standing army in America after the French and Indian War, James Otis asked: "Are all ambitious generals dead? Will no more rise hereafter? . . . The experience of past times will show that an army of 20 or 30 thousand veterans, half 3000 miles from Rome, were apt to proclaim Caesars. The first of the name, the assassin of his country, owed his false glory to stealing the affections of an army from the commonwealth." In 1768 John Dickinson also compared the British standing army with the standing armies that had destroyed Roman liberty. He had then quoted Demosthenes' second *Philippic* (out of context): "If any person considers these things, and yet thinks our liberties are in no danger, I wonder at that person's security." Similarly, in attacking the Boston Port Bill, Josiah Quincy cited Plutarch's *Lives* to demonstrate the tyranny inevitably produced by standing armies and the glory in resisting them.[35]

Likewise, Antifederalists John Tyler, "Veritas Politica," and John De Witt noted that it was with standing armies that sixth-century B.C. Athenian dictator Peisistratus and Julius Caesar had enslaved Athens and Rome respectively. (In Peisistratus' case, it was bodyguards armed with clubs.) "Brutus" naturally focused upon the Caesar analogy. Against the argument that the Continental Army, which had helped free America from British tyranny, could be trusted to act as a standing army, he noted that Julius Caesar's army, which had conquered Gaul for Rome, had also helped him enslave their own homeland. He quoted a British member of Parliament against standing armies: "Where was a braver army than that under Julius Caesar? Where was there ever an army that had served their country more faithfully? That army was commanded generally by the best citizens of Rome, by men of great fortune and figure in their country, yet that army enslaved their country. The affections of soldiers towards their country, the honor and integrity of the under officers, are not to be depended on." Soldiers, Brutus concluded, could be depended upon only to follow the orders of their immediate superiors. "An American" agreed. He asked: "And does anyone suppose that Americans, like the Romans, will submit to an Army merely because they have conquered a foreign enemy?"[36]

John Dawson argued that even a small standing army, like the Roman emperors' Praetorian Guard, posed a threat to liberty. He declared: "It was this, sir, which enabled the pretorian bands of Rome, whose number scarcely amounted to ten thousand, after having violated the sanctity of the throne by the atrocious murder of an excellent emperor, to dishonor the majesty of it, by proclaiming that the Roman empire—the mistress of the world—was to be disposed of, to the highest bidder, at public auction; and to their licentious frenzy may be attributed the first cause of the decline and fall of that mighty empire. We ought, therefore, strictly to guard against the establishment of an army." (This reference was rather odd: few historians would agree that Commodus was "an excellent emperor." Most consider the son of Marcus Aurelius to have been a disappointment and a disgrace.) "A Farmer" concurred with Dawson. He claimed that a standing army would pose a threat to its leaders, as well as to the general public: "The praetorian bands of the Roman . . . empire frequently stained the imperial purple with blood . . . Yet they were always the willing instruments of the cruelty of the Prince against all ranks of his subjects."[37]

But perhaps George Mason expressed the strongest fear when he predicted that a president would use the standing army to prevent his own removal from office. Mason explained: "When he is arraigned for treason, he has the command of the army and navy, and may surround the Senate with thirty thousand troops. It brings to my recollection the remarkable trial of Milo at Rome. We may expect to see similar instances here." T. Annius Milo was a gang leader who was arrested in 53 B.C. for killing Clodius, one of Caesar's underlings. Pompey, then an ally of Caesar, surrounded the courtroom with troops, intimidating Milo's attorney, Cicero, into losing the case. Milo was banished to Massilia (Marseilles).[38]

The Federalists retorted that since a standing army was necessary, to prohibit it was to encourage lawlessness. In *Federalist* No. 25 Alexander Hamilton noted that Pennsylvania had once ignored its own constitution and established a standing army. Similarly, the Spartans had been obliged, during the Peloponnesian War, to violate the spirit of the law prohibiting anyone from being admiral two years in a row, by making Lysander vice-admiral while allowing him, in reality, to command the navy. What lesson did Hamilton learn from this unlikely pair, the Pennsylvanians and the Spartans? He concluded: "Wise politicians will be cautious about fettering the government with restrictions that cannot be observed, because they know that every breach of the fundamental laws, though dictated by necessity, impairs that sacred reverence which ought to be maintained in the breast of the rulers towards the constitution, and forms a precedent for other breaches where the same plea of necessity does not exist at all, or is less urgent and palpable." Indeed, though James Madison conceded, in *Federalist* No. 41, that "the liberties of Rome proved the final victim to her military triumphs" and that societies ought to watch standing armies closely, he agreed with Hamilton that they were essential. He claimed that states without veteran armies fell swiftly before foreign powers who possessed them, noting: "The veteran legions of Rome were an overmatch for the undisciplined valor of all other nations, and rendered her the mistress of the world." Hence, Madison agreed that to prohibit standing armies was to encourage lawlessness, since such a clause could not be safely obeyed.[39]

The Republicans continued to utilize the Roman analogy against standing armies long after the Constitution was ratified. As late as 1814 John Taylor was still using the Caesar analogy against them.[40]

But the founders uncovered imperfections even in their favorite ancient republics. Although the republics served as rough models for the founders, they had obviously suffered from fatal flaws, else they would not have been replaced by tyrannies. Uncovering the cancers which had killed the republics was the principal obsession of the founders' leading coroners. During the constitutional debates, Federalists repeatedly cited the ancient Greek confederacies as examples of federal systems destroyed by decentralization, while Antifederalists cited the Roman republic as an example of a republic ruined by centralization. The founders had no choice but to turn to the ancient confederacies (and to the modern Dutch and Swiss confederacies) for lessons concerning federalism, since no such tradition existed in English history.

The first ancient confederacy invoked was the Amphictyonic League, a loose association of Greek city-states of the fifth and fourth centuries B.C. On the basis of statements by Greek historians Dionysius, Strabo, and Plutarch, the leading classicists of the eighteenth century believed that the council of the Amphictyonic League had served as a federal government. In actuality the league was never more than a religious body, without any coercive power. Both Federalists and Antifederalists accepted the misconception as fact, however, and no one ever questioned the league's credentials as a federal system.[41]

The Amphictyonic League was the focus of nearly as much discussion as the Constitution itself, especially among the Federalists, who seemed never to tire of recounting the league's history and attributing its downfall to decentralization. James Wilson first mentioned the league at the Constitutional Convention on June 6, 1787, citing it as an example of the dire consequences to a federal system of encroachment by constituent members. This brief statement sent Federalists scurrying to the obscure works which discussed the league. By June 18 Alexander Hamilton was prepared to lecture on the matter. He said: "The Amphictyonic Council had, it would seem, ample powers for general purposes. It had in particular the power of fining and using force against delinquent members. What was the consequence? Their decrees were mere signals of war . . . Philip [II of Macedon], at length taking advantage of their disunion, and insinuating himself into their Councils, made himself master of their fortunes." Americans could expect to be subjected to foreign domination as well, Hamilton insisted, if they remained a weak, disunited collection of republics similar to the Greek city-states of the Amphictyonic League. On the next day James Madison, who had spent the previous three years studying ancient and modern confederacies, reiterated the point: just as the disunity of the Amphictyonic League had allowed Philip II to "practice intrigues" resulting in its enslavement, so American disunity would produce the same result. On June 28 Madison added a second argument: "What was the condition of the weaker members of the Amphictyonic Confederacy? Plutarch (life of Themistocles) will inform us that it happened but too often that the strongest cities corrupted & awed the weaker." Decentralization might cause interstate warfare, as well as foreign invasion. Smaller states had the most to gain from a strong, centralized union, since they would suffer most from armed conflicts between the states.[42]

The Federalists did not forget the Amphictyonic League at the state ratifying conventions, nor would they allow anyone else to do so. At the New York ratifying convention Hamilton declared: "The council which managed the affairs of this league possessed powers of a similar complexion to those of our present Congress. The same feeble mode of legislation, and the same power of resistance in the members, prevailed. When a requisition was made, it rarely met a compliance; and a civil war was

the consequence. Those that were attacked called in foreign aid to protect them; and the ambitious Philip, under the mask of an ally to one,
invaded the liberties of each, and finally subverted the whole." At the
Virginia ratifying convention Madison repeated the message, comparing
the Amphictyonic League with the union formed by the Articles of
Confederation. Hence, Madison argued that the federal government
must be able to tax the people directly. He said: "Does not the history of
these confederacies coincide with the lesson drawn from our experience?
I most earnestly pray that America may have sufficient wisdom to avail
herself of the instructive information she may derive from a contemplation of the sources of their misfortunes, and that she may escape a similar
fate by avoiding the causes from which their felicity sprang. If the general
government is to depend on the voluntary contribution of the states for
its support, dismemberment of the United States may be the consequence." George Nicholas responded to Patrick Henry's refusal to believe that republican governments like the American states would wage
war against one another: "I refer the gentleman to the history of Greece.
Were not the republics which bordered on one another almost perpetually at war? . . . This proves the absolute necessity of the union."[43]

In response to Antifederalist contentions that no confederacy had ever
possessed the power to coerce its members, several federalists pointed,
incorrectly, to the Amphictyonic League. At the Connecticut ratifying
convention Oliver Ellsworth remarked: "It is said that other confederacies have not had the principle of coercion. Is this so? Let us attend to the
confederacies which have resembled our own." His first example was the
Amphictyonic League, which he claimed had once occupied Boeotia,
when the Boeotians refused to obey a federal order. Ellsworth did not
mention his source for this information. Neither did Francis Corbin cite
any source when he told the Virginia ratifying convention, "The coercive power of the Amphictyonic council was so great as to enable it to
punish disobedience and refractory behavior in the most severe manner,"
and cited instances of the Council's "carrying fire and sword through the
territories" of those who disobeyed it. Grasping this theme, Henry Lee
asked: "Had the Amphictyonic council had the power contained in that
paper [the Constitution], would they have sent armies to levy money?
Will the honorable gentleman [Patrick Henry] say that it is more eligible
and humane to collect money by carrying fire and sword through the
country, than by the peaceable mode of raising money of the people,
through the medium of an officer of [the] peace, when it is necessary?"[44]

Lest anyone escape hearing about the baneful effects of decentralization in ancient Greece, Federalists beat the Amphictyonic drum in published essays as well. John Jay assured his readers in *Federalist* No. 4 that
the history of Greece demonstrated that if the United States became disunited and a state were assaulted by foreign forces, other states would not
come to its aid. In *Federalist* No. 6 Hamilton attacked those who doubted
that decentralization would lead to warfare between the states: "A man
must be far gone in Utopic speculations who can seriously doubt that if
these States should either be wholly disunited, or only united in partial
confederacies, the subdivisions into which they might be thrown would
have frequent and violent contests with each other." Hamilton followed
this assertion with Plutarch's allegation that Pericles inaugurated the
Peloponnesian War, a war which "terminated in the ruin of the Athenian commonwealth," in order to deflect attention from his misuse of state
funds. Surely, American states could not remain free of such leaders forever. Madison finally exhausted the subject in *Federalist* No. 18. He began
by stating: "Among the confederacies of antiquity, the most considerable
was that of the Grecian republics, associated under the Amphictyonic
council. From the best accounts transmitted of this celebrated institution,
it bore a very instructive analogy to the present Confederation of the
American States." Members of both confederacies retained their sovereignty and possessed equal representation in the federal council. But the
council's powers, "like those of the present Congress, were administered
by deputies appointed wholly by the cities in their political capacities.
Hence, the weakness, the disorders, and finally the destruction of the
confederacy." As a result of the confederacy's weakness, Athens and
Sparta "became first rivals and then enemies; and did each other infinitely
more mischief than they had suffered from Xerxes." The final blow to
the confederacy came from Philip of Macedon, who became its master
"through intrigues and bribes."[45]

Though most Antifederalists preferred to ignore these allusions to the
Amphictyonic League than to read Strabo, they were not entirely silent
on the matter. James Monroe quarreled with the findings of the league's
Federalist coroners. Performing his own autopsy, Monroe concluded
that disunity had indeed caused the league's demise, but denied that a
lack of federal power had produced the disunity. Rather, the dissimilarity
of member governments had caused the dissension. Composed entirely
of republics, the United States would not face the same difficulties as a
confederacy which combined oligarchies and republics. Luther Martin of

Maryland argued, on the other hand, that the league had fallen prey to the intrigues of its larger states, machinations similar to those underlying the Virginia Plan. By allocating representation according to population in the House of Representatives, the Virginia Plan would give the larger states control of that body. Martin told the Constitutional Convention: "The Lacedemonians attempted, in the amphictionic council, to exclude some of the smaller states from a right to vote, in order that they might tyrannize over them. If the plan now on the table be adopted, three states in the union have the controul, and they may make use of their power when they please." The next day he added: "The basis of all ancient and modern confederacies is the freedom and independency of the states composing it. The states forming the amphictionic council were equal, though Lacedemon, one of the greatest states, attempted the exclusion of three of the lesser states from this right. The plan reported, it is true, only intends to diminish those rights, not to annihilate them—It was the ambition and power of the Grecian states which at last ruined this respectable council." Robert Barnwell of South Carolina agreed that "the ambition of a few of the states of Greece" had destroyed the league. "The Federal Farmer" suggested a third possible cause for the decline of the league. He claimed that the fatal weakness of the league was "that each member possessed power to league itself with foreign powers." Since the Articles of Confederation did not grant such power to American states, he concluded that there was no cause for concern.[46]

Some Antifederalists quarreled with the assertion that the Amphictyonic League was ineffective while it operated. Their chief argument rested upon the almost miraculous victory of the Greeks over the Persians in the Persian War (499–479 B.C.). After comparing the Amphictyonic League with the United States under the Articles of Confederation, Samuel Willard noted the league's remarkable defeat of the Persians. George Mason concurred, praising "the little cluster of Greek republics which resisted and almost constantly defeated the Persian monarchy." Indeed, the analogy between the Greeks' unexpected triumph over the mighty Persian empire and the Americans' surprising victory over the powerful British empire was a good one. Federalist John Dickinson's response was to carry the analogy further. He noted—correctly, by Herodotus' account—that just as the Greeks' disunity had nearly cost them their liberty against the Persians, the Americans' disunity had nearly cost them their freedom against the British.[47]

Indeed, though both the Federalists and Antifederalists were incorrect in viewing the Amphictyonic League as a federal system, their observations were shrewd. The Federalists were correct in noting that Greek disunity had opened the door to Macedonian domination. As Madison put it: "Had Greece, says a judicious observer on her fate, been united by a stricter confederation, and persevered in her union, she would never have worn the chains of Macedon; and might have proved a barrier to the vast projects of Rome." Conversely, the Antifederalists were correct in noting that the Greeks had proved in the Persian War—and Americans had proved in the recent Revolutionary War—that a small cluster of republics animated by patriotism and love of liberty could triumph over a large, centralized power. As Patrick Henry said, it was not "federal ideas" that led to American victory in the Revolutionary War, but "sons of Cincinnatus, without splendid magnificence or parade, going, with the genius of their just progenitor, Cincinnatus, to the plough; men who served their country without ruining it—men who had served it to the destruction of their private patrimony—their country owing them amazing amounts, for the payment of which no adequate provision was then made."[48]

The second ancient confederacy which the Federalists invoked was the Achaean League. Second only to the Amphictyonic League in references (and frequently mentioned in the same breath with it), the Achaean League was a confederacy of southern Greek city-states which existed from 280 to 146 B.C., at which time it was dissolved by the Romans. John Adams' *Defence of the Constitutions of Government of the United States* brought attention to the league in 1787. Having criticized Polybius, who was both the league's cavalry commander and its chief historian, for papering over "the revolutions they underwent for a course of ages," Adams contended: "Such is the passion for independence that this little commonwealth, or confederation of commonwealths, could not hold together." He concluded that Americans must adopt the sentiments of Aratus, one of the league's principal leaders, who, according to Plutarch, declared: "That small cities could be preserved by nothing else but a continual and combined force, united by the bond of common interest; and as the members of the body live and breathe by their mutual communication and connection, and when once separated pine away and putrify, in the same manner are cities ruined by being dismembered from one another, as well as preserved, when linked together into one great body."[49]

At the Constitutional Convention James Wilson also cited the

Achaean League as an instance of federal government gone awry as a result of "the encroachments of the constituent members." Madison noted that the same disunity which had paved the way for Macedonian conquest of the Amphictyonic League in the fourth century B.C. led to Roman subjugation of the Achaean League in the next century.[50]

Although Federalist appeals to the Achaean precedent were not as numerous as their appeals to the Amphictyonic example, they were equally persistent. At the Connecticut ratifying convention Oliver Ellsworth insisted that the Achaean League had used coercion to enforce its decrees. At the New York ratifying convention Hamilton declared regarding the Greek confederacies: "Weakness in the head has produced resistance in the members; this has been the immediate parent of civil war: auxiliary force has been invited; and foreign power has annihilated their liberties and name." The Romans subverted the Achaean League, just as the Macedonians had the Amphictyonic confederacy. Madison took great pains to ensure that the Virginia ratifying convention was not deprived of the same lesson.[51]

Hamilton and Madison referred to the Achaean League in their *Federalist* essays as well. In No. 16 Hamilton praised the league for being among the most centralized of the ancient confederacies, though it had not been centralized enough. In No. 18 Madison reviewed the "valuable instruction" which the league provided. The member states of the Achaean League, all of which were democracies, were equally represented in the federal council. The federal council exerted complete control over the league's foreign policy and appointed its chief magistrate. The chief magistrate commanded the army and administered the government with the advice of ten assemblymen. Madison claimed that "there was infinitely more of moderation and justice in the administration of its government, and less of violence and sedition in the people, than were to be found in any of the cities exercising singly all the prerogatives of sovereignty." He contended: "Popular government, so tempestuous elsewhere, caused no disorders in the members of the Achaean republic, because it was there tempered by the general authority and laws of the confederacy."[52]

Madison was not dissuaded from such assertions by the scarcity of knowledge concerning the Achaean League. True, he admitted: "It is much to be regretted that such imperfect monuments remain of this curious political fabric. Could its interior structure and regular operation be ascertained, it is probable that more light would be thrown by it on the science of federal government, than by any of the like experiments with which we are acquainted." Nonetheless, Madison contended that enough was known about the league to warrant his assertion that disunity caused by decentralization had produced its downfall. The Achaeans' Roman ally "seduced the members from the league, by representing to their pride the violation it committed on their sovereignty." Madison concluded: "By these arts this union, the last hope of Greece, the last hope of ancient liberty, was torn to pieces; and such imbecility and distraction introduced, that the arms of Rome found little difficulty in completing the ruin which their arts had commenced . . . It emphatically illustrates the tendency of federal bodies rather to anarchy among the members, than to tyranny in the head." He repeated the message in *Federalist* No. 45, pointing out that though the league had "a considerable likeness to the government framed by the convention," its downfall did not result from encroachments by the federal government, but from "the dissensions, and finally the disunion, of the subordinate authorities."[53]

John Dickinson ("Fabius") was even more vociferous in praise of the league, though equally aware of its fatal flaw. Whereas John Adams doubted Polybius' objectivity, seeing "the fond partiality of a patriot for his country" in the historian's praise of the league, Dickinson quoted Polybius enthusiastically: "From their incorporation may be dated the birth of that greatness, that by a constant augmentation, at length arrived to a marvelous height of prosperity." He also paraphrased Polybius' exaggerated claim that the members of the league "seemed to be but one state." Nevertheless, Dickinson concluded that even this prosperous and happy confederacy was destroyed by internal dissension fomented by a foreign power. Had it been more unified and had it comprised all the Greek republics, the outcome of history would surely have been different. Dickinson wrote: "Let any man of common sense peruse the gloomy but instructive pages of their mournful story, and he will be convinced that if any nation could have successfully resisted those conquerors of the world [Macedon and Rome], the illustrious deed had [could have] been achieved by Greece, that cradle of republics, if the several states had been cemented by some league such as the Achaean, and had honestly fulfilled its obligations." He added regarding the Achaean League and its lesson: "The glorious operations of its principles bear the clearest testimony to this distant age and people, that the wit of man never invented such an antidote against monarchical and aristocratical projects, as a strong combination of truly democratical republics . . . The reason is plain . . . [Since] the energy of the government pervaded all the parts in things relating to the whole, it counteracted for the common welfare the designs hatched by selfishness in separate councils." Dickinson concluded with an appeal to American pride: "How degrading would be the thought to a citizen of United America that the people of these states, with institutions beyond comparison preferable to those of the Achaean league, and so vast a superiority in other respects, should not have wisdom and virtue enough to manage their affairs with as much prudence and affection for one another as these ancients did."[54]

Even fewer Antifederalists responded to the Achaean analogy than replied to the Amphictyonic comparison. In fact, at the Constitutional Convention George Mason conceded that the Achaean League and the other ancient confederacies had suffered from decentralization, but contended that the Constitution went so far in the opposite direction as to create the threat of federal tyranny. James Monroe was not prepared to accept the Federalist interpretation of the league's demise, however. Equally pleased with the league—since members "retained their individual sovereignty and enjoyed a perfect equality," in marked contrast to the system proposed by the Constitution—Monroe argued that the confederacy had been overwhelmed by three great powers (Macedon, Sparta, and the Aetolian League), making Roman aid necessary and submission to the vast Roman power inevitable.[55]

A third confederacy invoked during the constitutional debates, though much less than the former two, was the Lycian League. This obscure confederacy of cities in Asia Minor, whose principal historian was Strabo, existed from 200 to 43 B.C., at which time it was incorporated into the Roman empire. Though no mention was made of the league at the Constitutional Convention, Hamilton and Madison discussed it in their *Federalist* essays. In No. 9 Hamilton noted that it was not true that all previous confederacies had operated on the principle of equal representation and that the proportional representation in the House of Representatives lacked precedent. Hamilton noted: "In the Lycian confederacy, which consisted of twenty-three cities or republics, the largest were entitled to three votes in the Common Council, those of the middle class to two, and the smallest to one." Hamilton added: "The Common Council had the appointment of all the judges and magistrates of the respective Cities. This was certainly the most delicate species of interference in their internal administration; for if there be anything that seems exclusively appropriate to local jurisdiction, it is the appointment of their own officers. Yet Montesquieu, speaking of this association, says: 'Were I to give a model of an excellent Confederate Republic, it would be that of Lycia.'" In No. 16 Hamilton wrote regarding decentralization: "Of all the confederacies of antiquity which history has handed down to us, the Lycian and Achaean leagues, as far as there remains vestiges of them, appear to have been the most free from the fetters of that mistaken principle, and were accordingly those which have best deserved, and have most liberally received, the applauding suffrages of political writers." Yet both fell as a result of decentralization.[56]

James Madison considered the Lycian League the ancient confederacy most similar to the federal system proposed by the Constitution. In *Federalist* No. 45, having made such a comparison with the Achaean League, Madison declared: "The Lycian Confederacy, as far as its principles are transmitted, must have born still greater analogy to it." Yet there was no evidence that the federal power of Lycia had encroached on the member states, and the ease of Roman conquest suggested otherwise. Regarding the Achaean and Lycian examples, Madison concluded ominously: "These cases are the more worthy of our attention, as the external causes by which the component parts were pressed together were much more numerous and powerful than in our case; and consequently less powerful ligaments within would have been sufficient to bind the members to the head, and to each other." Since the United States faced fewer immediate foreign threats than the ancient confederacies, it was even more susceptible to disunity. Consequently, the nation required an even stronger central government to hold it together.[57]

Few Antifederalists replied to the Lycian analogy. "Helvidius Priscus" argued, as he had concerning the Amphictyonic League, that it was not decentralization, but the encroachment of federal power, particularly monarchical power, which had destroyed the Lycian League. The Lycians were free "until the reign of Leomitian, when they fell under the Roman yoke, with the other cities of Greece [actually, much later], while the tyrant alleged the same excuse for his encroachment that we hear hacknied in the streets of our capitals for subjugating Americans to the arms of power, because they are no longer capable of enjoying their liberties." But perhaps the most interesting Antifederalist comment on the ancient confederacies was made by Melancthon Smith at the New York ratifying convention. The secretary paraphrased him thus: "It had been observed that no example of federal republics had succeeded. It was true that the ancient confederated republics were all destroyed; so were those which were not confederated; and all ancient governments, of every form, had shared the same fate." Virtually no one on either side of the constitutional debate ever specified the criteria according to which an ancient government should be termed a success or failure. If longevity meant success, as so many implied, how much time constituted longevity? The Romans were ruled by emperors for nearly half a millennium, yet no republican theorist deemed that government a success.[58]

The Antifederalists' chief response to the Greek confederacies analogy was the repetition of Montesquieu's assertion that republics must remain small in order to remain republics, an assertion which Montesquieu based largely on the failure of the Roman republic. Since Montesquieu had also lavished praise upon the fairly centralized Lycian confederacy, this amounted to using Montesquieu against himself. "Brutus" wrote: "History furnishes no example of a free republic any thing like the extent of the United States. The Grecian republics were of small extent; so also was that of the Romans. Both of these, it is true, in process of time, extended their conquests over large territories of country; and the consequence was that their governments were changed from that of free governments to those of the most tyrannical that ever existed in the world." Hence the United States must remain thirteen separate republics, uniting only for a few necessary purposes. "An Old Whig" concurred, noting: "But a few years elapsed from the time ancient Rome extended her dominions beyond the bounds of Italy, until the downfall of her Republic." He concluded: "The continent of North America can no more be governed by one Republic than the fabled Atlas can support the heavens." "A Farmer" remarked: "It was the extensive territory of the Roman republic that produced a Sylla [Sulla], a Marius, a Caligula, a Nero, and an Eliagabalus."[59]

The Federalists disagreed. John Dickinson ("Fabius") argued that Montesquieu's assertion applied only to the ancient republics, which, being ignorant of the crucial principle of representation, could only rule over their provinces. By contrast, the system proposed by the Constitution would "bear a remarkable resemblance to the mild features of patriarchal government [in the Roman family], in which each son ruled his own household, and in other matters the whole family was directed by the common ancestor." Alexander Hamilton agreed that the modern principle of representation invalidated Montesquieu's assertion. In the famous *Federalist* No. 10 James Madison not only argued that representation allowed republics to be large, but insisted that large republics would be more moderate, stable, and just than small republics. The Federalists considered the "modern improvement" of representation crucial to the survival of republicanism in the United States. As Hamilton pointed out, if the ancients' and Montesquieu's strictures on the size of republics were the final word on the matter, then there could be no republican government in the United States, since even the states were far too large.[60]

The founders perceived other flaws in the ancient republics. At the Constitutional Convention James Wilson opposed the establishment of a plural executive, citing conflict between the two Spartan kings and two Roman consuls. Alexander Hamilton agreed that a plural executive would create disunity and dissension in a branch of government in which unity and energy were vital. In *Federalist* No. 70 he wrote regarding ancient history: "It teaches us not to be enamoured of plurality in the Executive. We have seen that the Achaeans, on an experiment of two Praetors, were induced to abolish one." Roman history also revealed the disadvantages of a plural executive without revealing any advantages. Conflict between the two consuls would have been fatal to Rome, if the consuls had not made a strict division of power between them and if, as patricians, they had not been united by class interest.[61]

Noah Webster claimed that the president's mode of election and age requirement would be superior to the Roman consuls' as well. The popular election of consuls had "paved the way for such excessive bribery and corruption as are wholly unknown in modern times." The president, on the other hand, would be selected "by a few men—chosen by the several legislatures—under their inspection—separated at a vast distance—and holding no office under the United States." "Such a mode of election almost precludes the possibility of corruption," Webster claimed. The lower age requirement for the president (thirty-five, as opposed to forty-three for consuls) was appropriate, since "the improvements in science, and particularly in government, render it practicable for a man to qualify himself for an important office much earlier in life than he could among the Romans." Webster was twenty-nine when he made this assertion.[62]

Webster also concluded that the U.S. Senate term and the provisions for the new federal judiciary were superior to those of the Romans. Since American senators would not serve for life, as had Roman senators, they would be more responsible to their constituents. Yet, since their term would be a full six years, neither would they be dismissed as soon as they understood the job. Since federal judges would not be elected annually like Roman judges (praetors), but would be appointed by the president for life, they would be less prone to corruption.[63]

The Federalists also portrayed the large assemblies of the ancients as antimodels when defending the small size of the House of Representatives. In *Federalist* No. 55 James Madison contended: "In all very numerous assemblies, of whatever character composed, passion never fails to wrest the scepter from reason. Had every Athenian citizen been a Socrates, every Athenian assembly would still have been a mob." In No. 58 he noted that the greater the number of representatives in an assembly, "the fewer will be the men who will in fact direct their proceedings." He added: "In the ancient republics, where the whole body of the people assembled as one person, a single orator, or an artful statesman, was generally seen to rule with as complete a sway as if a scepter had been placed in his single hand." The reason for this phenomenon, Madison concluded, was that larger assemblies possessed a larger proportion of feeble-minded men. Hamilton agreed. At the New York ratifying convention he said: "The ancient democracies, in which the people themselves deliberated, never possessed one feature of good government. Their very character was tyranny; their figure, deformity. When they assembled, the field of debate presented an ungovernable mob, not only incapable of deliberation, but prepared for every enormity." By contrast, the five ephors of Sparta and the three tribunes of the early Roman republic had protected the people's rights effectively. Hamilton declared concerning the tribunes: "Every one acquainted with the history of that republic will recollect how powerful a check to the senatorial encroachments this small body proved; how unlimited a confidence was placed in them by the people, whose guardians they were; and to what a conspicuous station in the government their influence at length elevated the plebeians." "The Federal Farmer" retorted: "The most respectable assemblies we have any knowledge of and the wisest, have been those, each of which consisted of several hundred members; as the Senate of Rome, of Carthage."[64]

The argument spilled over onto the U.S. Senate. John Dickinson wanted proportional representation in the Senate as well as in the House, which would have made the Senate large. But as James Madison recorded regarding his own opposition to Dickinson's proposal: "He differed from Mr. D who thought that the additional number would give additional weight to the body. On the contrary; it appeared to him that their weight would be in an inverse ratio to their number. The example of the Roman Tribunes was inapplicable. They lost their influence and power, in proportion as their number was augmented." Madison explained that the larger the number of representatives, the more apt they were "to be divided among themselves either from their own indiscretions or the artifices of the opposite factions, and of course the less liable of fulfilling their trust." Dickinson's rebuttal was sharp: "If the reasoning of Mr. Madison was good it would prove that the number of the Senate ought to be reduced below ten, the highest number of the Tribunal corps."[65]

Antifederalists noted other imperfections in the ancient republics. In opposing the constitutional clause providing for the creation of a federal city Thomas Tredwell called the proposed municipality "this political hive, where all the drones in the society are to be collected to feed on the honey of the land." He added: "I pray God it may not prove to this western world what the city of Rome, enjoying a similar constitution, did to the eastern." Similarly, Patrick Henry opposed the clause giving Congress the power to determine "the time, place, and manner of elections." He claimed that this clause, through the operative word "manner," would allow Congress to make one wealthy man's vote worth those of a hundred poor men, just as Roman law had given the patricians disproportionate weight by having many votes taken by the Comitia Centuriata, rather than by the Comitia Tributa.[66]

Antifederalists objecting to the absence of a clause guaranteeing trial by jury recounted the evil effects of the absence of such a provision in the ancient republics. "A Farmer" quoted Blackstone: "Therefore, a celebrated writer (Montesquieu) who concludes that because Rome, Sparta, and Carthage have lost their liberties, therefore those of England in time must perish, should have recollected that Rome, Sparta, and Carthage, at the time when their liberties were lost, were strangers to the trial by jury." William Grayson agreed, arguing that it was the absence of trial by jury that led to the establishment of the client system in Rome, since the plebeians could not hope for justice from the patrician-dominated judicial system unless they possessed a wealthy patron. America could expect the same result without a constitutional clause guaranteeing trial by jury. (Christopher Gore answered that trial by jury in the same county in which a crime had been committed was not conducive to justice. It was much better if the jury did not know the defendant. Gore noted: "From such motives did the wise Athenians so constitute the famed Areopagus, that, when in judgment, this court should sit at midnight, and in total darkness, that the decision might be made on the thing, and not the person.")[67]

Antifederalists objecting to the difficulty in amending the Constitution also constructed classical analogies. Patrick Henry claimed that because of the requirement that three-quarters of the states ratify an amendment, one-eighth of the American people could block a badly needed amendment, much as a single Roman tribune could negate Senate legislation. "An Old Whig" went further, comparing the Federalists with Lycurgus, who had made the Spartans swear that they would make no alterations in his constitution until he returned from a voyage—and then failed to return.[68]

Ancient history provided the founders with a large body of information, knowledge which they used both to make sense of the confusing events of their day and to construct arguments for their political positions. Separating the real lessons which the founders learned from the mere ammunition which they used to support their positions is virtually impossible, since there was generally an element of both in any given analogy or contrast. For instance, the fact that James Madison feared decentralization before he first used the Greek confederacies analogy is not evidence that he was *only* using the analogy as ammunition. Although he probably read the history of the ancient confederacies with an eye toward corroborating his own views, as most people read most literature, the very addition of the analogy to his stock of knowledge probably reinforced those views. When faced with forceful arguments against his position, he was not defenseless. He could charge into battle, confident of the caliber of his ammunition. Conversely, Adams' unflattering contrasts between ancient and American military strategy, a result of his study of classical warfare while head of Congress' Board of War, is not evidence that he merely learned a lesson from ancient history. His fiery temperament undoubtedly also contributed to his support for more offensive action.

The founders' immersion in ancient history had a profound effect upon their style of thought. They developed from the classics a suspicious cast of mind. They learned from the Greeks and Romans to fear conspiracies against liberty. Steeped in a literature whose perpetual theme was the steady encroachment of tyranny on liberty, the founders became virtually obsessed with spotting its approach, so that they might avoid the fate of their classical heroes. It has been said of the American Revolution that never was there a revolution with so little cause. Whatever his faults, George III was hardly Caligula or Nero; however illegitimate, the moderate British taxes were hardly equivalent to the mass executions of the emperors. But since the founders believed that the central lesson of the classics was that every illegitimate power, however small, ended in slavery, they were determined to resist every such power. Even legitimate authority should be exercised sparingly, lest it grow into illegitimate powers. Young Thomas Jefferson copied into his commonplace book the warning of Tacitus: "The more corrupt the commonwealth the more numerous its laws." In 1767 John Adams declared regarding the "spirit of liberty": "Obsta Principiis [resist the beginnings (of tyranny)] is her motto and maxim, knowing her enemies are secret and cunning, making the earliest advances slowly, silently, and softly." He then cited Tacitus on the insidiousness of despotism. The following year his cousin Samuel used the Latin motto "Principiis Obsta" as a pseudonym for an essay warning against a British military dictatorship over America. John Dickinson echoed the sentiment, quoting Cicero: "Even though the ruler may not, at the time, be troublesome, it is a sad fact that he can be so, if he takes the fancy." Dickinson added that the smaller the illegitimate tax the larger the danger, since the more easily it would be accepted by the incautious, thereby establishing a precedent for greater encroachments. Dickinson concluded: "Nations, in general, are not apt to think until they feel . . . Therefore, nations in general have lost their liberty." John Adams' friend William Tudor also acknowledged the classical tradition of resistance to tyranny. In 1774 he wrote regarding the simple mechanic who said that he would prefer to eat acorns in the forests rather than submit to British tyranny: "What a Roman! By Heavens, I glory in being this Man's fellow Citizen. When I meet with such Sentiments from such a Person, I easily anticipate the Period when Bostonian shall equal Spartan Virtue, and the American colonies rival in Patriotism the most celebrated Grecian Republic."[69]

So prevalent was the founders' fear of conspiracies against liberty, a fear derived largely from their lifelong immersion in classical political horror stories, that they could seriously equate one another—their recent partners in the struggle against British tyranny—with Caesar and Catiline. The presence of these irrational analogies in private letters and diaries suggests that they were fervent beliefs, not mere rhetorical devices. Rufus King noted that the Antifederalists seemed more afraid of the Federalists than of the Constitution itself, fearing that "some injury is plotted against them." The classics had taught the Antifederalists that tyrants generally proceeded by small degrees. Did not the Federalists seek to enslave the nation through the same insidious expansion of federal power? Likewise, the Federalists genuinely believed that their opponents were Caesars and Catilines, demagogues prepared to reduce the nation to anarchy in order to seize dictatorial power. Had not the Roman dictators secured their power in such a fashion? George Washington wrote concerning Antifederalist opposition to the Constitution: "Whilst many ostensible reasons are assigned, the real ones are concealed behind the Curtains, because they are not of a nature to appear in open day." The Federalists perceived the marginal increase in federal power they proposed as an antidote to the absolute power which, ancient history taught, must follow anarchy. If federal power were insufficient to maintain law and order, disintegration must lead to interstate warfare, which must eventuate in the dictatorship of a Caesar or Catiline. The Federalists intended their booster shot to the federal arm of government as an inoculation against the full-fledged disease of dictatorship. Ancient history taught two diametrically opposed "lessons" regarding how tyrants acquired their power—sometimes through the gradual accretion of authority, but at other times through the fomentation of anarchy via the annihilation of legitimate government power. Federalists and Antifederalists each clung to their favorite classical lesson. The common denominator was the fear of conspiracy. The same conspiracy theories soon infected the Federalist and Republican parties, as evidenced by the seriousness with which Jefferson and Hamilton compared each other with Julius Caesar.[70]

Classical republicans feared conspiracies not so much because tyranny deprived citizens of their liberty as because it robbed them of their virtue. As we have seen, the founders repeatedly contended that tyranny corrupted citizens by dehumanizing and degrading them. Perhaps more than any argument this assumption produced the desire for independence from Great Britain. If the cunning prime ministers of Britain could ever convince the American public to accept the smallest unconstitutional tax, Americans would eventually lose not only the power, but the very will, to resist. Americans would then be no more than slaves, subject to the whims of distant masters. To stay within the British empire would be to witness the recreation of that horrifying degradation and depravity which Tacitus had so vividly described in imperial Rome. But to leave the empire and start anew would be to embrace the exciting possibility of creating a society so elevated and virtuous as to inspire future Plutarchs to immortalize the nation. The fear of witnessing another Roman empire was as essential to producing the revolution as the hope of creating another Roman republic. As Jefferson astutely noted in the Declaration of Independence, humans are not, by nature, rebels. Only genuine fear of the dire consequences of persisting in their current situation, joined with real hope in the possibility of achieving a better fate, can inspire people to disrupt their lives and undertake the arduous sacrifices and hazard the frightful dangers characteristic of revolutions.

Bernard Bailyn contended that the founders' fear of conspiracies against liberty originated in Whig literature. But, while certainly reinforced by Whig rhetoric against the "Court Party" of Britain, the theme was classical in origin. The founders understood the theme's ancient lineage, referred directly to the works which had introduced it, and took great pride in the antiquity of their august role as the guardians of liberty. Indeed, as Bailyn himself noted, both British and American Tories repeatedly described themselves as the victims of a great conspiracy of Catilines, who were attempting to foment rebellion in order to bring American society under their dictatorial control. It is doubtful that the Tories derived *their* obsession with conspiracies from Whig literature. Rather, it makes more sense to ascribe the obsession with conspiracy rampant among every British, American, and French faction to the one classical canon which united them all.[71]

Nevertheless, the founders did inherit from the Whigs a crucial innovation to classical theory. Classical authors had never feared government power in general, only the excessive accretion of power by its monarchical, aristocratic, or democratic branch. Although the classical historians and political theorists strenuously denounced ambitious individuals or groups who attempted to seize too much power, they did not object to "government encroachments on the people," a Whig formulation which would have made no sense to citizens of small societies possessing participatory governments. Power could be safely concentrated in the government, as long as it was properly balanced between the different orders of society. But, living in a large, modern society and alienated from the centers of government power in London, Whigs like Thomas Gordon naturally interpreted classical authors' attacks on the encroachments of individual rulers as a broader assault on government power in general. Such a view allowed the Whigs to perceive themselves as heirs to the venerable figures of antiquity in an eternal struggle against government power. Gordon's statement, "Whatever is good for the People is bad for their Governors, and what is good for the Governors is pernicious to the People,"[72] would have mystified his favorite historian, Tacitus, a fact which explains why Tories could be just as fond of the classical authors as Whigs.

During the American Revolution, when fighting the same centralized power as the old Whigs, it was only natural that the founders should have accepted the Whig interpretation of the classical authors. But the matter is not that simple. After the war had been won, in the 1780s, the actions of state legislatures (the inflation of currencies and measures to prevent debt collection) so disgusted Federalists that they attempted to concentrate more power in the federal government. Although a residue of the Whig fear of government power remained even in Federalist thought, the Federalists were becoming more classical and less Whiggish. Hence, while the founders were heavily influenced by the Whig interpretation of the classics, they were not enslaved by it. In assaulting the concept of judicial review Andrew Jackson once asserted that he could read the Constitution as well as John Marshall; in the same fashion, it might be said that many of the founders could read Tacitus as well as Thomas Gordon.

The same visceral fear of conspiracies which instilled in the founders a passionate love of liberty and a proper recognition of its fragility also fueled the tendency to see a conspiracy behind every well-intentioned blunder, a conspirator in every opponent. There was a dark side to the sense of identity and purpose which the classical authors bequeathed the founders. It required fresh threats of tyranny for sustenance. Where such threats did not exist, they must be created.

V

Mixed Government and Classical Pastoralism

In addition to models and antimodels, the classics provided the founders with mixed government theory, the ideological framework they often employed to distinguish between the two. Mixed government theory set the terms of the founders' political discourse. Federalists enshrined the theory in the U.S. Constitution, forcing Antifederalists either to assault it directly or to question its applicability to the American context. Although James Madison developed a modern alternative to the theory as a solution to the problem of majority tyranny, most Republicans preferred to rest their hopes for the success of the nation's new representative democracy upon its agricultural lifestyle, a lifestyle deified by classical poets and historians. While Madison argued that the multiplicity of interests in a modern commercial republic rendered representative democracy a safe alternative to mixed government, most other Republicans rested its defense upon the abundance of land in America, which allowed for a society of Virgilian farmers.

Although democracy first developed in Greece, no one would have been more astonished by its current worship than the average Greek of the classical period. Hardly egalitarian, the Greeks were intensely concerned with distinctions between humans and animals, males and females, free people and slaves, men who owned property and those who did not, and, of course, Greeks and non-Greeks. Few Greek city-states possessed democracy before the fifth century B.C., when imperial Athens began pressuring its new allies to adopt constitutions similar to its own.[1]

Democracy was a bold venture. One reason the Athenians were so elated by their victory over the Persians on the plain of Marathon, in 490 B.C., was that it soothed their apprehension that the gods simply would not allow the overthrow of aristocracy—of a government controlled by men whose ancestry might ultimately be traced to the gods. The Athenians used the lot to select their officials partly because this system permitted the gods to play a role in what seemed to many people a most ungodly state.[2]

Members of prominent Athenian families resented the new democracy's dilution of their power and prestige and developed elaborate constructs to demonstrate its unacceptability as a form of government. It was these aristocrats who forged the basis of the anti-Athenian tradition which the founders imbibed at an early age. The aristocrats maintained that Athenian democracy constituted the tyranny of the poor over the rich. The Athenian masses were irrational, unstable, ungrateful, and fickle. Pericles corrupted the citizens by offering them state pay for state service. Athens' situation worsened even further after the death of Pericles, when demagogues of lesser ability controlled the government. Athens was a horrifying example of what could happen if the inherent inequalities among men were disregarded and government were based upon a specious egalitarianism.

The leading forgers of the antidemocratic tradition which was to dominate western political theory for two millennia not only suffered from a class bias, but also had personal axes to grind. Thucydides had been exiled by the Athenian people for a military failure during the Peloponnesian War. Although the historian praised Pericles, he did so largely in order to contrast the Athenian statesman with the "demagogic" Cleon, the man most responsible for Thucydides' exile. Thucydides (2.65.5–13) emphasized that Pericles "restrained the people . . . He was not led by them, but they by him." Similarly, Plato and Xenophon, already critics of democracy and supporters of a Spartan-style aristocracy, were devastated by the public execution of their mentor, Socrates. Hence it is not surprising that Thucydides' *History of the Peloponnesian War* featured hair-raising descriptions of the chaos and violence of Athenian democracy, that Xenophon's *Memorabilia of Socrates* was antidemocratic, that Plato advocated a simple aristocracy of guardians (led by a philosopher-king) in the (in)famous *Republic,* or that Plato's chief pupil, Aristotle, equated democracy with mob rule.

In the fourth century B.C. Plato identified three simple forms of government: monarchy, aristocracy, and democracy—rule by the one, the few, and the many. Each of these forms, he claimed (*Laws,* 756e–757a, 832c; *Politicus,* 291d–e, 303c), deteriorated over time: monarchy into tyranny, aristocracy into oligarchy, and democracy into ochlocracy (mob rule). Plato suggested that the best form of government would be a mixed government, one which balanced the power of the three orders of society. (This theory represented a marked departure from the one elaborated in the *Republic* more than a decade earlier.) Aristotle then immortalized mixed government theory, making it the centerpiece of his *Politics* (3.7), in which he cited numerous examples of mixed government in the ancient world.

Polybius provided the most detailed analysis of mixed government theory (*Histories*, 6.5–18). The second-century B.C. Greek historian agreed that the best constitution assigned approximately equal amounts of power to the three orders of society. He explained that only a mixed government could circumvent the cycle of discord which was the inevitable product of the simple forms. Hence only a mixed government could provide a state with the internal harmony necessary for prosperity and for the defeat of external enemies. Polybius claimed that the cycle began when primitive man, suffering from chaos and violence, consented to be ruled by a strong and brave leader. Then, as men began to conceive of justice (by developing the habit of putting themselves in others' positions), they replaced the strong and brave leader with the just leader and chose his son to succeed him, in the expectation that the son's lineage and education would lead him to emulate his father. But the son, having been accustomed to a special status from birth, possessed no sense of duty toward the public and, soon after acquiring power, sought to distinguish himself from the rest of the people. Monarchy had deteriorated into tyranny. When the bravest and noblest of the aristocrats (for who else would risk their lives in such an endeavor?) overturned the tyranny, the people naturally chose them to succeed the king as rulers. The result was an aristocracy, "rule by the best." Unfortunately, the aristocrats' children were not "the best," but the most spoiled and, like the king's son, soon placed their own welfare above that of the people. Aristocracy had deteriorated into oligarchy. The oppressed people rebelled against the oligarchy and created a democracy. But the wealthy, seeking to raise themselves above the common level, soon corrupted the people with bribes and created factions. The result was the chaos and violence which always accompany ochlocracy. When these reached epic proportions, sentiment grew for a dictatorship. Monarchy reappeared. This cycle, Polybius contended, would repeat itself in every society indefinitely until the society had the wisdom to balance the power of the three orders.

Polybius considered the Roman republic the most outstanding example of mixed government. He claimed that the Roman constitution, which had been constructed slowly through trial and error and had reached perfection at the time of the Second Punic War, was the secret of Roman success. The interdependence between the one, the few, and the many minimized internal strife. The Roman consuls (in this case, "the two" rather than "the one") needed to maintain good relations with the senate because the senate could block the flow of grain, clothing, and money to them in military campaigns, could replace them in the middle of a campaign if their year in office had expired, and could withhold triumphs and other prestigious awards. The consuls needed to maintain good relations with the people, since they could find fault with the account which the consuls were required to submit at the end of their term and could reject the treaties which they negotiated. Similarly, the senate and the people were bound to one another by the senate's control of lucrative contracts, by its dominance of the judicial system, and by the people's ability (through the tribunes) to veto senate legislation. Likewise, the people needed to maintain good relations with the consuls, since they served under them in the army. Presented with the need to explain to his dazed and defeated compatriots how a group of western "barbarians" had managed to conquer "the whole inhabited world" (the Mediterranean basin), the Achaean historian understandably turned to a well-established Greek theory.[3]

But such was the beguiling clarity and simplicity of Polybius' analysis that he even convinced the Romans themselves that their complex system of balances was the chief cause of their success. Cicero (*Republic*, 2.23–30) seized upon Polybius' theory to thwart the increasing efforts of ambitious Romans to consolidate their own power at the republic's expense. Although Plutarch, Livy, Sallust, and Tacitus never formally endorsed mixed government, their sympathy toward the lost republic and criticism of absolute monarchy, combined with their disquisitions on the volatile nature of untutored mobs, suggested a strong sympathy for it.

It may be doubted that the Roman republic ever possessed a mixed government. Even at the peak of plebeian power, the patricians continued to hold the upper hand, for three reasons. First, since the senate controlled the treasury, it could use financial leverage to prevent the enforcement of such measures as the Gracchi's land redistribution laws. Second, vast economic inequalities allowed the patricians to control large blocks of plebeian votes through a client system. Third, most plebeians could not afford to hold office, since officials were not paid salaries. Hence it is debatable whether consuls, who were almost always patricians, who shared in the economic interests of that class, and who generally had relatives in the senate, can be considered to have served as an effective counterweight to the aristocratic assembly. In addition, Polybius' "balances" between the consuls and the people were of unequal weight. A consul's fear that he might have a treaty rejected hardly balanced the terror felt by plebeians at the thought of opposing someone who, as a military leader, would have the power of life and death over them. Indeed, the imbalance between the patricians and plebeians was becoming much worse at the very time Polybius and Cicero were writing. The further inequalities produced by the growth of the latifundia, plantations in the conquered provinces worked by slaves (mostly prisoners of war), increased the relative power of the patricians enormously.[4]

In any case, mixed government theory survived the collapse of the Roman empire. Thomas Aquinas, a follower of Aristotle in politics as well as in metaphysics and ethics, revived the idea. John Calvin expressed a similar preference for mixed government, reiterating the widespread belief in the instability of the simple systems.[5]

The antidemocratic rhetoric of displaced Athenian aristocrats, staid Romans, and cloistered clerics is more easily understandable than Renaissance humanists' revulsion against Athens. One would imagine that the Florentines, in particular, would have admired the creativity of the Athenians and rejected the anti-intellectualism of the Spartans. However, Florentine political theorists such as Niccolò Machiavelli and Francesco Guicciardini uniformly rejected Athens in favor of Sparta and Rome. Machiavelli practically copied Polybius' discussion of the degeneration of the simple forms of government into his *Discourses on Livy*. Machiavelli observed regarding mixed government:

> Lycurgus is one of those who have earned no small measure of praise for constitutions of this kind. For in the laws which he gave to Sparta, he assigned to the kings, to the aristocracy, and to the populace each its own function, and thus introduced a form of government which lasted for more than eight hundred years to his very great credit and to the tranquility of that city.
>
> It was not so in the case of Solon, who drew up laws for Athens, for he set up merely a democratic form of government, which was so short lived that he saw before his death the birth of a tyranny under Pisistratus; and though, forty years later, Pisistratus' heirs were expelled, and Athens returned to liberty, because it again adopted a democratic form of government in accordance with Solon's laws, it did not retain its liberty for more than a hundred years.

Like Polybius and Cicero, Machiavelli ascribed Roman greatness to the gradual development of mixed government there. His source for the information regarding Solon was Plutarch. Elsewhere, Machiavelli cited Aristotle, Cicero, Sallust, and Tacitus. Similarly, Guicciardini based his advocacy of a mixed government for Florence partly on Aristotle's *Politics*. So strong was the fear of instability among the city-states of Renaissance Italy that even the Florentines blinded themselves to the weaknesses of Sparta and accepted it as a model. In part, the Florentine position may be traced to the Renaissance worship of Plutarch.[6]

The dominance of the mixed-government tradition in western political thought was not challenged until the rise of absolutism in the seventeenth century. Even the Roman emperors had generally cloaked their edicts in the language and forms of the republic. But monarchists Jean Bodin, Robert Filmer, and Thomas Hobbes, who were as revolutionary, in their own way, as latter-day democrats, attacked the hallowed theory of mixed government with great zeal. Although they disliked democracy as much as the mixed government theorists, the monarchists preferred to attack the most sacred model of mixed government, the Roman republic, than to join their opponents in beating the dead horse of Athens. Taking care to refute Aristotle, Polybius, Cicero, and Machiavelli, Bodin denied the possibility of such a thing as mixed government, arguing that the Roman republic had been a simple democracy and Sparta a simple aristocracy. Since the only real choice lay between the simple systems, and since monarchy was the best of these systems (Bodin agreed with his opponents that democracy was the worst), reasonable men had no choice but to support monarchy. Filmer agreed. After grousing that the Greeks had possessed "learning enough to be seditious," Filmer made a half-hearted and dubious attempt to convert Aristotle into a monarchist. He then contrasted the paltry 480 years of the Roman republic with the millennia of ancient Middle Eastern monarchies. Even during those 480 years, the Roman republic's restlessness betrayed its inability to find a decent form of government. Filmer concluded: "Rome began her empire under Kings and did perfect it under Emperors; it did only increase under the popularity. Her greatest exultation was under Trajan, as her longest peace had been under Augustus . . . The murders by Tiberius, Caligula, Nero, Domitian, and Commodus put all together cannot match that civil tragedy which was acted in that one sedition between Marius and Sulla." Contending that effective government demanded the concentration of sovereignty in a monarch, Filmer concluded that mixed government was a vain "fancy." Similarly, Hobbes assaulted the hallowed system of classical education which instilled the absurd belief in mixed government. Hobbes contended:

> In these western parts of the world, we are made to receive our opinions concerning the institutions and rights of commonwealths from Aristotle, Cicero, and other men, Greeks and Romans that, living under popular states, derived those rights not from the principles of nature but transcribed them into their books out of the practice of their own commonwealths which were popular—as the grammarians describe the rules of language out of the practice of the time, or the rules of poetry out of the poems of Homer and Virgil . . . Cicero and other writers have grounded their civil doctrine on the opinions of Romans, who were taught to hate monarchy at first by them that, having deposed their sovereign, shared among them the sovereignty of Rome, and afterwards by their successors. And by reading of these Greek and Latin authors, men from their childhood have gotten a habit, under a false show of liberty, of favoring tumults and of [the] licentious controlling [of] the actions of their sovereigns and again of controlling the controllers, with the effusion of so much blood as I think I may truly say there was never anything so dearly bought as these western parts have bought the learning of the Greek and Latin tongues.

The fact that Hobbes was not dissuaded by such sentiments from calling Thucydides "the most politic historiographer that ever writ" and translating his work into English does not reveal inconsistency. Thucydides never advocated a specific government form, and his horrific depiction of Athens during the Peloponnesian War could be interpreted as a portrayal of Hobbes's state of nature, a state to which Hobbes believed any society without concentrated sovereignty would revert.[7]

English republicans responded to these unprecedented assaults on mixed government both by reasserting classical arguments against the simple systems and by adding Great Britain to their list of successful mixed governments. The king, the House of Lords, and the House of Commons joined the Spartan and Roman governments in the pantheon of mixed government theorists. Seventeenth-century Englishman James Harrington was the modern advocate of mixed government most influential in America. Not surprisingly, he treated Athens harshly, though incorporating several features of Athenian government into his ideal state of Oceana. Citing Aristotle and Machiavelli, he made the usual bow to Sparta and Rome. It was Harrington who contributed a concept essential to any American adaptation of mixed government theory, the concept of

"natural aristocracy." Even in a new country like Oceana, without a titled aristocracy, certain men would possess greater talent than others. In
any free society this natural difference in talent would produce unequal
wealth. Unequal wealth would, in turn, produce class conflict. Mixed
government, combined with a few laws limiting the size of landholdings,
was the only means of preventing violent struggles between the classes
and the tyranny which inevitably followed these civil wars. Hence,
Oceana's government consisted of a senate which represented the natural
aristocracy, a huge assembly elected from the common people, and an
executive to provide a balancing center of power. Harrington believed
that such a system would produce good laws, which would, in turn,
produce good men. Algernon Sidney shared Harrington's respect for
mixed government. He declared: "There never was a good government
in the world that did not consist of the three simple species of monarchy,
aristocracy, and democracy [mixed together]." He added: "And those
nations that have wanted the prudence rightly to balance the powers of
their magistrates have been frequently obliged to have recourse to the
most violent remedies, and with much difficulty, danger, and blood, to
punish the crimes which they might have prevented." Although Sidney
defended Athens' policy of ostracism, he agreed with Xenophon and
Thucydides "that Athens was more subject to disorder and had less stability than Sparta." Mixed government theory was used to justify both
the British system of government and the American colonial governments, which generally consisted of a governor, a few councillors, and an
assembly elected by the colonists.[8]

The founders had access to every level of this western tradition of
mixed government theory. Hence it was only natural that, when confronted by unprecedented parliamentary taxation during the 1760s and
1770s, they should turn to the most ancient and revered of political theories to explain this perplexing phenomenon. Patriot leaders such as
Richard Henry Lee, Samuel Adams, and John Adams ascribed the new
tyranny to a degeneration of the mixture of the English constitution.
Although the form of the British government remained the same, King
George III had destroyed its delicate balance by using his patronage powers to buy the House of Commons and to pack the House of Lords. This
corruption had then seeped into colonial governments, where royal governors generally possessed the power to appoint the upper branch of the
legislature. As in the nations of antiquity, the source of tyranny was an
inadequate mixture. As Gordon Wood noted: "The long wrangle with

England, for all that it touched in the realm of politics, had scarcely con-
tested, and indeed for most Americans, had only endorsed mixed-government theory." The theory was still so axiomatic among all but a few
absolute monarchists and radical democrats that it was very rarely questioned.[9]

The framers of the new state constitutions which emerged from the
Revolution never doubted that their governments should be mixed.
Rather, their real dilemma was how to mix them in a society which no
longer possessed a monarch and which had never possessed a titled aristocracy. The framers decided that these essential roles should be played
by an elective governor and a senate consisting of Harrington's "natural
aristocracy." Ten of the thirteen states created a senate, nearly all of them
establishing property qualifications for senate candidates which exceeded
those for members of the lower house. North Carolina and New York
even established special property qualifications for their senates' electors,
a practice which won James Madison's approval as late as 1788. Maryland
went even further, establishing an electoral college to select its senators.
When Virginia chose to have its upper house elected in the same manner
as its lower assembly, and when Pennsylvania chose to eliminate its upper
branch altogether, the resultant furor engulfed both states. Unmollified
by the creation of a long-termed Council of Censors (based on the
Spartan ephors and the Roman censors) to monitor the single, democratic assembly, obstructionists finally crippled the Pennsylvania Constitution, forcing a new constitution which mimicked the mixture of the
other state governments. Americans had decided that since education
and talent often accompanied wealth, and since wealth (unlike either talent or virtue) could be easily quantified, property was the most appropriate criterion for identifying the "natural aristocracy" which would provide their governments with the necessary senatorial stability. The state
senates were generally smaller than the lower houses, and senators generally served longer, staggered terms to diminish their vulnerability to popular pressure.[10]

Even Thomas Jefferson, the future champion of representative democracy, fervently embraced mixed government during the Revolution.
Young Jefferson had devoted more space in his legal and political commonplace book to Montesquieu, the most famous modern advocate of
mixed government, than to any other author. In 1776 Jefferson argued
that "the wisest men" should be selected to the Virginia Senate and
should be, "when chosen, perfectly independent of their electors." Ex-

perience taught Jefferson "that a choice by the people themselves is not generally distinguished for its wisdom," a sentiment echoed in his literary commonplace book quotations. Hence he disliked the Virginia Constitution's provision for the direct election of senators. The first draft of his own proposed constitution established a nine-year, nonrenewable term, so that senators would not always "be casting their eyes forward to the period of election (however distant) and be currying favor with the electors, and consequently dependent on them." Jefferson could even accept Edmund Pendleton's suggestion "to an appointment for life, or to any thing rather than a mere creation by and dependence on the people." In 1782 Jefferson was still complaining about the Virginia Senate. He noted: "The purpose of establishing different houses of legislation is to introduce the influence of different interests or different principles." But since both of Virginia's houses were elected in the same manner, Virginia could not derive "those benefits" of a mixed system which compensated for its inconvenience. Jefferson also deplored the weakness of Virginia's governor, remembering his own troubles as governor during the Revolutionary War. Jefferson's proposal for a new Virginia constitution the following year favored the indirect election of senators and the elimination of all previous restrictions on the Senate's power to originate or amend any bill. He added that the governor should appoint the state's judges, in order to make the jurists "wholly independent of the Assembly—of the Council—nay, more, of the people."[11]

John Adams was the most visible and most persistent proponent of mixed government in America. Adams was devoted to mixed government theory throughout his life. As early as 1763 he claimed, in "An Essay on Man's Lust for Power": "No simple Form of Government can possibly secure Men against the Violences of Power. Simple Monarchy will soon mould itself into Despotism, Aristocracy will soon commence on Oligarchy, and Democracy will soon degenerate into Anarchy, such an Anarchy that every Man will do what is right in his own Eyes, and no Man's life or Property or Reputation or Liberty will be safe." In 1772 he contended: "The best Governments of the World have been mixed. The Republics of Greece, Rome, and Carthage were all mixed Governments." In 1776 Adams published his *Thoughts on Government,* a series of essays urging the Virginia and North Carolina legislatures to establish mixed governments in their new constitutions. The pamphlet exerted a tremendous influence upon the framers of the state constitutions. In 1780 Adams played a leading role in drafting the Massachusetts Constitution, then widely considered the best of all the state constitutions. Under the Massachusetts Constitution representation in the Senate was based upon the amount of taxes paid by each district. A higher property qualification was required for the senators' electors than for the representatives' electors. An even larger amount of property was required of the governor's electors. The governor was a limited, elective monarch, possessing the veto power, a fixed salary, and broad powers of appointment. In 1787 Adams wrote the *Defence of the Constitutions of Government of the United States,* which remains the fullest exposition of mixed government theory by an American. He penned the three volumes partly in response to Turgot's *Letters,* which had endorsed the single-assembly government of Pennsylvania and had assaulted Adams' Massachusetts constitution, and partly in response to Shays's Rebellion, whose supporters had demanded single-assembly government. Shays's rebels, Massachusetts farmers angered by foreclosures resulting from a shortage of paper money, knew that a single, democratic assembly was more likely to yield to popular pressures to inflate the money supply.[12]

Adams turned directly to the ancients for mixed government theory. In the *Defence* he summarized the vague genesis of the theory in Plato's work and its development through Aristotle, Polybius, and Cicero. While respecting such modern authors as Niccolò Machiavelli, James Harrington, Algernon Sidney, John Locke, and Montesquieu, Adams considered these theorists (particularly Montesquieu) overrated, emphasizing that "the best part" of their writings came directly from the ancients. Indeed, Machiavelli's shady reputation and Harrington's support for "agrarian acts" (land redistribution legislation) could not have endeared these authors to the conservative New Englander.[13]

Garry Wills contends that few founders advocated mixed government, since it was inherently "at odds" with the separation of powers. This conclusion is the product of Wills's unique definition of mixed government. Wills claims that, according to mixed government theory, "all the interests should 'have a say' on all the issues." Though Wills does not attach a literal meaning to the phrase "all the issues," signifying only that each order of society must share in the executive, legislative, and judicial power, he is still incorrect. Neither Plato, nor Aristotle, nor Polybius, nor Cicero, nor any other mixed government theorist defined mixed government in such a fashion. In none of the numerous examples of mixed government cited by the ancient philosophers did each of the orders share in each of the three types of power. In fact, what is most striking about these examples is their rich variety, a variety which allowed for interminable disputes over which governments might be termed mixed. This variety of examples was possible only because theorists labeled as mixed any government in which the three orders possessed approximately equal power, balanced against one another. The specific powers held by each order were irrelevant, so long as a rough balance prevailed. Hence, while none of the governments cited by the philosophers possessed a full separation of powers, neither did their founders take care that each order possess some executive, some legislative, and some judicial power.[14]

Indeed, so far was John Adams from considering the separation of powers inconsistent with mixed government that he deemed the former necessary to the latter. In his *Defence of the U.S. Constitutions,* the first volume of which circulated at the Constitutional Convention, Adams claimed that since the time when Lycurgus (now considered mythical) first instituted mixed government in Sparta in the eighth century B.C., only three improvements had been made in the science of government: representation, the separation of powers, and the division of the legislature into "three independent, equal branches"—that is, the veto power for all three orders of society. Adams was particularly emphatic concerning the necessity of a high degree of separation of powers in a mixed government:

> If there is one certain truth to be collected from the history of all ages, it is this: That the people's rights and liberties, and the democratical mixture in a constitution, can never be preserved without a strong executive, or, in other words, without separating the executive power from the legislative. If the executive power, or any considerable part of it, is left in the hands of either an aristocratical or democratical assembly, it will corrupt the legislature as necessarily as rust corrupts iron, or as arsenic poisons the human body; and when the legislature is corrupted, the people are undone.[15]

What Adams feared most in the American states were single-assembly governments, which would inevitably be dominated by a natural aristocracy of wealth, birth, and talent. Hence the natural aristocracy should be segregated in a Senate, where their talent could benefit the country, while their ambition could be checked by the one executive and the representatives of the many. The consequence of the states' failure to maintain such a balance would be a repetition of Greek history—that is, "two factions, which will struggle in words, in writing, and at last in arms." Having cited Thucydides on the barbaric acts of "the aspiring few" and "the licentious many" in many of the Greek city-states during the Peloponnesian War, Adams ascribed this class conflict to their single-assembly governments. He then pleaded: "In the name of human and divine benevolence, is such a system as this to be recommended to Americans, in this age of the world? . . . Without three orders, and an effectual balance between them, in every American constitution, it must be destined to frequent, unavoidable revolutions." Adams further contended: "The history of Greece should be to our countrymen what is called in many families on the [European] continent a boudoir; an octagonal apartment in a house, with a full-length mirror on every side, and another in the ceiling." He added that a nation the size of the United States should fear simple governments even more than the tiny Greek republics had.[16]

The simple government to which Americans were most apt to fall prey was, of course, democracy. Adams claimed that democracy never had a patron among men of letters, because the people applauded "artifices and tricks . . . hypocrisy and superstition . . . flattery, bribes, [and] largesses." "It is no wonder then," he added, "that democracies and democratical mixtures are annihilated all over Europe, except on a barren rock, a paltry fen, an inaccessible mountain, or an impenetrable forest." Later in the same volume Adams expanded upon his view of democracy:

> An usurping populace is its own dupe, a mere under-worker, and purchaser in trust of some single tyrant, whose state and power they advance to their ruin, with as blind an instinct as those worms that die while weaving magnificent habits for beings of a superior order. The people are more dextrous at putting down and setting up than at preserving what is fixed; and they are not fonder of seizing more than their own than they are of delivering it up again to the worst bidder, with their own into the bargain. Their earthly devotion is seldom paid to above one at a time, of their own creation, whose oar they pull with less murmuring and more skill, than when they share the leading, or even hold the helm.

Democracy, Adams concluded in Polybian fashion, was a mere way station on the road to tyranny.[17]

Adams opposed the other simple forms of government as well. He marshaled an impressive array of examples, drawn largely from ancient history, to prove the crucial importance of a balance among the three orders of society. His favorite example of mixed government was

Polybius' favorite, the Roman republic. Adams claimed that in the eighth century B.C. Romulus (another mythical figure) had created a mixed government in Rome modeled upon the Spartan government instituted by Lycurgus. Unfortunately, Romulus failed to give the Roman king the full executive authority and a veto on the senate's legislation, and failed to balance the aristocratic senate with a regular assembly of the people. As a result, the aristocracy overturned the monarchy, as it must when the monarch lacks the aid of a popular assembly. There followed a harsh oligarchy. The two consuls replaced the one king. The consuls were elected annually, thereby allowing the senate much influence in their selection. In addition, the consuls, like the kings before them, lacked full executive authority and the veto power. Nevertheless, after suffering numerous popular revolts, the senate granted the plebeians the authority to elect tribunes, who possessed the power to veto senate legislation. As a result, the Roman government finally achieved the rough balance of the three orders which served as the basis for the city's unparalleled stability, prosperity, and growth. But the people were dissatisfied and grasped for more power. Since the consuls were too weak to moderate between the few and the many, open warfare ensued between the two groups. The leader of the many (Caesar) defeated the leader of the few (Pompey), as he must when aristocrats lack the aid of a powerful monarch. The horrible tyranny that succeeded Caesar's triumphs lasted until the fall of the Roman empire in the fifth century A.D.[18]

Adams also attributed the downfall of Carthage to its lack of a separation of powers and executive veto. Since the two Carthaginian suffetes, like the Roman consuls, shared executive authority with the senate and lacked the veto power, they were too weak to moderate between the few and the many. The popular assembly possessed too much power, settling all legislative questions on which the senate did not rule unanimously. The enormous power of the assembly was fatally increased when the term of the state's popularly elected chief judicial officers was reduced from life to one year. The dissension which resulted from the ensuing lack of balance between the few and the many undermined the Carthaginian war effort against the Romans. This was the reason that the Romans "finally destroyed their rival power so effectually that scarce a trace of it remains to be seen, even in ruins."[19]

Adams ascribed the fall of Sparta to the same lack of balance, resulting from the same causes. The Spartan senate (the *gerousia*, or "council of elders," consisting of twenty-eight members, aged sixty and older) had the whole executive power and most of the legislative authority. The two kings were merely religious and military leaders. The popular assembly could not debate, but could only confirm or reject senate proposals by acclamation. Hence the longevity of Lycurgus' constitution (eighth century to fourth century B.C.) could not be ascribed to a proper balance between orders, but must be ascribed to two other causes. First, the five ephors, who acted as the people's watchdogs over senate administration, swore an oath every month to maintain the kings' hereditary honors, while the kings swore to obey the laws. These solemn oaths, though a poor substitute for a royal and popular veto power, served to unite the kings with the people against the senate. Second, and more important, the Spartans' remarkable social system instilled in its citizens a deep attachment to the republic. This system featured "the equal division of property; the banishment of gold and silver; the prohibition of travel and intercourse with strangers; the prohibition of arts, trades, and agriculture [by citizens, not by the foreign helots]; the discouragement of literature; the public meals; the incessant warlike exercises; [and] the doctrine that every citizen was the property of the state, and that parents should not educate their own children." Not only was this system contrary to the personal happiness of the citizens, but the Spartan conquest of Athens and the rest of Greece, by introducing luxury and foreign manners into Sparta, destroyed the values the system had produced. The ephors, against their most solemn oath, killed a king. To Adams, the lesson was clear: proper balancing of the power of the three orders of society, not religious oaths or education, was the only practical method of achieving public happiness.[20]

Adams contended that Athens' downfall had also resulted from an improper balance of the orders. Athens was first ruled by an aristocracy of nine archons. By the seventh century B.C. the archons had become so tyrannical that Draco's harsh legal code allowed creditors to sell debtors into foreign servitude. Such laws would have incited revolution if Solon had not been made dictator in 594 B.C. Solon eased the plight of debtors and transferred power to the Athenian popular assembly. Though only the wealthy could hold office, because of high property qualifications, the majority held the supreme power. Adams wrote regarding Solon: "He had not, probably, tried the experiment of democracy in his own family before he attempted it in the city, according to the advice of Lycurgus; but was obliged to establish such a government as the people would bear, not that which he thought best, as he said himself." The result of Solon's democracy was the tyranny of Peisistratus and his son (561–510 B.C.). After a brief civil war the Athenians returned to democracy, which again failed to last "above one hundred years" (actually, by a fairer reckoning, close to two hundred). Like the Spartans, the Athenians toyed with empty solutions to the problem of tyranny, such as ostracism, which served only to banish Athens' best leaders. Adams asked: "What more melancholy spectacle can be conceived even in imagination, than that inconstancy which erects statues to a patriot or hero one year, banishes him the next, and the third erects statues to his memory?"[21]

The real solution to democracies' problems, Adams concluded, was their moderation by the other two orders. Adams declared: "Without this, they are but a transient glare of glory, which passes away like a flash of lightning, or like a momentary appearance of a goddess to an ancient hero, which by revealing but a glimpse of celestial beauties, only excited regret that he had never seen them." He added: "The republic of Athens, the school mistress of the whole civilized world, for more than a thousand years in arts, eloquence, and philosophy, as well as in politeness and wit, was, for a short period of her duration, the most democratical commonwealth in Greece." But through a proper balance of orders and through the modern innovations of representation, the separation of powers, and the veto power for each order, the United States could escape "the tumultuous comotions, like the raging waves of the sea, which always agitated the ecclesia [popular assembly] at Athens." Adams concluded regarding the American experiment: "This will be a fair trial, whether a government so popular can preserve itself. If it can, there is reason to hope for all the equality, all the liberty, and every other good fruit of Athenian democracy, without any of its ingratitude, convulsions, or factions."[22]

Adams received not only his general political theory, but also his principal supporting examples for that theory, from the ancients. Yet it was a theory substantially altered by the modern innovations Adams listed. Representation removed the people from direct participation in government. Based upon a suspicion of government alien to the ancients, Montesquieu's separation of powers balanced government branches rather than social orders. The executive veto injected a greater degree of monarchical power into modern republics than had existed in the ancient republics. Most significant, though it failed to make Adams' list of modern innovations, was Harrington's concept of "natural aristocracy," a concept essential to the American adaptation of mixed government.

The United States' eventual replacement of England's hereditary king and aristocrats with an elective monarch and an assembly of wealth necessarily increased the nation's distance from the classical polity. But the founders' general unwillingness to recognize the revolutionary nature of modern innovations to mixed government theory is yet another great testament to their reluctance to stray too far from the classical font of wisdom and authority.

At the end of Adams' first volume of the *Defence,* completed in January 1787, he declared himself satisfied with the existing structure of the federal government. Under the Articles of Confederation, the supreme federal legislative and executive authorities were lodged in a single assembly. But, Adams explained, since the state governments were the real powers in the system, their structure was a far greater concern than that of the federal government. Adams wrote: "The security against the dangers of this kind [tyranny] will depend upon the accuracy and decision with which the governments of the separate states have their own orders arranged and balanced." But when the U.S. Constitution shifted the balance of power from the state governments to the federal government, it became imperative that the latter be mixed. Hence Adams was exceptionally pleased with the Constitution, with its balance between the one president, the few senators, and the representatives of the many. At the conclusion of his third and final volume, completed in October, a month after the adjournment of the convention, he exulted: "It is now in our power to bring this work to a conclusion with unexpected dignity." He reprinted the text of the Constitution and heaped praise upon it. Years later, Adams recalled that the writings of Polybius "were in the contemplation of those who framed the American constitution."[23]

James Madison also endorsed the Constitution as establishing a mixed government. At the Constitutional Convention Madison argued for a nine-year term for senators, declaring: "Landholders ought to have a share in the government to support these invaluable interests and to balance and check the other [the many]. They ought to be so constituted as to protect the minority of the opulent against the majority. The senate, therefore, ought to be this body; and to answer these purposes, they ought to have permanency and stability. Various have been the propositions; but my opinion is, the longer they continue in office, the better will these views be answered." It was useless to deny the existence of an American aristocracy, though there were no "hereditary distinctions," and though inequalities of wealth were minor by comparison with Europe. Madison continued: "There will be debtors and creditors, and an unequal possession of property, and hence arises different views and different objects in government. This, indeed, is the ground work of aristocracy; and we find it blended in every government, both ancient and modern." Madison concluded that even in his own day America could not be regarded as "one homogeneous mass" and that there were recent "symptoms of a leveling spirit" which he feared might lead to "agrarian acts." Four years earlier, when Madison had chaired a committee to recommend books for congressional use, he had placed Aristotle's *Politics* at the top of his list of works concerning political theory.[24]

In *Federalist* No. 63 Madison asserted that "history informs us of no long-lived republic which had not a senate." He then related how the Spartan, Roman, and Carthaginian senates, whose members possessed lifetime terms, had acted as an "anchor against popular fluctuations." Madison further argued that the danger of a republic's being corrupted was "greater where the whole legislative trust is lodged in the hands of one body of men than where the concurrence of separate and dissimilar bodies is required in every public act." The operative word here is "dissimilar." Madison did not consider the Senate a mere redundancy, a democratic body which existed only to block any hasty legislation which might proceed from the other democratic body, the House of Representatives. Rather, it was obvious from the Senate's different manner of selection and much longer term of office that it would house a natural aristocracy. Thus, Madison took care to assuage fears that the Senate would convert the government into an oligarchy. He demonstrated that in Sparta, Rome, and Carthage, it was encroachment by the representatives of the people, and not by the senate, which had corrupted the republic. Madison concluded: "It proves the irresistable force possessed by that branch of a free government which has the people on its side." Evidently, the U.S. Senate was not that branch which was intended to "have the people on its side." In his notes for the essay Madison cited Aristotle, Polybius (whom he had just read regarding the Achaean League), and Cicero as his sources. In the previous essay, Madison had also referred to "the dissimilarity in the genius of the two bodies" that were to form the U.S. Congress. In the same year Madison warned Thomas Jefferson: "Wherever the real power in Government lies, there is the danger of oppression. In our Governments the real power lies in the majority of the Community, and the invasion of private rights is chiefly to be apprehended not from acts of Government contrary to the sense of its constituents, but from acts in which the Government is the mere instrument of the major number of the constituents." Even after the Constitutional Convention Madison continued to endorse a federal veto on state laws, claiming that without it, states would continue to be controlled by "interested majorities" trampling "on the rights of minorities and individuals."[25]

Madison agreed with Adams that the principle of representation and the separation of powers had improved mixed government. Although Madison skillfully demonstrated that "the principle of representation was neither unknown to the ancients nor wholly overlooked in their political constitutions," he recognized that their popular assemblies had consisted of the citizens themselves. In *Federalist* No. 10 Madison refuted Montesquieu's assertion that republics must remain small, in part by arguing that representative republics were more stable than the participatory democracies of ancient Greece and Rome. He reiterated this position in *Federalist* Nos. 14 and 39. In No. 47 he tied the separation of powers to the success of mixed government as well: "The accumulation of all powers, legislative, executive, and judicial, in the same hands, whether of one, a few, or many, and whether hereditary, self-appointed, or elective, may justly be pronounced the very definition of tyranny. Were the federal Constitution, therefore, really chargeable with the accumulation, no further arguments would be necessary to inspire a universal reprobation of the system."[26]

Alexander Hamilton was a third Federalist who advocated mixed government. Hamilton's outline for a speech given at the Constitutional Convention on June 18, 1787, a speech in which he advocated lifetime terms for both the president and the Senate, included these statements:

> Here I shall give my sentiments of the best form of government—not as a thing attainable by us, but as a model which we ought to approach as near as possible. British constitution best form. Aristotle—Cicero—Montesquieu—Neckar. Society naturally divides itself into two political divisions—the few and the many, who have distinct interests. If a government [is] in the hands of the few, they will tyrannize over the many. If [it is in] the hands of the many, they will tyrannize over the few. It ought to be in the hands of both; and they should be separated.

He added that the voice of the people was not the voice of God. Hamilton concluded: "Nothing but a permanent body [a lifetime senate] can check the imprudence of democracy." Eight days later, Hamilton opposed Roger Sherman's measure to reduce the senators' term of office, reminding him that the House of Representatives would act as "the democratic body." Hamilton further noted that the absence of legal distinctions in America between citizens did not mean that American society was homogeneous. Inequality of property still "constituted the great & fundamental distinction in Society." Making an analogy between the United States and the Roman republic, he asked: "When the Tribunitial power had leveled the boundary between the patricians and plebeians what followed?" He answered: "The distinction between rich and poor was substituted." He concluded pointedly: "If we incline too much to democracy, we shall soon shoot into a monarchy. The difference of property is already great among us. Commerce and industry will still increase the disparity." At the New York ratifying convention Hamilton declared: "There are few positions more demonstrable than that there should be, in every republic, some permanent body to correct the prejudices, check the intemperate passions, and regulate the fluctuations, of a popular assembly." Too many American states were "either governed by a single democratic assembly, or have a senate constituted directly upon democratic principles."[27]

But Hamilton was also as conscious as Adams and Madison of the "improvements" made upon mixed government theory since ancient times. In *Federalist* No. 9 he wrote: "The science of politics, however, like most other sciences, has received great improvement. The efficacy of various principles is now well understood, which were either not known at all, or imperfectly known, to the ancients." Such principles included representation and the separation of powers. Hamilton concluded regarding these: "They are means, and powerful means, by which the excellencies of republican government may be retained and its imperfections lessened or avoided."[28]

Other Federalists endorsed the Constitution as establishing a mixed government. Gouverneur Morris, George Wythe, and John Dickinson championed mixed government at the Constitutional Convention. Morris warned of the usual "encroachments of the popular branch of Government" and suggested an absolute veto by the president as the remedy. Wythe echoed Morris' concern. Dickinson insisted that the Senate should "consist of the most distinguished characters, distinguished for their rank in life and their weight of property, and bearing as strong a likeness to the House of Lords as possible," a Senate that would combine "the families and wealth of the aristocracy" in order to "establish a balance that will check the Democracy." To ensure that the Senate possessed such a character Pierce Butler and John Rutledge opposed the payment of salaries to its members. In a subsequent pamphlet Dickinson argued that the ambitions of the popular branch were most to be feared, having killed the republics of Carthage, Rome, and Athens. Noah Webster claimed that there were a thousand examples of the failure of "pure democracy," contended that the Roman masses had "extorted" powers from the senate, and concluded that the U.S. Constitution was similar, though superior, to the illustrious mixed constitutions of Britain and Rome.[29]

James Wilson was yet another Federalist advocate of mixed government. Ignorant of Greek political theory, he believed that his idol, Cicero, had been the first to propose this form of government. At the Pennsylvania ratifying convention Wilson appeared to repudiate mixed government theory, saying: "It would be an improper government for the United States, because it is inadequate to such an extent of territory, and because it is suited to an establishment of different orders of men." Wilson recognized that the Constitution would not establish mixed government in a strict classical sense: no branch of the government would be the province of a hereditary aristocracy. But Wilson also recognized that the Constitution did not propose a democracy, either. The indirect election and lengthy term of the senators would ensure that the Senate was dominated by a natural aristocracy. Hence, Wilson concluded: "What is the nature and kind of that government which has been proposed for the United States by the late Convention? In its principle, it is purely democratical. But the principle is applied in different forms, in order to obtain the advantages, and exclude the inconveniences, of the simple modes of government." Having defined mixed government narrowly, Wilson was left without a label for the new government, a predicament he might have avoided by simply calling it a new type of mixed government. Numerous other Federalists supported the government on that very basis.[30]

Recognizing that mixed government theory provided the theoretical foundation for the Constitution, most Antifederalists either assaulted it vigorously or denied its applicability to the American context. "Centinel" turned Adams on himself, writing regarding mixed government: "Mr. Adams, although he has traced the constitution of every form of government that ever existed, as far as history affords materials, has not been able to adduce a single instance of such a government." Adams' own examples proved that the balance between orders was constantly in jeopardy, if not wholly impossible to maintain. "Centinel" added that Great Britain, another highly touted example of mixed government, was also unbalanced. ("Centinel" was certainly correct on this point. Even as he wrote, George III's mental illness was undermining the British monarchy. In addition, the House of Commons remained a misnomer at least until the mid-nineteenth century as a result of high property qualifications for voting. Great Britain might more aptly have been termed a simple oligarchy than a mixed government.) "Centinel" concluded, in a fashion ironically similar to the seventeenth-century monarchists, that mixed government was a mirage. Furthermore, he argued, even if mixed government were possible, it would promote a lack of responsibility, since the various branches would blame one another for government inefficiency or corruption. By contrast, the most responsible government would be simple in structure, featuring one legislative body elected for a short term. The Articles of Confederation government, which the Federalists were seeking to displace, was, of course, just such a government.[31]

Other Antifederalists, stopping short of a complete repudiation of mixed government theory, simply denied its applicability to the American context. At the Constitutional Convention Charles Pinckney responded to expositions on mixed government theory: "The people of this country are not only very different from the inhabitants of any State we are acquainted with in the modern world; but I assert that their situation is distinct from either the people of Greece, or Rome, or of any State we are acquainted with among the antients." Pinckney then moved from the general to the specific: "Can the orders introduced by the institution of Solon, can they be found in the United States? Can the military habits & manners of Sparta be resembled to our habits & manners? Are the distinctions of Patrician & Plebeian known among us?" (Pinckney recanted his position the following year at the South Carolina ratifying convention, supporting the Constitution precisely because it proposed a mixed government. He declared: "Among the other honors, therefore, that have been reserved for the American Union, not the least considerable of them is that of defining a mixed system by which a people may govern themselves, possessing all the virtues and benefits, and avoiding all the dangers and inconveniences, of the three simple forms." He explained that the six-year Senate term would give "the system all the advantages of an aristocracy—wisdom, experience, and a consistency of measures.") James Monroe agreed with Pinckney's original argument that the United States was fundamentally different from the ancient republics. At the Virginia ratifying convention he claimed that although the Roman and British governments were based on mixed government theory, the American situation was entirely different, necessitating government "founded on different principles."[32]

But whatever disagreements existed among Antifederalists over the possibility of mixed government in the abstract, all agreed that the Constitution would not establish one. Rather, the Antifederalists claimed it would produce an oligarchy. "Centinel" called the Constitution the "most daring attempt to establish a despotic aristocracy among freemen that the world has ever witnessed." "Philadelphiensis" wrote that the "lordlings" of the Constitutional Convention were "unanimous in favoring a government that should raise the fortunes and respectability of the well born few, and oppress the plebeians." "Helvidius Priscus" compared the Constitution with the "draconian code" of Athens, while "Sidney" compared its supporters with the Athenian aristocrats of Solon's day who sold debtors into slavery. Patrick Henry claimed that "similar examples are to be found in ancient Greece and ancient Rome—instances of the people losing their liberty by their own carelessness and the ambition of a few." "A Columbian Patriot" declared that it was every citizen's duty "to resist the first approaches of tyranny, which at this day threaten to sweep away the rights for which the brave sons of America have fought with an heroism scarcely paralleled even in ancient republicks." "An Old Whig" concurred fully with this assessment, comparing the American people, should they ratify the document, with the tree in Aesop's story which furnished the handle for the ax of a man, who then cut down the tree. He added: "If we perish in America, we shall have no better comfort than the same mortifying reflection, that we have been the cause of our own destruction." "John Humble" wrote, with overbearing irony, that the "skillful physicians" at Philadelphia, "through the assistance of John Adams Esquire, in the profundity of their great political knowledge, found out and discovered that nothing but a new government consisting of three branches, kings, lords, and commons, or in the American language, president, senate, and representatives, can save this our country from inevitable destruction."[33]

Even the few Antifederalists who advocated mixed government denied that the Constitution would create one. "A Farmer" contended: "There is nothing solid or useful that is new. And I will venture to assert that if every political institution is not fully explained by Aristotle and other ancient writers, yet that, there is no new discovery in this the most important of all sciences, for ten centuries back." But "A Farmer" denied that the Constitution would create an Aristotelian mixed government. "The Federal Farmer" agreed, claiming that it would create an oligarchy. George Mason concurred. In the 1770s he had proposed the indirect election of Virginia senators from among men who possessed estates worth two thousand pounds or more. In 1787, at the Constitutional Convention, James Madison recorded: "Mr. Mason argued strongly for an election of the larger branch by the people. It was to be the grand depository of the democratic principle of the government. It was, so to speak, to be our House of Commons . . . He admitted that we had been too democratic, but was afraid we should incautiously run into the opposite extreme. We ought to attend to the rights of every class of the people." Unsatisfied that the Constitution had created a mixed government, Mason opposed it thereafter, predicting: "The government will set out a moderate aristocracy; it is at present impossible to foresee whether it will, in its operation, produce a monarchy or a corrupt, tyrannical aristocracy. It will probably vibrate some years between the two, and then terminate in the one or the other."[34]

As proof that the Constitution would institute an oligarchy rather than a mixed government, Antifederalists generally cited the small number of delegates to be elected to the House of Representatives and, hence, the large size of their electoral districts. As William Grayson put it: "If we look at the democratic branch, and the great extent of the country . . . it must be considered, in a great degree, to be an aristocratic representation." He feared that the House "might unite with the other two branches" against the people. Samuel Chase agreed. He asserted: "I object [to the Constitution] because the representatives will not be the representatives of the people at large, but really of a few rich men . . . In fact, no order or class of the people will be represented in the House of Representatives—called the Democratic branch—but the rich and wealthy. They will be ignorant of the sentiments of the middling (and much more of the lower) class of citizens." The large size of the House of Representatives' electoral districts was proof, Antifederalists felt, that the proponents of the Constitution were merely utilizing mixed government theory as a respectable cloak for shameless oligarchical schemes.[35]

The debate between the Federalists and Antifederalists regarding mixed government reveals their shared environmentalism. Both sides agreed that humans had acted in a depraved fashion in the past, and both sought to prevent future depravity through a rational rearrangement of the environment. While most Antifederalists believed that a virtuous society could be achieved through proper education, accompanied by majority rule, most Federalists believed it could be achieved through a balance in government between the three orders. John Adams expressed the latter view well. While far from deeming a nation's educational system irrelevant, he argued: "Millions must be brought up, whom no principles, no sentiments derived from education, can restrain from trampling on the laws: orders of men, watching and balancing each other, are the only security; power must be opposed to power, and interest to interest . . . Religion, superstition, oaths, education, laws, all give way before passions, interest, and power, which can be resisted only by passions, interest, and power." Having reviewed the horrors of the Peloponnesian War, Adams concluded: "Such things ever will be, says Thucydides, so long as human nature continues the same. But if this nervous historian had known a balance of three powers, he would not have pronounced the distemper so incurable, but would have added—so long as parties in cities remain unbalanced." Hence, even so pessimistic a man as John Adams—the same man who charged Polybius with excessive optimism for assuming that the first generation acquiring power would not be corrupted by it—could write that it was possible for a constitution to last forever, if it only possessed the proper balance among the orders. Adams explained in Polybian fashion: "The best republics will be virtuous and have been so; but we may hazard a conjecture, that the virtues have been the effect of the well-ordered constitution, rather than the cause: and perhaps it would be impossible to prove that a republic cannot exist even among highwaymen, by setting one rogue to watch another; and the knaves themselves may, in time, be made honest men by the struggle."[36]

Gordon Wood suggested that the framers of the U.S. Constitution possessed an understanding of mixed government different from the Whig conception which had prevailed during the American Revolution. According to Wood, the British Whigs had argued that republics consisted of one homogeneous mass united by a common interest. Hence, the purpose of aristocratic assemblies was not to protect the private property of the wealthy, but to provide a body of the most talented men to work for the common good. The threat posed by democracy was not majority tyranny, since the majority shared a common interest with the more affluent minority, but anarchy ("licentiousness"). The danger was a general and random violation of the law, which would endanger the life, liberty, and property of all citizens, rather than the calculated use of the law against the propertied. But in the 1780s, when mobs of debtors succeeded in pressuring several state legislatures into inflating their currencies and preventing the collection of debts, the Federalists were compelled to recognize that, far from being one homogeneous mass, American society was strictly divided by class. Since the interests of the few directly conflicted with those of the many, Federalists now perceived the real threat of majority rule in the legalized robbery of the wealthy by the poor. Hence they now considered aristocratic assemblies "bodies of the opulent," whose chief function was to block the confiscatory legislation which would inevitably emerge from the "democratic branch."[37]

Wood's dichotomy between these two types of mixed government theory is too strict. Both justifications for mixed government may be found in classical, British Whig, American Revolutionary, and Federalist writings. Both ancient and modern republican authors wavered between the idealistic yearning to rid society of divergent interests and the practical need to balance interests, as a result of the inevitable failure of efforts at homogenization. Hence, Harrington's Oceana possessed both Platonic limits on wealth and Aristotelian mixed government. Similarly, after the Revolution Alexander Hamilton applauded those patriots who had given their all for the cause, but opposed retribution against those who had not, since the latter were only human. Like most ancient and modern philosophers, Hamilton combined the hope for virtue with the recognition of its scarcity.[38]

Nevertheless, Wood's essential point, that the Federalists of the 1780s placed increasing emphasis upon class conflict, is valid—and would seem to indicate that they were becoming more classical and less Whiggish. While the classical historians and political theorists had always urged virtue, which they defined as enlightened service on behalf of the common good, the constant class conflict of Greek and Roman history had always made it clear to them that the immediate economic interests of the landed few and the landless many were often directly opposed. Within each polis, Plato wrote, there were "two cities at war with each other— the polis of the poor and that of the rich." Popular cries for the cancellation of debts and the redistribution of land never ceased. Attempts to eliminate inequalities of wealth through the safety valve of colonization and through restrictions on the size of estates never succeeded, and the Peloponnesian War produced open class warfare in many cities, with the few supporting Sparta, the many Athens.[39] Hence, no sane republic would base its safety exclusively on popular virtue and common interests. The motto of classical authors might have been: "Demand the best, but expect the worst." Although they assumed that aristocratic assemblies were composed of those men most capable of discerning society's common interests, they also considered such bodies necessary to check the "demagogues" who were always ready to persuade the masses to pass unjust legislation, or to lead them in lawless acts. Thucydides saw first-hand that, in an ancient democracy like Athens, where the people assembled to pass their own laws, the line between a mob and a tyrannical legislature was very fine. In a small, participatory republic there was no distinction between society and government. Yet there was always the Polybian hope that the habit of compromise necessitated by mixed government might itself produce virtuous men, by tempering men's souls. Paradoxically, institutional restraints on human selfishness might ultimately reduce (if never completely eliminate) their own necessity.

British Whigs found it much easier to distinguish between anarchy and majority tyranny and to perceive the former as the greater threat. Since the propertyless majority of Britain lacked a voice in the House of Commons, the "democratic branch" in Britain's alleged mixed government, the majority lacked any means to use the assembly as a tool of oppression. The Whigs were necessarily more preoccupied with the threats posed by monarchical despotism and general lawlessness than with the danger presented by majority tyranny.

This antimonarchical and antianarchical preoccupation suited American Revolutionary leaders equally well. Enmeshed in their own struggle against a monarch, and similarly lacking in experience with an empowered majority (even the so-called mobs of Revolutionary Boston marched in unison under the direction of aristocratic leaders), patriot leaders tended to emphasize the common interests of society. Such an emphasis was, of course, reinforced by the need for unity in a war against the most powerful nation on earth. It is equally understandable that this unity collapsed after the war, and that the conflicting interests of the few and the many reemerged in popular thought. Though the American aristocracy had possessed little direct experience with "majority tyranny" before the 1780s, their lifetime of classical reading evoked a shock of recognition when the state legislatures began redistributing wealth through inflation. Mixed government theory and its underlying conception of society had provided the Federalists with the intellectual tool necessary for interpreting yet another disturbing phenomenon. James Madison clearly reflected the equivocal quality of classical political theory when he stated in *Federalist* No. 56: "The aim of every political Constitution is or ought to be first to obtain for rulers men who possess the most wisdom to discern and the most virtue to pursue the common good of the society; and in the next place, to take the most effectual precautions for keeping them virtuous, whilst they continue to hold their public trust." While the people should certainly demand virtuous representatives, only institutional checks could ensure that their representatives remained virtuous, or at least, not vicious.[40]

John Adams' support for mixed government continued long after the adoption of the U.S. Constitution. In 1790 he penned the "Discourses on Davila," which analyzed Davila's history of the civil wars of sixteenth-century France. Adams argued that Davila's history revealed the dangers presented by an imbalance of power among the three orders. Adams' notes on Lord Bolingbroke defended mixed government. In 1805 Adams wrote to Benjamin Rush: "Believe me, my friend, a government in one center is as hostile to law, physic, and divinity, and even to pen, ink, and paper, inkhorns, standishes, and even to reading and ciphering, as it is to stars and garters, to crowns and scepters, or any other exclusive privileges." In 1810 Adams contended: "Aristocrats and Democrats have the same passions with kings and become tyrants from those passions whenever they have opportunity, as certainly and often more cruelly than kings . . . I can never too often repeat that aristocracy is the monster to be chained; yet so chained as not to be hurt, for he is a most useful and necessary animal in his place. Nothing can be done without him."[41]

Adams continued to argue, late in life, for the existence of a natural aristocracy. In August 1813 he contended regarding the influence of the "well-born": "Philosophers and Politicians may nibble and quibble, but they will never get rid of it. Their only resource is to controul it. Wealth is another Monster to be subdued. Hercules could not subdue both or either. To subdue them by regular approaches, by a regular Siege, and strong fortifications, was my Object in writing on Aristocracy." In the next month he wrote to Thomas Jefferson: "Now, my Friend, who are the aristoi [the best]? Philosophy may Answer, 'The Wise and Good.' But the World, Mankind, have, by their practice, always answered, 'the rich, the beautiful, and well-born.' And Philosophers themselves in marrying their Children prefer the rich, the handsome, and the well descended, to the wise and good. What chance have Talents and Virtues in competition with Wealth and Birth and Beauty?" It was certain that Washington's and Napoleon's "remotest Cousins will be sought and will be proud, and will avail themselves of their descent."[42]

Adams further contended that it was at best futile, and at worst harmful, to attempt to legislate the rich and well-born out of existence. Agrarian acts, designed to eliminate inequality of wealth, such as those proposed by the Gracchi at Rome, were ill advised. Adams wrote in 1787: "The rich have as clear a right to their liberty and property as the poor: it is essential to liberty that the rights of the rich be secured; if they are not, they will soon be robbed and become poor, and in turn rob their robbers, and thus neither the liberty nor the property of any will be regarded." Measures designed to destroy the influence of birth were equally futile. The consolidation of power and monopolization of loyalty which the family structure promoted had so terrified Plato that he had constructed his utopia so as to feature "a Community of Wives, a confusion of Families, [and] a total extinction of all Relations of Father, Son, and Brother." But such measures were counterproductive. In 1814 Adams responded to Plato's *Republic:* "Nothing can be conceived more destructive of human happiness, more infallibly contrived to transform Men and Women into Brutes, Yahoos, or Daemons than a Community of Wives and Property." A balance of orders was the only answer to the problem presented by the influence of birth and wealth.[43]

In *An Inquiry into the Principles and Policy of the Government of the United States* (1814) Republican economist John Taylor of Caroline challenged Adams' argument for the existence of a natural aristocracy by questioning the existence of human nature. Taylor wrote: "Superior abilities constitutes one among the enumerated causes of a natural aristocracy. This cause is evidently as fluctuating as knowledge and ignorance . . . The aristocracy of superior abilities will be regulated by the extent of the space between knowledge and ignorance. As the space contracts or widens, it will be diminished or increased; and if aristocracy may be thus diminished, it follows that it may be thus destroyed." The only real aristocracy, then, was the new and artificial aristocracy of "paper and patronage." While the ancient aristocracy had rested its authority upon superstition, and the medieval aristocracy had based its rule upon force, the new aristocracy of modern commercial nations like Great Britain based its power upon the control of governments through paper wealth stolen from the people. Taylor claimed facetiously: "If aristocracy is the work of nature, by deserting her accustomed constancy, and slyly changing the shape of her work, she has cunningly perplexed our defensive operations: to create the aristocracy of the first age, she used Jupiter [the chief god of Roman religion]; of the second, Mars [the god of war]; and of the third, Mercury [the god of commerce]. Jupiter is dethroned by knowledge; the usurpations of Mars are scattered by commerce and alienation; and it only remains to detect the impostures of Mercury."[44]

Taylor considered the new aristocracy worse than the old, since it provided nothing for the people. Taylor continued: "The aristocracy of Rome, for instance, did, at certain periods, possess a greater proportion of virtue, talents, and wealth than can be found in any cast or order of men at present, among commercial nations . . . Plebeian ignorance was both the cause and the justification of the Roman aristocracy. That might have been a worse magistrate than patrician knowledge, and the magic circle drawn by superstition around the conscript fathers, might have been necessary to restrain the excesses of a rude nation enclosed within a single city. But this supplies no argument in favor of an aristocracy in societies not of national aggregation, but of national intelligence; not sustained by superstition, but by a common interest." Since all aristocracy was artificial, it deserved destruction rather than protection. In the United States the destruction of aristocracy entailed the elimination of neomercantilist programs, the purpose of which was to foster aristocracy through theft. Taylor concluded that Adams' "whole political system is built with materials which have vanished, and it is as imaginary and romantick gravely to talk of patricians, plebeians, and feudal barons at this day, as it would be to propose the restoration of oracles, or the revival of chivalry." It was the uncritical acceptance of ancient theories that prevented politics from achieving the same degree of progress as the physical sciences.[45]

But, to Adams, Taylor's unkindest cut was his inaccurate depiction of Adams as an advocate of hereditary monarchy and aristocracy. Although Adams had written such works as the *Defence of the U.S. Constitutions* expecting that his views might be criticized, he did not expect to see them grossly distorted. To a proud man like Adams, who valued his reputation above all, slander was the worst crime. In 1809 he wrote: "The newspapers have represented my writings as monarchical . . . [and] as aristocratical . . . I answer to these charges, I only ask that they may be read." In anguish he wrote to Taylor in 1814: "Is it not a damper to any ardor in search of truth, to read the absurd criticism, the stupid observations, the jesuitical subtleties, the studied lies that have been printed concerning my writings, in this my dear, native country, for five-and-twenty years? . . . In fine, is it not humiliating to see a volume of six or seven hundred pages written by a gentleman of your rank, fortune, learning, genius, and eloquence, in which my system, my sentiments, and my writings, from beginning to end, are totally misunderstood and misrepresented? After all, I am not dead, like Harrington and Secondat [Montesquieu]." By that time Adams considered his *Defence of the U.S. Constitutions* the most misunderstood book ever written, with the sole exception of the Bible. In 1820 he noted: "My plain writings have been misunderstood by many, misrepresented by more, and vilified and anathematized by multitudes who never read them."[46]

The misrepresentations were especially painful to Adams, since he secretly yearned for popularity. In 1813 he complained to Jefferson: "In Truth, my 'defence of the Constitutions' and 'Discourses on Davila' laid the foundation of that immense Unpopularity which fell like the Tower of Siloam upon me. Your steady defense of democratical Principles, and your invariable favourable Opinion of the french Revolution laid the foundation of your Unbounded Popularity . . . Now, I will forfeit my Life, if you can find one instance in my Defence of the Constitutions, or the Discourses on Davila, which, by a fair construction, can favour the introduction of hereditary Monarchy or Aristocracy into America. They were all written to support and strengthen the Constitutions of the United States." To Adams, a public servant who lived his long life on a meager income, it was galling to be accused of "oligarchical tendencies" by wealthy men like Taylor and Jefferson, who owned plantations and hundreds of slaves. Ironically, he considered his chief opponents in the dispute, the Virginia planters, the greatest examples of the very natural aristocracy of birth, wealth, and talent whose existence they so vehemently denied.[47]

Adams' critics might have employed their time better by exploring the real vulnerabilities of mixed government theory. First, it is debatable whether a mixed government (using Adams' rigid definition) has ever existed for any substantial period. The diffusion of power which would characterize such government might lead, at best, to irresponsibility or, at worst, to paralysis. Second, if human nature is as ambitious as mixed government theory maintains, the theory cannot explain why "the one" should not forsake the balancing role envisioned by the theorists and join with either "the few" or "the many" to destroy the other. John Taylor correctly noted that kings and nobles were not always the natural enemies Adams claimed. They had in fact worked together quite effectively against the liberties of the masses for thousands of years. Finally, mixed government theory cannot explain the longevity of such simple systems as the monarchies of the ancient Middle East and of the Roman empire.[48]

Adams' reaction to the calumny against him was varied. Although he sometimes responded by exaggerating his own influence on federal and state constitutions, as well as on European and Latin American history, more often he patiently explained and defended his position. In 1814 he expressed wonder at Taylor's refusal to admit the existence of a natural aristocracy:

> Will any man say . . . that all men are born equal in strength? Was Hercules not stronger than his neighbors? . . . Socrates called beauty a short-lived tyranny; Plato, the privilege of nature; Theophrastus, a mute eloquence; Diogenes, the best letter of recommendation . . . It is genuine aristocracy; for it has as much influence in one form of government as in any other; and produces aristocracy in the deepest democracy that ever was known or imagined as infallibly as in any other form of government . . . Is not beauty, a privilege granted by nature, according to Plato and to truth, often more influential in society, and even upon laws and government, than stars, garters, crosses, eagles, golden fleeces, or any hereditary titles or other distinctions? . . . The Grecian sages wondered not at the Trojan war when they saw Helen.

Since it was futile to deny the existence of a natural aristocracy, one could only hope to restrain it through a balance of the orders of society. In addition, Adams challenged Taylor's claim that the U.S. Constitution had established a simple democracy, pointing out the great powers of the president and Senate, both indirectly elected for long terms. Noting that hereditary descent was "not an essential ingredient in the definition of monarchy or aristocracy," Adams claimed that the Constitution had established a mixed government, possessing monarchical, aristocratic, and democratic branches.[49]

John Taylor was not the only Republican now distancing himself from mixed government theory. As early as 1788 James Madison had begun expressing ambivalence concerning the theory. Though taking a clear mixed government position at the Constitutional Convention and in *Federalist* Nos. 47, 62, and 63, Madison's *Federalist* No. 10 proposed a different solution to the problem of majority tyranny. Madison suggested that, unlike the ancient republics, a modern commercial nation like the United States possessed more than two factions, "the few" and "the many." For instance, planters and merchants, though both large propertyholders, possessed different interests. Furthermore, Madison recognized that religious and ideological considerations would also create factions. Hence the number of factions in the United States would be so great that majorities must be weak coalitions, incapable of prolonged tyranny. (Representation would enhance this effect by preventing majorities from acting on sudden impulse.) As the years passed, Madison clung ever more fervently to this solution to the problem of majority tyranny, a solution which not only seemed more appropriate to the American situation, but which justified a form of government more popular with the public.[50]

Indeed, some historians have gone so far as to claim that Madison's theory concerning the multiplicity of modern interests, an insight he derived partly from David Hume, formed the new Constitution's principal foundation. But, as we have seen, although most Federalists recognized that modern commercial nations possessed numerous interests, they continued to consider the division between the few and the many the most important such division. In *Federalist* No. 10, the very essay in which Madison introduced his theory of the multiplicity of interests, he concluded: "But the most common and durable source of factions has been the various and unequal distribution of property. Those who hold, and those who are without property, have ever formed distinct interests in society." In fact the Antifederalists accepted the dichotomy as well. They merely reversed virtue and vice, siding with "the many" instead of "the few." In the 1790s members of both political parties continued to employ the same distinction. Indeed, such is the dichotomy's emotional power that it continues to infuse political rhetoric even today, when the nation's interests are far more numerous and varied than even Madison could have predicted.[51]

By 1791 Madison's conversion to representative democracy was complete. Under the pressure of John Quincy Adams' pamphlet war with Thomas Paine, Madison's ambivalence toward John Adams' *Defence of the U.S. Constitutions* hardened into bitter denunciation. In 1787, though justly faulting the first volume of Adams' work for its lack of originality and style, and though misperceiving some statements as "unfriendly to republicanism," Madison concluded: "The book also has merit." In 1791, however, Madison wrote regarding the same work: "Under a mock defence of the Republican Constitutions of this Country, he [Adams] attacked them with all the force he possessed, and this in a book with his name to it whilst he was the Representative of his Country at a foreign court." The next year Madison concluded, erroneously, that Adams' "Discourses on Davila," which Madison termed "that voluminous and ponderous work," supported the institution of hereditary orders.[52]

Madison's opposition to mixed government hardened as a result of Hamilton's fiscal measures, such as the debt-funding plan, the Bank of the United States, and the protective tariff, policies Madison believed designed to create an oligarchy. In a 1792 *National Gazette* essay Madison attacked mixed government theory. He wrote regarding the British model of mixed government: "Those who ascribe the character of the British Government to the form alone in which its powers are distributed & counterpoised forget the changes which its form has undergone." The simple oligarchy of feudal Britain had lasted longer than its newly-balanced government had thus far. The form of government was less important than public opinion, which determined the form. (Public opinion was itself influenced by the form of government, but not entirely.) Madison added concerning Britain: "If the nation were in favour of absolute monarchy, the public liberty would soon be surrendered by their representatives. If a republican form of government were preferred, how could the monarch resist the national will?" In his notes for the essay Madison added classical examples: "Not only Theoretical writers [such] as Plato (Republic), but more practical ones [such] as Swift & c. remark that the natural rotation in Government is from the abuses of Monarchy to Aristocracy, from the oppression of aristocracy to democracy, and from the licentiousness of Democracy back to Monarchy. Many examples . . . shew this tendency. Yet it appears from Aristotle that under the influence of public opinion, the rotation was very different in some of the States of Greece." A month earlier Madison had declared: "Public opinion sets bounds to every government, and is the real sovereign in every free one." Madison seemed not to consider that if he were correct, his own favorite institutional checks, such as the separation of powers and the balance between federal and state governments, were equally futile.[53]

Whatever Madison's degree of ambivalence concerning mixed government, by 1792 he was certain that the Federalists' use of it was both irrational and self-serving. He began another *National Gazette* essay in a familiar manner: "In all political societies, different interests and parties arise out of the nature of things, and the great art of politicians lies in making them checks and balances to each other." He then paraphrased the Federalists: "Let us then increase these *natural distinctions* by favoring an inequality of property; and let us add to them *artificial distinctions,* by establishing *kings* and *nobles,* and *plebeians.*" The first reference was to

Hamilton's fiscal policies, whose purpose, Madison believed, was to redistribute income from the poor to the wealthy. The second reference was to Adams' support for titles for federal officials, in order to attract talented people to those positions. Madison concluded: "This is as little the voice of reason, as it is that of republicanism."[54]

When arranging his notes on the Constitutional Convention for posthumous publication, in 1821, Madison clearly repudiated mixed government theory. He admitted that he had been wrong to support a property qualification for the electors of the House of Representatives, since such a qualification would enable the propertied to oppress the landless, who Madison knew must one day be the majority. He added that an alternate plan to confine the right of suffrage for one branch to the propertied and for the other branch to the propertyless was also a bad idea. He explained: "The division of the State into the two Classes, with distinct & independent Organs of power, and without any intermingled Agency whatever, might lead to contests & antipathies not dissimilar to those between the Patricians & Plebeians at Rome." Madison now believed that the division between the propertied and propertyless need not overshadow all others and, in so doing, endanger the republic. But to separate the two into distinct branches would be to highlight the distinction. It would be much better to allow these two large groups to fragment on the basis of other considerations. This statement represented a marked departure from those made by Madison at the Constitutional Convention, when he had urged the creation of a "body of the opulent" to protect the propertied from "agrarian acts."[55]

Thomas Jefferson, the other leader of the Republican Party, also shifted his support from mixed government to representative democracy in the 1790s. Jefferson's support for the U.S. Constitution had been lukewarm at best; he had told James Madison, its leading drafter, that he considered it an interesting first effort, but not the best constitution the nation could obtain. By 1790 he had turned against the revered Montesquieu, repudiating the Frenchman's "falsehoods" and "heresies." In 1816 Jefferson expressed his new attitude concerning ancient political theory: "The introduction of this new principle of representative democracy has rendered useless almost everything written before on the structure of government; and, in a great measure, relieves our regret, if the political writings of Aristotle, or of any other ancient, have been lost, or are unfaithfully rendered or explained to us." This opinion constituted a significant change from 1787, when Jefferson had recommended that

John Adams study ancient confederacies for what they might reveal about federal systems, and when he had sent copies of Polybius to James Madison at the Constitutional Convention.[56]

But Jefferson and most other Republicans did not base their endorsement of representative democracy on Madison's theory regarding the advantages of modern commercial republics. Rather, most Republicans sought the support of the classical pastoral tradition, a heritage as ancient and revered as mixed government theory. In order to muster the courage necessary to endorse an unprecedented form of government, Republican leaders enveloped themselves in the myth of classical pastoralism, much as the supporters of the Constitution had wrapped themselves in the myth of mixed government. Republicans comforted themselves with the notion that the United States could safely adopt a democracy, however vilified by classical political theorists, partly because it would feature such "modern improvements" as representation and the separation of powers, but largely because the abundance of land in the United States would allow a citizenry of Virgilian farmers. When cutting the trusty anchor of mixed government theory, Republicans assuaged their anxiety by fastening the anchor of classical pastoralism with even greater firmness. However ingenious they might be, theories concerning the superiority of modern institutions were, by their very nature, untested, and hence lacked the authority required to reassure a generation raised on ancient verities. Just as the old myth of mixed government had proven a necessary catalyst for the new reality of the U.S. Constitution, so the ancient legend of classical pastoralism proved essential to creating the new reality of representative democracy.

Aside from its novelty, there was another, equally important, reason why most Republicans found it difficult to embrace Madison's hypothesis. Taken to its logical conclusion, the theory encouraged the very neomercantilist policies Republicans were most anxious to avoid. If a republic's level of justice and stability depended upon the number of its interests, the best policy must be to multiply that number. In a nation of farmers like the United States such a policy would inevitably entail government measures to redistribute wealth from agriculture to infant industries—the very fiscal program that Alexander Hamilton had introduced and the pro-agricultural Republican Party bitterly opposed. Ill-suited to the Republican Party, the theory Madison had proposed in *Federalist* No. 10 would have been ideal for the Federalist Party, had the Federalists been able to transcend the aristocratic cosmology that so attracted them to mixed government theory and its distinction between the few and the many.

No theme was more ubiquitous in classical literature than that of the superiority of the rural, agricultural existence, a lifestyle wedged comfortably between the extremes of "savage" and "sophisticated." A motif of some Greek poets, like Hesiod and Theocritus, pastoralism became the central theme of Virgil, Horace, and Ovid, the leading poets of Rome's Augustan Age. Convinced that farmers were the backbone of Rome, Virgil's *Georgics* (2.458–474) exhorted his fellow Romans to regenerate the community after a century of civil war by returning to the plow:

> How lucky the farmers are—I wish they knew!
> The Earth herself, most just, pours forth for them
> An easy living from the soil, far off
> From clashing weapons. Though the farmer has
> No mansion with proud portals which spits out
> A monster wave of morning visitors
> From every room, nor do his callers gasp
> At inlaid columns, bright with tortoiseshell,
> Or gold-embroidered clothes or bronzes from
> Ephyre, nor in his house is plain white wool
> Dyed with Assyrian poison, nor does he
> Corrupt his olive oil with foreign spice,
> He has untroubled sleep and honest life.
> Rich in all sorts of riches, with a vast
> Estate, he has all the leisure to enjoy
> A cave, a natural pond, a valley where
> The air is cool—the mooing of the cows
> Is ever present, and to sleep beneath
> A tree is sweet. Wild animals abound
> For hunting, and young people grow up strong,
> Hardworking, satisfied with poverty:
> Their gods are holy; parents are revered.
> Surely, when Justice left the earth she stayed
> Last with these folk, and left some tokens here.

The farmer's lifestyle was the source of republican virtue.[57]

The pastoral theme was as much a staple of classical political theory and history as of Greek and Roman poetry. Aristotle argued that the best republics were predominantly agricultural. Polybius, Plutarch, Livy,

Tacitus, and Sallust considered Sparta and republican Rome models not merely because they had possessed mixed governments, but also because they had been agricultural societies. These historians credited the triumph of Sparta and Rome over their vice-ridden, commercial adversaries, Athens and Carthage, as much to their pastoral virtues as to their government forms. Both produced virtue, the agricultural life by fostering frugality, temperance, and independence, the balanced constitution by encouraging moderation, cooperation, and compromise. The plow was both the symbol and the cause of Cincinnatus' "Roman virtue." Furthermore, classical historians attributed the fall of the Roman republic to "the Punic Curse," the commercialization of Rome which had resulted from the republic's conquest of the Carthaginian empire. The curse of commercial wealth had transformed Rome from a modest village into an imperial city. Whether by choice or necessity, farmers had abandoned the soil for the iniquitous life of the city. Deprived of that dignity which an independent means of sustenance affords the farmer, these former bastions of republicanism had become the clients of dictators, prepared to sell the once-glorious republic for the paltry price of bread and circuses. Disgruntled by their forced subservience to emperors, the aristocratic poets and historians who painted this compelling portrait idealized an epoch which their class had dominated, though their own luxurious lifestyles would hardly have suited them to the rustic existence their works immortalized. Like most worshipers of agriculture who succeeded them, the Roman pastoralists lived a life distant from the manual labor they extolled. Far less romantic about their lot, many of the farmers the pastoralists glorified preferred the freedom from "noble toil" which life in the city afforded—hence Virgil's need to tell the farmers how lucky they were. As in the case of mixed government, these Roman aristocrats offered an ideal whose simple beauty remains powerful, however unreflective of reality and however self-interested in origin.[58]

As with mixed government also, the founders derived the pastoral tradition both directly from the ancients, who formed the core of the classical curriculum, and through the medium of modern authors. Having spread throughout the Middle Ages and the Renaissance, pastoralism achieved a virtual cult status in seventeenth- and eighteenth-century England and France. James Harrington praised farmers for their love of liberty, moderated by a stability which he found lacking in the city-dwellers of Athens. An enthusiastic supporter of agriculture, King George III was fond of his nickname "Farmer George." Both Farmer Georges, the king and the rebel Washington, corresponded with Arthur Young, one of the high priests of the eighteenth-century pastoral movement. Young declared: "Perhaps we might, without any great impropriety, call farming the reigning taste of the present times." Ironically, pastoralism inspired many of the early classical economists, whose ideas proved the eventual ruin of classical republicanism. The French Physiocrats, the economists who first coined the term "laissez-faire," fondly cited Socrates on the greater morality, as well as the greater prosperity, produced by agriculture. It is no accident that Adam Smith began his career as a moral philosopher and that his brand of laissez-faire economics favored agriculture over industry, in sharp contrast to the later theories of David Ricardo. Early economists of all varieties were motivated as much by moral as by economic concerns. While laissez-faire economics was, indeed, something very new, it was developed, at least in part, to protect something very old: the agricultural lifestyle.[59]

Republicans failed to note the extent to which the new classical economics subverted the old classical republicanism. Although laissez-faire arguments could be used to defend agriculture against the debilitating tariffs favored by industrial interests, the same arguments justified its transformation from subsistence to commercial farming. The "luxury" produced by commerce, the great enemy without, was surreptitiously introduced within. Classical economics (along with natural rights) proved to be the Trojan horse which destroyed classical republicanism. But Republicans delayed classical republicanism's eventual destruction by arming themselves with the invincible weapon of inconsistency. They simply refused to take sides between the competing ideologies. They sometimes praised agriculture for its greater productivity and sometimes for its greater virtue. They sometimes celebrated the prosperity produced by commerce and sometimes vilified it as the source of corruption.

Thomas Jefferson cherished the pastoral tradition. His favorite books concerning agriculture were Columella's *De re rustica* and Adam Dickson's *Husbandry of the Ancients*. Like other Virginia aristocrats, Jefferson designed his estate to resemble the Roman villas Pliny and Varro had described. He also planned the inscription of a Latin passage from Horace (*Epodes*, 2.1–4, 7–8, 23–34, 39–40, 43–48, 61–66) near a small temple which he hoped to build on his burial ground. The excerpt, which he had copied into his literary commonplace book as a young man, exulted:

> Happy the man who, free from business worries, like the men of the old days, tills with his oxen his ancestral fields without being harassed by mortgages . . . He keeps away from the Forum and the proud threshold of the

powers that be . . . He likes to recline now under an ancient oak, now on the thick grass. Meanwhile the brooks flow between the high banks, birds warble in the woods, and springs bubble with running water, a sweet invitation to repose. But when the wintry season of thundering Jove brings back rains and snows, either with his pack of hounds he drives the fierce boars into the traps, or arranges large meshed nets on polished sticks to snare the greedy thrushes; . . . If a modest wife, who does her part in tending the house and her dear children, piles high the sacred hearth with dry firewood waiting for the return of her tired husband, gathers in a pen made of wattles the fat ewes in order to milk their distended udders, and drawing from the keg new sweet wine, prepares a meal which she had not to pay for . . . amid such feasts what joy to see the tired oxen dragging along the upturned ploughshare and the young slaves, industrious swarm of an opulent house, seated around the resplendent Lares.

As Gilbert Chinard noted, Jefferson removed from the text of Horace's epode those parts which described elements absent from eighteenth-century Virginia life (shrill war clarions and vineyards, for example). By condensing a poem of seventy-two lines into thirty-two, he presented a picture, however idealized, of his own time and place. By 1819 Jefferson was inclined to write in Latin of "the bond of the sweet natal soil."[60]

Though certainly aware of classical economists' arguments for the greater productivity of agriculture, Jefferson generally emphasized its moral and political benefits. Jefferson knew that the Physiocrats had demonstrated the superior efficiency of large plantations, but he continued to champion the small farm. In a famous passage in the *Notes on the State of Virginia* Jefferson glorified agriculture in a manner reminiscent of the *Georgics*:

Those who labor in the earth are the chosen people of God, if ever he had a chosen people, whose breasts He has made His peculiar deposit for genuine and substantial virtue. He keeps alive that sacred fire, which otherwise might escape from the face of the earth. Corruption of morals in the mass of cultivators is a phenomenon of which no age nor nation has furnished an example. It is the mark set on those, who, not looking up to heaven and to their own soil and industry as does the husbandman, for their subsistence, depend for it on casualties and caprices of customers. Dependence begets subservience and venality suffocates the germ of virtue and prepares fit tools for the designs of ambition . . . The mobs of great cities add just so much to the support of pure government, as sores do to the strength of the human body. It is the manners and spirit of a people which preserve a republic in vigor. A degeneracy in these is a canker which soon eats to the heart of its laws and constitution.

The secret of the ancient republics' success was not their mixed governments, but their pastoral societies. Jefferson later wrote: "Cultivators of the earth are the most valuable citizens. They are the most vigorous, the most independent, the most virtuous, and they are tied to their country, and wedded to its liberty and interests by the most lasting bonds . . . I consider the class of artificers as the panders of vice, and the instruments by which the liberties of a country are overturned." Hence, Jefferson predicted: "I think our governments will remain virtuous for many centuries; as long as they are chiefly agricultural; and this will be as long as there shall be vacant lands in any part of America."[61]

Ironically, the same pastoralism that excited dread and sorrow in Jefferson's favorite classical poets and historians inspired hope and confidence in the Virginian. Jefferson expected that centuries must pass before the vast lands of the West were fully settled. Hence the same ideology which evoked nostalgia from the imperial literati of Rome could be a source of encouragement to an American sitting on the edge of a fertile and lightly settled continent.

Jefferson's passionate embrace of the pastoral tradition colored his perceptions of the world. So determined was he to perpetuate the agricultural character of the United States that he was willing to violate strict construction of the Constitution, one of the core principles of the Republican Party, in order to purchase Louisiana. When the absence of a constitutional provision allowing Jefferson to buy foreign territory threatened the future of the republic's agricultural base, and hence its virtue and longevity, Jefferson reluctantly sacrificed constitutional scruples in order to extend the life of the republic. The Virginian frequently compared the British commercialism he detested with that of the Carthaginians, implying an analogy between the United States and the frugal Roman republic. In 1810 he scoffed at the suggestion that an alliance be made with Great Britain: "The faith of a nation of merchants! The *Punica fides* of modern Carthage." Later that year, after predicting a mutiny in the British navy, Jefferson further claimed that if the mutineers were unable to establish a military dictatorship, they would become individual pirates, and "the modern Carthage will end as the old one has done"—a reference to the Barbary pirates of North Africa. In 1815, a few months after the end of the War of 1812, Jefferson turned from predictions of doom to threats of violence. If the modern Carthage, Great Britain, did not stop injuring the United States, she would force Americans to adopt the famous motto of Cato the Elder, who had ended all his speeches in the Roman senate with: "Carthago delenda est!"—"Carthage must be destroyed!" Jefferson added a dark reference to the brilliant Roman general Scipio Africanus, who had issued a lethal blow to Carthage at Zama in 201 B.C.: "And some Scipio Americanus will leave to posterity the problem of conjecturing where stood once the ancient and splendid city of London." In 1813 and 1815 Jefferson used Cato's motto against the Federalist financial interests that profited from the national debt. He was determined to prevent his Federalist adversaries from transforming the frugal Rome of the United States into another modern Carthage like Britain. Ironically, his very hatred of the modern Carthage forced him, however reluctantly, to adopt some of its policies. After the War of 1812 Jefferson reluctantly recognized that the United States would have to possess some industry in order to maintain its independence from British manufacturers. But Jefferson remained optimistic as long as agriculture held the predominant position in the national economy.[62]

Similarly, John Taylor, the leading Republican economist, championed Adam Smith's laissez-faire economics largely in order to preserve the cherished agricultural lifestyle against the onslaughts of the commercial and financial elites, who sought government aid to industry at the expense of agriculture. M. E. Bradford has noted that Taylor's famous handbook on agriculture, the *Arator,* bears a remarkable resemblance to Roman agricultural treatises, such as Cato the Elder's *De agricultura,* Varro's *Rerum rusticarum,* and Columella's *De re rustica,* treatises widely read by eighteenth-century Virginians. Like the Roman aristocrats, Taylor ladled out large portions of practical advice regarding the care of fields, crops, fences, animals, and slaves, while advancing a broader theme: the necessity of preserving the rural values which served as the backbone of the republic and of resisting urban temptations. Cato the Elder had written: "And when they would praise a worthy man their praise took this form: 'good husbandman, good farmer'; one so praised was thought to have received the greatest commendation." Taylor agreed, even referring to the pastoral tradition in *Arator* No. 59: "Poetry, in allowing more virtue to agriculture than to any other profession has abandoned her privilege of fiction, and yielded to the natural moral effect of the absence of temptation." In defense of agriculture Taylor tied the classical heritage to the biblical tradition: "The divine intelligence, which selected an agricultural state as a paradise for its first favourites has . . . prescribed the agricultural virtues as the means for the admission of their posterity into heaven."[63]

Even the sober Madison occasionally fell into this romanticism regarding agriculture. In 1792 Madison wrote what for him must be considered a rhapsody:

> The life of the husbandman is pre-eminently suited to the comfort and happiness of the individual. Health, the first of blessings, is an appertenance of his property and his employment. Virtue, the health of the soul, is another part of his patrimony, and no less favored by his situation. Intelligence may be cultivated in this as well as in any other walk of the life. If the mind be less susceptible of polish in retirement than in a crowd, it is more capable of profound and comprehensive effort . . . Competency is more universally the lot of those who dwell in the country, where liberty is at the same time their lot. The extremes, both of want and waste, have other abodes. 'Tis not the country that peoples either the Bridewells or the Bedlams. These mansions of wretchedness are tenanted from the distresses and vices of overgrown cities . . . The classes of citizens who provide at once their own food and their own raiment, may be viewed as the most truly independent and happy. They are more; they are the best basis of public liberty and the strongest bulwark of public safety. It follows that the greater the proportion of this class to the whole society, the more free, the more independent, and the more happy must be the society itself.

If Madison differed from Jefferson in placing a greater reliance upon the balancing of interests as the favored remedy in combating the decay which had claimed all previous republics, it was because he was haunted by a specter which seemed to Jefferson but a distant cloud. From the time of the Constitutional Convention, if not before, Madison feared and prepared for the day when the continent would be filled, and the numbers of the landless would exceed those of the landed. American cities would then resemble imperial Rome, both in its squalor and in its opulence. What else but a balance of interests would then save the republic from destruction by social vice? While Madison's belief in pastoral virtue separated him from most Federalists, his tendency to place greater reliance upon institutional checks as a republican preservative separated him from most of his fellow Republicans.[64]

But even some Federalist merchants failed to escape the grasp of the pervasive classical pastoralism and its deprecation of commercial profit. Some early republican merchants worked hard and saved their money so that they could retire to a country estate and play the role of the "gentleman farmer." Stigmatized by his commercial fortune, John Hancock expended his vast inheritance in a lifelong attempt to prove that he did not care about wealth. Robert Morris, the superintendent of finance who moved mountains to keep the United States afloat during the latter part of the Revolutionary War and who first proposed many of the fiscal programs later associated with Alexander Hamilton, ended in debtors' prison as the result of an attempt to shed the image of the money-grubbing merchant for that of the landed gentleman. Rather than assault the classical stigma on commercial wealth, some wealthier merchants looked forward to the day when they could live without it. Such was their desire to be a true "gentleman" that too many made the move too soon. The same ethic prevented Alexander Hamilton, when suffering fnancial diffculties in 1795, from using his political connections to make money.[65]

This suspicion of all wealth produced by commerce, political connections, or anything other than agriculture produced some odd results. George Washington, Benjamin Franklin, and Thomas Jefferson all argued vehemently against salaries for members of Congress. Public service should not be debased by any monetary gain. As secretary of state, Thomas Jefferson often refused to issue patents, expecting inventors to contribute their inventions to the world without profit, as he himself did. Even Thomas Paine, the great friend of commerce, could write with great concern in *Common Sense:* "Commerce diminishes the spirit both of patriotism and military defense . . . The more men have to lose, the less are they willing to venture."[66]

The ancient and august tradition of classical pastoralism provided the essential service of legitimizing the Republican shift toward a representative democracy. The near-unanimous judgment of ancient political theorists against democracy could be overcome only by resorting to an equally revered tradition. Only by arguing that the liberty of the ancient republics had been founded on their agricultural lifestyle, rather than on their mixed governments, could Republicans succeed in persuading both themselves and others that a new and unprecedented system of government might be safely adopted.

Faced with the increasing unpopularity of mixed government theory among the reigning Republicans, John Adams' pessimism grew. By the first decade of the nineteenth century, he had come to the terrifying conclusion that the mixed government established by the Constitution of 1787 was being transformed, in substance if not in form, into a simple democracy. Divisions between political parties were replacing the intended divisions between branches. In 1806 Adams declared: "I once thought our Constitution was quasi or mixed government, but they have now made it, to all intents and purposes, in virtue, in spirit, and effect, a democracy. We are left without resources but in our prayers and tears, and having nothing that we can do or say, but the Lord have mercy upon us." By "they," Adams meant the Republicans, and particularly President Jefferson, whose administration Adams considered subversive of the intent of the drafters of the Constitution. Ironically, since Jefferson had quickly reinterpreted the Constitution as having established a representative democracy, he had himself complained, in the 1790s, that Adams' administration of the government was subversive of the spirit of the document. Jefferson wrote: "If Mr. Adams could be induced to administer the government on its true principles, quitting his bias for an English constitution, it would be worthy of consideration whether it would not be for the public good to come to a good understanding with him as to future elections." It was of little consolation to Adams that his interpretation of the intent of the drafters was more accurate than Jefferson's. It was Jefferson's that prevailed.[67]

Nevertheless, Adams' judgment was overly pessimistic. The modern American political system is a hybrid of democracy and mixed government. The rise of political parties, combined with other developments, has democratized American politics. (These other developments include the linkage of the selection of the Electoral College with the popular vote, accomplished before Adams' death in 1826, and the ratification of the Seventeenth Amendment, which provided for the direct election of senators, in 1913.) Yet elements of mixed government remain. The Supreme Court, whose power has grown steadily, is still appointed for life by the president, who is still indirectly elected. The senators' larger electoral districts still foster a more aristocratic representation than the House of Representatives, while the equality of states in the Senate favors small states. Hence the passage of congressional legislation requires more than simple majority support. Ironically, in their effort to emulate the systems of Sparta, Rome, and Great Britain, whose status as mixed governments was dubious at best, the founders of the United States may have created the first real mixed government in history—though mixed in a modern sense.

But classical mixed government, as defined by purists like Adams, was more the victim of its own fundamental inadequacy than of latter-day changes. The rise of political parties so soon after the inauguration of the new government, parties which failed to follow class lines and which received support from members of each branch of government, was proof that Adams' understanding of the interests which divided the United States was too simplistic. Adams failed to see that mixed government, in its rigid Polybian form, was unsuited to a modern commercial nation like the United States. James Madison was correct in noting that modern commercial nations were heterogeneous, possessing more than Polybius' two interests, the few and the many. Ironically, when John C. Calhoun later incorporated Madison's insight into his political theory, he did so with the object of introducing a new form of mixed government theory. Calhoun posited the theory of concurrent majority, the theory that each "major interest" in a nation should have a veto on legislation. But, fraught with practical difficulties and undermined by the reverence which the Constitution of 1787 had come to command, Calhoun's theory failed to win wide currency. The result, for better or worse, was a civil war.

Nothing better exemplifies the founders' shrewdness than their adaptation of mixed government theory to the American context. Though based on the same ancient principle of society's need for a balance of power among its factions, mixed government theory had undergone important changes—from Polybius' rigid system, to Adams' modern version, to Calhoun's concurrent majority—by the time of the Civil War. Thoughtful men, the founders resisted slavishness. They refused to establish a simple democracy, despite the urging of leading philosophes such as Turgot. Yet neither did they simply copy the mixture of the old colonial governments, borrow the proposals of Enlightenment philosophers, or ape the ancients themselves, though anxious to learn from each of the three primary sources which comprised their collective "experience." Rather, the founders established a political system which bears their own indelible stamp. It is, to borrow a phrase from Alexander Hamilton, "neither Greek nor Trojan, but purely American."[68]

VI

Philosophy

Although the founders were politicians, not systematic philosophers, classical philosophy exerted as great an influence upon them as mixed government theory. Stoicism contributed much to their conception of human nature, the theory of natural law on which they based the federal and state bills of rights, much of their understanding of the nature and purpose of virtue, their appreciation of society's essential role in its production, and the solace necessary to face the numerous hardships of eighteenth-century life with courage. The eclectic Thomas Jefferson added an element of Epicureanism to his cosmology. Classical philosophy proved an essential intellectual tool, an ancient and respectable vehicle through which the founders could reconcile their Christianity with the new naturalism introduced by the Scientific Revolution. Furthermore, the Stoic version of natural law theory and the optimistic conception of human nature which undergirded it furnished the raw materials for the modern doctrines of natural rights and social progress, which in turn served as the principal bridges between classical republicanism and modern liberalism.

The germ of natural law theory may be found in the writings of Plato. In Plato's *Meno* (77c–78b) Socrates argued that the desire for good "belongs to our common nature." The understanding of good and evil was accessible through intuition, rather than through reason (logic) acting upon experience. In Plato's *Phaedo* (63c–68b) Socrates explained that the body is an "obstacle" to knowledge. Socrates contended: "And the best sort of thinking occurs when the soul is not disturbed by any of these things—not by hearing, or sight, or pain, or pleasure—when she leaves the body and is alone and, doing her best to avoid any form of contact with it, reaches out to grasp what is truly real." Aristotle also believed in natural law. In the *Rhetoric* (1.1375a.25–b.1–8) he accepted the legitimacy of the "higher law" argument in court, whenever the law conflicted with justice. But Aristotle believed that humans used their reason to deduce natural law from experience. In Book 1 of the *Politics* he claimed regarding the human: "Justice which is his salvation belongs to the polis; for justice, which is the determination of what is just, is an ordering of the political association." Virtue was not innate, but the product of training by the polis. Epicurus (Diogenes Laertius, *History of Philosophy*, 10.122–135) supported Aristotle's position. He claimed: "It is wise, however, to evaluate all these things by measuring one against another and discovering what is beneficial and what is harmful. For sometimes we consider good to be evil and also the opposite." Reason, not intuition, led humans to moral truth.

But it was the Stoics who placed natural law theory at the center of their philosophy. Cleanthes, a third-century B.C. disciple of Zeno, the fourth-century B.C. founder of Stoicism, taught that virtue lay in "living agreeably to nature in the exercise of right reason." In Cleanthes' "Hymn to Zeus," God's reason flowed through the universe, giving order to everything. Humans were distinct from other species in possessing a reason of their own, though it was connected to the divine reason. Many were destined to spurn the divine gift and lead a senseless, wicked life. (In this view, humans appear at a disadvantage to the other species. They are made distinct not only by consciousness but also by their ability to err.) Cicero concurred. In *De legibus* (1.33) he defined law as "right reason applied to command and prohibition." He conceived of the universe as "one commonwealth of which both gods and men are members." Natural law was not handed down by the gods, but was the glue which connected them to humans in the one great organism of the universe. Reason and matter were two parts of the same whole, the former acting upon the latter. The first-century Roman philosopher and statesman Seneca (*Epistles*, 65.2) defined God as "creative reason," both the "First Cause" and the universal glue. Both Cicero and Seneca found evidence of God's existence in the alleged consensus concerning it. Seneca wrote: "In our eyes the fact that all men agree upon something is proof of its truth. For instance, we infer that the gods exist, for this reason, among others—that there is implanted in everyone an idea concerning deity, and there is no people so far beyond the reach of laws and customs that it does not believe at least in gods of some sort." Cicero added: "On every matter the consensus of all peoples is to be regarded as the law of nature." Similarly, Epictetus (*Discourses,* 1.22.1) believed that humans were born with common, consistent preconceptions. Two of these pre-conceptions were that righteousness is good, and that good is more profitable and worthy of choice than evil.[1]

The Stoics assumed a middle position between Plato and Aristotle concerning the mechanics of natural law. Although the Stoics portrayed natural law as embedded in human nature through a sort of intuition, they argued that it could be accessed only with the help of reason acting upon sensory information. Maryanne Cline Horowitz aptly summarized this aspect of Stoic philosophy: "They believed that the mind is born predisposed to certain ideas which are not yet consciously held. These ideas are evoked and developed through the stimulus of sense impressions and the development of reason." Cicero wrote regarding nature and man: "It is true that she gave him a mind capable of receiving every virtue, and implanted at birth and without instruction some small intimations of the greatest truths, and thus, as it were, laid the foundation for education and instilled into those faculties which the mind already had what may be called the germs of virtue. But of virtue itself she merely furnished the rudiments; nothing more. Therefore it is our task (and by when I say 'our' I mean that it is the task of art) to supplement those mere beginnings by searching out the further developments which were implicit in them, until what we seek is fully attained." Cicero used the two analogies of sparks and seeds to clarify his position. At one point he stated that human souls were all sparks temporarily separated from the Great Flame (the World Soul), but that a spark might be extinguished by a bad upbringing. At another he argued (*De legibus,* 26.4) that the seeds of virtue manifested themselves in the social nature of humans, in their "gregarious impulses." (The two analogies differed somewhat: nurturing a seed into a full-grown plant generally requires more conscious effort than keeping a flame lit.) Similarly, Seneca claimed (*Epistles,* 49.11): "At our birth, nature made us teachable, and gave us reason, not perfect, yet capable of being perfected." He added: "Every living thing possessed of reason is inactive if not first stirred by some external impression; then the impulse comes, and finally assent confirms the impulse." Regarding virtue he wrote (120.4–8): "Nature could not teach us this directly; she has given us the seeds of knowledge, but not knowledge itself." He contended (110.46): "Even in the best of men, before you refine them by instruction, there is but the stuff of virtue, not virtue itself." The Stoics believed that humans possessed the requisite experience to trigger innate impulses by about age seven. Only Epictetus seemed to favor the Platonic doctrine of innate ideas. He asked (*Discourses,* 2.11.3): "Who has come into being without an innate concept of what is good and evil, honorable and base, appropriate and inappropriate?" Epictetus insisted (1.22.1; 4.1.41–3) that disagreements between humans did not concern general principles, but merely regarded their application to specific situations. Everyone understood the idea of evil, but only through the aid of philosophy could humans learn that death was not evil. Even so, this was an admission that only through the medium of reason could natural law be brought down to earth and play a meaningful role in human life.[2]

Paul and the early Christians accepted the concept of natural law. Paul wrote (Romans 2:14–5): "When Gentiles who do not possess the law [of Moses] carry out its precepts by the light of nature, then, although they have no law, they are their own law, for they display the effect of the law inscribed on their hearts." The theory of natural law persisted through the Middle Ages, though subordinated to divine law, as revealed by scripture and by the canon law of the Roman Catholic church. Thomas Aquinas affirmed: "There is in man an inclination to good . . . Man has a natural inclination to know the truth about God, and to live in society; and in this respect, whatever pertains to this inclination belongs to the natural law." But, while there were some self-evident truths, such as the fact that every whole is greater than each part, "some are self-evident only to the wise, who understand the meaning of the terms of such propositions." Aquinas concluded: "In some few cases it [reason] may fail . . . Thus, at one time, although it is expressly contrary to natural law, theft was not considered wrong among the Germans, as Julius Caesar relates . . . Sin blots out the law of nature in particular cases, not universally, except perchance in regard to the secondary principles of the natural law, in the way stated above." Divine law was superior to natural law as a guide to ethics, for two reasons. First, as a product of direct revelation, divine law was a clearer expression of God's will than natural law, which required the use of greater deductive powers. Second, though fully consistent with natural law, divine law was a broader representation of God's will.[3]

Though restricting divine law to scripture alone, the Protestant reformers agreed with Aquinas that divine law was superior to natural law as a guide to ethics. Martin Luther instructed that if two men in a dispute were unwilling to forgive each other: "Announce to them that they are acting against God and the law of nature, even though they may obtain absolute justice through human law. For nature, like love, teaches that I should do as I would have done by." The Golden Rule was the best expression of natural law. But scripture remained the best ethical guide. John Calvin agreed. He contended:

> I feel pleased with the well-known saying which has been borrowed from the writings of Augustine, that man's natural gifts were corrupted by sin, and his supernatural gifts withdrawn; meaning by supernatural gifts the light of faith and righteousness, which would have been sufficient for the attainment of heavenly life and everlasting felicity . . . These, when restored to us by Christ, are to be regarded as adventitious and above nature. If so, we infer that they were previously abolished. On the other hand, soundness of mind and integrity of heart were, at the same time, withdrawn, [and] it is this which constitutes the corruption of natural gifts. For although here is still some residue of intelligence and judgment as well as will, we cannot call a mind sound which is both weak and immersed in darkness . . . Therefore, since reason, by which man discerns between good and evil, and by which he understands and judges, is a natural gift, it cannot be entirely destroyed; but being partly weakened and partly corrupted, a shapeless ruin is all that remains.

Renaissance political theorist Niccolò Machiavelli seemed to agree. While not denying the existence of natural law, he doubted the ability of humans to apply it to the field of politics.[4]

Meanwhile, jurists like Coke equated English common law with natural law. They declared that custom, the basis of the common law, was the product of natural law. Often unconsciously, humans wrote into law those customs which worked best—that is, which best conformed to experience and nature. The passage of time refined the law through trial and error, making it ever more compatible with natural law. The process was a form of legal natural selection.[5]

But English monarchist Thomas Hobbes raised doubts similar to those raised by the medieval and Reformation theologians concerning the ability of humans to understand natural law. Hobbes questioned the existence of intuition and the reliability of reason. The infinite variety of interpretations of natural law seemed a recipe for perpetual conflict. Claiming some special ability to deduce the vaporous law, aristocrats incited the common people to rebellion, producing chaos and violence. Hobbes contended: "Good and evil are names that signify our appetites and aversions which in different tempers, customs, and doctrines of men are different . . . Nay, the same man in divers times differs from himself, and one time praises—that is, calls good—what another time he dispraises and calls evil; from whence arise disputes, controversies, and at last war." The proper path for humans was to submit themselves to the positive law of their rulers in dealing with the state, as Paul had commanded (Romans 13:1–4), and to the divine law in dealing with one another. Both the positive and divine law were clearer than natural law, which relied too much on the flawed faculty of reason. (Of course, Hobbes and the earlier clerics ignored the fact that, though somewhat clearer than the vague natural law, statutes and biblical passages are subject to interpretation as well.)[6]

In refuting Hobbes and other monarchists modern republicans contributed a new emphasis on natural rights, a deduction from natural law rarely pursued by the ancients. The Huguenots first summarized these natural rights as the right to life, liberty, and property. Algernon Sidney appealed to ancient English liberties and to the existing legal system, as though it somehow comprehended all of natural right. The product of an "ultimate reason," natural law was universal, rooted in the human conscience, and "above all passion, void of desire and fear, lust and anger." Sidney suggested that humans could make certain inferences from the common characteristics of all organized societies, adding that certain legal axioms were as obvious as Euclidean geometry. Sidney trusted Parliament, as the true representative of the people, to deduce natural law. John Locke wrote that a nation's laws "are only so far right as they are founded on the Law of Nature, by which they are to be regulated and interpreted." He added: "The Law of Nature stands as an Eternal Rule to all Men, legislators as well as others." He argued that men did not surrender their natural rights to government when forming the social contract, only their prerogative of enforcing natural law. If government threatened natural rights, its citizens were morally obligated to uphold natural law by opposing the government which violated it. Since such citizens resisted tyranny on behalf of law, they were in no sense rebels. The influential Dutch commentator Enrich de Vattel attempted to apply the principles of natural law to international trade and communications. Montesquieu began his *L'esprit des lois* with a discussion of natural law. He claimed that God must surely exist, since intelligent beings could not have arisen by accident. Montesquieu declared: "God is related to the universe as Creator and Preserver; the laws by which He created all things are those by which he preserves them. He acts according to these rules, because He knows them; He knows them, because He made them; and He made them, because they are in relation of His Wisdom and power . . . The law which, impressing on our minds the idea of a Creator, inclines us toward Him, is the first in importance, though not in order, of natural laws."[7]

Although the founders had access to every level of the western discourse on natural law, they frequently quoted the Stoics in support of the theory. The founders generally derived their Stoicism not from the systematic Greek philosophers Zeno and Epictetus, but from the works of the two ill-fated Roman republicans Cicero and Seneca, and from the Roman historians. As early as 1759 John Adams exhorted himself, in his diary: "Labour to get distinct Ideas of Law, Right, Wrong, Justice, Equity. Search for them in your own mind, in Roman, grecian, French, English Treatises of natural, civil, common, Statute Law . . . Study Seneca, Cicero, and all other good moral Writers." In the 1760s Samuel Adams praised the British constitution, then threatened by parliamentary measures, as founded "On the Law of God and the Law of Nature," as interpreted by Cicero, the Stoics, and James Otis. Near the end of his life, Jefferson wrote regarding the Declaration of Independence: "All its authority rests, then, on the harmonizing sentiments of the day, whether expressed in conversation, in letters, in printed essays, or in the elementary books of public right, [such] as Aristotle, Cicero, Locke, Sidney, etc." In his *Letters from a Pennsylvania Farmer* John Dickinson cited Sophocles' *Antigone* (lines 453–457), a pre-Stoic work filled with "stoicisms":

> . . . I never could think
> A mortal's law of power or strength sufficient
> To abrogate the unwritten law divine,
> Immutable, eternal, not like those
> Of yesterday, but made ere time began.

Even Benjamin Rush and Thomas Paine, alleged critics of the classics, frequently cited Cicero's expositions on natural law.[8]

Typical was James Wilson's admiration for the Stoic philosophy of his idol, Cicero. Like most of the founders, Wilson was completely persuaded by Cicero's misrepresentation of Epicureanism. In a 1790 lecture to the law students at the College of Philadelphia, part of a series attended by President Washington, Vice-President Adams, Secretary of State Jefferson, and many other dignitaries, Wilson declared: "If the opinion of

Epicurus concerning his divinities—that they were absolutely indifferent to the happiness and interests of men—were admitted for a moment, the inference would unquestionably be that they were not entitled to human obedience." He followed this statement with a quotation from Cicero: "Epicurus, in fact, takes away the gods, though he professes to leave them. In fine, if god is precisely such as is held by no sense of gratitude, by no love of mankind, then goodbye to him! For why should I say 'may he be gracious toward me'?" Having quoted Cicero's misrepresentation of Epicurus' view of the gods, Wilson then misrepresented Epicurus' view of human nature: "Epicurus, as well as some modern advocates of the same philosophy, seem to have taken their estimates of human nature from its meanest and most degrading exhibitions; but the noblest and most respectable philosophers of antiquity have chosen, from a much wiser and better purpose, to view it on the brightest and most advantageous side. 'It is impossible,' says the incomparable Addison, 'to read a passage in Plato or Tully and a thousand other ancient moralists without being a greater and better man for it.'"⁹

Having destroyed his Epicurean straw man, Wilson then repeatedly quoted Cicero in support of the Stoic concept of natural law. He contended that humans possessed a sort of intuition, variously called "conscience" or "moral sense," which led them to the right moral conclusions. Wilson asserted: "Morality, like mathematicks, has its intuitive truths, without which we cannot make a single step in our reasonings upon the subject." He then quoted Cicero: "What nation, what species of man is there which does not have, without teaching, some sort of foreknowledge, that is, a certain image of the thing conceived beforehand by the mind, without which nothing can be understood, investigated, or discussed?" Wilson added: "This law, or right reason, as Cicero calls it, is thus beautifully described by that eloquent philosopher." Wilson again quoted Cicero: "It is, indeed, a true law, conformable to nature, diffused among all men, unchangeable, eternal. By its commands, it calls men to their duty; by its prohibitions, it deters them from vice. To diminish, to alter, much more to abolish this law, is a vain attempt. Neither by the senate, nor by the people, can its powerful obligation be dissolved. It requires no interpreter or commentator. It is not one law at Rome, another at Athens; one law now, another hereafter: it is the same eternal and immutable law, given at all times and to all nations." This intuition was implanted by God, "the author and promulgator" of natural law. Wilson quoted Cicero: "That first and final law, they used to say, is the mind of God, who forces or prohibits everything by reason." Intuition was evident in our universal need for community. Wilson quoted Cicero yet again, preceding the citation with the comment, "How beautiful and energetick are the sentiments of Cicero on this subject": "If we could suppose ourselves transported by some divinity into a solitude, replete with all the delicacies which the heart of man could desire, but excluded, at the same time, from every possible intercourse with our kind, there is not a person in the world of so unsocial and savage a temper as to be capable, in these forlorn circumstances, of relishing any enjoyment . . . If a man were to be carried into heaven, and see the beauties of universal nature displayed before him, he would receive but little pleasure from the wonderful scenes, unless there was some person to whom he could relate the glories which he had viewed. Human nature is so constituted as to be incapable of solitary satisfaction."[10]

Like most advocates of natural law, Wilson was far bolder in asserting its existence than in establishing its contents. He did assert a natural right of self-preservation, again quoting Cicero: "There exists, Judges, this law which is not written, but inborn; we have not learned it, received it, or read it, but from nature herself we have snatched, imbibed, and extorted it; a law to which we are not trained, but in which we are made; in which we are not instructed, but with which we are imbued; the law, namely, that whenever our life falls into some ambush, is attacked, or is set upon by brigands or enemies, there is every honest reason for saving one's self: for amid arms the laws are silent, and they do not order a man to wait around, since he who will wait must suffer an unjust penalty before he obtains a just retribution." In addition, Wilson asserted, once again on Cicero's authority, the right "that no one, contrary to his inclination, should be deprived of his right of citizenship; and that no one, contrary to his inclinations, should be obliged to continue in that relationship."[11]

The founders shared the Stoic belief that both intuition and reason were necessary to understand natural law. Often citing Cicero, the founders spoke of the existence of a "moral sense." Having read and copied the Stoics long before he became familiar with Scottish moral philosophy, Jefferson believed that everyone possessed a "moral sense," which God had implanted in humans to ensure the preservation of their race. Not everyone listened to that moral sense; a plowman might decide a moral case better than a professor, if the professor were "led astray by artificial rules." But if people listened to their moral sense, they would find that it spoke the same things to each of them. Thus, Jefferson wrote that ethics should be taught at the University of Virginia as "moral obligations . . . in which all sects agree," and praised the Quakers for rallying around their common ethics rather than fragmenting over theological points. Similarly, John Adams, like his Stoic hero, Cicero, found proof of the existence of God in the universality of human reason. He argued: "The human Understanding is a revelation from its Maker which can never be disputed or doubted. There can be no Sceptism, Pyrrhonism, or Incredulity, or Infidelity here. No Prophecies, no Miracles are necessary to prove this celestial communication. This revelation has made it certain that two and one make three; that one is not three; nor can three be one." To Adams, the very universality of reason implied interconnection with a universal mind. The Stoic concept of the interconnectedness of individual souls with the World Soul, for which philosophes substituted the Judaeo–Christian God, lay at the very heart of the Enlightenment belief in natural law, a universal code of ethics. Using a circular logic, philosophes deduced a common God from the existence of universal laws, both physical and moral, and the existence of universal laws from a common God.[12]

Yet the founders also considered history ("experience") an essential means of teaching virtue. Intuition could not be awakened without the aid of reason and experience. When seeing virtue represented in present and past examples, children instinctively recognized its inherent beauty and sought to reproduce it. Conversely, children who rarely experienced virtuous behavior could not develop their moral sense to its full potential. Jefferson used an enlightening analogy to explain this Stoic concept of the moral sense: "The moral sense, or conscience, is as much a part of a man as his leg or arm. It may be strengthened by exercise, as may any particular limb of the body . . . In this branch, therefore, read good books, because they will encourage as well as direct your feelings." Such "good books" included Xenophon's *Memorabilia,* Cicero's philosophical writings, Marcus Aurelius' *Meditations* (another Stoic work), and Seneca's essays. But at times Jefferson seemed not to appreciate the implications of this analogy: that any faculty which requires exercise can be considered neither infallible nor equally possessed by all.[13]

James Wilson agreed that both intuition and reason were necessary to comprehend natural law. In the same law lectures in which Wilson quoted Cicero repeatedly concerning intuition, he referred to "the divine law, as discovered by reason and the moral sense," and added: "We discover [the will of God] by our conscience, by our reason, and by the Holy Scriptures." Although Wilson emphasized intuition, he refused to exempt reason from a role in uncovering natural law. He concluded: "The cases that require reasoning are few, compared with those that require none; and a man may be very honest and virtuous, who cannot reason, and who knows not what demonstration means . . . Our instincts are no other than the oracles of eternal wisdom; our conscience, in particular, is the voice of God within us." Odd that "the voice of God" should be silent in "a few cases." But most of the founders felt little need to elucidate the precise relationship between reason and intuition, perhaps because they possessed such an optimistic view of the powers of reason and the senses that they considered this road to knowledge as likely to end in success as that employing the engine of intuition.[14]

Such optimism concerning the possibility of progress was not entirely inconsistent with the ancients' cyclical view of history. Many of the founders' favorite ancient historians implied that the very purpose of studying history was to break the cycle of the past. Indeed, anyone who truly considers historical cycles unbreakable must conclude that the study of history is an idle amusement, but this was neither the position of most of the ancients nor of most of the founders. Thucydides wrote regarding his *History of the Peloponnesian War* (1.22): "If it be judged useful by those inquirers who desire an exact knowledge of the past as an aid to the interpretation of the future, which in the course of human things must resemble if it does not reflect it, I shall be content." History was not merely a pleasant pastime, but a guide to action. Knowledge of the past might prevent its repetition. Polybius seemed to concur, writing (*Histories*, 1.14): "For just as a living creature, if it is deprived of the truth, is rendered completely helpless, so if history is deprived of the truth, we are left with nothing but an idle, unprofitable tale." Polybius' opposition to "idle, unprofitable tales" suggests that he considered history a tool, rather than an end in itself. Indeed, Polybius sometimes seemed to suggest that, through a perfectly mixed government, the Roman republic had broken the cycle and had transcended history. Livy declared: "What chiefly makes the study of history wholesome and profitable is this, that you behold the reasons for every kind of experience set forth as on a conspicuous monument: from these you may choose for yourself and for your own state to imitate, from these marks for avoidance what is shameful in the conception and shameful in the result." Similarly, Plutarch used history to teach morality.[15]

Likewise, since the founders rejected any endeavor which was not "useful," their arguments for history centered on its utility in breaking the cycles of the past. It was not a morbid curiosity which motivated the founders, in their role as coroners, to plunge their scalpels into the decayed remains of the ancient republics. Their search was purposeful. They searched for a vaccine which would forestall the ravages of old age, with the confidence of physicians who believed that they had already discovered the basis of the remedy and who knew that the patient was still young and healthy.

Classical republicanism was not a completely closed system, an intellectual black hole from which no ray of hope could escape. The Stoic conception of human nature, which exerted a profound influence upon the founders' favorite Roman statesmen and historians, held the potential for a doctrine of social progress. True, the Stoics had chosen to interpret the theory pessimistically. They had viewed the world as a place of pain and suffering in which only a fortunate few—those whose "seeds" of innate goodness were properly cultivated by capable gardeners—were destined to achieve any peace of mind, and that in solitude.

That most philosophers of the eighteenth century chose to interpret the theory more optimistically was perhaps the result of the Scientific, Commercial, and Technological Revolutions. When combined with startling advances in knowledge of the universe, the unprecedented prosperity and mechanical innovations of the era seemed to provide ample evidence that humans were rational animals, capable of unfathomable progress. By contrast, the lifestyle of the ancients had changed little from one generation to the next, in part as a result of the Greeks' notorious disdain for applied science. By and large, the Greek scientists, whose ingenious deductions remain the object of wonder, considered the mechanical arts a base study, fit only for the lower classes, and preferred to speculate concerning things above the heavens and beneath the earth. Hence they considered progress of any kind unusual and ephemeral.

The fact that classical republicanism was the parent of liberalism—that modern Whigs had deduced the doctrine of natural rights and social progress from the ancient theory of natural law and its positive conception of human nature—made it easier for the founders to ignore the fundamental differences between the two ideologies and to borrow freely from both. The founders failed to note that the ancients had been less individualistic and more pessimistic than the Whigs. This evasion was understandable, since the differences between classical republicanism and liberalism, however significant, were minor at the outset. Not until the nineteenth century did liberals develop a conception of individual rights broad enough and consistent enough to constitute a clear rejection of classical republicanism. Even British Whigs had emphasized "the rights of the people" against the monarch, rather than individual rights against the majority. Having inherited this outlook, the American Revolutionaries believed that the people possessed the right to speak against the king, but denied that individuals had the right to slander the representatives of the people, as the Tories soon discovered. Even the Bill of Rights, which Antifederalists sought in order to limit the powers of the federal government, was as much a states'-rights document as a protector of individual rights. Modern individualism developed very slowly.[16]

To have highlighted the distinction between the ancient and the modern philosophers—between the modern theory of natural rights and the classical doctrine of natural law from which it derived—would not only have threatened unity during the Revolutionary era, since some patriots adhered more closely to one doctrine than to the other, but would also have forced the founders to confront contradictions in their own beliefs. In the early days of the republic the founders' attraction to liberalism grew. But they neither relinquished their attachment to classical republicanism nor noted the logical problems posed by their attempt to live in both intellectual worlds simultaneously.

In any event, the founders' advocacy of natural law can be placed in the broader context of an eighteenth-century movement, led by the Scots, to encroach upon the privileged position of English common law, in preference for Roman civil law, which they considered more truly based on natural law. Like America, Scotland was a society geographically removed and emotionally alienated from English society and self-conscious about its lack of refinement. Hence, both societies embraced the classics as a vehicle for respectability. James Wilson was himself a Scottish immigrant, Jefferson studied under the Scot William Small at the College of William and Mary, and James Madison learned from the Scot John Witherspoon at the College of New Jersey. In his first lecture at the College of Philadelphia, Wilson, then an associate justice of the Supreme Court, urged resistance to the slavish adoption of English models and called for "the foundation, at least, of a separate, an unbiased, and an independent law education" in the United States. Sixth-century Byzantine emperor Justinian's *Institutes* and *Digest,* the leading textbooks on Roman law, became more popular with American law students as both criticism of Britain and praise of France grew during the Revolutionary War, and as it became clear that the common law could not provide federal courts with a model for addressing their most crucial cases, those concerning the relationship between federal and state governments. Even before the Revolution, in the late 1750s, John Adams had studied Justinian so closely that he claimed regarding Massachusetts provincial law: "I know much less than I do of the Roman Law." In 1800 Samuel Chase, Supreme Court justice and signer of the Declaration of Independence, wrote regarding the beginning law student: "He should next contemplate the maxims of the Law of Nature reduced to a practical system in the Laws of Imperial Rome, for he will find that the principles of the Common Law of England were borrowed from the Civil Law."[17]

The civil law was popular in Virginia state courts. In 1790 George Wythe, head of the Virginia High Court of Chancery, began citing Justinian's Roman law as precedents, though at first somewhat apologetically. By 1795 he was prepared to inveigh against slavish adherence to English authorities, endorsing Roman law as a more rational model. In the twenty-one cases Wythe reviewed in the 1790s he alluded to classical figures eighty-five times. In one case Wythe compared justice with three of Aeneas' ships (*Aeneid*, 1.112), run aground by "the torrent of authority" of English precedent. By contrast, though English judges were as classically trained as the American judiciary, classical allusions were exceedingly rare in English courts, since Roman precedents were irrelevant to the common law.[18]

Other founders endorsed a greater role for the civil law. Fond of French experts on commercial law, Alexander Hamilton introduced his friend James Kent to civil law works. Kent employed them in the first law lectures delivered at Columbia. Thomas Jefferson expressed a popular view when, in an 1812 memorandum on Edward Livingston's Louisiana Civil Code, he called Roman law "a system carried to a degree of conformity with natural reason attained by no other." A few years later Jefferson urged the appointment of Thomas Cooper, who had published a translation of Justinian's *Institutes,* as the first professor of law at the University of Virginia.[19]

But though the founders may have first learned to appreciate natural law and its alleged product, civil law, from Scottish teachers, most had both the ability and the inclination to turn directly to the Roman Stoics themselves. As in so many other areas, there was a symbiotic relationship between classical and Whig works. Reading a Whig work generally motivated the founders to refer to relevant classical texts, and vice versa. To the founders, there was but one worthy tradition, the tradition of liberty, and they would not have understood the modern historian's need to distinguish between the classical and Whig traditions and to measure the influence of one against the other.

Stoicism also proved an important source of solace for the founders, giving them the courage to face old age, death, and other hardships. Late in life, John Dickinson identified himself with Seneca. Upon returning home in 1798 and surveying his estate after a long and distinguished political career, Dickinson wrote to his wife: "Seneca, when about my age, in a letter to a friend, says, 'I have lately been to my villa. There, objecting to the expense of repairs, the manager said, that with all he had done he could scarcely keep the house from falling on his head. Immediately I said to myself—what then am I who saw the first stone of that building laid? Walking in the orchards, I took notice to him how knotty and mossy the trees were grown. No wonder, replied he, for they are mere dotards and worn out with age. I said to myself, what then am I, who helped to plant the first tree of that orchard?' This is the substance of the story, and every part of it is strictly applicable to myself, except the complaint about the expense." But Seneca had consoled his readers with the knowledge that old age was but a temporary and bearable condition.[20]

The Stoics even helped the founders cope with the death of loved ones. The Stoics helped Jefferson endure the passing of his father (in 1752), his favorite sister (in 1765), and his wife (in 1782). Young Jefferson's literary commonplace book overflows with Stoic quotations regarding the certainty of sorrow in this world and the need to endure it patiently. For instance, in the late 1750s Jefferson quoted Euripides, a pre-Stoic stoic (*Orestes*, 1–3): "There is naught so terrible to describe, be it physical pain or heaven-sent affliction, that man's nature may not be able to bear the burden of it." He also quoted the Roman poet Horace (*Satires*, 2.7.83–88): "Who then is free? The wise man, who is lord over himself, whom neither poverty nor death nor bonds affright, who bravely defies his passions and scorns ambition, who in himself is a whole, smoothed and rounded, so that nothing from outside can rest on the polished surface, and against whom Fortune in her onset is ever maimed." He quoted Cicero (*Tusculan Disputations*, 1.49 and 3.16): "For the man who is afraid of the inevitable cannot live with a soul at peace; but the man who is without fear of death, not simply because it is unavoidable, but also because it has no terrors for him, secures a valuable aid toward rendering life happy . . . He is the happy man who can think no human occurrence insupportable to the point of dispiriting him, or unduly delightful to the point of rousing him to ecstasy." The aged Cicero had penned these words in the wake of his daughter's death, and the adolescent Jefferson copied them, along with others, in the wake of his father's passing. As Douglas L. Wilson, the editor of the commonplace book, notes: "This encounter with Cicero and the consolations of stoic philosophy, in the shadow of his father's death, may well have been pivotal in the development of the young man's personality." Jefferson certainly maintained a Stoic stance toward death for the rest of his life. It was no coincidence that the first volume of Seneca's works lay on his reading table when he himself died.[21]

The Stoics comforted other founders as well. John Adams derived comfort from the Stoic argument that the universality of belief in the afterlife proved its existence. In 1816 Adams echoed Cicero: "All Nations, known in History, or in Travels, have hoped, believed, and expected a future and better State. The Maker of the Universe, the Causer of all Things, whether we call it Fate or Chance or God, has inspired this Hope." In 1820 he wrote to Samuel Miller: "That you and I shall meet in a better world, I have no more doubt than I have that we now exist on the same globe. If my natural reason did not convince me of this, Cicero's dream of Scipio, and his essays on friendship and old age would have been sufficient for the purpose." By then, Adams' beloved Abigail had died, making the subject of the afterlife one of great concern. Likewise, Supreme Court justice Joseph Story became attracted to Cicero's philosophical works following the death of one of his children. Samuel Eliot Morison has even suggested that George Washington's Stoicism was a source of solace to him in his dealings with Sally Fairfax, the wife of his best friend, a woman whom he loved but could not have. Morison claimed that Washington's Stoicism enabled him to exercise restraint and to follow the "practical solution" of marriage to Martha Custis.[22]

Since the founders derived their conception of classical virtue principally from the martyrs and historians of the late Roman republic and the early empire, the zenith of Stoic popularity, Stoicism contributed much to their conception of virtue as well. Influenced by Cicero, Seneca, and the Roman historians, as well as by modern philosophers influenced by these Stoics, the founders perceived the nature and purpose of virtue in Stoic terms. Even George Washington, unphilosophical by nature, imbibed Stoicism at an early age. The Fairfaxes, whom Washington considered his second family, read Marcus Aurelius and the other Stoics. At the age of seventeen, Washington read Sir Roger L'Estrange's English translation of Seneca's principal dialogues. As Samuel Eliot Morison noted: "The mere chapter headings are the moral axioms that Washington followed through life." As a result of their Stoicism, the founders equated "Roman virtue" with frugality, simplicity, temperance, fortitude, love of liberty, selflessness, and honor.[23]

These qualities were not incompatible with traditional Christian ethics. Indeed, the classics had been an integral part of Christian education for centuries. Puritan ministers like Charles Chauncy had defended the classics against their few detractors by citing biblical passages (Timothy 1:12; Acts 17:28; and 1 Corinthians 15:33) which quoted the "heathens" and by arguing that "great moral truths may be found in Plato, Aristotle, Plutarch, Seneca, etc." Cotton Mather, a student of Ezekiel Cheever, had been an ardent classicist. Mather's eulogy of Cheever, who had never missed a school day in seventy years of teaching, bristled with classical allusions. In his *Considérations sur les causes de la grandeur et de la decadence des Romains* (1734), Montesquieu gushed: "If I could for a moment cease to think that I am a Christian, I should not be able to hinder myself from ranking the destruction of the sect of Zeno among the misfortunes that have befallen the human race." Latter-day Puritans like Samuel Adams conceded that "the pagans" had been as virtuous as any Christian. Indeed, the whole concept of an eighteenth century classical "revival" (and of a Renaissance classical "revival," for that matter) is dubious at best. How could something which never waned have been revived? The founders differed from medieval monks in their greater access to a somewhat wider variety of classics, in their ability to obtain translations, and in the different manner in which they perceived and used the classics. But the clerics, whose principal language was Latin, had been no less classically oriented than the founders.[24]

But while Christian and Stoic ethics were similar, their conceptions of the purpose of ethical behavior differed markedly. Forrest McDonald has noted that Washington was "a man of honor, not religion" (we might say a man with a Stoic, rather than a Christian, conception of ethics), explaining: "The one considers vice as offensive to the Divine Being, the other as something beneath him." To the Stoic, the "man of honor," virtue was rewarded here, as well as in the next life, through self-respect and the respect of others. In 1787 Thomas Jefferson assured his nephew regarding his examination of religious questions: "If it ends in a belief that there is no god, you will find incitements to virtue in the comfort and pleasantness you feel in its exercise, and the love of others which it will procure you." Since virtue brought earthly rewards, it was nothing more than wisdom, vice nothing more than folly. Young James Madison copied into his commonplace book Seneca's equation of vice with folly: "Why does no man confess his vices? Because he yet continues in them: it is for a man who is awake to tell his dream." Fame, virtue's greatest reward, was a praiseworthy end. But "fame" referred to the praise of one's few virtuous contemporaries and of posterity, the respect of the "best men" of the age and the commendation of a presumably transcendent "History," not mere "popularity," the immediate applause of the misguided multitude. John Adams expressed the common view when, as a young man, he inscribed in his diary this line from Tacitus: "Contemptu Famae, contemni Virtutem. A Contempt of Fame generally begets or accompanies a Contempt of Virtue." Like Cicero at Lilybaeum, the founders considered themselves always onstage, subject to the scrutiny of their peers and successors. Obsessed with their own reputations, they were acutely aware that historians would scrutinize their motives and actions. The founders' emphasis upon fame as the principal reward of virtue was incompatible with the traditional Christian emphasis upon the need for humility, the need to recognize that pride was folly. It was also inconsistent with the traditional Christian emphasis upon the utter insignificance of this world when set against the tremendous importance of the eternal afterlife.[25]

The founders were never fully classical, however. Although they rejected the abject humility of orthodox Christianity, they retained enough Christian modesty to regard the full-fledged egotism of classical heroes with embarrassment. Hence John Adams was at pains to defend Cicero against the charge of vanity, a quality which no Roman would have considered a vice. Similarly, Benjamin Franklin audaciously paired Socrates with Jesus as the two greatest models of humility. Whatever Socrates' virtues, humility had never been one of them. The gleeful arrogance with which the Athenian philosopher had enticed his opponents into admissions of inconsistency persuaded few Athenians to consider him a humble truth-seeker. However eloquent and frank his final speech to the Athenian jury, its condescension probably contributed substantially to his death sentence. Socrates boasted that he had too much dignity and wisdom to plead for his life in the fashion typical of most Athenians facing capital punishment (38d2–e5). Just as the founders interwove classical mixed government theory with modern innovations to produce a unique political system, they interwove Stoic philosophy with Christian values to produce a unique cosmology.[26]

Thomas Jefferson added a large portion of Epicurus to this potent mixture of Stoicism and Christianity. Although on one occasion the empiricist Jefferson accused one of his favorite British authors, Lord Kames, of being "too metaphysical," and on another called theology "charlatanerie of the mind," he did not lack metaphysical or theological views. Jefferson considered Epicurus and the Stoic philosophers the two best guides for metaphysics, Jesus the best guide for ethics. In 1803 Jefferson wrote regarding the classical philosophers: "Their precepts related chiefly to ourselves, and the government of those passions which, unrestrained, would disturb our tranquility of mind. In this branch of philosophy they were really great. In developing our duties to others, they were short and defective." In 1819 he declared: "Epictetus and Epicurus give laws for governing ourselves, Jesus a supplement of the duties and charities we owe to others."[27]

Jefferson's favorite philosopher was Epicurus, the Athenian whom John Stuart Mill would later acknowledge as the founder of Utilitarianism. In 1800 Jefferson compiled "A Syllabus of the Doctrines of Epicurus." In 1816 he termed the Epicurean philosophy "the most rational system remaining of the philosophy of the ancients, as frugal of vicious indulgence, and fruitful of virtue as the hyperbolic extravagancies of rival sects." In an 1819 letter, having stated that the doctrines of Epicurus contained "everything rational in moral philosophy which Greece and Rome have left us," Jefferson summarized these doctrines:

> The Universe eternal . . . Matter and Void alone . . . Gods, an order of beings next superior to man, enjoying in their sphere, their own felicities; but not meddling with the concerns of the scale of beings below them . . . Happiness the aim of life. Virtue the foundation of happiness. Utility the test of virtue . . . The *summum bonum* [ultimate good] is to be not pained in body, nor troubled in mind . . . To procure tranquility of mind we must avoid desire and fear, the two principal diseases of the mind. Man is a free agent. Virtue consists in: 1. Prudence. 2. Temperance. 3. Fortitude. 4. Justice. To which are opposed, 1. Folly. 2. Desire. 3. Fear. 4. Deceit.[28]

There is some evidence that Jefferson was an Epicurean long before he compiled the syllabus of Epicurean doctrines in 1800. As early as the 1750s Jefferson had copied into his literary commonplace book two corporealist passages from Cicero (who, though largely a Stoic, denied the existence of spirit). The first passage (*Tusculan Disputations,* 1.11) declared: "For if the soul is the heart or blood or brain, then assuredly, since it is material, it will perish with the rest of the body; if it is breath it will perhaps be dispersed in space; if fire it will be quenched." The second (1.16) exclaimed: "And such was the extent of deception . . . that though they knew that the bodies of the dead were consumed with fire, yet they imagined that events took place in the lower world which cannot take place and are not intelligible without bodies." By 1786 Jefferson's library contained the first-century Roman philosopher Lucretius' *De rerum natura,* one of the few surviving ancient summaries of Epicurean doctrines. In that year Jefferson wrote an anguished letter to his love interest, Maria Cosway, from whom he had just parted. Jefferson included in the letter a touching dialogue between his head and his heart. His head contended: "The art of life is the art of avoiding pain . . . The most effectual means of being secure against pain is to retire within ourselves . . . For nothing is ours which another may deprive us of. Hence the inestimable value of intellectual pleasures. Ever in our power, always leading us to something new, never cloying, we ride sublime above the concerns of this mortal world, contemplating truth and nature, matter and motion, the laws which bind up their existence, and that eternal being who made and bound them up by these laws."[29]

Although Jefferson accepted the Stoic belief in intuition (the "moral sense," in the terminology of eighteenth-century Scottish philosophy) and the resultant doctrine of moral equality, and although he found comfort in their emphasis upon the patient endurance of misfortune, Jefferson vehemently disapproved of certain aspects of Stoicism. He rejected the Stoics' doctrine of a separable soul and their fatalism and was angered by their misrepresentation of the Epicurean philosophy as mere hedonism. In 1819 Jefferson argued: "Epictetus, indeed, has given us what was good of the Stoics; all beyond, of their dogmas, being hypocrisy and grimace. Their great crime was in their calumnies of Epicurus and misrepresentations of his doctrines; in which we lament to see the candid character of Cicero engaging as an accomplice . . . Seneca is indeed a fine moralist, disfiguring his work at times with some Stoicisms."[30]

Although Jefferson differed from Epicurus in accepting the Stoic doctrine of intuition, he applauded the Epicurean emphasis upon reason. Jefferson considered reason and intuition the two guides which God had implanted in humans for the preservation of the race. While both reason and intuition were ethical guides, reason alone was the guide for metaphysics. In 1814 Jefferson claimed: "Dispute as long as we will on religious tenets, our reason at last must ultimately decide, as it is the only oracle which God has given us to determine between what really comes from Him and the phantasms of a disordered or deluded imagination." Although reason had to act upon information provided by the senses, Jefferson was equally convinced of their reliability. In 1820 he declared: "A single sense may indeed be sometimes deceived, but rarely: and never all our senses together." Hence Jefferson regarded religious liberty as crucial; for if men were free to think as they chose, reason would surely lead them in the same direction. In 1813 he asserted: "If thinking men would have the courage to think for themselves, and to speak what they think, it would be found that they do not differ in religious opinions as much as is supposed." What would such "thinking men" believe? They would believe in a Creator, not on the basis of a superstitious acceptance of revelation, but on the basis of the intricate design of the universe. Furthermore, they would adopt a particular brand of Christianity. In 1822 Jefferson made a prediction regarding the future religion of his free country: "I trust there is not a young man now living in the United States who will not die an Unitarian." Just as free inquiry in the Roman empire had produced Christianity, free inquiry in America would produce Christian Epicureanism. Thinking men freely using their reason would be Thomas Jefferson![31]

Although Jefferson's chief guide for ethics was Jesus, it was Jesus viewed through an Epicurean lens. Taking his cue from a book called *Jesus and Socrates Compared,* written by his friend Joseph Priestley, Jefferson frequently made the same comparison. He contended that the doctrines of both Socrates and Jesus had been corrupted. Plato had used "the name of Socrates to cover the whimsies of his own brain," and his dialogues were "libels on Socrates." Xenophon's *Memorabilia of Socrates* was the only source for the unadulterated philosophy of the Athenian.[32]

The doctrines of Jesus, on the other hand, had been corrupted by three groups: his inept and superstitious biographers, conniving Platonists, and illogical Calvinists. This corruption was tragic, Jefferson lamented, because, "Had the doctrines of Jesus been preached always as pure as they came from his lips, the whole civilized world would now have been Christian." Jefferson contended that "fragments only of what he did deliver have come to us mutilated, misstated, and often unintelligible," and complained of "the follies, the falsehoods, and the charlatan-isms" that Jesus' biographers had foisted upon him. Jefferson trusted, however, that "the dawn of reason and freedom of thought in the United States" would tear down "the artificial scaffolding" set up by these biographers. He concluded: "And the day will come when the mystical generation of Jesus by the supreme being as his father in the womb of a virgin will be classed with the fable of the generation of Minerva in the brain of Jupiter."[33]

Worse yet, Platonists, intent on establishing and maintaining power for a dissolute class of priests, had afterward engrafted onto Christianity the "sophisms" of that pernicious philosopher. After reading Plato's *Republic* in 1814, Jefferson subjected Adams to this diatribe:

> While wading thro' the whimsies, the puerilities, and unintelligible jargon of this work, I laid it down often to ask myself how it could have been that the world should have so long consented to give reputation to such nonsense as this? . . . In truth, he [Plato] is one of the race of genuine Sophists, who has escaped the oblivion of his brethren, first by the elegance of his diction, but chiefly by the adoption and incorporation of his whimsies into the body of artificial Christianity. His foggy mind is forever presenting the semblances of objects which, half seen thro' a mist, can be defined neither in form or dimension. Yet this which should have consigned him to early oblivion really procured him immortality of fame and reverence. The Christian priesthood, finding the doctrines of Jesus leveled to every understanding, and too plain to need explanation, saw in the mysticisms of Plato, materials with which they might build an artificial system which might, from its indistinctness, admit everlasting controversy, give employment for their order, and introduce it to profit, power, and pre-eminence. The doctrines which flowed from the lips of Jesus himself are within the comprehension of a child; but thousands of volumes have not yet explained the Platonisms engrafted on them: and for the obvious reason that nonsense can never be explained . . . It is fortunate for us that Platonic republicanism has not obtained the same favor as Platonic Christianity; or we should now have been all living, men, women, and children, pell mell together, like beasts of the field or forest.

Jefferson concluded that it was such Platonists, appealing to mystical and absurd doctrines like that of the Holy Trinity, in their effort to establish their individual sects as the national religions of the United States and Great Britain, who were slandering him and his friend Priestley for their religious opinions. But Jefferson hoped that Christians would not, in the end, "give up morals for mysteries, and Jesus for Plato."[34]

Jefferson believed that Calvinists had further obscured matters by adding the absurd doctrine of predestination to the Christian baggage. In his beloved Bill for Establishing Religious Freedom (1779) Jefferson had emphasized the Epicurean doctrine of free will, writing: "Almighty God hath created the mind free . . . [and] being lord of both body and mind, yet chose not to propagate it by coercions on either, as was in his Almighty power to do, *but to extend it by its influence on reason alone.*" (The Virginia Senate deleted the italicized words.) In a clearer attack on Calvinism in 1823, Jefferson told Adams: "I can never join Calvin in addressing his god . . . If ever man worshipped a false god, he did. The being described in his 5 points is not the God whom you and I acknolege and adore, the Creator and benevolent governor of the world; but a daemon of malignant spirit. It would be more pardonable to believe in no god at all, than to blaspheme him by the atrocious attributes of Calvin." In the previous year Jefferson had caricatured the "5 points of Calvin" as: "1. That there are three Gods. 2. That good works, or the love of our neighbor, are nothing. 3. That faith is everything, and the more incomprehensible the proposition, the more merit in its faith. 4. That reason in religion is of unlawful use. 5. That God, from the beginning, elected certain individuals to be saved, and certain others to be damned; and that no crimes of the former can damn them; no virtues of the latter save." Unfortunately, Jefferson substituted such ridicule for a rational explanation of the sense in which the human will could be free—perhaps because his position on free will conflicted with his penchant for environmentalism.[35]

In short, Jefferson concluded that both Jesus and Socrates had been Epicureans like himself. In 1820 he wrote dogmatically: "To speak of an immaterial soul or god is to say there is no soul or god; it is to be an atheist. Jesus taught none of it." Jesus had been a materialist: "He told us indeed that 'God is a spirit,' but he has not defined what a spirit is, nor said that it is not matter. And the ancient fathers, generally, if not universally, held it to be matter." Similarly, in 1824 Jefferson contended that Jesus had taught that the Resurrection was one of the body, and not of a separable soul. On this point Jefferson was only partially Epicurean: although Epicurus, like Jefferson, denied the existence of a separable soul, he also denied the existence of an afterlife, maintaining that death was nothingness (Lucretius, *De rerum natura*, 3.323–358, 417–458). This is one of the few areas in which Jefferson's Christianity got the better of his Epicureanism. Jefferson also rejected the view that Jesus had held any pretensions to supernatural powers. In 1803 Jefferson wrote: "I am a Christian, in the only sense in which he wished any one to be; sincerely attached to his doctrines, in preference to all others; ascribing to himself every human excellence; and believing he never claimed any other." The *logos* which had been with God from the beginning, as related in the first chapter of John, did not refer to the other members of a peculiar Holy Trinity ("the Word"), but to reason. In the same fashion Jefferson speculated that the *daemon* (divine entity) which Socrates claimed spoke to him was also reason: "He was too wise to believe, and too honest to pretend, that he had real and familiar converse with a superior and invisible being. He probably considered the suggestions of his conscience, or reason, as revelations, or inspirations from the Supreme mind, bestowed, on important occasions, by a special superintending providence."[36]

How was Jefferson able to extract the true Epicurean meaning of the doctrines of Jesus and Socrates from their corrupt texts—to separate the diamonds from the dung hill? Through the use of "reason," of course. In 1813 Jefferson explained how he had compiled his famous Bible: "We must reduce our volume to the simple evangelists, select, even from them, the very words only of Jesus, paring off the Amphibologisms into which they have been led by forgetting often, or not understanding what had fallen from him, by giving their own misconceptions as his dicta, and expressing unintelligibly for others what they had not understood themselves. There will be found remaining the most sublime and benevolent code of morals which has ever been offered to man." In 1820 Jefferson contended that he was trying to "rescue His [Jesus'] character." He wrote regarding Jesus' perfect morals (as manifested in "humility, innocence, and simplicity of manners, neglect of riches, [and] absence of worldly ambition and honors"): "These could not be the invention of the grovelling authors who relate them. They are far beyond the powers of their feeble minds." True, even after completing the distillation process, one was left with some objectionable passages, but these might be explained by Jesus' need to escape the clutches of bloodthirsty priests. Jefferson then performed the same operation on Socrates, paring away the same fatty tissue with the same scalpel (reason) to reach the same Epicurean heart: "When, therefore, Plato puts into his mouth such paralogisms, such quibbles on words, and sophisms as a schoolboy would be ashamed of, we conclude they were the whimsies of Plato's own foggy brain and acquit Socrates of puerilities so unlike his character."[37]

Jefferson ignored conflicting evidence. John clearly intended the *logos* to signify Jesus. He concluded his discussion of the *logos* with, "And the Word became flesh and dwelt among us," and followed this with a narrative of Jesus' life. In addition, both Plato and Xenophon related prominent instances in which Socrates demonstrated faith in the oracle of Delphi. In Plato's *Apology of Socrates* (20d–21b) Socrates stated that it was faith in the oracle which had launched him on his mission to examine others, leading ultimately to his trial. When the oracle, a priestess who served as the voice of Apollo, had declared that Socrates was the wisest man in the world, the statement had seemed so odd to the philosopher that he had been determined to discover what the god really meant. The Athenian did not doubt for a moment that Apollo spoke through the oracle. "What does the god mean, and what riddle does he pose?" the philosopher asked himself. "For I am not conscious of being wise, either in great or in small things. What does he mean, then, in saying that I am the wisest? For he certainly does not lie." In Xenophon's *Memorabilia* (3.1.5–7), a work Jefferson highly recommended,[38] Socrates urged Xenophon to seek the oracle's advice before embarking on his ill-fated Persian expedition. Socrates' faith in the oracle proves that he believed in divine intervention in human affairs, contrary to the doctrines of Epicurus, and that he may well have believed that a god spoke directly to him. Central to the works which contain them, these famous passages could hardly have escaped Jefferson's notice.

Why did Jefferson ignore these conspicuous passages? The answer seems to lie in his desire to "save Jesus' character"—and Socrates' as well. Enamored of their ethics (particularly Jesus'), which possessed a warmth and sense of benevolence absent from utilitarian calculus, Jefferson was determined that their metaphysics should also match his own Epicurean metaphysics. In this way alone could he feel comfortable in defending their ethics against the onslaughts of materialist detractors. In Jefferson's dialogue between his Epicurean head and his Christian heart, the heart informed the head that happiness was not "the mere absence of pain" and that the warmth of friendship was a necessary comfort in life. Here we catch a glimpse of why Jefferson's Christianity, with its emphasis on loving others, was as necessary to his emotional health as Greek philosophy, which merely taught the avoidance of self-injury and the injury of others. But Jefferson was too much the rationalist to surrender complete control of his head to his heart. Instead, he twisted and contorted the two to make them compatible. Jefferson was a true "heretic" in the original sense of the Greek word: "one who picks and chooses" those elements of a philosophical system which he likes, discarding the others. Ironically, Jefferson's reconciliation of Epicureanism and Christianity required an immense leap of faith from this leading figure of the Age of Reason.[39]

While the intricacies of Jefferson's theology were unique, many of the other founders shared its most essential elements: fondness for Jesus' ethics and rejection of his divinity. Benjamin Franklin stated that while he did not believe in the divinity of Jesus, he did not mind others so believing, since it would make them more likely to follow Jesus' moral teachings. Rather than completely rejecting Christianity and adopting Stoicism or Epicureanism, the founders interwove Christianity and classical philosophy. Under the shadow of new scientific theories which had reduced the universe to a set of natural laws, many of the founders could no longer accept the traditional Christian belief in direct divine intervention in the world. They now required rational "proofs" for the existence of God and the afterlife, as well as earthly rewards for virtue, in case the afterlife proved an illusion. But the psychological need to retain some elements of Christianity proved just as strong, for three reasons. First, like the early Christian converts of the Roman empire, the founders preferred the warmth and benevolence of Christianity to the cold obligations of classical philosophy. After reminding his Epicurean head of the numerous times in which the head had chosen safety over aiding those in need, Thomas Jefferson's Christian heart concluded: "In short, my friend, as far as my recollection serves me, I do not know that I ever did a good thing on your suggestion, or a dirty one without it." After expressing admiration for *The Golden Verses of Pythagoras,* with its maxims on the sanctity of oaths, the respect due to parents, affection for friends, and connection to humankind, Adams nevertheless added: "How dark, mean, and meagre are these Golden Verses, however celebrated and really curious, in comparison with the Sermon on the Mount and the Psalm of David or the Decalogue!" Second, the doctrine of the Resurrection and the afterlife provided tremendous comfort in an age of lower life expectancies. Epicureanism rejected the concept of the afterlife, and the Stoic afterlife was much too abstract for most people's taste. By reinterpreting Christianity in a classical light, the founders could expect to have their cake of earthly progress and eat it in heaven. Finally, the reconciliation of Christianity with classical philosophy served a vital emotional function: it saved the founders from the painful necessity of abandoning the religion of their ancestors and of their countrymen.[40]

The founders responded to unprecedented philosophical needs as they responded to unprecedented political needs: by returning to the same font of classical wisdom which had quenched their thirst in youth. Joyce Appleby was only half right when she wrote concerning the founders: "Science became the lodestar for those who thought they were at the dawn of a new age; modern scientists, not ancient philosophers, guided them into the future." *Both* modern scientists and ancient philosophers guided the founders, and it is precisely this fact which reveals so much about them. Isaac Newton's success in employing the scientific method had proved that reason and experience were partners in the quest for truth. To the founders, reason and tradition need not be opposed. The two were joined in the classical heritage, a tradition formed by rational men, whose wisdom had stood the test of time. How else can one account for the paradoxical fact that when the designers of the Great Seal of the United States proudly proclaimed the year 1776 the beginning of a "new order of the ages," they engraved the date in Roman numerals and inscribed the phrase in Latin, without the slightest sense of irony?[41]

VII

The Myth of Classical Decline

Despite abundant evidence for the persistence of classical republicanism throughout the early national period, Meyer Reinhold hypothesizes
a decline in classical influence during that era. Reinhold bases his claim
chiefly on the efforts made by such prominent figures as Benjamin Franklin, Benjamin Rush, and Thomas Paine to abolish the classical languages
requirement in the schools. To these efforts Reinhold adds nineteenth-
century statements, made by Thomas Jefferson and a few others, which
deny the validity of classical analogies. But in fact nothing better illustrates the classics' hold on the founders than the ambivalence of their
most prominent "critics" and the fierce resistance which blocked even
their most modest attempts at educational reform. The opposition of
Franklin, Rush, and Paine to the classical languages requirement did not
imply opposition to the classics themselves. Rather, these men, who read
and used classical works in the same fashion as the other founders, generally argued that freedom from Greek and Latin would allow students
more time to study the classics in translation. Mainstream opposition to
these modest reforms proved so bitter that the ambivalent reformers
were forced to fall back upon even milder proposals. While the
reformers' unprecedented assaults on the classical languages reflected the
rise of liberalism, their own ambivalence and utter defeat signified its inability to displace classical republicanism in the founders' lifetime.[1]

Benjamin Franklin opposed the classical languages requirement. As
early as 1722, in the guise of "Silence Dogood," the teenager satirized the
study of Greek and Latin. Franklin related a dream in which he had entered the "Temple of Learning," which represented Harvard College.
There, on the right hand of Learning, "sat English with a pleasant, smil-
ing Countenance, and handsomely attired." By contrast, Latin, Greek,

and Hebrew, on her left hand, "were very much reserv'd and seldom or never unvail'd their Faces here, and then to few or none, tho' most of those who have in this Place acquir'd so much Learning as to distinguish them from English, pretended to an intimate Acquaintance with them."[2]

In 1749 Franklin reiterated his belief that the classical languages were useless to many students. In a proposal for a Philadelphia academy, published in his own *Pennsylvania Gazette,* Franklin argued that while all students should be required to study English grammar, only divinity, medical, and law students should be compelled to study Greek and Latin. He quoted no less an authority than John Locke (*Treatise on Education*):

> He [The student] ought to study Grammar, among the other Helps of Speaking well, but it must be the Grammar of His Own Tongue, of the Language he uses, that he may understand his own Country Speech nicely, and speak it properly, without shocking the Ears of those it is addressed to with Solecisms and offensive Irregularities . . . Whereas the Languages whose Grammars they have been so much employed in are such as probably they shall scarce ever speak or write; or if upon Occasion this should happen, they should be excused for the Mistakes and Faults they make in it. Would not a Chinese who took Notice of this Way of Breeding be apt to imagine that all our young Gentlemen were designed to be Teachers and Professors of the dead Languages of foreign Countries, and not to be Men of Business in their own?

Locke concluded: "To speak or write better Latin than English may make a Man to be talk'd of, but he will find it more to his Purpose to express himself well in his own Tongue, that he uses every Moment, than to have the vain Commendation of others for a very insignificant Quality." Franklin added educator George Turnbull's indignant statement: "Few think their Children qualified for a Trade till they have been whipt at a Latin School for five or six years, to learn a little of that which they are oblig'd to forget."[3]

Franklin questioned the utility of Greek and Latin throughout his life. In 1760 he told David Hume that any new words deemed necessary should be constructed by compounding English words, rather than by borrowing from Greek and Latin. Franklin had the traditional classical curriculum in mind in 1781, when he related a story concerning the Iroquois. Several English commissioners offered to give six of the brightest Iroquois boys a traditional college education. Franklin wrote: "The Indians, after consulting on the proposals, replied that it was remembered that some of their youths had formerly been educated at that [unspecified] college, but that it had been observed that for a long time after they returned to their friends that they were *absolutely good for nothing,* being neither acquainted with the true methods of killing deer, catching beavers, or surprising an enemy." Grateful for this "mark of kindness and good will," however, the Iroquois offered to educate a dozen or two English boys "in what was really the best manner and make men of them." In his autobiography Franklin complained that "many of those who begin with Latin quit the same after spending some years without having made any great proficiency, and what they have learned becomes almost useless so that their time has been lost." He claimed that modern languages were easier to learn. In 1789 Franklin referred to the classical languages as "the Chapeau bras of modern Literature." Just as the *chapeau bras* had once been useful as a head covering but was now a mere decorative item carried on the arm, so Greek and Latin had once been vital depositories of all knowledge but were now a mere badge of pedantry. Franklin complained: "But there is in Mankind an unaccountable Prejudice in favour of ancient Customs and Habitudes which inclines to a Continuance of them after the Circumstances which formerly made them useful cease to exist."[4]

Franklin passed the reform mantle to Benjamin Rush, the tireless Philadelphia physician and signer of the Declaration of Independence. In 1788 Rush, an avid classicist, suddenly turned against the classical languages with unaccountable fury. As late as 1786 he had declared: "I do not wish the Learned or Dead Languages, as they are commonly called, to be reduced below their present just rank in the universities of Europe, especially as I consider an acquaintance with them as the best foundation for a correct and extensive knowledge of the language of our country." But two years later Rush omitted Greek and Latin from his "Plan for a Federal University." Rush concluded: "Should this plan of a federal university or one like it be adopted, then will begin the golden age of the United States. While the business of education in Europe consists in lectures upon the ruins of Palmyra and the antiquities of Herculaneum, or in disputes about Hebrew points, Greek particles, or the accent and quantity of the Roman language, the youth of America will be employed in acquiring those branches of knowledge which increase the conveniences of life, lessen human misery, improve our country, promote population, exalt the human understanding, and establish domestic, social, and political happiness."[5]

In 1789 Rush launched a fervent assault upon the Greek and Latin requirement. He denounced "the strong and universal prejudice in favour of the Latin and Greek languages as a necessary branch of liberal education" and proclaimed the necessity of "combating this formidable enemy of human reason . . . this tyrant." He lamented: "How few boys relish Greek and Latin . . . Many sprightly young boys of excellent capacities for useful knowledge have been so disgusted with the dead languages as to retreat from the drudgery of schools to low company, whereby they have become bad members of society and entailed misery upon all who have been connected with them . . . The Latin and Greek languages are the first tests of genius in schools. Where boys discover a want of capacity for them, they are generally taken from school, or remain there the butts of their companions." Not content with attributing criminal behavior to the study of the classical languages, Rush then charged the classically based educational system with fostering elitism "because it confines education to the few, whereas universal education is necessary for the very preservation of the republican form of government." He explained that since Greek and Latin were unpopular with the masses, their elimination from the schools would destroy the prejudices of common people against formal education, thereby spreading knowledge. Rush ascribed modern authors' alleged lack of originality to their passion for the classics, noting: "A judicious critic has observed the descriptions of Spring which are published every year in England apply chiefly to the climates of Greece and the neighborhood of Rome. This is the natural effect of a servile attachment to the ancient poets. It insensibly checks invention and leads to imitation." Furthermore, Rush castigated the languages for hindering the development of useful sciences: "We occupy a new country. Our principal business ought to be to explore and apply its resources, all of which press to enterprize and haste. Under the circumstances, to spend four or five years in learning two dead languages is to turn our backs upon a gold mine in order to collect butterflies." Posterity would be astounded that in the age of the American Revolution "the human understanding was fettered by prejudice in favor of the Latin and Greek languages." "But I hope," Rush added, "with the history of this folly, some historian will convey to future generations that many of the most active and useful characters in accomplishing this revolution were strangers to the formalities of a Latin and Greek education." Rush did not provide any examples of such men; he himself was certainly not one. Rush concluded: "The rejection of Latin and Greek from our schools would produce a revolution in science and in human affairs. That nation which shall first shake off the fetters of these ancient languages will advance further in knowledge and in happiness in twenty years than any nation in Europe has done in a hundred."[6]

Rush's crusade against the classical languages continued through the next two decades. In 1789 he wrote to John Adams that republican government had never been given a fair trial. He urged: "Let us try what the influence of general science and religion diffused in early life will have upon our citizens. Let us try the effect of banishing the Latin and Greek languages from our country." A month later Rush asked: "Who are guilty of the greatest absurdity—the Chinese, who press the feet into deformity by small shoes, or the Europeans and Americans, who press the brain into obliquity by Greek and Latin? Do not men use Latin and Greek as the scuttlefish emit their ink, on purpose to conceal themselves from an intercourse with common people?" At times Rush seemed engaged in a simile contest. He also claimed that the classical languages were as "useless in America as the Spanish great-coat on the island of Cuba, or the Dutch foot-stove at the Cape of Good Hope." In 1790 Rush asserted: "I do not reject the modern languages as part of academical education. I have found much more benefit from the French than I ever found from the Latin or Greek in my profession." Italian and Spanish were also beneficial. He continued: "My partiality to these languages is one of the reasons of my having quarreled with the dead languages of Greece and Rome." In a 1791 *American Museum* article Rush claimed: "Much more, in my opinion, might be said in favour of teaching our young men to speak the Indian languages of our country than to speak or write Latin." A knowledge of Indian tongues might help whites to civilize Indians, but of what use was Latin? The same year Rush replied gleefully to the claim of James Muir, head of an academy at Alexandria, Virginia, that only nineteen of his ninety students had chosen to study the classical languages: "It gives me great pleasure to find . . . that the young gentlemen who compose your academy had discovered so much good sense in preferring useful to useless, or, at best, ornamental literature." In a 1796 eulogy for the celebrated astronomer David Rittenhouse, Rush ascribed his extensive knowledge and good character "to his having escaped the pernicious influence of monkish learning upon his mind in early life." A classical education "would probably have consumed the force of his genius." Rush concluded: "Rittenhouse the Philosopher, and one of the luminaries of the eighteenth century, might have spent his hours of study in composing syllogisms, or in measuring the feet of Greek and Latin poetry."[7]

Rush questioned the utility of the classical languages the rest of his life. In 1807 he contended that even divinity students required little Greek and Latin: "No more Latin should be learned in these schools than is necessary to translate that language into English, and no more Greek than is necessary to read the Greek Testament. One-half or two-thirds of the time now misspent in learning more of those two languages should be employed in learning Hebrew and in studying Jewish antiquities, Eastern customs, Eastern geography, ecclesiastical and natural history, and astronomy, all of which are calculated to discover the meaning and establish the truth of many parts of the Scriptures." In 1809 Rush noted in his commonplace book:

> Habit continues after what occasioned it ceases. Latin and Greek [were] useful to monks when all knowledge [was] shut up in them. Not so now. As well might continue the spade since the invention of the plough, or skins and fig leaves since the discovery of silk, cotton, and woolen clothing . . . Dead languages [are] less necessary now than formerly. All that is available in them [is] diffused through other and modern books . . . As medicine and law cannot be learned by all, but are necessary to all, why [can] not the dead languages [be] confined like medicine and law to certain persons only? Teaching dead languages [is] irritating to the tempers of Schoolmasters. [There should be] No ears pulled, no swearing, no calling [students] beasts for ignorance or dullness of apprehension in teaching other things.

In 1810 he lectured Adams again: "It is folly and madness to spend four or five years in teaching boys the Latin and Greek languages . . . Were every Greek and Latin book (the New Testament excepted) consumed in a bonfire, the world would be the wiser and better for it. All of them that are good for anything are translated into modern languages. Even their beauties and fine thoughts are to be met with in an improved state in modern books. A passion for what are called the Roman and Greek classics may be compared to a passion for their coins. They are well enough to amuse the idle and the rich in their closets, but they should have no currency in the modern pursuits and business of mankind."[8]

Rush's opposition to the classical languages stemmed in part from medical concerns. Rush believed that both the transmission of medical knowledge in Latin and the universal veneration of ancient physicians had hindered progress in the field and feared a similar result in other areas. In 1801 Rush listed two of the chief obstacles to medical progress: "3. The publication of systems and discoveries in medicine in the Latin language. Our science is interesting to all mankind; but by locking it up in a dead language, which is but partially known, we have prevented its associating with other sciences, and precluded it from attracting the notice and support of ingenious men of other professions . . . 4. An undue attachment to great names. Hippocrates, Galen, and Araetus, among the ancients . . . have all, in their turns, established a despotism in medicine, by the popularity of their names, which has imposed a restraint upon free inquiry, and thereby checked the progress of medicine, particularly in the ages and countries in which they lived." Regarding the latter obstacle, Rush had written as early as 1774: "I honour the name of Hippocrates: But forgive me ye votaries of antiquity, if I attempt to pluck a few grey hairs from his venerable head. I was once an idolater at his altar, nor did I turn apostate from his worship, till I was taught that not a tenth part of his prognostics corresponded with modern experience or observation." In 1806 he added: "It is impossible to calculate the mischief which Hippocrates has done by first marking nature with his name, and afterwards letting her loose upon sick people."[9]

Though lacking Franklin's affiliation with an academy and Rush's fervor on the subject, Thomas Paine added his voice to the cause of educational reform. In *The Age of Reason* (1794) Paine contended that the classical languages had become useless, "and the time expended in teaching and in learning them is wasted." He explained: "In general, a youth will learn more of a living language in one year than of dead languages in seven; and it is but seldom that the teacher knows much of it himself. The difficulty of learning the dead languages does not arise from any superior abstruseness in the languages themselves, but in their being dead, and the pronunciation entirely lost . . . The best Greek linguist that now exists does not understand Greek so well as a Grecian plowman did, or a Grecian milkmaid . . . and with respect to pronunciation and idiom, not so well as the cows that she milked." The study of classical languages destroyed a child's natural curiosity. Paine argued: "It [the child] afterwards goes to school, where its genius is killed by the barren study of a dead language, and the philosopher is lost in the linguist." He further contended that early Christians had established the standard system of classical education out of the conviction that real learning posed a grave threat to their absurd beliefs. These early Christians had decided "to cut learning down to a size less dangerous to their project, and this they effected by restricting the idea of learning to the dead study of dead languages," while persecuting those pursuing useful scientific study.[10]

Nevertheless, in spite of such rhetoric, the three reformers used the classics in precisely the same ways as the defenders of the classical languages. Like the other founders, Franklin derived great pleasure from reading classical literature. Lacking money for a college education for the youngest of his ten children, Franklin's father had removed him from Boston Latin School at age eight, after less than a year, and had placed him under George Brownell, a tutor of mathematics and writing. Yet Ben relished an English translation of Plutarch's *Lives,* later recording in his autobiography: "I still think that time spent to great advantage." Indeed, the book was among the first which Franklin ordered, in 1737, for what was to become the Library Company of Philadelphia. While acting as his brother's apprentice, Ben also read a translation of Xenophon's *Memorabilia of Socrates,* which convinced him of the superiority of the Socratic method of argumentation. Franklin later recalled that he had "found this method the safest for myself and very embarrassing to those against whom I used it; therefore, I took delight in it, practiced it continually, and grew very artful and expert in drawing people, even of superior knowledge, into concessions the consequences of which they did not foresee, entangling them in difficulties out of which they could not extricate themselves, and so obtaining victory that neither myself nor my causes always deserved." The first essay Franklin read to the Junto, his famous debating club, was just such a dialogue, between "Socrates" and "Crito," attempting to prove that "a man of vice" could not logically be called "a man of sense."[11]

Although Franklin never learned Greek, he resurrected his childhood Latin in the 1730s, helped his son learn the language, and often quoted Roman authors in the original Latin. In 1768, when castigating the British for assuming that an American revolt would be easy to suppress, he quoted a Latin translation of Euripides which translates: "Whom God would destroy he first makes mad." In a 1774 essay Franklin warned the British people that the Coercive Acts would produce a shortage of the New England whale oil which lighted London streets. He added: "But if we should be so blind as to adopt the above Plan, we can hardly be injured by remaining in the Dark; nor shall we be afraid of Robbers after our Money is gone." He then quoted Juvenal (*Satires,* 10.22): "The empty-handed traveler will sing in the robber's face." In 1775 Franklin cited Horace (*Odes,* 2.10.15–18) to cheer a friend suffering as a result of the British closing of the port of Boston: "Jupiter brings back the horrid winters and also removes them; what is bad now may not always be." In the same year Franklin wrote that, although "as yet the Muses have scarcely visited these remote Regions," he hoped that the proceedings of Congress would "furnish materials for a future Sallust." In 1784 Franklin wrote conversantly about various Latin mottos.[12]

Benjamin Rush also enjoyed the classics. Rush received so rigorous a classical training during his four years at Samuel Finley's boarding school in Nottingham, Maryland, that he was admitted to Princeton as a junior in 1759, while only fifteen years old, and graduated in less than a year. Having read Hippocrates in 1765 and having revived his Latin in 1767, Rush maintained the usual prejudice in favor of classical authors throughout his life. According to Rush's eulogist, William Staughton, Tacitus was his favorite author. Indeed, long after beginning his crusade against the classical languages, Rush copied into his commonplace book extracts from Tacitus' *Annals* and compared the Roman historian's descriptions with the paintings of "the best artists." In 1813, near the end of his life, Rush praised Samuel Miller's *Memoirs of Dr. John Rogers* in the best fashion he knew: "You have given an importance to the most minute incidents in his life by your reflections upon them. In doing so, you have happily imitated the manner of Tacitus."[13]

Tacitus was not the only classical author Rush admired. Rush praised Virgil in 1769: "In painting, as well as poetry, the attention should always be directed to some object, to which every other part of the work should be subservient; Virgil's Aenead would cease to please us unless our eyes were kept constantly fixed upon the illustrious hero of the poem." Rush and his friend Ebenezer Hazard always exchanged a handclasp originally described by Virgil (*Aeneid,* 1.408–409). In 1765 Rush had declared that the New Testament and Horace were the "two books that in my opinion contain the marrow of the Greek and Latin languages." He called Horace "the Venusian poet who was blest by Genius and Philosophy." In his autobiography (1800) Rush praised Arthur Middleton as "a critical Latin and Greek scholar" who "read Horace and other classicks during his recess from Congress." In the previous year Rush had cited the blind poets Homer and John Milton as evidence that "the energy of the mind is increased by the absence of impressions upon the organs of vision." In 1769 he had cited Demosthenes and Cicero as evidence that oratorical eloquence thrives only in societies favored by free speech. Finally, in

1809 Rush cited Homer, Demosthenes, Plato, Aristotle, Cicero, Horace, and Virgil as evidence against hereditary brilliance. Were any of their sons great philosophers, orators, or poets, he demanded?[14]

No one, not even Thomas Jefferson or John Adams, quoted Roman authors in the original Latin more often than Benjamin Rush. In 1765 he quoted Horace (*Ars poetica*, 1.397), imploring a friend: "Let us then be more diligent in preparing ourselves to serve our generation. The world in a few years will expect our services, and you know we have both of us ever been taught 'publica, privatis secernere' [to distinguish between public and private concerns]." In the next year Rush quoted Livy (37.6) on the grief caused by the parting of a family: "The mind is horrified to recall it and shrinks from mourning." While studying medicine at the University of Edinburgh, Rush complained of the city's waste disposal system, writing: "Unhappy they who are obliged to walk out after ten or eleven o'clock at night. It is no uncommon thing to receive what Juvenal says he did, in his first Satire [actually, 3.276–277], from a window in Rome. This is called here being naturalized. As yet I have happily escaped being made a freeman of the city in this way." In 1767 Rush called John Witherspoon "a man to his very fingertips" (Horace, *Satires*, 1.5.32–33) and exulted over his appointment as president of the College of New Jersey with a line from Virgil's *Eclogues* (4.6.52): "The reign of Saturn returns."[15]

Far from diminishing, Rush's propensity for citing Roman authors intensified during his anticlassical campaign. In 1792 he called his firstborn son, John, "the spes gregis" (the hope of the flock; Virgil, *Eclogues*, 1.15). In 1808 he memorialized Dr. John Redman, whom he had served as an apprentice for six years, by quoting Ovid (*Amores*, 1.3.17–18): "So may it be our fortune to live and so to die." Disturbed by the corruption of American morals caused by commerce, Rush twice quoted the famous line of an equally disgusted Sallust (*Jugurtha*, 35): "O City soon to perish if you find a buyer." In the following year, envious of his son James's sojourn in Edinburgh, Rush quoted Virgil (*Aeneid*, 8.560): "O! If Jupiter would but restore to me the years that are gone!" He admitted to some nationalism, explaining with a line from Horace (*Epistles*, 1.10.24): "Though you drive out nature with a fork, it will incessantly return." A supporter of the War of 1812, he altered Horace's statement (*Satires*, 1.9.59–60), "The gods have given nothing to mortals without much labor" to read "The gods have given nothing to mortals without not only labor, but also war." But Rush lamented the defeats of 1813, quoting

Virgil (*Georgics,* 1.199–200): "Everything is rushing to deterioration." In this last year of his life, once again decrying "a nation debased by love of money," Rush again quoted Virgil (*Aeneid,* 1.462): "Hence are there tears for things." He also copied into his commonplace book the statement of his favorite, Tacitus (*Annals,* 3.18): "When we review what has been doing in the world, is it not evident in all transactions, whether of ancient or modern date, that some strange caprice of fortune turns all human wisdom to a jest?"[16]

Though his few years of grammar school in England did not familiarize him with the Greek and Latin languages, Thomas Paine enjoyed translations of the classics. Paine later recalled: "I did not learn Latin, not only because I had no inclination to learn languages, but because of the objection the Quakers had against the books in which the language is taught. But this did not prevent me from being acquainted with the subjects of all the Latin books used in the school." He cited the genius of Homer and Euclid against hereditary rule: "I know not whether Homer or Euclid had sons; but I will venture an opinion that if they had, and had left their works unfinished, their sons could not have completed them." In *The Age of Reason* (1794) Paine called the writings of Homer, Plato, Aristotle, Demosthenes, and Cicero "works of genius."[17]

The three reformers employed classical symbols whenever the opportunity arose. When Franklin assumed the editorship of his brother's newspaper in 1723, while James languished in prison for criticizing the government, Benjamin announced: "Gentle readers, we design never to let a paper pass without a Latin motto, which carries a charm in it to the Vulgar, and the Learned admire the pleasure of construing." For the first issue he selected an apt line from Ovid (*Tristia,* 2.563): "I have never injured anybody with a mordant poem, not a letter of mine is dipped in poisoned jest." Franklin began each of his "Silence Dogood" essays with Latin mottos. He used such classical pseudonyms as "Americanus," "Benevolus," "Fabius," "Philomath" (a lover of learning), and "Theophilus" (a lover of God). In 1782 Franklin commissioned the French engraver Augustin Dupré to strike a medal commemorating American victory in the Revolutionary War. Under Franklin's plan the face of the medal would depict an energetic young woman carrying over her shoulder a cap at the end of a pole. Her flowing hair would give the impression of forward movement, and the Latin words "Libertas Americana" would serve as her caption. The back of the medal would depict Hercules in his cradle (the United States) strangling two serpents (the armies of Burgoyne and Cornwallis) while Minerva (France) sat by the infant's side as a nurse. Franklin chose for the motto the same line from Horace (*Odes*, 3.4.20) which John Adams so loved, "Non sine dis animosus infans" (Not without divine help is the child courageous). Franklin once even proposed that Thomas Paine, his fellow critic of the classical languages, be painted in a toga.[18]

Benjamin Rush demonstrated a familiarity with classical symbols as well. In 1769 he exulted over a painting with a classical theme: "In the palace of the Duke of Orleans is to be seen painted in the most masterly manner, everything remarkable in the History of Aeneas, from the destruction of Troy to his arrival in Italy. Nothing struck me more than the moving story of his leaving Dido at Carthage. You behold grief mixed with resentment in the countenance of the queen, while Aeneas expresses in every feature of his face all the passionate fondness of a lover, mingled at the same time with all that manly heroism which the prospect of establishing a kingdom and being the author of an illustrious race of heroes in a distant country naturally fired his soul." He added an explanation for the popularity of Roman statues: "There Trajan, Pompey, and most of the illustrious genii of Rome appear in all their wonted glory, and seem to tell the traveler in every feature of their faces, the history of their lives and illustrious actions." He then complained about absurd Parisian statues, based upon Ovid's *Metamorphoses,* which depicted women transformed into fish or trees. Rush also appropriated the name of Leonidas, the Spartan king and hero who fell at Thermopylae, for several essays during the Revolution.[19]

Thomas Paine also employed classical symbols. When first meeting Franklin in London, he impressed the old man with a Latin proverb which translates: "Every man is the artisan of his own fortunes." In 1775 Paine penned a fanciful story about how Cupid (love) must triumph over Plutus (money), signing the essay "Esop," after the Greek fable writer. In other essays he used the pseudonyms "Vox Populi" and "Atlanticus." In a patriotic pamphlet Paine had Richard Montgomery, the patriot hero killed in the Battle of Quebec (1775), return from the Elysian Fields, the Homeric afterlife for heroes, to urge independence.[20]

Despite the reformers' campaigns against the classical languages requirement, there is strong evidence to suggest that they agreed with the defenders of Greek and Latin that the classics provided appropriate models and antimodels of personal behavior and government form. Franklin certainly revered classical models. As early as 1722 he cited the mythical

Roman heroes Horatius, Publius Valerius, and Cincinnatus as examples of rulers who welcomed free speech because they had nothing to hide. In 1728 Franklin wrote: "He that is acquainted with Cato, as I am, cannot help thinking as I do now, and will acknowledge that he deserves the Name [of 'great man'] without being honour'd by it. Cato is a Man whom Fortune has plac'd in the most obscure Part of the Country. His circumstances are such as only put him above Necessity, without affording him many Superfluities. Yet, who is greater than Cato? . . . In fine, his Consummate Virtue makes him justly deserve to be esteem'd the Glory of his Country." In 1730 Franklin noted approvingly that the Roman senate once erected a statue to a sixty-year-old Egyptian priest for his honesty, but denied the burial, and banished the family, of the Roman Pamphilius for having been an "irreclaimable Liar." Franklin asked: "Can there be a greater Demonstration of Respect to Truth than this of the Romans, who raised an Enemy to the greatest Honour, and exposed a Citizen's Family to the greatest Contumely?" In 1740 he insisted: "Thou hadst better eat salt with the Philosophers of Greece than sugar with the Courtiers of Italy." In the next year he added some advice on acquiring virtue: "Think Cato sees thee"—an interesting substitute for, "Think God sees thee." In 1749, in the guise of Poor Richard, Franklin quoted Cicero on the importance of work: "There never was any great man who was not an industrious man." In the same year Franklin quoted Pliny the Younger (*Letters,* 4.13) on the superiority of local education over boarding schools in instilling virtue in youth. He also praised the ancients for recognizing the role of frequent exercise "in the Formation of a liberal Character."[21]

Franklin continued to admire classical models well after his first onslaughts against the classical languages. In 1751 he congratulated the Romans for recognizing the importance of swimming for youth, quoting John Locke: "The Romans thought it so necessary that they rank'd it with Letters; and it was the common phrase to mark one ill educated, and good for nothing, that he had neither learnt to read nor to swim." In the same year Franklin cited Cicero's *Orations* on the duty of people to administer to the ill. In 1756 he called Lucan's *Pharsalia* (19.587–593) "a glorious Picture of Cato leading his Army thro' the parched Desarts of Libya." Franklin recalled that Cato had not touched water until even the slaves had drunk. In 1758 Franklin recommended daily self-examination using the ethical maxims contained in the *Golden Verses of Pythagoras*. He contended: "These golden Verses, as translated by Rowe, are well worth your Reading, and even getting by Heart." In 1760, rebutting the English eccentrics who argued that British security from American independence lay in returning Canada to France, Franklin retorted that it lay in emulating Roman justice. Citing Livy (33.30), Franklin wrote: "The Romans well understood that policy which teaches the security arising to the chief government from separate states among the governed, when they restored the liberties of the states of Greece (oppressed but united under Macedon) by an edict that every state should live under its own laws." The Romans ruled many provinces without governors or standing armies. In 1764, following a white massacre of Indians, Franklin noted regarding Homer: "He frequently speaks of what he calls not only the Duties, but the sacred Rites of Hospitality (exercised towards Strangers, while in our House or Territory), as including, besides all the common Circumstances of Entertainment, full Safety and Protection of Person, from all Dangers of Life, from all Injuries, and even Insults." The gods took vengeance upon the inhospitable.[22]

Franklin's praise of classical virtue continued unabated during the last two decades of his life. In 1771, after noting that a group of Australian aborigines had been deemed stupid for declining gifts, Franklin wrote: "But if we were dispos'd to compliment them, we might say, Behold a Nation of Philosophers! such as him whom we celebrate [Socrates] for saying as he went thro' a Fair, 'How many things there are in the World that I don't want!'" In 1773 Franklin recalled his earlier attempt to get someone to reproduce a set of copper plates, taken from a translation of Horace's *Ars poetica,* onto square tiles. Franklin hoped that the illustrations on the tiles, "being about our Chimneys and constantly in the Eyes of Children when by the Fire-side, might give Parents an Opportunity, in explaining them, to impress moral Sentiments." In the famous section of his autobiography in which he described his attempt to achieve moral perfection, Franklin stated his last (and most difficult) virtue as: "Humility: Imitate Jesus and Socrates." He then quoted both Addison's *Cato* and Cicero on the importance of virtue.[23]

Naturally, Franklin also found antimodels in the classics. In 1722 he castigated the Roman emperors for repressing free speech, remarking about Tiberius: "The public Censure was true, else he had not felt it bitter." Twice, in 1747 and 1764, he compared the wealthy and ambitious courtiers favored by the Pennsylvania proprietors with the lazy and inept Roman aristocrats of the late republic, as described by Sallust in *Catiline's War.* In 1767 he compared English Tories who supported violent action against America with Athenian demagogues, like Alcibiades, who had urged the ill-fated invasion of Sicily during the Peloponnesian War. Franklin argued ominously: "Athens had her orators. They did her sometimes a great deal of good, at other times a great deal of harm; the latter particularly when they prevailed in advising the Sicilian war, under the burthen and losses of which war that flourishing state sunk, and never again recovered itself. To the haranguers of the ancients succeed among the moderns your writers of political pamphlets and newspapers and your coffee-house talkers." In the next year Franklin compared these demagogues with Cato the Elder. He argued that those who claimed that Bostonians were as much an enemy to Britain as Carthage was to Rome were implying that Britain should adopt Cato the Elder's slogan and leave not "a Carthaginian or Bostonian alive upon the face of the earth." In 1770 he added: "Indeed, an Empire composed of half Freemen, half Slaves (in a very few Years the British Subjects in America will equal the Number of those in the Mother Country) would resemble the Roman Empire in its ruinous State." In the previous year he had castigated Roman imperialism, writing to Lord Kames: "There seems to be but three ways for nations to acquire wealth. The first is by war, as the Romans did, in plundering their conquered neighbors. This is robbery. The second by commerce, which is generally cheating. The third is by agriculture, the only honest way." Both in 1768 and in 1770 Franklin complained that the Townshend Acts were as harsh as the Carthaginian law forcing the Sardinians to purchase all their corn from Carthage.[24]

By 1775 Franklin's analogies were bitter. He lambasted Britain, writing: "When I consider the extream Corruption prevalent among all Orders of Men in this old rotten State, and the glorious publick Virtue so predominant in our rising Country, I cannot but apprehend more Mischief than Benefit from a closer Union . . . To unite us will only be to corrupt and poison us also. It seems like Mezentius [Medzentius, an Etruscan king] coupling and binding together the dead and the living." He then quoted Virgil (*Aeneid*, 8.487–488): "Truly torture: as they floated in the poisonous, putrid blood in vile embrace, he slew them with a lingering death." In 1776, after George III employed Hessian mercenaries against the rebellious American colonies, Franklin portrayed the king as Xerxes, putting these words into his mouth: "Do you remember that of the 300 Lacedaemonians who defended the defile at Thermopylae, not one returned? How happy could I be if I could say the same of my brave Hessians!"[25]

Benjamin Rush also perceived models in the ancient world. True, he sometimes opposed classical mythology and philosophy on moral grounds. In 1789 he charged these studies with the promotion of vice, paganism, and militarism: "The study of some of the Latin and Greek classics is unfavorable to morals and religion. Indelicate amours, and shocking vices of gods and men, fill many parts of them. Hence, [they impart] an early dangerous acquaintance with vice; and hence, from an association of ideas, a diminished respect for the unity and perfections of the true God." He wrote to John Adams: "I shall class them hereafter with Negro slavery and spiritous liquors and consider them as, though in a less degree, unfriendly to the progress of morals, knowledge, and religion in the United States." He explained: "If the years spent teaching boys the Greek and Roman mythology were spent in teaching them Jewish antiquities and the connection between the types and prophecies of the Old Testament with the events of the New, don't you think we should have less infidelity and, of course, less immorality and bad government in the world? . . . Men love royalty, titles, and the Latin and Greek languages. They make wars, enslave their fellow creatures, distill and drink rum, all because they are not formed by Reason." In 1799 Rush singled out Epicurus' doctrine of divine noninterference for refutation, arguing that "the continuance of animal life, no less than its commencement [is] the effect of the constant operation of divine power and goodness [which] leads us to believe that the whole creation is supported in the same manner." In 1800 he added reprovingly: "Deism [is] derived from partiality to Greek and Roman writers—morality enough supposed to be found in them." In 1807 Rush wrote regarding divinity schools: "No one of the Latin nor Greek poets or historians should be read in these schools, by which means a pious ignorance will be preserved of the crimes of the heathen gods and men related not only without censure, but often with praise . . . Nor should [classical] moral philosophy be taught in these schools. It is . . . infidelity systematized." In 1809 he added concerning the Romans: "Consult the Pantheon for marks of their immoral tendency." In 1811 Rush derided "the pagan doctrines of Aristotle and Plato." He even advanced the peculiar theory that the evil Napoleon was behind the classical revival in Europe, writing: "It is one among many other of his acts that are calculated and perhaps intended to bring back the darkness and ignorance of the fourteenth and fifteenth centuries."[26]

But, with the exception of the 1807 statement, Rush concentrated his assaults upon classical mythology and philosophy. It is not surprising that Rush exempted ancient history from these attacks, since he himself derived models from it. In 1773 Rush applauded the patriotism of Themistocles, writing: "Themistocles ordered his body to be removed from Persia after his death in order that it might mix with his native dust in Greece, although he had been banished from that country." In the next year he praised some of the medical practices of the ancients. He cited Tacitus and Caesar for his assertion that the ancient Germans had seldom married before thirty, a practice which maintained their youthful vigor and ensured a "more certain fruitfulness to their wives." He also applauded the simplicity, temperance, and reliance on natural cures of the Romans, Spartans, and Egyptians. In a lecture he strongly praised Hippocrates' careful attention to recording detail, though his reasoning had sometimes been flawed. He honored Hippocrates and Galen for their piety and humanitarianism. Rush wrote: "Hippocrates, who furnished the earliest, has likewise exhibited the most prominent example of this divine form of humanity of any physician that ever lived." He quoted Galen regarding Hippocrates: "There was but one sentiment in his soul, and that was the love of doing good, and in the course of his long life, but a single act, and that was the relieving [of] the sick."[27]

Like the other founders, Rush formulated numerous analogies during the Revolution. In 1776, while in Congress, Rush wrote to his wife: "I hope, my dear, we shall see many happy days in Philadelphia together, notwithstanding we have precluded ourselves from the society of a few tory families. 'I should have blushed,' says Cato, 'if Cato's house had stood secure and flourished in a civil war.' I should have blushed much more to have heard it said that I shook hands or drank Madeira with men who would have sacrificed their country to ambition or avarice." A month later, having spoken in Congress for the first time, Rush praised the assembly as another Roman senate, explaining: "I felt that I was not thundering like Cato in the Uttica of our [local] committee of inspection. The audience [in Congress] is truly respectable." In 1777, as medical officer for the Continental Army, he praised ancient generals for seeing to the medical care of their soldiers, writing: "Had it not been for this eminent quality, Xenophon would never have led ten thousand Greeks through sixteen months through a cold and most inhospitable country, nor would Fabius have kept that army together . . . which conquered Hannibal and delivered Rome." In the same year he referred to "the integrity of Aristides" as the epitome of that quality. In opposing the new state constitution of Pennsylvania, Rush argued: "Of so much consequence did the wise Athenians view the force of ancient habits and customs in their laws and government that they punished all strangers with death who interfered in their politics. They knew well the effects of novelty upon the minds of the people, and that a more fatal stab could not be given to the peace and safety of their state than by exposing its laws to frequent or unnecessary innovations."[28]

Rush's respect for classical models outlived his campaign against the Greek and Latin requirement. In 1789 he praised the Roman republicans for avoiding titles: "Caesar was Caesar, and Scipio was Scipio in all companies." In the following year he applauded Cicero for deploring the tendency of people to concentrate their admiration and political support on one man. Soon after he appeared to believe in classical virtue when he criticized those who "ascribe Roman attainments in virtue to those men only, who, by consuming an undue proportion of their time in writing, talking, or debating upon politics, bequeath the maintenance of their families to their country." In 1798 he praised the Spartan understanding of the importance of training children, writing: "The policy of the Lacedaemonians is well worthy of our imitation. When Antipater demanded fifty of their children as hostages for the fulfillment of a distant engagement, those wise republicans refused to comply with his demand, but readily offered him double the number of their adult citizens, whose habits and prejudices could not be shaken by residing in a foreign country." He added: "The black broth of Sparta and the barley broth of Scotland have been alike celebrated for their beneficial effects upon the minds of young people." Rush concluded that "the history of the commonwealths of Greece and Rome show that human nature, without the aid of Christianity, has attained these [high] degrees of perfection." Both in 1800 and in 1812 Rush implicitly compared himself with Brutus, quoting the Roman: "I early devoted myself to my country, and I have ever since lived a life of liberty and glory." Through this analogy Rush indulged his own frustration for John Adams: "Your correspondent early devoted himself to the cause of humanity. He has lived in a constant succession of contests with ignorance, prejudice, and vice, in all which his only objects were to lessen the miseries and promote the happiness of his fellow men, and yet he has lived a life constantly exposed to malice and persecution." In 1809 Rush contrasted the intelligence of Augustus with the ignorance of Congress, which had passed the Embargo Act against Britain and France. He wrote: "Had our legislators been better historians, they would have promptly saved their honor and preserved the peace of our country. Augustus repealed a law to compel bachelors to marry, as soon as he discovered that it could not be carried into effect."[29]

Likewise, Rush shared the same antimodels with the defenders of the classics. In opposing the death penalty he raised the specter of the Roman empire: "From whence arose the conspiracies, with assassinations and poisonings, which prevailed in the decline of the Roman Empire? Were they not favored by the public executions of the amphitheatre?" Similarly, in 1778, when Rush argued that, contrary to popular opinion, America's lack of a military genius was not harmful, he used a Roman analogy: "Rome was on the eve of ruin when Pompey alone could make war on Mithridates, destroy the pirates, bring corn to Rome, and oppose the invasion of Caesar. General Gates's success [at Saratoga] has rescued this country in a degree from its idolatry to one man [George Washington]." In the next year, when opposing Congress' inflationary measures, Rush used yet another Roman analogy: "None of you can be unacquainted with the depravity of morals and manners that preceded the overthrow of the Commonwealth of Rome. The effects of universal vice are the same whether produced by plentiful emissions of money or by the artful designs of a Marius or Sylla. Are you sure we have no Caesars nor Cromwells in this country?" When decrying the monopolization of knowledge by kings in the early 1790s, Rush singled out Alexander of Macedon for special condemnation. He cited Plutarch for the story that Alexander had once reprimanded Aristotle, his tutor, for publishing certain books, saying, "For what is there now that we excel others in, if those things which we have been particularly instructed in be laid open to all?"[30]

Rush's ambivalence toward the classics was, in part, the product of an erratic nature. When encountering the fierce resistance of the defenders of the classical languages, Rush was inclined to carry the counterattack further than in his calmer moments. For instance, in 1810 he admitted to Adams that the study of ancient history was not detrimental to the morals of society: "Napoleon would have been just what he is had he never read a page of ancient history. Rulers become tyrants and butchers from instinct much oftener than from imitation. As well we might suppose the human race would have been extinct had not Ovid bequeathed to modern nations his 'arte amandi' so suppose that modern villains are made by ancient examples." A whirlwind of erratic activity, Rush engaged in a one-man crusade to remake America after 1783. In the words of L. H.

Butterfield, the editor of Rush's papers: "He wrote dozens of public letters, broadsides, and pamphlets attacking strong drink, slavery, war, capital punishment, public punishments, test laws, tobacco, oaths, and even country fairs; and, on the other hand, advocating beer and cider, free schools, education for women, a college for the Pennsylvania Germans, a national university, the study of science rather than Greek and Latin, free postage for newspapers, churches for Negroes, and the cultivation of the sugar-maple tree."[31]

Thomas Paine was similarly ambivalent regarding classical models. In the third "American Crisis" essay (1776) he declared: "The wisdom, civil government, and sense of honor of the states of Greece and Rome are frequently held up as objects of excellence and imitation. But why do we need to go back two or three thousand years for lessons and examples? Clear away the mists of antiquity!" He added: "The Grecians and Romans were strongly possessed of the spirit of liberty, but not the principle, for at the time that they were determined not to be slaves themselves, they employed their power to enslave the rest of mankind. But *this* distinguished era is blotted by no one misanthropical vice . . . A good opinion of ourselves is exceedingly necessary in private life, but absolutely necessary in public life, and of the utmost importance in supporting national character. I have no intention of yielding the palm of the United States to any Grecians or Romans that were ever born. We have equalled the bravest in times of danger, and excelled the wisest in the construction of civil governments." In the thirteenth essay of the series Paine contrasted the glorious establishment of the United States with the ignoble founding of Rome by "a band of ruffians." In *The Age of Reason* he criticized the writings of Homer and Aesop on moral grounds: "I am not contending for the morality of Homer; on the contrary, I think it is a book of false glory, tending to inspire immoral and mischevious notions of honor; and with respect to Aesop, though the moral is in general just, the fable is often cruel; and the cruelty of the fable does more injury to the heart, especially in a child, than the moral does good to the judgment." Evidently, Paine regretted his selection of "Esop" as a pseudonym almost two decades earlier.[32]

But Paine did not disdain all classical models. In a 1775 essay against dueling, he cited the Greeks and Romans on the need to maintain unity within an army. In a subsequent essay Paine had the ghost of James Wolfe say to British General Thomas Gage: "If you have any regard for the glory of the British name, and if you prefer the society of Grecian,

Roman, or British heroes in the world of spirits to the company of Jef-
fries, Kirk, and other royal executioners, I conjure you immediately to
resign your commission. Only in a commonwealth can you find every
man a patriot or a hero. Aristides, Epaminondas, Pericles, Scipio,
Camillus, would have been nobodies if they had lived under royal governments." In 1776 Paine cited the first book of Thucydides to contrast
the Greek policy of colonial independence with the British policy of
tyrannizing over their colonies. In the same year he responded to William Smith's rebuttal of *Common Sense* by questioning his right to use
"Cato" as a pseudonym: "What pretensions the writer . . . can have to
the signature, the public will best determine; while, on my own part, I
prophetically content myself with contemplating the similarity of their
exits." In 1792 Paine declared that America, blessed by the modern principle of representation, would be an improved version of Athens: "What
Athens was in miniature America will be in magnitude. The one was the
wonder of the ancient world; the other is becoming the admiration, the
model of the present." Paine was fond of quoting Solon's dictum that the
best government was one in which "the least injury done to the meanest
individual was considered as an insult to the whole Constitution."[33]

Paine, too, shared antimodels with the defenders of the classics. He
particularly disliked Alexander of Macedon. In 1775 Paine betrayed
a somewhat ghoulish satisfaction in portraying Alexander as a bug in
Hades, "a most contemptible figure of the downfall of tyrant greatness."
Paine fantasized: "Affected with a mixture of concern and compassion
(which he was always a stranger to) I suffered him to nibble on a pimple
that was newly risen on my hand, in order to refresh him; after which I
placed him on a tree to hide him, but a Tom Tit coming by, chopped
him up with as little ceremony as he put whole kingdoms to the sword."
In 1776 Paine compared Great Britain with Alexander, writing: "Like
Alexander, she has made war her sport, and inflicted misery for
prodigality's sake." He added: "The histories of Alexander and Charles
[XII] of Sweden are the histories of human devils; a good man cannot
think of their actions without abhorrence, nor of their deaths without
rejoicing." When urging Virginia to surrender its claim to western lands,
he asked if the state could make such claims any more than "Alexander
could have taken it into his head to bequeath away the world?" A democrat, Paine also abhorred the classical mixed government which many
of the other founders idolized. He wrote regarding freedom: "If the ancients ever possessed her in a civil state, it is a question well worth

enquiring into, whether they did not lose her through the bolts, bars, and checks under which they thought to keep her?" Paine objected to Roman and Greek militarism as well.[34]

Indeed, one of the reformers' most ingenious arguments against the Greek and Latin requirement was that Americans should emulate the Greeks and Romans, who had become great not by wasting time on older languages, but by concentrating upon the mastery of their own. In 1749 Franklin quoted John Locke regarding the ancients: "They made it a Part of Education to cultivate their own, not foreign Tongues. The Greeks counted all other Nations barbarous, and had a Contempt for their Languages. And though the Greek Learning grew in Credit amongst the Romans towards the End of their Commonwealth, yet it was the Roman Tongue that was made the Study of their Youth: Their own Language they were to make Use of, and therefore it was their own Language they were instructed and exercised in." Franklin reinforced the point with a quotation from George Turnbull (*Observations on a Liberal Education,* 1742): "The Greeks perhaps made more early Advances in the most useful Sciences than any Youth have done since, chiefly on this Account, that they studied no other Language but their own. This no Doubt saved them very much Time . . . The Roman Youth, though they learned the Greek, did not neglect their own Tongue, but studied it more carefully than we now do Greek and Latin, without giving ourselves any Trouble about our own Tongue." Pliny had advised a lady seeking a tutor for her son to hire a capable master of Latin rhetoric, though the Greeks were superior in that branch of knowledge.[35]

In 1794 Paine espoused the same argument: "From what we know of the Greeks, it does not appear that they knew or studied any language but their own, and this was one cause of their becoming so learned; it afforded them more time to apply themselves to better studies. The schools of the Greeks were schools of science and philosophy, and not of languages; and it is in the knowledge of the things that science and philosophy teach that learning consists. Almost all the scientific learning that now exists came to us from the Greeks."[36]

In 1798 Rush joined the chorus. He argued: "Too much pains cannot be taken to teach our youth to read and write our American language with propriety and elegance. The study of the Greek language constituted a material part of the literature of the Athenians, hence the sublimity, purity, and immortality of so many of their writings." Nothing more clearly demonstrates the depth of the founders' attachment to the classics than their leading reformers' employment of classical models as an argument against the teaching of Greek and Latin. In fact Rush once even had the audacity to use the Latin language against the Latin language: "Delenda, delenda est lingua Romana should be the voice of reason and liberty and humanity in every part of the world."[37]

The classics also provided the reformers with important ideas. As a child Franklin read Pliny the Elder's *Natural History* and was intrigued by his account of sailors stilling the waves in a storm by pouring oil into the sea. As an adult, Franklin personally validated the hypothesis with an experiment. He concluded that "it has been of late too much the Mode to slight the Learning of the Ancients [in science]." Furthermore, both Franklin's conception of virtue and his recognition of the educational system's role in its production was quintessentially classical.[38]

Benjamin Rush was an advocate of mixed government. In 1777 he objected to the single-assembly government created by the new Pennsylvania constitution, claiming that "all the dissentions of Athens and Rome, so dreadful in nature, and so fatal in their consequences, originated in single Assemblies possessing all the power of those commonwealths." He added: "Socrates and Barnevelt were put to death by Assemblies that held their powers at the election of the people. The same Assemblies would have shed oceans of tears to have recalled those illustrious citizens to life again, in less than half a year after they imbrued their hands in their blood." Power should not be concentrated in the hands of the majority alone. He concluded: "All history shows us that the people soon grow weary of the folly and tyranny of one another. They prefer one to many masters, and stability to instability. They prefer a Julius Caesar to a Senate, and a Cromwell to a perpetual Parliament." In 1788 Rush endorsed the federal constitution as establishing a mixed government. He asked: "Is not history as full of the vices of the people as it is the crimes of the kings? What is the present moral character of the citizens of the United States? I need not describe it. It proves too plainly that the people are as much disposed to vice as their rulers, and that nothing but a vigorous and efficient government can prevent their degenerating into savages or devouring each other like beasts of prey. A simple democracy has been very aptly compared by Mr. [Fisher] Ames of Massachusetts to a volcano that contained within its bowels the fiery materials of its own destruction . . . [It is] the devil's own government." In 1810 Rush confided to a sympathetic John Adams: "The politicians hate me for being neither a democrat nor a monarchist, neither a Frenchman nor an Englishman."[39]

Like most of the other founders, Rush often cited Cicero concerning natural law. He once quoted the Roman statesman and philosopher: "This, my lords, is not a written but an innate law. We have not been taught it by the learned; we have not received it from our ancestors; we have not taken it from books; it is derived from nature and stamped in invisible characters upon our very frame. It was not conveyed to us by instruction but wrought into our Constitution: It is the dictate of instinct."[40]

Thomas Paine endorsed Cicero's arguments for the use of "right reason" in religion, for a rational God, and for natural law. In 1804, using Middleton's biography as his source, Paine claimed: "In Cicero we see that vast superiority of the mind, that sublimity of right reasoning and justness of ideas, which man acquires, not by studying bibles and testaments, and the theology of schools built thereon, but by studying the creator in the immensity and unchangeable order of his creation, and the immutability of his law." He quoted Cicero: "There cannot be one law now, and another hereafter; but the same eternal immutable law comprehends all nations, at all times, under one common master and governor of all—God." Paine then used this theory to assault the doctrine that God had propounded two very different laws, one vested in the Old Testament, the other in the New. Paine also praised the "sublime treatment" of the afterlife by such ancient philosophers as Socrates, Plato, Xenophon, Cicero, "and other of the ancient theologists, whom the abusive Christian Church calls heathen." Paine seemed to forget that he had earlier accused the church of imposing the classics on society in order to "cut learning down to size." Given that Rush sometimes assaulted the classics because they violated Christian orthodoxy, while Paine sometimes opposed them because they reinforced it, it is clear that the classics were susceptible to a great variety of interpretations.[41]

The real target of the reformers' educational proposals was not the classics themselves, but the requirement of the classical languages. As early as 1735, Franklin, then a printer, demonstrated his support for English translations of the classics by publishing James Logan's translation of *Cato's Moral Distichs,* a collection of Roman maxims. Franklin was "extreamly pleased" with the translation, writing: "For certainly, such excellent Precepts of Morality, contain'd in such short and easily-remember'd Sentences, may to Youth particularly be serviceable in the Conduct of Life, since there can scarce happen any Affair of Importance to us, in which we may need Advice, but one or more of these Distichs suited to the Occasion, will seasonably occur to the Memory, if the Book has been read and studied with proper Care and Attention." Franklin's own *Poor Richard's Almanac* bore a close resemblance to such collections of classical maxims. In 1744, when Franklin published Logan's translation of *Cato Major,* one of Franklin's most popular publications, he prefaced it with a reference to his true desire: "I shall add to these few Lines my hearty Wish that this first Translation of a Classic in this Western World may be followed with many others performed with equal Judgment and Success; and be a happy Omen that Philadelphia shall become the Seat of the American Muses."[42]

In his proposal for the Philadelphia Academy Franklin emphasized the need for students to study ancient history in English translation. He asked: "But if History be made a constant Part of their Reading, such as the Translations of the Greek and Roman Historians, and the modern Histories of ancient Greece and Rome & c., may not almost all Kinds of useful Knowledge be that Way introduc'd to Advantage, and with Pleasure to the Student?" The students should learn classical oratory, law, and agricultural practices as well. Furthermore, those who genuinely desired to study Greek and Latin should not be denied. Franklin explained:

> When Youth are told that the Great Men whose Lives and Actions they read in History, spoke two of the best Languages that ever were, the most expressive, copious, beautiful; and that the finest Writings, the most correct Compositions, the most perfect Productions of human Wit and Wisdom, are in those Languages, which have endured Ages, and will endure them while there are Men; that no Translation can do them Justice, or give the Pleasure found in Reading the Originals; that those Languages contain all Science; that one of them is become all universal, being the Language of Learned Men in all Countries; that to understand them is a distinguishing Ornament & c. they may be thereby made desirous of learning those Languages, and their industry sharpen'd in the Acquisition of them. All intended for Divinity should be taught the Latin and Greek; for Physick, Latin, Greek, and French; for Law, the Latin and French; Merchants, the French, German, and Spanish: And though all should not be compell'd to learn Latin, Greek, or the modern foreign Languages; yet none that have an ardent Desire to learn them should be refused; their English, Arithmetick, and other Studies absolutely necessary being at the same Time not neglected.

Franklin inconsistently quoted Locke's nervous and inconsistent disclaimer: "I am not speaking against Greek and Latin. I think Latin at least ought to be understood by every Gentleman."[43]

Benjamin Rush also proposed the study of English translations of the classics. In his "Plan for a Federal University" (1788), the opening salvo in his campaign against Greek and Latin, Rush ranked history, both ancient and modern, high on his list of priorities. In 1790 he expressed pleasure that his eldest son was reading Charles Rollin's *Ancient History*. In a 1795 lecture to medical students at the College of Philadelphia he claimed that ancient historians and philosophers "contain much useful knowledge, capable of being applied to the many useful purposes in life." In 1798 Rush declared: "The science of government, whether it relates to constitutions or laws, can only be advanced by a careful selection of facts that are to be found chiefly in history. Above all, let our Youth be instructed in the history of the ancient republics, and the progress of liberty and tyranny in the different states of Europe." Rush's opinion on this question did not change. In 1810 his argument against the study of Greek and Latin emphasized the availability of translations.[44]

Although Thomas Paine never advanced a specific curriculum, there is evidence he agreed with the other reformers that the classics should be read in translation. Paine wrote: "As there is now nothing new to be learned from the dead languages, all the useful books being already translated, the languages are become useless, and the time expended in teaching and in learning them is wasted." He proposed the creation of "a society for enquiring into the ancient state of the world and the state of ancient history, so far as history is connected with systems of religion, ancient and modern." Like the other founders, he considered the study of ancient governments a valuable pursuit, enabling one "to make a proper use of the errors or improvements which the history of it presents."[45]

Yet so fierce was the resistance against even the moderate proposals of Franklin and Rush that the reformers were compelled to retreat to more conservative ground. Within two years of Franklin's original plan to eliminate the Greek and Latin requirement at the academy in Philadelphia, he was forced to compromise, demanding only that an English grammar requirement be added to that of the classical languages. He even proposed that Rollin's histories and various translations of Homer, Virgil, and Horace occupy some of the students' time in the English School, though the students would be reading some of the same works in the original languages at the Latin School. Even so, disgruntled traditionalists sabotaged Franklin's mild reform. They so weakened the English School in favor of the Latin that Franklin felt compelled to issue a pitiful diatribe, a year before his death, against the trustees of the academy. He complained bitterly that the trustees had displayed excessive favoritism toward the Latin master in the disbursal of salaries, titles, teaching materials, and duties. Having forced several English masters into retirement by such treatment, the trustees had then turned the English School over to the Latin masters, who had neglected it. Franklin demanded an equitable separation of the stock so that the advocates of English could establish their own school. He wrote emotionally: "I seem here to be surrounded by the Ghosts of my dear departed Friends, beckoning and urging me to use the only Tongue now left us in demanding that Justice to our grandchildren that our children have been denied, and I hope they will not be sent away discontented." Completely unrepentant, the leading trustee, Richard Peters, declared that Greek and Latin were essential for the "Instruction of Youth in Piety, Virtue, and Useful Knowledge" and claimed that there was "an Abundance of Useful Knowledge which can be acquired in no other Language."[46]

The passionate assaults of the classicists overwhelmed Rush as well. His earliest anticlassical letter received a sharp reply from his close friend John Adams: "I should as soon think of closing all my window shutters to enable me to see as of banishing the Classicks to improve Republican ideas." In 1810 Adams declared, in response to another of Rush's tirades: "But now I must tell you a great and grave truth. I am one among your most serious haters of the philological species. I do most cordially hate you for writing against Latin, Greek, and Hebrew. I never will forgive you until you repent, retract, and reform. No never! It is impossible." In the next month, having thanked Rush for sending him a "tranquilizer" device, Adams lectured: "But, to be serious, if I were possessed of sovereign power over your hospital . . . I would put you into your own tranquilizer till I cured you of your fanaticism against Greek and Latin . . . My friend, you will labor in vain. As the love of science and taste for the fine arts increases in the world, the admiration of Greek and Roman science and literature will increase. Both are increasing very fast. Your labors will be as useless as those of Tom Paine against the Bible, which are already fallen dead and almost forgotten." To Jefferson, Adams concluded: "Classicks, in spight of our Friend Rush, I must think indispensable." Adams was preaching to the faithful. Despite having read his share of Rush's anticlassical missives, Jefferson insisted, as late as 1825, that students at the University of Virginia read ancient history in the original languages. But at least Adams and Jefferson were polite. Others were so passionate in defense of what they considered a precious heritage that their attacks assumed a personal character. Josiah Quincy suggested that the reformers hated the classics because they had been poor students.[47]

Suffering the brunt of the classical counteroffensive, Rush retreated. He aborted his planned anticlassical appeal to the ladies of America. As early as 1791, only three years after beginning his campaign, Rush conceded that, since the force of tradition was too powerful to resist, the best that could be achieved was to require students only to read the classical languages, and not to write them. He explained: "This will cut off one half the difficulty of learning them, and enable a boy to acquire as much of both in two years as will be necessary for him. He will, moreover, by this plan, be able to read more of the classics than are read at present in our schools. The classics are now read only for the sake of acquiring a knowledge of the construction of the languages in which they are written, but by the plan I have proposed they would be read for the sake of the matter they contained, and there would be time enough to read each book from its beginning to its end. At present, what boy ever reads all of the *Aeneid* of Virgil or the *Iliad* of Homer? In short, few boys ever carry with them from school anything but a smattering of the classics." This softening of Rush's position was reflected in his instruction to his twelve-year-old son Richard the following year, to "Go on with your class in learning Latin," though he added that the boy should spend at least half his time on English and mathematics. In 1811 Rush reiterated his position that "the dead languages" should be read, but not written, to save time for "the knowledge of *things* instead of the sounds and relations of *words*." Ever alert, John Adams seized the opening to proclaim victory: "By reading them, no doubt you meant that they should so read them as to understand them, and they can be read to be understood in no way so well as by writing and speaking them."[48]

Franklin, Rush, and Paine were not the only critics of the classical languages. As early as 1769 John Wilson had resigned as Latin master at the Friends' Latin School of Philadelphia, partly because he believed that English and mathematics were more useful studies (except for students of medicine and law), and partly on moral grounds. His resignation letter contained the tirade:

Is it not surprizing? Is it not monstrous? That Christian Children intended to believe and relish the Truths of the Gospel should have their early and most retentive years imbued with the shocking Legends and abominable

Romances of the worst of Heathens and should be obliged to be Pimps of the detestable Lusts of Jupiter & Mars, attend the thefts & Villainy of Mercury, or follow Aeneas on his Murdering Progress, while the Actions and Sufferings of the great and worthy Propagators of our Holy Religion that Succeeded the Apostles are totally hid from their Eyes. Is Bacchus preferable to Ignatius, Apollo to Origin or will Helena and Clytemnestra yield an affecting Instruction or warm our Hearts with the Love of Virtue like the Virgin Martyrs & Heroines of Christian Story?

But Wilson's moral criticisms, like those of most other anticlassicists, were aimed exclusively at classical mythology. Obviously, he would not have become a Latin master had he believed that most classical works had exerted a deleterious influence on children. Though unsuccessful in diminishing classical education, such moralistic criticisms led ultimately to the bowdlerization of Ovid's *Metamorphoses* by Victorian editors.[49]

Most other critics of the classical languages betrayed the same ambivalence, and their efforts suffered the same fate. Although Noah Webster admired classical models, he complained in 1783 that "the whispers of common sense in favor of our native tongue have been silenced amid the clamour of pedantry in favour of Greek and Latin." In 1788 he explained that translations had divested the classical languages of their utility. In 1790 he argued that the classics were useless to merchants, farmers, and mechanics, although he also conceded that Greek and Latin were superior to English in softness, harmony, energy, and construction. Indeed, he complained that classical training was too superficial for those who should legitimately study the languages. He cited Tacitus and Middleton's *Life of Cicero* to support his favorite educational theories. Even so, by 1800 Webster, like Rush, had been forced to recant his mild form of heresy. Others, like John Trumbull, spared the languages themselves and contented themselves with attacking the unimaginative pedagogical methods commonly employed in teaching them. But although English grammar and the physical sciences began to appear in school curricula, grammar schools and colleges continued to emphasize Greek and Latin throughout the nineteenth century. As late as 1844 the only subjects taught at Boston Latin School were Greek, Latin, ancient history, mathematics, and English composition and declamation. Every college maintained proficiency in Latin as a requirement for graduation.[50]

The ambivalence of the classical critics demonstrates the inability of even the most independent-minded to escape the conditioning of eighteenth-century society. It is significant that two of the three most prom-

inent critics, Franklin and Paine, were men who had possessed little formal schooling. Yet even they could not completely escape socialization
in the cult of the classics. In the end, they too were made to kiss the
classical icons.

But even the most zealous defenders of the classics experienced occasional lapses of faith. In 1782 Jefferson complained that twice during desperate periods in the recent war (1776 and 1781) men, "seduced in their
judgment by the example of an ancient republic, whose constitution and
circumstances were fundamentally different," had attempted to create a
temporary dictatorship. But republican Rome was not the United States,
because the Roman government had consisted of "a heavy-handed aristocracy" ruling "over a people ferocious and rendered desperate by poverty and wretchedness." The government and the people of the United
States, on the other hand, were too enlightened to need a dictator.
Again, in 1819, Jefferson claimed that the Romans had never possessed
good government, because they had always possessed a "degenerate Senate" and had always lacked the "enlightened, peaceable, and really free"
citizens America possessed. The Romans' only hope had lain in the production of virtue through education: "But this would have been an operation of a generation or two at least, within which period would have
succeeded many Neros and Commoduses, who would have quashed
the whole process." Yet Jefferson must have recovered from this notion
fairly quickly, for in this same period he plumbed the depths of Roman
history for examples of republican virtue. In 1821, for instance, he expressed the hope that "the human mind will some day get back to the
freedom it enjoyed 2000 years ago."[51]

Alexander Hamilton also occasionally argued against the propriety of
classical models. In 1782, when arguing that a modern commercial nation such as the United States required a large, well-paid magistracy, he
contended:

> We may preach till we are tired of the theme, the necessity of disinterest-
> edness in republics, without making a single proselyte. The virtuous de-
> claimer will never persuade himself nor any other person to be content
> with a double mess of porridge [the Spartan reward for newly elected sen-
> ators, according to Plutarch], instead of a reasonable stipend for his ser-
> vices. We might as soon reconcile ourselves to the Spartan community of
> goods and wives, to their iron coin, their long beards, or their black broth.
> There is a total dissimulation in the circumstances, as well as the manners,
> of society among us; and it is as ridiculous to seek for models in the simple

ages of Greece and Rome, as it would be to go in quest of them among the Hottentots and Laplanders.

In 1787, when advocating New York's recognition of Vermont's independence, Hamilton retorted to Richard Hanson's contention that the Romans would never have allowed "an inconsiderable part of their citizens" to declare themselves independent: "Neither the manners nor the genius of Rome are suited to the republic or age in which we live. All her maxims and habits were military, [and] her government was constituted for wars. Ours is unfit for it, and our situation still less than our constitution invites us to emulate the conduct of Rome, or to attempt a display of unprofitable heroism." In 1795 he branded Roman law "a relic of ancient barbarism with too many precedents of imitation," adding that it was inconsistent with both English common law and natural law. He seemed to have forgotten that only four years earlier he had appealed to the same "barbaric" Roman law to prove the legality of government-created corporations, namely, the Bank of the United States. Furthermore, in the same period he was scouring Plutarch for extraordinarily apt pseudonyms and constructing numerous analogies between the ancient world and the present, analogies implying a respect for Greek and Roman models.[52]

What should we make of the few remarks which appear to reject all classical models, deluged, as they are, in a sea of statements which clearly embrace them? Some such remarks may be dismissed as mere rhetoric. It was a common tactic, when a politician's back was against the wall and he was staring down the barrels of classical guns, with little time for thought, to disarm his opponent by denying the validity of all classical analogies. The use of such a stratagem was understood not to bind the tactician beyond the hour; hence, it was not uncommon to hear the same politician using classical analogies later in the same day. The same James Wilson who argued passionately, one day at the Constitutional Convention, that the ancient leagues had fallen from decentralization, and who claimed on another that they had fallen because their legislatures were unicameral, declared, a few months later at the Pennsylvania ratifying convention, that "the situation and dimensions of the confederacies, and the state of society, manners, and habits" of the Greeks were too different from those of Americans to warrant analogy with their republics. As we have seen, this conclusion did not stop Wilson from making such comparisons his whole life. Nathaniel Gorham, a delegate at the Massachu-

setts ratifying convention, set a record for the least amount of time between the wholesale criticism and use of classical analogies. He "exposed
the absurdity of conclusions and hypotheses drawn from ancient governments which bore no relation to the confederacy proposed," but warned,
in the same breath, "against the evil which ruined these states, which he
thought was the want of an efficient government."[53]

Other anticlassical statements reflected national pride and expressed the
hope that the United States could transcend history. Even John Adams,
who so admired the ancient orators, was anxious to exalt American
statesmen above them. He wrote of James Otis' famous speech against
the British writs of assistance: "No harangue of Demosthenes or Cicero
ever had such effects upon the globe." In a 1788 speech celebrating the
ratification of the U.S. Constitution, James Wilson contrasted ancient republican constitutions, imposed by the fiat of temporary dictators like
Numa, Lycurgus, and Solon, with the U.S. Constitution, drafted and
ratified by conventions specifically elected for that purpose. He concluded
that although the ancients had introduced the theory of popular sovereignty, only the United States had put it into practice. In 1790 Wilson
criticized those who considered their country inferior to the Greek and
Roman republics. Though great, Greece was overrated because "their
virtues [have been] transmitted to posterity by writers who excelled those
of every other country in abilities and elegance." He added: "Alexander,
when master of the world, envied the good fortune of Achilles, who had
a Homer to celebrate his deeds." Wilson declared: "But, in real worth
and excellence, I boldly venture to compare them [the United States]
with the most illustrious commonwealths which adorn the records of
fame. When some future Xenophon or Thucydides shall arise to do justice to their virtues and their actions; the glory of America will rival—it
will outshine the glory of Greece." He noted: "In the European temple
of fame, William Penn is placed by the side of Lycurgus. Will America
refuse a temple to her patriots and heroes?" Much of Thomas Paine's
anticlassicism can be traced to nationalism. In the *Crisis* essays, designed
to improve patriots' morale during the Revolutionary War by appealing
to national pride, Paine wrote regarding the Greeks: "We do great injustice to ourselves by placing them in such a superior line . . . Could the
mist of antiquity be cleared away, and men and things be viewed as they
really were, it is more than probable that they would admire us, rather
than we them."[54]

But the founders' classical conditioning generally got the better of their nationalist sentiment. As Edwin A. Miles aptly noted: "One must not be misled by the [founders'] constant claims of American superiority over the Greeks and Romans; the fact that such comparisons were deemed necessary is of weightier significance." The founders were like the son who idolizes his father, though striving to surpass him. However great the son's success, his measuring stick remains the achievements of the father, his boastful claims reassuring himself that he has proven a worthy successor.[55]

Oddly enough, few anticlassical statements were based upon doubts regarding the integrity of the historical record or the objectivity of ancient historians. John Adams frequently complained about the loss of large portions of Aristotle's *Politics* and Cicero's *Republic,* two of the greatest works concerning mixed government theory. These works had been destroyed, Adams claimed, by "lying priests or knavish politicians." Adams even irrationally ascribed to such priests and politicians the destruction of the famous library at Alexandria, destroyed by Muslims in the early seventh century, as well as the destruction of the missing works of Livy and Tacitus, and the laws framed by Seleucus for the Greek polis of Locris. In addition, like Jefferson, he complained about the ancient historians' habit of composing fictitious speeches for their statesmen. But these fleeting reflections hardly deterred Adams from citing the ancients regarding mixed government theory and most other matters. Jefferson expressed regret that no historian had given an account of the Punic Wars from the Carthaginian point of view and deduced from Carthage's "wealth, power, and splendor" that "she must have had a very distinguished policy and government." But such momentary doubts concerning the objectivity of Roman historians did not prevent Jefferson from calling the British and American commercial elites he despised "modern Carthaginians." Indeed, neither Adams nor Jefferson ever expressed the skepticism of Rush or John Taylor. In 1790 Rush asked: "What trash may we not suppose has been handed down to us from antiquity, when we detect such errors and prejudices in the history of events of which we have been eyewitnesses and in which we have been actors? . . . I suspect the well-concerted plans of battles recorded by Livy to have been picked up in the barbers' shops of Rome or from deserters from the Roman armies." In 1814, forgetting Tacitus and Suetonius, Taylor claimed that as a result of Augustus' supreme power, he was known only through "his sycophants and slaves." Taylor concluded: "The history of the ancient times is hardly more weighty, opposed to living evidence, than the wanderings of fancy; it is invariably treacherous in some degree, and comes, like an oracle, from a place into which light cannot penetrate. We are to determine whether we will be intimidated by apparitions of departed time, frightfully accoutred for that purpose, to shut our eyes, lest we should see the superiority of our policy displayed, not in theory, but in practice; not in history, but in sight." Such skepticism, considered healthy by modern classicists, was all too rare, and prevented no one from utilizing the works of ancient historians in public and private disputes.[56]

Some anticlassical statements reflected a genuine recognition of the irrationality involved in perceiving the ancient republics as exact models for modern government. Jefferson felt, for instance, that the direct democracy of Athens was not only impractical for a large republic like the United States, but would lead to administrative incompetence. While Jefferson was convinced that the general public was best qualified to elect those representatives most capable of managing the daily affairs of government, it certainly should not attempt, assuming it were possible, to manage those affairs directly. In addition, Jefferson criticized Athens (and, by extension, Rome) for ruling over foreign territory. It was not expansion that bothered the purchaser of Louisiana. Nor was Jefferson even bothered, like Voltaire and other philosophes, by the use of warfare to achieve expansion. He explained to Abigail Adams that he was not ashamed of having bought her a figurine of Mars, the Roman god of war, because this god had "rocked the cradle of our birth . . . and has shewn himself the patron of our rights and the avenger of our wrongs." What bothered Jefferson about the Athenians and Romans was that they had not allowed their conquered peoples representation, in part a result of their alleged ignorance of the "principle of representation." Expansion was proper only if the inhabitants of the new territories were given equal representation. This principle, which distinguished American expansion from European colonialism, had been enshrined in the Northwest Ordinance of 1787.[57]

Finally, some anticlassical statements were themselves manifestations of a deep-seated classicism. The founders believed that the best way to honor men famous for their independence of thought and action was to exhibit the same quality. Idolized for their intellectual courage and lonely virtue, classical heroes could not be honored by the slavish acceptance of all their theories. Since slavishness was the very antithesis of classical virtue, the founders could equal their ancient heroes only by opposing classical authority whenever it seemed warranted. In 1790 James Wilson expressed a common view when he quoted Grotius: "Among philosophers, Aristotle deservedly holds the chief place, whether you consider his method of treating subjects, or the acuteness of his distinctions, or the weight of his reasons. I could only wish that the authority of this great man had not, for some ages past, degenerated into tyranny, so that truth, for the discovery of which Aristotle took so great pains, is now oppressed by nothing more than by the very name of Aristotle." Similarly, it was with obvious pain that Wilson criticized Cicero for defending the principle that sons should be punished for the crimes of their parents. With an almost audible sigh Wilson wrote: "Amicus Cicero—sed magis amica veritas," meaning, "Dear is Cicero, but dearer is Truth." He added in English: "For the high authority of Cicero I certainly entertain a proportionate degree of respect; but implicit deference should be paid to no one." John Adams paused, even in the midst of heckling John Quincy into studying his classics, to warn his eldest son: "These great Masters of Antiquity you must sooner or later be able to judge of critically. But you must never imitate them. Study nature, and write accordingly, and you will resemble them. But it is nature, not the Ancients, that you are to imitate and Copy." (Of course, since the very concept of natural law which was to serve as the measuring stick was classical, Greek and Roman heroes tended to fare well in such judgments.) In the wake of the Stamp Act Adams had enumerated the various branches of knowledge which could illuminate the nation's path: "Let us study the law of nature; search into the spirit of the British Constitution; read the histories of the ancient ages; contemplate the great examples of Greece and Rome; set before us the conduct of our British ancestors, who have defended for us the inherent rights of mankind against foreign and domestic tyrants and usurpers . . . Let every sluice of knowledge be opened and set a-flowing." Likewise, Thomas Jefferson replied to the pedant, who would argue that *only* the classics were useful: "I answer, everything is useful which contributes to fix us in the principles and practice of virtue."[58]

Although the founders considered the classics an important source of enlightenment, they understood that the highest expression of classical virtue was independence of thought and action. The statesmen and philosophers of Greece and Rome had demonstrated the intellectual courage necessary to flout the absolutism and superstition which dominated the rest of the ancient world and to establish their theories on the solid foundations of reason and republicanism. Hence, neither the Ciceros of the past nor the Plutarchs of the future would respect slavishness.

The fact that the early national period witnessed an unprecedented challenge to the requirement of Greek and Latin in the schools is as important as the fact that it was roundly defeated. The first fact signifies the rise of liberalism, an ideology which emphasized the differences between past and present, while the second fact reflects its inability to displace classical republicanism during the founders' lifetime. Similarly, the intimations of ambivalence among even the staunchest supporters of the classics presaged the ultimate victory of liberalism. The transition from classical republicanism to liberalism was an evolution, not a revolution. It proceeded in fits and starts, sometimes taking two backward steps for every lurch forward.

Conclusion

It is clear that the classics exerted a formative influence upon the founders. Classical ideas provided the basis for their theories of government form, social responsibility, human nature, and virtue. The authors of the classical canon offered the founders companionship, solace, and the models and antimodels which gave them a sense of identity and purpose. The classics facilitated communication by furnishing a common set of symbols, knowledge, and ideas, a literature select enough to provide common ground, yet rich enough to address a wide range of human problems from a variety of perspectives. Although it is true that the founders' unique concerns helped shape their interpretation of the classics, it is equally true that the classical themes which pervaded their world helped identify and define those concerns.

Above all, the classics gave the founders the courage to face the great challenges of their time. During the Revolutionary era, the classics provided an indispensable illusion of precedent for actions that were essentially unprecedented. In 1775 John Adams had been able to write regarding the popular sovereignty theory which underlay American resistance to British measures: "These are what are called revolution-principles. They are the principles of Aristotle and Plato, of Livy and Cicero, of Sidney, Harrington, and Lock.—The principles of nature and eternal reason." In an age in which rebellion was considered an act of the darkest villainy, and rebels were summarily hanged, ancient history (interwoven with British Whig and American colonial history) enabled the conservative American revolutionaries to argue that they were preserving past liberties rather than presumptuously tinkering with the natural order. Classical republican ideology allowed them to cast George III as Nero or Caligula, George Washington and Thomas Jefferson as Cato and Cic-

ero—in other words, to portray the king as the real rebel, the violator of
that natural law which lawful patriots would die to defend. Without this
illusion of precedent it is unlikely that the founders could have persuaded
themselves and many other Americans to rebel against the mother country. The American Revolution was a paradox: a revolution fueled by
tradition.[1]

The success of the Revolution raised other unprecedented questions:
what form should the new federal government take, and how much
power should it possess? The Federalists again turned to the classics for
answers. In seeking to emulate Sparta and Rome, two republics possessing dubious reputations for mixed government, the founders created
something entirely new, a government truly mixed, though not by class.
Furthermore, they strengthened the federal government in an effort to
avoid the fate of the ancient Greek confederacies, at least one of which
had never really operated as a federal system. Again, old myths served as
the essential catalysts for the creation of a new reality.

The most remarkable aspect of the debates surrounding the drafting
and ratification of the U.S. Constitution was not the Federalists' narrow
victory over the Antifederalists, but the classicists' rout of the anticlassicists. The classical tidal wave carried all before it. When Benjamin
Franklin, annoyed by the plethora of classical allusions at the Constitutional Convention, suggested daily prayer as an alternative (enlightenment from God rather than from the ancients), the response was an embarrassed silence and a hasty adjournment. The resolution died a silent
death, and the next day, the delegates were locked in classical combat
once again. Benjamin Randall's claim, at the Massachusetts ratifying convention, that "the quoting of ancient history was no more to the purpose
than to tell how our forefathers dug clams at Plymouth," merely incited
James Bowdoin to lecture on the Roman decemvirate. Henry Abbot's
sarcastic response to classical allusions at the North Carolina ratifying
convention, "Some are desirous to know how and by whom they are to
swear, since no religious tests are required, by Jupiter, Juno, Minerva,
Proserpina, or Pluto," met with cold silence.[2]

The ancients were invoked at every level of debate—at the Constitutional Convention and at state ratifying conventions, concerning general
political theory and regarding specific clauses of the Constitution—by
Federalists and by Antifederalists. Indeed, the Antifederalists put themselves at a disadvantage by playing the classical game. They might have
noted that all the classical historians and their modern disciples, then

practically the sole source of knowledge about ancient history, had been aristocrats, and might have thus dismissed "ancient history" as elitist. Or they might have argued consistently what they only infrequently suggested—that classical analogies were inapplicable to the American context. Instead, because of their own reverence for the classics and because of the lack of any opposing tradition, they played the game, even arguing defensively that their classicists were as good as the opposition's. As a result, the deck was stacked against them. It was much easier for John Adams to find a thousand quotations and historical examples from the ancients in support of mixed government than for any Antifederalist to find even one endorsing simple democracy. The Antifederalists attempted to argue that they were more closely aligned with the ancients on the other great issue facing the nation: the federal government's relationship to the states. They cited Montesquieu and classical sources in support of their contention that republics must remain small in order to remain republics and claimed that a loose confederacy of thirteen small republics best achieved that purpose. But, as Alexander Hamilton noted, and as all could clearly see, the ancients would have been as appalled by a republic the size of New York as by one the extent of the United States. On the question of the size of republics, neither side was classical; both emphasized the innovation of representation.[3]

On the two great issues facing the United States in 1787 and 1788 the Antifederalists did not have a classical leg to stand on. There was no tradition of representative democracy to which they could appeal, and direct democracies, like Athens, bore the stigma of instability, violence, corruption, and injustice which the ancient historians and political theorists had so brilliantly fastened upon them. So vivid, in particular, was Thucydides' description of the Athenian mobs during the Peloponnesian War, in what was considered the definitive history of Athens, that even many friends of democracy in America avoided using the word. Like the advocates of mixed government, they used the word "republic" and emphasized the stability fostered by representation. The unwillingness of the Antifederalists to shatter classical icons, to insist upon different rules of engagement, left them with motley and inferior fragments of rhetorical ammunition and thus helped to ensure their defeat.

Such a view conflicts, of course, with Gordon Wood's famous and influential judgment that the ratification of the Constitution represented the "end of classical politics." Though skillfully demonstrating the framers' allegiance to mixed government theory, Wood emphasizes that

the theory had become so unpopular by the time the Constitution issued from the convention that they were compelled to defend the document on very different grounds. According to Wood, in their public pronouncements, as distinct from their private correspondence or their speeches behind the closed doors of the Constitutional Convention, the framers defended the presidency and the Senate as perfectly democratic institutions, intended as mere precautions against abuse of power by the House of Representatives. Sometimes James Madison and other Federalists opportunistically defended the Senate as the representative of small states, though they had staunchly opposed equal representation for the states for most of the convention and had only reluctantly accepted the "Great Compromise" in its final days. Wood explains:

> The Constitution was intrinsically an aristocratic document, designed to check the democratic tendencies of the period . . . [Yet] out-of-doors few Federalists dared to ascribe any sort of aristocratic character to the Senate . . . There is something decidedly disingenuous about the democratic radicalism of their arguments. In effect, they appropriated and exploited the language that more rightfully belonged to their opponents . . . Actually, given the nature and pressures of American society in 1787, the Federalists had little choice in the matter. For they were not detached intellectuals free from the constraints of power and the demands of the electorate; they were public officials and social leaders fully immersed in the currents of American politics—a politics that would no longer permit the members of an elite to talk to each other. Because of the increasing emergence of a broader audience, the Federalists could not ignore George Mason's warning that the genius of the American people was in favor of democracy.

According to Wood, John Adams' *Defence of the U.S. Constitutions* was outdated when it appeared in 1787 not so much because Adams misread the intentions of the framers as because he refused to employ the new democratic rhetoric: "Perhaps he was too honest, too much the scientist and too little the politician . . . He refused to pervert the meaning of language, and he could not deny or disguise, without being untrue to everything he felt within himself, the oligarchic nature of American politics." In his most recent book Wood reiterates: "The Constitution, the new federal government, and the development of independent judiciaries and judicial review were certainly meant to temper majoritarianism."[4]

Wood has certainly captured a crucial development in the evolution of American political thought. The wave of egalitarianism produced by

the American Revolution did indeed eventually overwhelm mixed government theory (though the theory's core conviction, the need to balance society's interests, remained). A significant and growing number of
Americans were beginning to abandon mixed government theory for a
democratic bicameralism which reinterpreted state and national execu-
tives and senates as representatives of the majority, a development all the
more remarkable for its lack of plausibility. If the framers of the Constitution had intended that the president and the Senate be as representative
of the majority as the House of Representatives, why had they insulated
these officials from majority pressures through indirect election and
lengthy terms? Antifederalists certainly understood the real reasoning behind the Constitution. Yet by the antebellum period most Americans
had reinterpreted the Constitution as a democratic document.

But Wood exaggerates the popularity of the new, democratic ideology in 1787 and 1788. His claim that the Federalists refused to embrace
mixed government theory publicly simply does not hold. John Adams,
John Dickinson, Alexander Hamilton, James Madison, Noah Webster,
and numerous other Federalists frequently and eloquently cited mixed
government theory in defense of the Constitution in their public ad-
dresses and pamphlets. When some denied that the Senate would be another House of Lords, they meant that it would house a natural aristocracy of the talented and virtuous, rather than the kind of unworthy
aristocracy of birth that dominated Britain's upper house. A rejection of
the House of Lords, or even of "aristocracy" itself (depending on the
definition), was not equivalent to a repudiation of mixed government
theory. Federalists justly prided themselves on the ingenuity they had
demonstrated in adapting mixed government theory to the American
context. Even some Antifederalists publicly endorsed mixed government
theory, simply denying that the Constitution had created one.

It is true that few Federalists were willing to criticize publicly the vices
of the majority with the vehemence of a John Adams. But, as Wood
himself notes, even Adams suffered no immediate penalty for his famous
and passionate defense of the state and federal constitutions on mixed
government grounds. While the Antifederalists and even a few supporters
of the Constitution (most of whom later joined the Republican
Party) criticized Adams, numerous Federalists of various economic
classes agreed with Adams' *Defence of the U.S. Constitutions*. As Benjamin
Rush later noted: "The book and the new federal Constitution became
linked in men's thinking." James Madison's principal criticism of the

work was that "men of learning find nothing new in it." If Adams' widely read book and its arguments had been so peculiar and frightening to most Americans in the late 1780s and the 1790s, how could he have won the vice-presidency and presidency in these years? As Wood himself states, both the Federalists and Antifederalists noted, the former with approval, the latter with disgust, that many ordinary Americans still maintained a deference for the educated classes and a firm adherence to older and better-established modes of thought. If this had not been so, the Federalist Party could not have maintained its preeminence during the 1790s. Not until the first few decades of the nineteenth century, at the earliest, did the ideology of representative democracy completely displace that of mixed government theory.[5]

It is not surprising that even those founders friendly to representative democracy were unwilling to adopt Athenian democracy as their model. The founders were not exceptionalists, but followers of the one classical canon which comprehended the whole western world. Even the French revolutionaries of the 1790s were unwilling to embrace Athenian democracy. Claiming Plutarch as their idol, most of the French republicans proclaimed the merits of Solon and Lycurgus, not Pericles. Madame Roland often spoke of herself as Cato's wife, remarked that she ought to have been a Roman or a Spartan woman, and thought that French theater should devote itself to *Catiline,* The *Death of Caesar,* and other neo-Roman plays. Having read Plutarch, Tacitus, and Cicero, Charlotte Corday believed that she acted as a Roman in assassinating Marat. Imprisoned Girondists contemplated the martyrdoms of Phocion and Cato. The French republicans cast themselves in the role of Cicero, their enemies in the role of Catiline, and the new citizen-army in France as the Roman republican army. On the rare occasions when radicals spoke of democracy, people shuddered. It was long remembered that the awful word was once heard on the lips of Robespierre. Napoleon adopted the title of "First Consul" (not "Strategos") and wisely maintained the republican forms, in imitation of Augustus. No wonder that the far more conservative Antifederalists could not accept Athens as a model and, consequently, were left without one.[6]

In the early national period Republicans confronted yet another unprecedented problem: how to justify the transition from the mixed government created by the Constitution to a representative democracy. They did so by attributing the success of ancient republics to their agricultural societies, rather than to their mixed systems. It was as if pure

classical republicanism died in the 1790s, and its heirs divided the intellectual legacy. The Federalists retained custody of mixed government
theory, while the Republicans kept the classical pastoralism. Each party
became half-classical, half-liberal: the Federalists remained aristocratic
but embraced the new industry; the Republicans remained pastoral but
embraced the new democracy. Each had reason to fear that the republic
was degenerating. John Adams, Alexander Hamilton, and other Federalists feared the spread of democracy. Thomas Jefferson, Samuel Adams,
Benjamin Rush, and other Republicans feared the growth of industry.
Samuel Adams' hope that the Revolutionary War would produce a
"Christian Sparta" proved as tragically ill-founded as Rush's dream that
the War of 1812 would restore frugality, patriotism, and other classical
values to the young nation. In fact both wars had the opposite effect,
increasing American manufacturing. But most founders mingled their
fears with hope.[7]

The Republican leaders who endorsed the new laissez-faire economics preferred Adam Smith's pro-agricultural version to David Ricardo's
pro-industrial brand. They supported free trade largely in order to preserve the agricultural way of life, frequently citing Greek and Roman
pastoral poets on its moral and political benefits and Roman historians on
the evils of the luxury produced by commerce. (The mere fact that these
leaders supported innovations in agricultural techniques does not mean,
as Joyce Appleby would have it, that they rejected pastoralism. Republican leaders clearly recognized that the most essential elements of agricultural life transcended innovation. Jefferson often justified technological
innovations on the quintessentially classical grounds that they left the
farmer more time for contemplation and public service.) Conversely, the
Federalist leaders who endorsed government intervention in the economy hoped to use a strengthened federal government to protect the
rights of the natural aristocracy from propertyless mobs. Both parties
continued to urge devotion to public service and to denounce selfishness.[8]

John T. Agresto misses the point when he notes that, in practice,
"Americans clearly loved profit more than frugality, comfort more than
sacrifice, and liberty more than duty." Who doesn't, in practice? But the
fact that the founders failed to live up to their classical ideals does not
mean that they lacked them. Though inherently unattainable, the ideals
to which a society lays claim are important because they determine the
way in which the society views the world, and because they occasionally

triumph over narrow self-interest. The founders' occasional criticism, late in life, of what they sometimes considered a society degenerating as a result of the accumulation of wealth, reveals an understandable frustration with their own failure to build the classical utopia. The very criticism reveals that both their ideals and its corresponding cosmology remained intact. Even had the founders felt the need to do so, they could not have completely reshaped their own minds. They could not have removed the imprint left by their conditioning in the classics.[9]

Yet the founders betrayed a touch of ambivalence toward classical republicanism. They often spoke confidently of social progress. They sometimes celebrated the unprecedented prosperity around them. They even occasionally questioned the validity of analogies between ancient and contemporary societies. One must take seriously Paul Rahe's observation that ancient societies were fundamentally different from modern societies. Citizens of Greece and Rome led far richer public lives than we, who entrust to our representatives the power to deliberate for us, but led far poorer private lives than we, who possess an almost infinite variety of physical comforts and diversions. As a result, while the ancients granted politics primacy, defining humans as rational and deliberative animals and subordinating private to public concerns, we grant our private lives primacy, defining humans as acquisitive beings and identifying the protection of life, liberty, and property as the chief purpose of government. Perhaps this distinction corroborates, at least in part, Gordon Wood's contention that the founders possessed a greater devotion to classical republicanism than did most other Americans of the early republic. As the nation's political class, the founders could more easily approach the classical ideal which the modern republic denies most of its citizens. They could experience firsthand the excitement of deliberation upon crucial questions, the satisfaction of significant legislative achievements, and the enjoyment of fame secured by thinking and speaking well for important causes. Had Aristotle wanted to paint a portrait of man as a political animal, he could have found a large number of suitable models in the legislative halls of the early American republic. Yet the founders had neither the inclination nor the ability to isolate themselves from an increasingly egalitarian and commercial society. Hence they exhibited divided minds. Only by ignoring or slighting half of the historical evidence and by oversimplifying the process of human thought can historians of the founders deny either their classical republicanism or their liberalism.[10]

During the antebellum period, classical republicanism was weakened by the rise of mass political parties, which introduced a new rhetorical style targeted at the uneducated voter; by the advent of romanticism, which emphasized enjoyment of the present over study of the past and stressed nature over books as the source of enlightenment; by the revivalism of the Second Great Awakening, which emphasized emotional attachment to Christianity over the rationalism of classical philosophy and which fueled prudish objections to classical works; and by the Industrial Revolution, which increased the gap between ancient and modern lifestyles, making the classics seem less relevant to contemporary concerns. Ironically, the founders themselves were perhaps most responsible for this decline of classical influence. Antebellum Americans were able to assert a greater degree of independence from the classics because the founders had given them something that they themselves had lacked: a set of American national heroes to replace the Greek and Roman idols. In seeking to match the achievements of Cato and Cicero, the founders inadvertently pushed them from the center of the American pantheon and assumed their positions. As Edwin A. Miles noted: "When they discovered their own history, Americans simply talked less of Thermopylae and Marathon, more of Lexington and Concord; less of Cato and Cicero, more of Washington and Jefferson." But the Roman republicans were not dashed from their pedestals; they retained secondary positions. Just as the Greeks and Romans had distinguished between primary and secondary gods, antebellum Americans differentiated the semidivine founders from their more flawed classical heroes. Indeed, the new mythology constructed around the founders was itself tinged with classical themes.[11]

Because antebellum Americans' idealization of the founders extended to their handiwork, the Constitution, it changed the nature of American political debate in a manner which lessened the utility of the classics. Not surprisingly, the effect of this shift was most evident in the career of James Madison, the last surviving founder. In the 1780s Madison had spent three years compiling evidence that the ancient Greek confederacies had fallen because of decentralization, evidence which he had wielded with great effect at the Constitutional Convention and in the *Federalist* essays. But by the 1830s, when the Nullification Crisis in South Carolina reawakened his fear of national disintegration, Madison had so completely abandoned the classics that he made no mention of the confederacies. Madison understood that American political debate was no longer a search for truth, with the history of nations as the guide, but a search for legitimacy, with the hallowed Constitution as the authority. As the sole surviving founder, Madison's role had shifted from that of a scholar, whose task was to distill the wisdom of the ancients, to that of a high priest, whose duty was to recount the intent of the demigods. Ironically, this Constitution of 1787, drafted by the most ardently rationalist statesmen in human history, became the focus of the same passionate devotion which the Greeks had reserved for the *patrioi nomoi,* the Romans for the *mos maiorum,* "the ways of our fathers."[12]

But it would be a mistake to banish classical republicanism entirely from the antebellum period, and even its decline hardly left liberalism an open field. Antebellum southerners seized upon Athens, now rehabilitated by pro-democratic historians, as a model society. Southern social critics attributed the greatness of the polis to slavery, which had presumably reinforced in citizens' minds the importance of liberty and equality within their own ranks and had provided them the leisure to produce astonishing literary and artistic works. Although the founders had been horrified by the "democratic excesses" of the Athenian political system and, consequently, had ignored the connection between democracy and the great intellectual achievements of Athens, southern antebellum social critics embraced both by ascribing both to slavery. It is ironic that when Athens finally achieved the popularity it had been denied for thousands of years because of its political egalitarianism, that popularity (at least in the South) was based upon its social inequalities. Furthermore, while liberalism benefited from a moderate decline in classical republicanism during the antebellum period, the evangelical Christianity encouraged by the Second Great Awakening, however liberalized in form, established a sense of social cohesion which tempered liberalism's individualist extremes. Perhaps Aristotle was right. Humans are, at least in part, social animals, who crave a sense of participation in something larger than themselves—though not because they are defined by reason, as Aristotle alleged, but because they are defined by powerful emotional needs. If so, liberalism can never be fully victorious, even in those nations most susceptible to its appeal.[13]

In our own age, when educational reform is again a salient issue, it is important to learn what we can from the system of education which produced the founders. Certainly, a case may be made for an expanded role for the classics in our educational system. Henry Steele Commager was probably correct when he cited study of the classics as one of five reasons Revolutionary Virginia produced so many political prodigies in a single generation. The classics taught a love of liberty, an understanding of human motivation, an appreciation for the written and spoken word, a respect for order, symmetry, and harmony, and a sense of belonging to an ancient and noble tradition. The latter feeling brought purpose to the founders' lives and gave them a sense of kinship with the world. Although other forms of literature may perform the same functions, few do it so well. One can do worse than to learn about poetry from Homer and Virgil, drama from Aeschylus, Sophocles, and Euripides, philosophy from Plato, politics from Aristotle, rhetoric from Demosthenes and Cicero, and history from Thucydides and Tacitus—all of whom are available in translation.[14]

But the reformers were correct when they contended that the learning of the Greek and Latin languages should not be mandatory for all students, since it greatly reduces the amount of material which can be read. Rather, students should read the classics in the best modern translations. Furthermore, the unimaginative techniques of rote memorization employed in the eighteenth century, techniques emphasizing fine grammatical points over the beauty and substance of the works, too often robbed the classics of their meaning and fostered frustration in those students who cared most about them. The masterpieces of Greek and Roman literature were presented as little more than a series of pegs on which to hang Cheever's grammatical rules. Surely, modern teachers of the classics should (and generally do) employ more enlightened pedagogical methods.

Undoubtedly we can also learn much from the founders' appreciation for history. Patrick Henry expressed a common view when he stated: "I have but one lamp by which my feet are guided, and that is the lamp of experience. I know of no way of judging the future but by the past." At the Constitutional Convention John Dickinson reiterated the point: "Experience must be our only guide. Reason may mislead us." In *The Federalist* Alexander Hamilton called history "the least fallible guide of human opinions," and Madison termed it "the oracle of truth," adding that "where its responses are unequivocal they ought to be considered conclusive and sacred." Immersion in the best works of ancient history made the founders shrewd judges of political and social affairs, contributing to success, against tremendous odds, in their quest for independence and a durable constitution. As Colyer Meriwether put it: "They knew how to build an argument, to construct a logical fortress; that been their pastime since youth. They could marshal words, they could explore the past . . . They had been doing that for years." The founders' constant use of their classical tools strengthened their logical and rhetorical faculties.[15]

Forrest McDonald has suggested that the founders had a much more highly developed sense of history than modern Americans because the latter believe that the dramatic technological changes of this century have created an impassable gulf between the past and the present. There is some merit to McDonald's assertion, although even in the eighteenth century some observers argued that the changes wrought by the Scientific and Commercial Revolutions had created a similar gulf. (Likewise, as early as the thirteenth century Machiavelli complained that the founders of republics and kingdoms often neglected history because they considered their countrymen too "different from what they were in ancient times" to warrant analogy.) David M. Kennedy has shown the illogic of dismissing history in such a fashion, contending that even if the past is so different from the present that it cannot enlighten it (a claim which he doubts), such a claim can be authenticated only through a thorough knowledge of the past.[16]

If studied critically, the shrewd ancients who founded western civilization can still teach us a great deal. While the oppressive thought systems of the world (such as sexism, ethnocentrism, class bigotry, and absolutism) are by no means uniquely classical (racism is not classical at all), the principal ideological tools which have been used to combat them (the theories of popular sovereignty, natural law, and mixed government) are all classical in origin. Even the characteristic of the classics most troublesome to modern Americans, their antidemocratic tenor, can serve as a reminder of the need to reconcile minority rights with majority rule.

Notes

Introduction

1. Carl Becker in Becker, J. M. Clark, William E. Dodd, eds., *The Spirit of 1776 and Other Essays* (Washington, D.C.: Robert Brookings Graduate School of Economics and Government, 1927), pp. 12–13; Merle Curti, *The Growth of American Thought* (New York: Harper and Brothers, 1943), p. 29; C. Dewitt Hardy and Richard Hofstadter, *The Development and Scope of Higher Education in the United States* (New York: Columbia University Press, 1952), p. 10; Howard Mumford Jones, *O Strange New World: American Culture, The Formative Years* (New York: Viking Press, 1952), p. 251; Henry Steele Commager, "Leadership in Eighteenth-Century America and Today," *Daedalus* 90 (Fall 1961):652–673.

2. Clinton Rossiter, *Seedtime of the Republic: The Origin of the American Tradition of Liberty* (New York: Harcourt, Brace, 1953), pp. 356–357; Bernard Bailyn, *The Ideological Origins of the American Revolution,* 2d ed. (Cambridge, Mass.: Harvard University Press, 1992), pp. 23–27, 44; Charles F. Mullett, "Classical Influences on the American Revolution," *Classical Journal* 35 (November 1939):92–104.

3. Gordon S. Wood, *The Creation of the American Republic,* 1776–1787 (Chapel Hill: University of North Carolina Press, 1969), pp. 47, 606; Joyce O. Appleby, *Capitalism and a New Social Order: The Republican Vision of the 1790s* (New York: New York University Press, 1984), pp. 8–23, 46; Appleby, *Liberalism and Republicanism in the Historical Imagination* (Cambridge, Mass.: Harvard University Press, 1992), pp. 183–184, 217, 223, 257–258, 334–335.

4. Meyer Reinhold, *Classica Americana: The Greek and Roman Heritage in the United States* (Detroit: Wayne State University Press, 1984), p. 108. Collections of essays by classicists include: Richard M. Gummere, *The American Colonial Mind and the Classical Tradition: Essays in Comparative Culture* (Cambridge, Mass.: Harvard University Press, 1963); Susan Ford Wiltshire, ed., *The Usefulness of Classical Learning in the Eighteenth Century* (Washington, D.C.: American Philo-

logical Association, 1975); John W. Eadie, ed., *Classical Traditions in Early America* (Ann Arbor: Center for the Coordination of Ancient and Modern Studies, 1976).

5. J. G. A. Pocock, *The Machiavellian Moment: Florentine Political Thought and the Atlantic Political Tradition* (Princeton: Princeton University Press, 1975), pp. ix, 529–533; "Virtue and Commerce in the Eighteenth Century," *Journal of Interdisciplinary History* 3 (Summer 1972):120, 133–134; Lance Banning, *The Jeffersonian Persuasion: Evolution of a Party Ideology* (Ithaca: Cornell University Press, 1978), pp. 13–18, 92–93, 273–274; Drew R. McCoy, *The Elusive Republic: Political Economy in Jeffersonian America* (Chapel Hill: University of North Carolina Press, 1980), pp. 189–195, 253.

6. Lance Banning, "Jeffersonian Ideology Revisited: Liberal and Classical Ideas in the New American Republic," *William and Mary Quarterly,* 3d ser., 43 (January 1986):4; Michael Lienesch, *New Order of the Ages: Time, the Constitution, and the Making of Modern American Political Thought* (Princeton: Princeton University Press, 1988), p. 7; Gordon S. Wood, *The Radicalism of the American Revolution* (New York: Alfred A. Knopf, 1992), pp. 233, 265, 335, 365–369; Paul A. Rahe, *Republics, Ancient and Modern: Classical Republicanism and the American Revolution* (Chapel Hill: University of North Carolina Press, 1992), p. x.

I. The Classical Conditioning of the Founders

1. Robert Middlekauff, *Ancients and Axioms: Secondary Education in Eighteenth-Century New England* (New Haven: Yale University Press, 1963), pp. 76–77. For Webster's statement see Frederick Rudolph, ed., *Essays on Education in the Early Republic* (Cambridge, Mass.: Harvard University Press, 1965), "On the Education of Youth in America, 1790," p. 65. For reference to Massachusetts' law regarding the maintenance of grammar schools see Sheldon D. Cohen, *A History of Colonial Education, 1607–1776* (New York: John Wiley and Sons, 1974), p. 83.

2. Middlekauff, *Ancients and Axioms,* pp. 80–90, 154, 164; Richard M. Gummere, *The American Colonial Mind and the Classical Tradition: Essays in Comparative Culture* (Cambridge, Mass.: Harvard University Press, 1963), p. 58.

3. Wilson Smith, ed., *Theories of Education in Early America, 1655–1819* (New York: Bobbs-Merrill, 1973), "John Clarke's Classical Program of Studies, 1730," pp. 67–71, 74–76, 88, 93–96. For reference to the divinity backgrounds of many masters and the turnover which resulted see James Axtell, *The School upon a Hill: Education and Society in Colonial New England* (New Haven: Yale University Press, 1974), pp. 187–188. On the overloading of classes and the burdensome duties of schoolmasters see Jean S. Straub, "Teaching in the Friends' Latin School of Philadelphia in the Eighteenth Century," *Pennsylvania Magazine of History and Biography* 91 (Winter 1976):438, 448–449.

4. Patrick Critwell, "The Eighteenth Century: A Classical Age?" *Arion* 7 (Spring 1968):117–118.

5. Pauline Holmes, *A Tercentenary History of the Boston Latin School, 1635–1935* (1935; reprint, Westport, Conn.: Greenwood Press, 1970), pp. 80, 83; Axtel, *The School upon a Hill*, p. 196; Richard Beale Davis, *Intellectual Life in Jefferson's Virginia, 1790–1830* (Chapel Hill: University of North Carolina Press, 1964), p. 40.

6. Axtell, *The School upon a Hill*, pp. 186–187.

7. James McLachlan, "Classical Names, American Identities," in John W. Eadie, ed., *Classical Traditions in Early America* (Ann Arbor: Center for the Co-ordination of Ancient and Modern Studies, 1976), p. 84; Edwin A. Miles, "The Old South and the Classical World," *North Carolina Historical Review* 48 (1971):262.

8. Holmes, *A Tercentenary History of the Boston Latin School*, pp. 61, 71.

9. Silvio A. Bedini, *Thomas Jefferson: Statesman of Science* (New York: Macmillan, 1990), p. 16; Irving Brant, *James Madison* (New York: Bobbs-Merrill, 1941–1961), vol. 1, pp. 64–65; Robert A. Rutland et al., eds., *The Papers of James Madison* (Chicago: University of Chicago Press, 1962–1977; Charlottesville: University Press of Virginia, 1977–), Commonplace Book, 1759–1772, vol. 1, p. 5; Merrill D. Peterson, *James Madison: A Biography in His Own Words* (New York: Harper and Row, 1974), pp. 16, 18; Davis, *Intellectual Life in Jefferson's Virginia*, p. 36.

10. Lawrence A. Cremin, *American Education: The Colonial Experience, 1607–1783* (New York: Harper and Row, 1970), pp. 506–509; Theodore Sizer, ed., *The Autobiography of Colonel John Trumbull, Patriot Artist, 1756–1843* (New Haven: Yale University Press, 1953), pp. 5, 9–10.

11. Gummere, *American Colonial Mind*, pp. 56–57; Gilbert Chinard, *Honest John Adams* (Boston: Little, Brown, 1933), pp. 11–12; Richard Hofstadter and Wilson Smith, eds., *American Higher Education: A Documentary History* (Chicago: University of Chicago Press, 1961), "Laws and Orders of King's College, 1755," vol. 1, p. 117; James Thomas Flexner, *The Young Hamilton: A Biography* (Boston: Little, Brown, 1978), pp. 52–60; Forrest McDonald, *Alexander Hamilton: A Biography* (New York: W. W. Norton, 1979), pp. 11–12.

12. Hofstadter and Smith, *American Higher Education*, "Laws and Orders of King's College, 1755," vol. 1, p. 120; "John Witherspoon's Account of the College of New Jersey, 1772," ibid., p. 141; Gummere, *American Colonial Mind*, pp. 55, 64, 72, 75; Martha W. Hiden, "Education and the Classics in the Life of Colonial Virginia," *Virginia Magazine of History and Biography* 49 (January 1941):26; Robert Middlekauff, "A Persistent Tradition: The Classical Curriculum in Eighteenth-Century New England," *William and Mary Quarterly*, 3d ser., 18 (January 1961):65.

13. Howard Mumford Jones, *Revolution and Romanticism* (Cambridge, Mass.:

Harvard University Press, 1974), pp. 121–123, 343. For reference to the persistence of the medieval methodology see Middlekauff, "A Persistent Tradition," p. 56. On the medieval origins of the system and the methods, authors, hours, discipline, and private status of English grammar schools see Cohen, *A History of Colonial Education,* pp. 11, 22–24.

14. Chinard, *Honest John Adams,* pp. 13–14, 19; Charles Francis Adams, ed., *The Works of John Adams* (Boston: Little, Brown, 1850–1856), Diary, May 31, 1760, vol. 2, p. 86; L. H. Butterfield, ed., *The Diary and Autobiography of John Adams* (Cambridge, Mass.: Harvard University Press, 1961), Autobiography, 1802, vol. 3, p. 262; Robert J. Taylor, ed., *The Papers of John Adams* (Cambridge, Mass.: Harvard University Press, 1977–), vol. 1, p. 7; Douglas Adair and John A. Schutz, eds., *The Spur of Fame: Dialogues of John Adams and Benjamin Rush, 1805–1813* (San Marino, Calif.: Huntington Library, 1966), Adams to Rush, December 4, 1805, p. 44.

15. Hofstadter and Smith, *American Higher Education,* "Julian M. Sturtevant on the Quality of Teaching at Yale in the 1820s," vol. 1, p. 275.

16. Bedini, *Thomas Jefferson,* pp. 24–25, 29, 33; Jurgen Herbst, "The American Revolution and the American University," *Perspectives in American History* 10 (1976):279–354; Douglas L. Wilson, "What Jefferson and Lincoln Read," *The Atlantic* 267 (January 1991):54.

17. Hofstadter and Smith, *American Higher Education,* "Robert Finley on National Uniformity in Textbooks, 1815," vol. 1, pp. 220–221.

18. McLachlan, "Classical Names, American Identities," pp. 87–91; James McLachlan, "The Choice of Hercules," in Lawrence Stone, ed., *The University in Society* (Princeton: Princeton University Press, 1974), vol. 2, pp. 474, 478; Meyer Reinhold, *Classica Americana: The Greek and Roman Heritage in the United States* (Detroit: Wayne State University Press, 1984), p. 154.

19. John E. Pomfret, "Student Interests at Brown University, 1789–1790," *New England Quarterly* 5 (January 1932):138–140, 145.

20. Hofstadter and Smith, *American Higher Education,* "John Witherspoon's Account of the College of New Jersey, 1772," vol. 1, p. 142; Gummere, *American Colonial Mind,* p. 69; Paul Lewis, *The Grand Incendiary: A Biography of Samuel Adams* (New York: Dial Press, 1973), p. 10.

21. Pomfret, "Student Interests at Brown University," p. 145; Edwin A. Miles, "The Young American Nation and the Classical World," *Journal of the History of Ideas* 35 (April–June 1974):265n25.

22. Stanley E. Godbold and Robert H. Woody, *Christopher Gadsden and the American Revolution* (Knoxville: University of Tennessee Press, 1982), p. 7; Geoffrey Seed, *James Wilson* (Milkwood, N.Y.: KTO Press, 1978), pp. 3–4; Martin R. Zahniser, *Charles Cotesworth Pinckney: Founding Father* (Chapel Hill: University of North Carolina Press, 1967), pp. 12–15.

23. Taylor, *Papers of John Adams,* vol. 1, p. 7; Butterfield, *Diary and Autobiography of John Adams,* Diary, April 1778, vol. 4, p. 61; Adams, *Works of John*

Adams, Adams to Francis Dana, March 15, 1782, vol. 7, p. 544; Lester J. Cappon, ed., *The Adams-Jefferson Letters: The Complete Correspondence between Thomas Jefferson and Abigail and John Adams* (Chapel Hill: University of North Carolina Press, 1959), John Adams to Jefferson, February 3, 1812, vol. 2, p. 295.

24. Rutland et al., *Papers of James Madison,* Commonplace Book, 1759–1772, vol. 1, pp. 5–6, 17–18.

25. Ibid., pp. 21–22.

26. Ibid., "A Brief System of Logick," 1766–1772, pp. 35, 37, 39–41.

27. Harold C. Syrett, ed., *The Papers of Alexander Hamilton* (New York: Columbia University Press, 1961–1979), Pay Book, 1777, vol. 1, pp. 390–407; Flexner, *Young Hamilton,* p. 47.

28. Douglas L. Wilson, ed., *Jefferson's Literary Commonplace Book* (Princeton: Princeton University Press, 1989), pp. 7, 24–55, 106–110, 113, 115–116, 198–199; Gilbert Chinard, ed., *The Commonplace Book of Thomas Jefferson: A Repertory of His Ideas on Government* (Baltimore: Johns Hopkins Press, 1926).

29. Louis B. Wright, "Thomas Jefferson and the Classics," *Proceedings of the American Philosophical Society* 87 (1943–44):231; Bedini, *Thomas Jefferson,* p. 440; Julian P. Boyd, ed., *The Papers of Thomas Jefferson* (Princeton: Princeton University Press, 1950–), Jefferson to Thomas Mann Randolph, February 28, 1788, vol. 12, p. 632; Jefferson to John Pemberton, July 16, 1791, vol. 20, p. 635; Karl Lehmann, *Thomas Jefferson: American Humanist* (Chicago: University of Chicago Press, 1964), pp. 34, 75; Merrill D. Peterson, *Thomas Jefferson and the New Nation: A Biography* (New York: Oxford University Press, 1970), p. 927; Albert Ellery Bergh and Andrew A. Lipscomb, eds., *The Writings of Thomas Jefferson* (Washington, D.C.: Thomas Jefferson Memorial Association, 1903), Jefferson to Samuel H. Smith, September 21, 1814, vol. 14, p. 193; Dickinson W. Adams, ed., *Jefferson's Extracts from the Gospel* (Princeton: Princeton University Press, 1983), Jefferson to William Short, October 31, 1819, p. 389.

30. Cappon, *Adams-Jefferson Letters,* John Adams to Jefferson, July 9, 1813, vol. 2, p. 350; Jefferson to John Adams, March 21, 1819, ibid., p. 537–538; September 12, 1821, ibid., pp. 575–576; Bergh and Lipscomb, *Writings of Thomas Jefferson,* Jefferson to David Howell, December 15, 1810, vol. 12, p. 437; Jefferson to Nathaniel Macon, January 12, 1819, vol. 15, p. 179; Jefferson to John Brazier, August 24, 1819, ibid., pp. 208–211; Jefferson to Nathaniel Moore, September 22, 1819, ibid., pp. 216–218; Jefferson to William B. Giles, January 9, 1826, vol. 16, p. 150; "Thoughts on English Prosody," vol. 18, pp. 414–451.

31. Bergh and Lipscomb, *Writings of Thomas Jefferson,* Jefferson to John de Crevecoeur, January 15, 1787, vol. 11, p. 44; Jefferson to Joseph Priestley, January 27, 1800, vol. 10, p. 147; Jefferson to John Waldo, August 16, 1813, vol. 13, pp. 340–341; Jefferson to John Brazier, August 24, 1819, vol. 15, p. 208; "Thoughts on English Prosody," vol. 18, pp. 414–451.

32. Bergh and Lipscomb, *Writings of Thomas Jefferson,* Jefferson to George A. Otis, December 25, 1820, vol. 18, p. 307; Jefferson to John Wayles Eppes, Jan-

uary 17, 1810, vol. 12, p. 343; Jefferson to Abraham Small, May 20, 1814, vol. 14, p. 138; Jefferson to David Harding, April 20, 1824, vol. 16, p. 30; Jefferson to George W. Summers and John B. Garland, February 27, 1822, vol. 15, p. 353; Cappon, *Adams-Jefferson Letters,* Jefferson to John Adams, August 10, 1815, vol. 2, pp. 452–453; May 5, 1817, ibid., p. 513. Jefferson was not concerned only about *ancient* historians composing such speeches: a historian of the American Revolution had recently put words in his and other founders' mouths.

33. Wilson, *Jefferson's Literary Commonplace Book,* p. 71; Bergh and Lipscomb, *Writings of Thomas Jefferson,* Jefferson to John Wayles Eppes, January 17, 1810, vol. 12, p. 343; Jefferson to David Harding, April 20, 1824, vol. 16, p. 30; Gilbert Chinard, "Thomas Jefferson as a Classical Scholar," *Johns Hopkins Alumni Magazine* 18 (1929–30):296; Winfred E. Bernhard, *Fisher Ames: Federalist and Statesman, 1758–1808* (Chapel Hill: University of North Carolina Press, 1965), p. 28; Robert Ernst, *Rufus King: American Federalist* (Chapel Hill: University of North Carolina Press, 1968), p. 20; Davis, *Intellectual Life in Jefferson's Virginia,* p. 367; Charles F. Mullett, "Classical Influences on the American Revolution," *Classical Journal* 35 (November 1939):104.

34. Chinard, *Honest John Adams,* pp. 11–12; L. H. Butterfield, ed., *The Earliest Diary of John Adams* (Cambridge, Mass.: Harvard University Press, 1966), John Adams to Tristram Dalton, October–November 1758, p. 66; Adams, *Works of John Adams,* Diary, January 3, 1759, vol. 2, p. 56; Gummere, *American Colonial Mind,* p. 101; Reinhold, *Classica Americana,* p. 232; L. H. Butterfield, ed., *Letters of Benjamin Rush* (Princeton: Princeton University Press, 1951), Rush to John Adams, December 19, 1812, vol. 2, p. 1170; Adair and Schutz, *Spur of Fame,* John Adams to Benjamin Rush, December 27, 1812, p. 264. On Adams' poor writing style and his loss of Greek see Taylor, *Papers of John Adams,* Adams to James Warren, December 22, 1773, vol. 2, p. 3; Cappon, *Adams-Jefferson Letters,* John Adams to Jefferson, July 9, 1813, vol. 2, p. 350. For reference to his translation of classical authors in the late 1750s and early 1760s see Butterfield, *Diary and Autobiography of John Adams,* Diary, July 26–28, 1756, vol. 1, pp. 37–38; October 5, 1758, ibid., p. 45; Spring 1759, ibid., 94; June 1, 1760, ibid., p. 131; August 19, 1760, ibid., p. 152; October 17, 1761, ibid., p. 221.

35. Reinhold, *Classica Americana,* p. 233; Taylor, *Papers of John Adams,* Committee of the Boston Sons of Liberty to John Wilkes, June 6, 1768, vol. 1, pp. 215–216; Adams to William Tudor, September 29, 1774, vol. 2, pp. 176, 178; Adair and Schutz, *Spur of Fame,* John Adams to Benjamin Rush, April 12, 1807, p. 78; Zoltan Haraszti, *John Adams and the Prophets of Progress* (Cambridge, Mass.: Harvard University Press, 1952), p. 15; Chinard, *Honest John Adams,* p. 11.

36. Robert A. Rutland, ed., *The Papers of George Mason* (Chapel Hill: University of North Carolina Press, 1970), vol. 1, p. cxxvi; George Mason to John

Mason, December 18, 1788, vol. 3, p. 1138; Flexner, *Young Hamilton,* p. 47; William Wirt Henry, ed., *Patrick Henry: Life, Correspondence, and Speeches* (New York: Burt Franklin, 1969), vol. 1, pp. 9–10; Robert Douthat Meade, *Patrick Henry* (Philadelphia: J. B. Lippincott, 1957–1969), vol. 1, p. 57; Milton E. Flower, *John Dickinson: Conservative Revolutionary* (Charlottesville: University Press of Virginia, 1983), pp. 21–22, 271; Paul Leicester Ford, ed., *The Political Writings of John Dickinson, 1764–1774* (1895; reprint, New York: Da Capo Press, 1970), pp. 9, 406; Bernard Bailyn, ed., *Pamphlets of the American Revolution* (Cambridge, Mass.: Harvard University Press, 1965), "Introduction," vol. 1, p. 56; Richard M. Gummere, "The Classical Ancestry of the United States Constitution," *American Quarterly* 14 (Spring 1962): 4; James Madison, *Letters and Other Writings of James Madison* (New York: R. Worthington, 1884), Madison to Buckner Thruston, March 1, 1833, vol. 4, p. 279; Gaillard Hunt, ed., *The Writings of James Madison* (New York: G. P. Putnam's Sons, 1901–1910), Madison to Thomas Cooper, December 26, 1826, vol. 9, pp. 266–267.

37. L. H. Butterfield, ed., *Adams Family Correspondence* (Cambridge, Mass.: Harvard University Press, 1963), vol. 3, p. xii; Adams, *Works of John Adams,* Diary, April 25, 1779, vol. 3, p. 197.

38. Butterfield, *Adams Family Correspondence,* John Adams to John Quincy Adams, March 17, 1780, vol. 3, p. 309; John Adams to Monsieur Perchigny, May 16, 1780, ibid., p. 348; John Adams to John Quincy Adams, December 23, 1780, vol. 4, p. 48; vol. 3, pp. xv, xxxvii.

39. Ibid., John Adams to John Quincy Adams, May 29, 1781, vol. 4, p. 144.

40. Adrienne Koch and William Peden, eds., *The Selected Writings of John and John Quincy Adams* (New York: Alfred A. Knopf, 1946), John Adams to Benjamin Waterhouse, April 24, 1785, p. 72; Adair and Schutz, *Spur of Fame,* John Adams to Benjamin Rush, July 23, 1806, p. 59.

41. Reinhold, *Classica Americana,* pp. 149, 151, 233; Peter Shaw, *The Character of John Adams* (Chapel Hill: University of North Carolina Press, 1976), p. 317; Haraszti, *John Adams and the Prophets of Progress,* p. 16.

42. William Peden, ed., *Notes on the State of Virginia* (Chapel Hill: University of North Carolina Press, 1955), pp. 147–148; Bergh and Lipscomb, *Writings of Thomas Jefferson,* Jefferson to William C. Nicholas, April 2, 1816, vol. 14, p. 452; Smith, *Theories of Education in Early America,* "Thomas Jefferson's Design for His State University, 1818," p. 329; Saul K. Padover, ed., *The Complete Jefferson: Containing His Major Writings, Published and Unpublished, except for His Letters* (New York: Duell, Sloan, and Pearce, 1943), p. 1101; Gummere, *American Colonial Mind,* p. 57; Lehmann, *Thomas Jefferson,* p. 197; Boyd, *Papers of Thomas Jefferson,* Thomas Jefferson to Martha Jefferson, March 28, 1787, vol. 11, p. 251.

43. Henry, *Patrick Henry,* vol. 1, pp. 4, 8; Gummere, *American Colonial Mind,* p. 62; Meade, *Patrick Henry,* vol. 1, pp. 56–57.

44. Godbold and Woody, *Christopher Gadsden,* p. 48.

45. Syrett, *Papers of Alexander Hamilton,* Hamilton to Philip A. Hamilton, December 5, 1791, vol. 9, p. 560; Gummere, *American Colonial Mind,* p. 61; Richard M. Gummere, "The Heritage of the Classics in Colonial North America," *Proceedings of the American Philosophical Society* 99 (January 1955):76; Reinhold, *Classica Americana,* p. 157. It is true that in 1779 Jefferson had proposed eliminating the study of classical languages at the College of William and Mary; but that was only because he felt that students ought to have thoroughly mastered Greek and Latin by the time they entered college. See ibid., p. 124.

46. John C. Fitzpatrick, ed., *The Writings of George Washington* (Washington, D.C.: U.S. Government Printing Office, 1931–1940), Washington to John Didsbury, October 21, 1761, vol. 2, p. 371; Washington to Capel and Osgood Hanbury, July 25, 1969, ibid., pp. 515–517; Washington to Jonathan Boucher, January 2, 1771, vol. 3, pp. 36–37; July 9, 1771, ibid., p. 51.

47. Linda K. Kerber, *Women of the Republic: Intellect and Ideology in Revolutionary America* (Chapel Hill: University of North Carolina Press, 1980), pp. 215, 218.

48. Gummere, *American Colonial Mind,* p. 62; Herbert W. Benario, "The Classics in Southern Higher Education," *Southern Humanities Review* 11 (1977):17; Richard J. Hoffman, "Classics in the Courts of the United States, 1790–1800," *American Journal of Legal History* 22 (January 1978):56; Bergh and Lipscomb, *Writings of Thomas Jefferson,* Autobiography, 1821, vol. 1, p. 167; Richard Barry, *Mr. Rutledge of South Carolina* (New York: Duell, Sloan, 1942), pp. 10–13; Paul MacKendrick, "This Rich Source of Delight: The Classics and the Founding Fathers," *Classical Journal* 72 (Winter 1972–73):103; James Thomas Flexner, *George Washington* (Boston: Little, Brown, 1965–1969), vol. 1, pp. 17, 29, 153.

49. Adams, *Works of John Adams,* April 21, 1778, vol. 3, p. 139; Butterfield, *Adams Family Correspondence,* John Adams to John Quincy Adams, May 18, 1781, vol. 4, p. 117.

II. Symbolism

1. Richard Walsh, ed., *The Writings of Christopher Gadsden, 1746–1805* (Columbia: University of South Carolina Press, 1966), "To Sylvanus," March 28, 1769, p. 76; Paul Lewis, *The Grand Incendiary: A Biography of Samuel Adams* (New York: Dial Press, 1973), pp. 93, 100, 126, 128; John Cary, *Joseph Warren: Physician, Politician, and Patriot* (Urbana: University of Illinois Press, 1961), p. 29n20.

2. Herbert J. Storing, ed., *The Complete Antifederalist,* 7 vols. (Chicago: University of Chicago Press, 1981), vol. 2, pp. 11n3, 110, 358; vol. 3, pp. 58, 65, 199–200; vol. 4, pp. 41, 71, 124, 148, 151, 160n7; vol. 6, p. 16. For reference to "A Plebeian" (Melancthon Smith) see Paul Leicester Ford, ed., *Pamphlets on the*

Constitution of the United States: Published during Its Discussion by the People (1888; reprint, New York: Burt Franklin, 1971), p. 87. For reference to "Cassius" see Forrest McDonald, *Novus Ordo Seclorum* (Lawrence: University Press of Kansas, 1985), p. 68.

3. Ford, *Pamphlets on the Constitution,* pp. 167, 217; Storing, *The Complete Antifederalist,* vol. 2, p. 10. Dickinson had earlier used "Rusticus" in an essay against the British tea tax. See Paul Leicester Ford, ed., *The Political Writings of John Dickinson, 1764–1774* (1895; reprint, New York: Da Capo Press, 1970), "Letter on the Tea Tax," November 1773, p. 463.

4. Linda K. Kerber, *Women of the Republic: Intellect and Ideology in Revolutionary America* (Chapel Hill: University of North Carolina Press, 1980), p. 281; George R. Dangerfield, *Robert R. Livingston of New York, 1746–1813* (New York: Harcourt, Brace, 1960), pp. 260, 272.

5. Harold C. Syrett, ed., *The Papers of Alexander Hamilton* (New York: Columbia University Press, 1961–1979), "A Letter from Phocion to the Considerate Citizens of New York," January 1784, vol. 3, p. 488. True, Hamilton occasionally lapsed into such trite pseudonyms as "Civis," "Amicus," "Pacificus," and "Americanus." See vol. 12, pp. 320, 354; vol. 15, pp. 33, 669. But these were the exceptions, not the rule.

6. Ibid., "Publius Letter I," October 16, 1778, vol. 1, p. 563.

7. Ibid., "Catullus," September 15, 1792, vol. 12, p. 379; "Metellus," October 24, 1792, ibid., p. 613. It is far more likely that Hamilton was referring to Catulus Lutatius, though misspelling his name, than to Catullus the poet.

8. Ibid., "Tully No. I," August 23, 1794, vol. 17, p. 132.

9. Ibid., "The Defence No. I," July 22, 1795, vol. 18, p. 475; Horatius No. II, July 1795, vol. 19, p. 74.

10. Ibid., "The Stand No. I," March 30, 1798, vol. 21, p. 387.

11. Ibid., "For the Evening Post," February 8, 1803, vol. 26, p. 82.

12. Ibid., Hamilton to Rufus King, June 3, 1802, vol. 26, p. 13; Douglass Adair, "A Note on Certain of Hamilton's Pseudonyms," *William and Mary Quarterly,* 3d ser., 12 (April 1955):286–287.

13. Syrett, *Papers of Alexander Hamilton,* Hamilton to Gouverneur Morris, 1792, vol. 11, pp. 545–546; Richard M. Gummere, *The American Colonial Mind and the Classical Tradition: Essays in Comparative Culture* (Cambridge, Mass.: Harvard University Press, 1963), p. 13.

14. Karl Lehmann, *Thomas Jefferson: American Humanist* (Chicago: University of Chicago Press, 1964), p. 172; Martin D. Snyder, "The Icon of Antiquity," in Susan Ford Wiltshire, ed., *The Usefulness of Classical Learning in the Eighteenth Century* (Washington, D.C.: American Philological Association, 1975), p. 33; Albert Ellery Bergh and Andrew A. Lipscomb, eds., *The Writings of Thomas Jefferson* (Washington, D.C.: Thomas Jefferson Memorial Association, 1903), "An Account of the Capitol in Virginia," vol. 17, p. 353; Julian P. Boyd, ed.,

The Papers of Thomas Jefferson (Princeton: Princeton University Press, 1950–), Jefferson to James Madison, September 1, 1785, vol. 8, p. 462; September 20, 1785, ibid., pp. 534–535; Jefferson to Edmund Randolph, September 20, 1785, ibid., pp. 537–538; Jefferson to James Currie, January 28, 1786, vol. 9, p. 240; Jefferson to Madame de Tesse, March 20, 1787, vol. 11, p. 226.

15. For reference to Jefferson's maintenance of the proportion, despite the enlargement of the building, see Bergh and Lipscomb, *Writings of Thomas Jefferson,* "An Account of the Capitol in Virginia," vol. 17, p. 353. On the change from Doric to Ionic columns see Fiske Kimball, *Thomas Jefferson, Architect* (Boston: Riverside Press, 1916), p. 41. For the portico reduction controversy see Merrill D. Peterson, *Thomas Jefferson and the New Nation: A Biography* (New York: Oxford University Press, 1970), p. 341. For reference to the window innovation see Snyder, "The Icon of Antiquity," p. 33.

16. For reference to Jefferson's initial suggestions for the President's House, his desire for a model of approbation for the Capitol, and his advocacy of brick see Boyd, *Papers of Thomas Jefferson,* Jefferson to Pierre Charles L'Enfant, April 10, 1791, vol. 20, p. 86; Jefferson to Thomas Johnson, David Stuart, and Daniel Carroll, March 8, 1792, vol. 19, p. 90. For Palladio's influence on Jefferson and for a description of Thornton's original plan and Jefferson's and Latrobe's renovations see Fiske Kimball, *Thomas Jefferson,* pp. 45, 55, 64–65. On the Villa Rotunda and the burning of the Capitol see Peterson, *Thomas Jefferson and the New Nation,* pp. 539, 743. For Jefferson's 1793 and 1812 statements see Bergh and Lipscomb, *Writings of Thomas Jefferson,* Jefferson to David Stuart, January 21, 1793, vol. 9, p. 1; Jefferson to Benjamin H. Latrobe, July 12, 1812, vol. 13, p. 179.

17. Lehmann, *Thomas Jefferson,* pp. 169–172, 186. For Jefferson's praise of the Pantheon see Bergh and Lipscomb, *Writings of Thomas Jefferson,* "An Account of the Capitol in Virginia," vol. 17, p. 353. For reference to his desire for southern and western students to appreciate Roman architecture and to his restoration of the Pantheon podium see William Howard Adams, *Jefferson and the Arts: An Extended View* (Washington, D.C.: National Gallery of Art, 1976), pp. 180–181. For his adaptation of the Temple of Nerva Trajan and the Theatre of Marcellus see Eleanor Davidson Berman, *Thomas Jefferson among the Arts: An Essay in Early American Esthetics* (New York: Philosophical Library, 1947), p. 142.

18. For Jefferson's 1826 statement regarding Palladio, for reference to the Romans' recommendation of a high position, and for Jefferson's reference to the Italian language see Lehmann, *Thomas Jefferson,* pp. 168–169, 182–183. On his use of the Palladian basement, stories, mezzanines, and porticoes see Adams, *Jefferson and the Arts,* p. 177. For Palladio's influence concerning the white columns and the detail see Berman, *Thomas Jefferson among the Arts,* p. 119. For reference to Palladio's recommendation of construction on a *monticello* see Marie Kimball, *Jefferson: The Road to Glory,* 1743–1776 (New York: Coward-McCann,

1943), p. 151; Silvio A. Bedini, *Thomas Jefferson: Statesmen of Science* (New York: Macmillan, 1990), p. 52.

19. For reference to the Aeolian harp see Marie Kimball, *Jefferson,* pp. 162–163. On the other items proposed for his burial ground and on Pliny's influence see Lehmann, *Thomas Jefferson,* pp. 52, 183–184. For Jefferson's fish pond see Bedini, *Thomas Jefferson,* p. 410. For reference to Jefferson's triumphal column see Fiske Kimball, *Thomas Jefferson,* pp. 25–27.

20. Bedini, *Thomas Jefferson,* p. 382; Fiske Kimball, *Thomas Jefferson,* pp. 25–27.

21. Fiske Kimball, *Thomas Jefferson,* pp. 23, 45, 56; Peterson, *Thomas Jefferson and the New Nation,* pp. 24–25; Lehmann, *Thomas Jefferson,* p. 166.

22. Garry Wills, *Cincinnatus: George Washington and the Enlightenment* (Garden City, N.Y.: Doubleday, 1984), pp. 111–112.

23. Lehmann, *Thomas Jefferson,* pp. 173–175; Boyd, *Papers of Thomas Jefferson,* Jefferson to Madame de Tesse, March 20, 1787, vol. 11, p. 226; "Notes of a Tour into the Southern Part of France & c.," March–June 1787, ibid., pp. 423–425.

24. For Jefferson's statement against painting and sculpture see Bergh and Lipscomb, *Writings of Thomas Jefferson,* Traveling Notes for Mr. Rutledge and Mr. Shippen, June 3, 1788, vol. 17, p. 292. For his opposition to modern depictions of the ancients based on speculation see Lehmann, *Thomas Jefferson,* p. 92. For reference to his 1771 list, 1782 additions, *Democritus and Heraclitus, Ariadne,* pyramid model, fifty-eight paintings, Ceracchi busts, and "Diogenes" paintings see Adams, *Jefferson and the Arts,* pp. 109–110, 112, 121–122, 124–125. The *Ariadne* was long misidentified as Cleopatra, the reason Jefferson placed it beside the pyramid model. For the rest see Berman, *Thomas Jefferson among the Arts,* pp. 77, 84, 96, 107.

25. Lehmann, *Thomas Jefferson,* pp. 31–33; Gummere, *American Colonial Mind,* p. 15; Boyd, *Papers of Thomas Jefferson,* "The Virginia Cession of Territory Northwest of the Ohio," vol. 6, p. 605.

26. Gilbert Chinard, ed., *The Literary Bible of Thomas Jefferson: His Commonplace Book of Philosophers and Poets* (1928; reprint, New York: Greenwood Press, 1969), p. 8.

27. L. H. Butterfield, ed., *The Adams Family Correspondence* (Cambridge, Mass.: Harvard University Press, 1963–1973), vol. 2, p. ix; John Adams to Abigail Adams, August 14, 1776, ibid., pp. 96–97; April–May 1780, vol. 3, p. 333; L. H. Butterfield, ed., *The Diary and Autobiography of John Adams* (Cambridge, Mass.: Harvard University Press, 1961), Diary, 1759, vol. 1, p. 72; May 1778, vol. 4, p. 105; Peter Shaw, *The Character of John Adams* (Chapel Hill: University of North Carolina Press, 1976), pp. 37–38. The first version of the fable of Hercules appeared in Hesiod's *Works and Days,* and Cicero later mentioned it in *De Officiis* (3.5.25).

28. Richard Beale Davis, *Intellectual Life in Jefferson's Virginia, 1790–1830* (Chapel Hill: University of North Carolina Press, 1964), p. 227; Howard Mumford Jones, *O Strange New World: American Culture, the Formative Years* (New York: Viking Press, 1952), p. 253; Gummere, *American Colonial Mind*, pp. 15–17; James Thomas Flexner, *George Washington* (Boston: Little, Brown, 1965–1969), vol. 4, p. 357; Richard Barry, *Mr. Rutledge of South Carolina* (New York: Duell, Sloan, 1942), p. 243; Richard J. Hoffman, "Classics in the Courts of the United States, 1790–1800," *American Journal of Legal History* 22 (January 1978):56; Edwin A. Miles, "The Young American Nation and the Classical World," *Journal of the History of Ideas* 35 (April–June 1974):263.

29. Gordon S. Wood, *The Radicalism of the American Revolution* (New York: Alfred A. Knopf, 1992), pp. 197, 200–202, 402n17.

30. Ibid., p. 355.

III. Models

1. Robert A. Rutland et al., eds., *The Papers of James Madison* (Chicago: University of Chicago Press, 1962–1977; Charlottesville: University Press of Virginia, 1977–), Commonplace Book, vol. 1, p. 20; Meyer Reinhold, *Classica Americana: The Greek and Roman Heritage in the United States* (Detroit: Wayne State University Press, 1984), p. 258; John Taylor, *An Inquiry into the Principles and Policy of the Government of the United States* (New Haven: Yale University Press, 1950), p. 341.

2. Albert Ellery Bergh and Andrew A. Lipscomb, eds., *The Writings of Thomas Jefferson* (Washington, D.C.: Thomas Jefferson Memorial Association, 1903), Jefferson to Anne Cary Bankhead, December 8, 1808, vol. 18, p. 255; Jefferson to Edward Everett, February 24, 1823, vol. 15, p. 415; Douglass Adair, *Fame and the Founding Fathers,* ed. H. Trevor Colbourn (New York: W. W. Norton, 1974), p. 22; Peter Shaw, *The Character of John Adams* (Chapel Hill: University of North Carolina Press, 1976), p. 220; Paul Leicester Ford, ed., *The Political Writings of John Dickinson, 1764–1774* (1895; reprint, New York: Da Capo Press, 1970), "A Speech on a Change of Government of the Colony of Pennsylvania," May 24, 1764, p. 24; Bernard Bailyn, ed., *Pamphlets of the American Revolution* (Cambridge, Mass.: Harvard University Press, 1965), "Introduction," vol. 1, p. 34; Reinhold, *Classica Americana,* p. 41.

3. William Gribbin, "Rollin's Histories and American Republicanism," *William and Mary Quarterly,* 3d ser., 29 (October 1972):612–616; Henry F. May, *The Enlightenment in America* (New York: Oxford University Press, 1976), p. 39. For John Adams' statement see Linda K. Kerber, *Federalists in Dissent: Imagery and Ideology in Jeffersonian America* (Ithaca: Cornell University Press, 1970), p. 123. For the American Whig Society's reading of Rollin see James McLachlan, "The Choice of Hercules," in Lawrence Stone, ed., *The University in Society* (Princeton: Princeton University Press, 1974), vol. 2, p. 478.

4. Richard M. Gummere, *The American Colonial Mind and the Classical Tradition: Essays in Comparative Culture* (Cambridge, Mass.: Harvard University Press, 1963), pp. 18, 114; Silvio A. Bedini, *Thomas Jefferson: Statesman of Science* (New York: Macmillan, 1990), p. 297; Lester J. Cappon, ed., *The Adams-Jefferson Letters: The Complete Correspondence between Thomas Jefferson and Abigail and John Adams* (Chapel Hill: University of North Carolina Press, 1959), Jefferson to John Adams, March 25, 1826, vol. 2, p. 614.

5. Robert J. Taylor, ed., *The Papers of John Adams* (Cambridge, Mass.: Harvard University Press, 1977–), Adams to William Tudor, June 24, 1776, vol. 4, p. 336; Harry Olonzo Cushing, ed., *The Writings of Samuel Adams* (1908; reprint, New York: Octagon Books, 1968), Adams to James Warren, October 24, 1780, vol. 4, pp. 213–214; Cappon, *Adams-Jefferson Letters,* John Adams to Jefferson, May 11, 1794, vol. 1, p. 255.

6. Max Farrand, ed., *The Records of the Federal Convention of 1787* (New Haven: Yale University Press, 1966), June 5, 1787, vol. 1, p. 125; Bergh and Lipscomb, *Writings of Thomas Jefferson,* Jefferson to Du Pont de Nemours, April 24, 1816, vol. 14, p. 492; Jefferson to William Lee, January 16, 1817, vol. 15, p. 101; Robert Green McCloskey, ed., *The Works of James Wilson* (Cambridge, Mass.: Harvard University Press, 1967), "Of the Nature of Courts," vol. 2, p. 510; "Oration Delivered on the Fourth of July," 1788, ibid., p. 805.

7. Karl Lehmann, *Thomas Jefferson: American Humanist* (Chicago: University of Chicago Press, 1964), p. 93; Bedini, *Thomas Jefferson,* p. 194; Julian P. Boyd, ed., The Papers of Thomas Jefferson (Princeton: Princeton University Press, 1950–), Jefferson to John Page, December 10, 1775, vol. 1, p. 270; Taylor, *Papers of John Adams,* "U" to the Boston Gazette, August 29, 1763, vol. 1, p. 77; Adams to James Warren, July 17, 1774, vol. 2, p. 109; July 25, 1774, vol. 2, p. 117.

8. L. H. Butterfield, ed., *The Adams Family Correspondence* (Cambridge, Mass.: Harvard University Press, 1963–1973), Abigail Adams to Elbridge Gerry, July 20, 1781, vol. 4, p. 182; Bergh and Lipscomb, *Writings of Thomas Jefferson,* Autobiography, 1821, vol. 1, p. 169; Gordon S. Wood, *Radicalism of the American Revolution* (New York: Alfred A. Knopf, 1992), p. 199; James Thomas Flexner, *George Washington* (Boston: Little, Brown, 1965–1969), vol. 1, p. 242.

9. Frederick W. Litto, "Addison's *Cato* in the Colonies," *William and Mary Quarterly,* 3d ser., 23 (July 1966):431–432, 434–435. For reference to the events at the play's debut see Henry C. Montgomery, "Addison's *Cato* and George Washington," *Classical Journal* 55 (February 1960):210–211. For Pope's statement concerning Cato see Flexner, *George Washington,* vol. 1, p. 242.

10. For reference to Washington's affection for *Cato* and its performance at Valley Forge see Forrest McDonald, *Novus Ordo Seclorum* (Lawrence: University of Kansas Press, 1985), pp. 69, 195. For Washington's "'Tis not in mortals" statement see Paul Leicester Ford, *Washington and the Theater* (1899; reprint, Dunlap Society, 1967), p. 1. For Washington's criticism of his overseer see Garry Wills,

Cincinnatus: George Washington and the Enlightenment (Garden City, N.Y.: Doubleday, 1984), p. 186. On Thomas' threat to resign see Flexner, *George Washington*, vol. 1, p. 242; vol. 2, p. 30.

11. John C. Fitzpatrick, ed., *The Writings of George Washington*, "To the Officers of the Army," March 15, 1783, vol. 26, pp. 222–223, 225; A. C. Guthkelch, ed., *The Miscellaneous Works of Joseph Addison* (1914; reprint, St. Clair Shores: Scholarly Press, 1978), *Cato*, Act III, Scene 5, vol. 1, p. 395.

12. Fitzpatrick, *Writings of George Washington*, "To the Officers of the Army," March 15, 1783, vol. 26, pp. 226–227; Guthkelch, *Miscellaneous Works of Joseph Addison*, *Cato*, Act I, Scene 4, vol. 1, p. 316; Act III, Scene 5, ibid., p. 396.

13. Fitzpatrick, *Writings of George Washington*, "To the Officers of the Army," March 15, 1783, vol. 26, p. 222n38; Guthkelch, *Miscellaneous Works of Joseph Addison*, *Cato*, Act III, Scene 5, vol. 1, pp. 396–397.

14. Ford, *Washington and the Theater*, p. 1.

15. Guthkelch, *Miscellaneous Works of Joseph Addison*, *Cato*, Act II, Scene 4, vol. 1, p. 357; Act IV, Scene 4, ibid., p. 432; Litto, "Addison's *Cato* in the Colonies," p. 448.

16. L. H. Butterfield, ed., *The Earliest Diary of John Adams* (Cambridge, Mass.: Harvard University Press, 1966), October–November, 1758, p. 65; Butterfield, ed., *The Diary and Autobiography of John Adams* (Cambridge, Mass.: Harvard University Press, 1961), Diary, December 21, 1758, vol. 1, p. 63; December 30, 1758, ibid., p. 65; January 24, 1765, ibid., pp. 251, 253; February 21, 1765, ibid., p. 255; Taylor, *Papers of John Adams*, Adams to William Tudor, August 4, 1774, vol. 2, pp. 126–127.

17. Butterfield, *Diary and Autobiography of John Adams*, Diary, July 1, 1776, vol. 3, pp. 396–397.

18. Shaw, *The Character of John Adams*, p. 246n34; Kerber, *Federalists in Dissent*, p. 122.

19. Zoltan Haraszti, *John Adams and the Prophets of Progress* (Cambridge, Mass.: Harvard University Press, 1952), p. 60; Douglass Adair and John A. Schutz, eds., *The Spur of Fame: Dialogues of John Adams and Benjamin Rush, 1805–1813* (San Marino, Calif.: Huntington Library, 1966), Adams to Rush, December 4, 1805, p. 44; Shaw, *The Character of John Adams*, p. 272.

20. For reference to Adams' reading of *De Senectute* see Shaw, *The Character of John Adams*, p. 270. On Adams' avoidance of war with France and its political cost see Ralph Ketcham, *Presidents above Party: The First American Presidency, 1789–1829* (Chapel Hill: University of North Carolina Press, 1984), p. 98. For the rest see Adair and Schutz, *Spur of Fame*, John Adams to Benjamin Rush, March 23, 1809, pp. 139–140; December 19, 1811, p. 203; December 27, 1812, p. 263.

21. Ketcham, *Presidents above Party*, pp. vii, x, 3–4, 92, 121–124, 140. On the patriots' hatred of Tory "courtiers" see Gordon S. Wood, *Creation of the Amer-*

ican Republic, 1776–1787 (Chapel Hill: University of North Carolina Press, 1787), p. 78. For further reference to the antipartyism of the early republican period see Wood, *Radicalism of the American Revolution,* pp. 298–303. For further reference to the Whig Party's antiparty sentiment see Daniel Walker Howe, *The Political Culture of the American Whigs* (Chicago: University of Chicago Press, 1979), p. 8.

22. Butterfield, *Adams Family Correspondence,* Abigail Adams to John Quincy Adams, January 19, 1780, vol. 3, p. 268.

23. McCloskey, *Works of James Wilson,* "Introduction," vol. 1, p. 50; "The Study of Law," ibid., p. 85; "Of Man as a Member of the Commonwealth of Nations," ibid., p. 273; "Of the Common Law," ibid., p. 342; "Of the Nature and Philosophy of Evidence," ibid., p. 378; "Of Juries," vol. 2, p. 511; "Of the Natural Rights of Individuals," ibid., p. 598; "Of Crimes against the Rights of Individuals to Their Property," ibid., p. 643; "Of the Different Steps Prescribed by the Law for Apprehending, Detaining, Trying, and Punishing Offenders," ibid., pp. 694–695; "On the History of Property," ibid., p. 712, 716.

24. Taylor, *Papers of John Adams,* "A Dissertation on the Canon and Feudal Law," October 21, 1765, vol. 1, p. 125; "Humphrey Ploughjogger to Philanthrop," January 1767, ibid., p. 194; Adams to Elbridge Gerry, December 9, 1777, vol. 5, p. 353; Charles F. Mullett, "Classical Influences on the American Revolution," *Classical Journal* 35 (November 1939):97; McCloskey, *Works of James Wilson,* "Of Government," vol. 1, p. 297. For reference to Hancock's largesse and its effect on his estate see Wood, *Radicalism of the American Revolution,* p. 210.

25. Taylor, *Papers of John Adams,* Adams to Mercy Otis Warren, November 25, 1775, vol. 3, p. 319; Adams to Henry Knox, June 2, 1776, vol. 4, p. 226; Adams to Nathanael Greene, April 13, 1777, vol. 5, p. 151.

26. Butterfield, *Diary and Autobiography of John Adams,* Adams to William Tudor, September 26, 1776, vol. 3, p. 439; Adams to Samuel Holden Parsons, August 19, 1776, ibid., p. 448.

27. Adair and Schutz, *Spur of Fame,* John Adams to Benjamin Rush, September 19, 1806, p. 67.

28. Butterfield, *Adams Family Correspondence,* Abigail Adams to John Adams, April 10, 1782, vol. 4, p. 306; Milton E. Flower, *John Dickinson: Conservative Revolutionary* (Charlottesville: University Press of Virginia, 1983), p. 70; John Cary, *Joseph Warren: Physician, Politician, and Patriot* (Urbana: University of Illinois Press, 1961), p. 151; Robert Douthat Meade, ed., *Patrick Henry* (Philadelphia: J. B. Lippincott, 1957–1969), vol. 1, pp. 6–7, 326; Kate M. Rowland, ed., *The Life and Correspondence of George Mason* (New York: Russell and Russell, 1964), Mason to Martin Cockburn, May 26, 1774, vol. 1, p. 169; Howard Mumford Jones, *O Strange New World: American Culture, the Formative Years* (New York: Viking Press, 1952), p. 247.

29. For reference to Kant's analogy and for the analogies of Shipley and the Frenchman see Leonard W. Labaree, ed., *The Papers of Benjamin Franklin* (New Haven: Yale University Press, 1959–), vol. 20, p. 490n6; Georgiana Shipley to Franklin, February 11, 1777, vol. 23, p. 305; Jean-Hyacinthe Magellan to Franklin, June 20, 1778, vol. 26, p. 663. For Turgot's statement see L. Jesse Lemisch, ed., *Benjamin Franklin: The Autobiography and Other Writings* (New York: Penguin Books, 1961), p. 216. For Fragonard's painting see Wills, *Cincinnatus,* p. 73. For Adams' account of Franklin's meeting with Voltaire see Butterfield, *Diary and Autobiography of John Adams,* Diary, April 1778, vol. 4, pp. 80–81.

30. Charles Francis Adams, ed., *The Works of John Adams* (Boston: Little, Brown, 1850–1856), vol. 1, p. 637.

31. Stephen Botein, "Cicero as Role Model for Early American Lawyers: A Case Study in Classical 'Influence,'" *Classical Journal* 73 (Spring 1778):318; Garry Wills, *Explaining America: The Federalist* (New York: Penguin Books, 1981), p. 60; Reinhold, *Classica Americana,* p. 258; John Frederick Schroeder, ed., *Maxims of George Washington* (New York: D. Appleton, 1855), p. 315; Wills, *Cincinnatus,* pp. 35, 51.

32. For Wallis' statement and for reference to the changes from Phidias' *Zeus* see Wayne Craven, "Horatio Greenough's Statue of Washington and Phidias's Zeus," *Art Quarterly* 26 (Winter 1963):429–430. The fifth-century B.C. Athenian *Zeus* held a staff, rather than an inverted sword, in his left hand, while his right hand held the goddess Victory, rather than pointing upward. On the weight of the statue and for Hose's statement see Jones, *O Strange New World,* p. 265. For the other works which portrayed Washington as Cincinnatus see Wills, *Cincinnatus,* pp. 12–13, 70, 118.

33. Marcus Cunliffe, *George Washington: Man and Monument* (Boston: Little, Brown, 1959), pp. 16, 129; Wills, *Cincinnatus,* pp. 13, 241.

34. For reference to Washington's resignation from the vestry see Wood, *Radicalism of the American Revolution,* p. 206. On Washington's use of the term *villa* and for his Horatian statement see Cunliffe, *George Washington,* p. 130. For the rest see Wills, *Cincinnatus,* pp. 3, 12–13, 142, 162, 241.

35. Wood, *Radicalism of the American Revolution,* pp. 207–209.

36. McCloskey, *Works of James Wilson,* "The Study of Law," vol. 1, pp. 88–89.

37. Reinhold, *Classica Americana,* p. 157; Taylor, *An Inquiry,* p. 80; Ford, *Political Writings of John Dickinson, Letters from a Pennsylvania Farmer,* 1768, p. 324; Bedini, *Thomas Jefferson,* p. 466.

38. For Jefferson's and Hamilton's see Paul A. Rahe, *Republics, Ancient and Modern: Classical Republicanism and the American Revolution* (Chapel Hill: University of North Carolina Press, 1992), pp. 155, 324. For Ames's quotation of Alcibiades see McDonald, *Novus Ordo Seclorum,* p. 73. For Adams' statements see Haraszti, *John Adams and the Prophets of Progress,* pp. 122, 136.

39. McCloskey, *Works of James Wilson*, "Of Man as a Member of a Confederation," vol. 1, p. 265; "Citizens and Aliens," vol. 2, p. 581; Oration Delivered on the Fourth of July, 1788, ibid., p. 777.

40. Bailyn, *Pamphlets of the American Revolution*, "The Rights of the British Colonies Asserted and Proved," 1764, vol. 1, p. 422; Taylor, *Papers of John Adams*, Adams to James Warren, June 25, 1774, vol. 2, p. 99; Cappon, *Adams-Jefferson Letters*, Jefferson to John Adams, February 6, 1795, vol. 1, p. 260; McCloskey, *Works of James Wilson*, "Law and Obligation," vol. 1, pp. 122–123; "Of Government," ibid., p. 289; "Of the Nature and Philosophy of Evidence," ibid., p. 400; Richard J. Hoffman, "Classics in the Courts of the United States, 1790–1800," *American Journal of Legal History* 22 (January 1978):63; Taylor, *An Inquiry*, pp. 141, 413.

41. Taylor, *Papers of John Adams*, "Letters of Novanglus," March 6, 1775, vol. 2, pp. 311–312; Ford, *Political Writings of John Dickinson*, "Letter to the Philadelphia Merchants concerning Nonimportation," July 1768, pp. 444–445.

42. Gummere, *American Colonial Mind*, p. 106; Gilbert Chinard, ed., *The Commonplace Book of Thomas Jefferson: A Repertory of His Ideas on Government* (Baltimore: Johns Hopkins Press, 1926), pp. 181–185.

43. Bailyn, *Pamphlets of the American Revolution*, "The Rights of the British Colonies Asserted and Proved," 1764, vol. 1, pp. 437–438; "A Vindication of the British Colonies," 1765, ibid., p. 570; Harry Alonzo Cushing, ed., *The Writings of Samuel Adams* (1908; reprint, New York: Octagon Books, 1968), "Valerius Poplicola," October 28, 1771, vol. 2, p. 262.

44. Harold C. Syrett, ed., *The Papers of Alexander Hamilton* (New York: Columbia University Press, 1961–1979), "A Full Vindication of the Measures of Congress," December 15, 1774, vol. 1, p. 53; "The Farmer Refuted," February 23, 1775, ibid., pp. 104–105; Rutland, *Papers of George Mason*, Mason to Unidentified Correspondent, October 2, 1778, vol. 1, p. 435; Jonathan Elliot, ed., *Debates in the Several State Conventions on the Adoption of the Federal Constitution* (1888; reprint, New York: Burt Franklin, 1968), vol. 3, p. 282.

45. Taylor, *Papers of John Adams*, Adams to Nathan Webb, October 12, 1755, vol. 1, p. 5; Adams to James Warren, July 17, 1774, vol. 2, p. 109; Lorne Baritz, "The Idea of the West," *American Historical Review* 66 (April 1961):618–640; Butterfield, *Diary and Autobiography of John Adams*, Diary, June 20, 1779, vol. 2, p. 385.

46. Ford, *Political Writings of John Dickinson*, "An Address Read to a Meeting of Merchants to Consider Nonimportation," April 25, 1768, p. 416; Cary, *Joseph Warren*, p. 108.

47. Elliot, *Debates on the Adoption of the Federal Constitution*, vol. 3, p. 491; Herbert J. Storing, ed., *The Complete Antifederalist* (Chicago: University of Chicago Press, 1981), vol. 2, p. 311; Taylor, *An Inquiry*, pp. 186–188.

48. Storing, *The Complete Antifederalist*, vol. 5, pp. 27, 182; William V. Harris,

War and Imperialism in Republican Rome, 327–70 B.C. (Oxford: Clarendon Press, 1979), p. 10; Bergh and Lipscomb, *Writings of Thomas Jefferson,* Jefferson to Thomas Cooper, September 10, 1814, vol. 14, p. 185.

49. Max Farrand, ed., *The Records of the Federal Convention of 1787* (New Haven: Yale University Press, 1966), vol. 1, pp. 322–323; Alexander Hamilton, John Jay, and James Madison, *The Federalist: A Commentary on the Constitution of the United States* (New York: Random House, 1941), No. 34, p. 204.

50. Chinard, *Commonplace Book of Thomas Jefferson,* pp. 31–35, 118, 136, 190, 234. Dalrymple notes that these nonfeudal Anglo-Saxons owned slaves. See p. 170.

51. For Gordon's quote on German frugality see H. Trevor Colbourn, "Thomas Jefferson's Use of the Past," *William and Mary Quarterly,* 3d ser., 15 (January 1958):61–62. For his statement of purpose, for the inconsistency of his translation, and for Pope's statement see Herbert W. Benario, "The Classics in Southern Higher Education," *Southern Humanities Review* 11 (1977):15–20. For further reference to the importance of Gordon and Trenchard see Bernard Bailyn, *The Ideological Origins of the American Revolution,* 2d ed. (Cambridge, Mass.: Harvard University Press, 1992), pp. 35–36.

52. Boyd, *Papers of Thomas Jefferson,* Draft Instructions to the Virginia Delegates in the Continental Congress, July 1774, vol. 1, pp. 121–135.

53. Ibid., Jefferson to Edmund Pendleton, August 13, 1776, vol. 1, p. 492; Bergh and Lipscomb, *Writings of Thomas Jefferson,* Jefferson to Unidentified Correspondent, October 25, 1825, vol. 16, pp. 127–128; Jefferson to J. Evelyn Denison, November 9, 1825, ibid., p. 131; "An Essay on the Anglo-Saxon and Modern Dialects of the English Language," vol. 18, pp. 365–404; Chinard, *Commonplace Book of Thomas Jefferson,* p. 62.

54. Gummere, *American Colonial Mind,* p. 106; McCloskey, *Works of James Wilson,* "Of Man as a Member of a Confederation," vol. 1, pp. 253–254; "Of Government," ibid., p. 288; "Of the Common Law," ibid., pp. 349–350; "Of the Nature and Philosophy of Evidence," ibid., p. 425; "Of the Judicial Department," vol. 2, p. 470; "Of the Nature of Courts," ibid., p. 494; "Of the Natural Rights of Individuals," ibid., p. 597; "Of the Nature of the Crimes and the Necessity and Proportion of Punishments," ibid., pp. 626–627.

55. Taylor, *Papers of John Adams,* "A Dissertation on the Canon and Feudal Law," August 12, 1765, vol. 1, pp. 114, 117.

56. James McLachlan, "Classical Names, American Identities," in John W. Eadie, ed., *Classical Traditions in Early America* (Ann Arbor: Center for the Coordination of Ancient and Modern Studies, 1976), p. 93. For the statements of *Bickerstaff's Almanac* and Adams see Richard M. Gummere, "The Heritage of the Classics in Colonial North America," *Proceedings of the American Philosophical Society* 99 (January 1955):76.

57. Cappon, *Adams-Jefferson Letters,* Jefferson to John Adams, June 27, 1813, vol. 2, p. 335.

58. Cushing, *Writings of Samuel Adams*, Adams to Thomas Young, October 17, 1774, vol. 3, p. 163; Taylor, *Papers of John Adams*, "Thoughts on Government," April 1776, vol. 4, p. 92. Adams originally wrote this treatise in the form of a letter to George Wythe in 1776. Several copies of it circulated in 1776 and 1777, including one in the form of a 1777 letter to Richard Henry Lee. For Charles Lee's statement see Reinhold, *Classica Americana*, p. 41. For the statements of Pendleton and Washington see Gummere, *American Colonial Mind*, p. 18. For Tucker's statement see Gummere, "The Heritage of the Classics in Colonial North America," p. 71. For John Adams' 1805 statement see Adair and Schutz, *Spur of Fame*, Adams to Benjamin Rush, December 4, 1805, p. 44.

IV. Antimodels

1. Julian P. Boyd, ed., *The Papers of Thomas Jefferson* (Princeton: Princeton University Press, 1950–), "A Bill for the More General Diffusion of Knowledge," 1779, vol. 2, pp. 526–528. For Jefferson's opposition to a European education see Jefferson to John Banister, Jr., October 15, 1785, vol. 8, pp. 636–637. For another letter stressing the importance of studying ancient history see Jefferson to Thomas Mann Randolph, Jr., August 27, 1786, vol. 10, p. 307. For Jefferson's coupling of history with politics and law see Saul K. Padover, ed., *The Complete Jefferson: Containing His Major Writings, Published and Unpublished, except His Letters* (New York: Duell, Sloan, and Pearce, 1943), p. 1100. For the "usual suite" statement see Albert Ellery Bergh and Andrew A. Lipscomb, eds., *The Writings of Thomas Jefferson* (Washington, D.C.: Thomas Jefferson Memorial Association, 1903), Jefferson to Unidentified Correspondent, October 25, 1825, vol. 16, p. 124.

2. L. H. Butterfield, ed., *The Earliest Diary of John Adams* (Cambridge, Mass.: Harvard University Press, 1966), Adams to Unidentified Correspondent, 1758, p. 71; Douglass Adair and John A. Schutz, eds., *The Spur of Fame: Dialogues of John Adams and Benjamin Rush, 1805–1813* (San Marino, Calif.: Huntington Library, 1966), Adams to Rush, October 13, 1810, pp. 170–171; January 18, 1811, p. 177.

3. John Taylor, *An Inquiry into the Principles and Practices of the Government of the United States* (New Haven: Yale University Press, 1950), p. 68; Richard M. Gummere, "John Dickinson, Classical Penman of the Revolution," *Classical Journal* 52 (November 1956):82.

4. For reference to the primacy of politics in Greece, the denigration of lyric poets, and the medieval revision of history see Paul A. Rahe, *Republics, Ancient and Modern: Classical Republicanism and the American Revolution* (Chapel Hill: University of North Carolina Press, 1992), pp. 24, 94, 220.

5. Lester J. Cappon, ed., *The Adams-Jefferson Letters: The Complete Correspondence between Thomas Jefferson and Abigail and John Adams* (Chapel Hill: University of North Carolina Press, 1959) John Adams to Jefferson, February 3, 1812, vol. 2, p. 295.

6. Karl Lehmann, *Thomas Jefferson: American Humanist* (Chicago: University of Chicago Press, 1964), p. 116; Bergh and Lipscomb, *Writings of Thomas Jefferson,* Jefferson to Samuel Brown, July 14, 1813, vol. 13, p. 311; Autobiography, 1821, vol. 1, p. 152; Jefferson to William Duane, April 4, 1813, vol. 13, p. 320. Ironically, one of Jefferson's most famous statements was a paraphrase of Tiberius. When Jefferson declared, "In slavery we have the wolf by the ears. We can neither hold him nor safely let him go," he paraphrased Tiberius' explanation of why he could not surrender his power and restore the republic. See Rahe, *Republics,* p. 636.

7. Paul Leicester Ford, ed., *The Political Writings of John Dickinson, 1764–1774* (1895; reprint, New York: Da Capo Press, 1970), *Letters from a Pennsylvania Farmer,* 1768, p. 346; Harry Alonzo Cushing, ed., *The Writings of Samuel Adams* (1908; reprint, New York: Octagon Books, 1968), "The Town of Boston to Dennys De Berdt," October 22, 1766, vol. 1, p. 96; Adams to Christopher Gadsden, December 11, 1766, ibid., p. 109; Robert J. Taylor, ed., *The Papers of John Adams* (Cambridge, Mass.: Harvard University Press, 1977–), "Letters of Novanglus," February 20, 1775, vol. 2, p. 272.

8. Herbert J. Storing, ed., *The Complete Antifederalist,* 7 vols. (Chicago: University of Chicago Press, 1981), vol. 2, pp. 146, 157; vol. 4, pp. 190–191; vol. 6, p. 185.

9. Ibid., vol. 3, pp. 117–118; vol. 4, p. 618.

10. Harold C. Syrett, ed., *The Papers of Alexander Hamilton* (New York: Columbia University Press, 1961–1979), "A Letter from Phocion to the Considerate Citizens of New York," January 1784, vol. 3, pp. 488, 496.

11. Taylor, *Papers of John Adams,* Adams to Nathanael Greene, May 24, 1777, vol. 5, p. 202; Richard M. Gummere, *The American Colonial Mind and the Classical Tradition: Essays in Comparative Culture* (Cambridge, Mass.: Harvard University Press, 1963), p. 101; Ford, *Political Writings of John Dickinson,* p. 274; Richard Walsh, ed., *The Writings of Christopher Gadsden, 1746–1805* (Columbia: University of South Carolina Press, 1966), Gadsden to Samuel Adams, April 4, 1779, p. 164; Bergh and Lipscomb, *Writings of Thomas Jefferson,* Jefferson to John Langdon, December 22, 1806, vol. 19, p. 157; Cappon, *Adams-Jefferson Letters,* John Adams to Jefferson, September 3, 1816, vol. 2, p. 488; Lehmann, *Thomas Jefferson,* p. 90; Zoltan Haraszti, *John Adams and the Prophets of Progress* (Cambridge, Mass.: Harvard University Press, 1952), p. 59.

12. Bernard Bailyn, ed., *Pamphlets of the American Revolution* (Cambridge, Mass.: Harvard University Press, 1965), "The Rights of the British Colonies Asserted and Proved," 1764, vol. 1, p. 422; Robert Douthat Meade, ed., *Patrick Henry,* (Philadelphia: J. B. Lippincott, 1957–1969), vol. 1, pp. 31, 173–178; L. H. Butterfield, ed., *The Diary and Autobiography of John Adams* (Cambridge, Mass.: Harvard University Press, 1961), Diary, June 13, 1771, vol. 2, p. 35; Dorothy M. Robathan, "John Adams and the Classics," *New England Quarterly* 19

(March 1946):94; Stanley E. Godbold and Robert H. Woody, *Christopher Gadsden and the American Revolution* (Knoxville: University of Tennessee Press, 1982), p. 49; Charles F. Mullett, "Classical Influences on the American Revolution," *Classical Journal* 35 (November 1939):97.

13. Robathan, "John Adams and the Classics," pp. 97–98; Adair and Schutz, *Spur of Fame,* John Adams to Benjamin Rush, December 4, 1805, p. 45; Bergh and Lipscomb, *Writings of Thomas Jefferson,* Jefferson to Benjamin Rush, January 16, 1811, vol. 13, p. 4; Thomas P. Govan, "Alexander Hamilton and Julius Caesar: A Note on the Use of Historical Evidence," *William and Mary Quarterly,* 3d ser., 32 (July 1975):475–480. For Jefferson's opinion that Caesar had the greatest corrupting influence on republican Rome see Cappon, *Adams-Jefferson Letters,* Jefferson to John Adams, December 10, 1819, vol. 2, p. 549.

14. Syrett, *Papers of Alexander Hamilton,* Hamilton to Lieutinent Colonel John Laurens, September 11, 1779, vol. 2, p. 168; Hamilton to George Washington, August 18, 1792, vol. 12, p. 252; "Catullus No. III," September 29, 1792, ibid., pp. 500–501.

15. Ibid., vol. 12, pp. 504–505; Alexander Hamilton to Unidentified Correspondent, September 26, 1792, ibid., p. 480.

16. James McLachlan, "Classical Names, American Identities," in John W. Eadie, ed., *Classical Traditions in Early America* (Ann Arbor: Center for the Coordination of Ancient and Modern Studies, 1976), pp. 91–92.

17. Taylor, *Papers of John Adams,* "Humphrey Ploughjogger to Philanthrop," January 5, 1767, vol. 1, p. 179; Bergh and Lipscomb, *Writings of Thomas Jefferson,* Jefferson to Thomas Mann Randolph, February 2, 1800, vol. 10, p. 150; Jefferson to John Langdon, March 5, 1810, vol. 12, p. 374; Jefferson to Nathanael Macon, January 12, 1819, vol. 15, p. 179; Robathan, "John Adams and the Classics," pp. 97–98; Charles Francis Adams, ed., *The Life and Works of John Adams* (Boston: Little, Brown, 1850–1856), vol. 10, p. 419.

18. For reference to Washington's childhood reading of Caesar and his later lack of interest in Alexander see James Thomas Flexner, *George Washington* (Boston: Little, Brown, 1965–1969), vol. 1, p. 31; vol. 4, p. 357. For Fairfax's letter and Washington's ordering of the busts see John C. Fitzpatrick, ed., *The Writings of George Washington* (Washington, D.C.: Government Printing Office, 1931–1940), William Fairfax to Washington, May 13, 1756, vol. 1, p. 385n73; Washington to Robert Cary, September 20, 1759, vol. 2, pp. 333–334. On Washington's Farewell Address see Garry Wills, *Cincinnatus: George Washington and the Enlightenment* (Garden City, N.Y.: Doubleday, 1984), p. 87.

19. Robert Green McCloskey, ed., *The Works of James Wilson* (Cambridge, Mass.: Harvard University Press, 1967), "The Study of Law," vol. 1, pp. 84–85.

20. Kate M. Rowland, ed., *The Life and Correspondence of George Mason* (New York: Russell and Russell, 1964), Mason to the Committee of Merchants in

London, June 6, 1766, vol. 1, p. 386; Ford, *Political Writings of John Dickinson, Letters from a Pennsylvania Farmer,* 1768, p. 327.

21. Syrett, *Papers of Alexander Hamilton,* "Americanus No. I," January 31, 1794, vol. 15, p. 671; "The Stand No. III," April 7, 1798, vol. 21, p. 408; "The Stand No. IV," April 12, 1798, ibid., pp. 412–415; Milton E. Flower, *John Dickinson: Conservative Revolutionary* (Charlottesville: University Press of Virginia, 1983), p. 278.

22. Rowland, *Life and Correspondence of George Mason,* "Scheme for Replevying Goods under Distress for Rent," December 23, 1765, vol. 1, p. 378; Max Farrand, ed., *The Records of the Federal Convention of 1787,* 3d ed. (New Haven: Yale University Press, 1966), vol. 2, pp. 370–372.

23. William Peden, ed., *Notes on the State of Virginia* (Chapel Hill: University of North Carolina Press, 1955), p. 138.

24. Ibid., pp. 138–143.

25. Bergh and Lipscomb, *Writings of Thomas Jefferson,* Jefferson to Joel Barlow, December 25, 1808, vol. 12, p. 217; Jefferson to Unidentified Correspondent, October 25, 1825, vol. 16, p. 124; Edward Gibbon, *The History of the Decline and Fall of the Roman Empire* (New York: Begelow, Brown, 1854), vol. 1, p. 266.

26. Susan Ford Wiltshire, "Aristotle in America," *Humanities* 8 (Winter 1987):8–11; David Brion Davis, *The Problem of Slavery in the Age of Revolution, 1770–1823* (Ithaca: Cornell University Press, 1975), pp. 42–43; Peden, *Notes on the State of Virginia,* pp. 59–64, 142–143. Jefferson continued to advocate colonization throughout his life. See Bergh and Lipscomb, *Writings of Thomas Jefferson,* Jefferson to Thomas Cooper, September 10, 1814, vol. 14, p. 184; Autobiography, 1821, vol. 1, pp. 72–73.

27. Cappon, *Adams-Jefferson Letters,* Jefferson to John Adams, January 22, 1821, vol. 2, p. 570.

28. Taylor, *An Inquiry,* pp. 88, 261–262, 265.

29. McCloskey, *Works of James Wilson,* "Of the Natural Rights of Individuals," vol. 2, pp. 599–600.

30. Cushing, *Writings of Samuel Adams,* "Candidus," October 14, 1771, vol. 2, pp. 251, 254; Taylor, *Papers of John Adams,* "Letters of Novanglus," February 6, 1775, vol. 2, p. 251; April 17, 1775, ibid., pp. 376–377.

31. Storing, *The Complete Antifederalist,* vol. 4, pp. 148, 237; Jonathan Elliot, ed., *Debates in the Several State Conventions on the Adoption of the Federal Constitution* (1888; reprint, New York: Burt Franklin, 1968), vol. 2, p. 160.

32. Storing, *The Complete Antifederalist,* vol. 5, p. 57.

33. Ibid., pp. 58–60.

34. Paul Leicester Ford, ed., *Pamphlets on the Constitution of the United States: Published during Its Discussion by the People* (1888; reprint, New York: Burt Franklin, 1971), p. 171; Farrand, *Records of the Federal Convention,* vol. 1, p. 290.

35. Bailyn, *Pamphlets of the American Revolution,* "The Rights of the British

Colonies Asserted and Proved, 1764," vol. 1, p. 470; Ford, *Political Writings of John Dickinson, Letters from a Pennsylvania Farmer,* 1768, pp. 392–395; Meyer Reinhold, *Classica Americana: The Greek and Roman Heritage in the United States* (Detroit: Wayne State University Press, 1984), p. 254.

36. Elliot, *Debates in the Several State Conventions,* vol. 3, p. 455; Storing, *The Complete Antifederalist,* vol. 2, p. 413; vol. 3, p. 76; vol. 4, pp. 38, 227.

37. Elliot, *Debates in the Several State Conventions,* vol. 3, p. 611; Storing, *The Complete Antifederalist,* vol. 5, p. 58.

38. Elliot, *Debates in the Several State Conventions,* vol. 3, p. 494; H. H. Scullard, *From The Gracchi to Nero: A History of Rome from 133 B.C. to A.D. 68* (London: Merithen, 1959), pp. 117–120. Having failed his client, Cicero had the audacity to send Milo a copy of the speech which the troops had prevented Cicero from delivering in Milo's defense.

39. Alexander Hamilton, John Jay, and James Madison, *The Federalist: A Commentary on the Constitution of the United States* (New York: Random House, 1941), Nos. 25 and 41, pp. 157–158, 262.

40. Taylor, *An Inquiry,* p. 176.

41. On the true nature of the Amphictyonic League and the reasons for the misunderstanding see Edward A. Freeman, *History of Federal Government in Greece and Italy* (New York: MacMillan, 1893), pp. 95–100.

42. Farrand, *Records of the Federal Convention,* vol. 1, pp. 143, 285, 317, 319, 448–449; Robert A. Rutland et al., eds., *The Papers of James Madison* (Chicago: University of Chicago Press, 1962–1977; Charlottesville: University Press of Virginia, 1977–), "Notes on Ancient and Modern Confederacies," 1784–1787, vol. 9, pp. 3–8.

43. Elliot, *Debates in the Several State Conventions,* vol. 2, p. 234; vol. 3, pp. 129–132, 181, 242.

44. Ibid., vol. 2, p. 187; vol. 3, p. 106.

45. Hamilton, Jay, and Madison, *The Federalist,* Nos. 4, 6, and 18, pp. 21, 27–28, 106–109.

46. Elliot, *Debates in the Several State Conventions,* vol. 3, pp. 209–210; vol. 4, p. 239; Farrand, *Records of the Federal Convention,* vol. 1, pp. 441, 453–454; Storing, *The Complete Antifederalist,* vol. 2, p. 333.

47. Elliot, *Debates in the Several State Conventions,* vol. 2, p. 68; Gummere, *American Colonial Mind,* p. 180; Ford, *Pamphlets on the Constitution,* pp. 191–193.

48. Hamilton, Jay, and Madison, *The Federalist,* No. 18, p. 109; Elliot, *Debates in the Several State Conventions,* vol. 3, p. 162.

49. John Adams, *A Defence of the Constitutions of Government of the United States of America* (1787–88; reprint, New York: Da Capo Press, 1971), vol. 1, pp. 296, 298, 305. For modern scholarship on the Achaean League see J. A. O. Larsen, *Greek Federal States: Their Institutions and History* (Oxford: Clarendon Press, 1968), pp. 217–237.

50. Farrand, *Records of the Federal Convention,* vol. 1, pp. 143, 317, 319.

51. Elliot, *Debates in the Several State Conventions,* vol. 2, pp. 187, 235; vol. 3, p. 130.

52. Hamilton, Jay, and Madison, *The Federalist,* Nos. 16 and 18, pp. 95, 109–110.

53. Ibid., Nos. 18 and 45, pp. 110–112, 299–300.

54. Adams, *A Defence,* vol. 1, p. 296; Ford, *Pamphlets on the Constitution,* pp. 191–194, 201–202.

55. Farrand, *Records of the Federal Convention,* vol. 1, pp. 159–160; Elliot, *Debates in the Several State Conventions,* vol. 3, pp. 209–210.

56. Larsen, *Greek Federal States,* pp. 240–262; Hamilton, Jay, and Madison, *The Federalist,* Nos. 9 and 16, pp. 52–53, 95.

57. Hamilton, Jay, and Madison, *The Federalist,* No. 45, pp. 299–300.

58. Storing, *The Complete Antifederalist,* vol. 4, pp. 153; Elliot, *Debates in the Several State Conventions,* vol. 2, p. 224.

59. Storing, *The Complete Antifederalist,* vol. 2, p. 368; vol. 3, p. 32; vol. 5, p. 31.

60. Ford, *Pamphlets on the Constitution,* pp. 204–208; Elliot, *Debates in the Several State Conventions,* vol. 2, p. 352; Hamilton, Jay, and Madison, *The Federalist,* Nos. 9 and 10, pp. 41–42, 54–62.

61. Farrand, *Records of the Federal Convention,* vol. 1, p. 254; Hamilton, Jay, and Madison, *The Federalist,* number 70, pp. 456–457.

62. Ford, *Pamphlets on the Constitution,* pp. 35–36.

63. Ibid., pp. 37–38.

64. Hamilton, Jay, and Madison, *The Federalist,* Nos. 55 and 58, pp. 361, 381–382; Elliot, *Debates in the Several State Conventions,* vol. 2, pp. 253–254; Storing, *The Complete Antifederalist,* vol. 2, p. 284.

65. Farrand, *Records of the Federal Convention,* vol. 1, pp. 151–153.

66. Elliot, *Debates in the Several State Conventions,* vol. 2, p. 402; vol. 3, pp. 175–176.

67. Storing, *The Complete Antifederalist,* vol. 4, p. 213; Elliot, *Debates in the Several State Conventions,* vol. 2, p. 113; vol. 3, p. 568.

68. Elliot, *Debates in the Several State Conventions,* vol. 3, p. 595; Storing, *The Complete Antifederalist,* vol. 3, p. 19.

69. Gilbert Chinard, ed., *The Commonplace Book of Thomas Jefferson: A Repertory of His Ideas on Government* (Baltimore: Johns Hopkins Press, 1926), p. 27; Taylor, *Papers of John Adams,* "Governor Winthrop to Governor Bradford," February 9, 1767, vol. 1, p. 200; William Tudor to Adams, September 26, 1774, vol. 2, p. 175; Paul Lewis, *The Grand Incendiary: A Biography of Samuel Adams* (New York: Dial Press, 1973), p. 100; Richard M. Gummere, "John Dickinson, Classical Penman of the Revolution," *Classical Journal* 52 (November 1956):83; Bernard Bailyn, *The Ideological Origins of the American Revolution,* 2d ed. (Cam-

bridge, Mass.: Harvard University Press, 1967), pp. 99–100; Gordon S. Wood, *The Creation of the American Republic, 1776–1787* (Chapel Hill: University of North Carolina Press, 1969), p. 5.

70. For the statements of King and Washington see Wood, *Creation of the American Republic,* pp. 487, 494.

71. Bailyn, *Ideological Origins of the American Revolution,* pp. 150–153, 157.

72. Wood, *Creation of the American Republic,* p. 18.

V. Mixed Government and Classical Pastoralism

1. Thucydides, *History of the Peloponnesian War,* 3.82.

2. Jennifer Tolbert Roberts, *Reinventing Athens: History, Politics, and the Anti-Athenian Tradition* (Princeton: Princeton University Press, forthcoming, 1994).

3. For an excellent line-by-line analysis of Polybius' sixth book see F. W. Walbank, *A Historical Commentary on Polybius* (Oxford: Oxford University Press, 1957), vol. 1, pp. 635–746.

4. H. H. Scullard, *From the Gracchi to Nero: A History of Rome from 133 B.C. to A.D. 68* (London: Merithen, 1959), pp. 18–21, 27.

5. Paul K. Conkin, *Self-Evident Truths* (Bloomington: University of Indiana Press, 1974), p. 146; John Calvin, *Institutes of the Christian Religion,* trans. Henry Beveridge, 2 vols. (Grand Rapids: William B. Eerdman, 1970), vol. 2, pp. 656–657.

6. Niccolò Machiavelli, *The Discourses of Nicollò Machiavelli,* trans. Leslie J. Walker (New Haven: Yale University Press, 1950), vol. 1, pp. 212–215; vol. 2, pp. 7–12, 271–315; Francesco Guicciardini, *Maxims and Reflections of a Renaissance Statesman,* trans. Mario Domandi (New York: Harper and Row, 1965), p. 13.

7. Jean Bodin, *Method for the Easy Comprehension of History,* trans. Beatrice Reynolds (New York: W. W. Norton, 1945), pp. 179–187, 267, 282; Peter Laslett, ed., *Patriarcha and Other Political Works of Sir Robert Filmer* (Oxford: Basil Blackwell, 1949), pp. 85–87, 91, 93; Thomas Hobbes, *Leviathan, Parts I and II* (New York: Bobbs-Merrill, 1958), p. 175. For Hobbes's statement concerning Thucydides see Paul A. Rahe, *Republics, Ancient and Modern: Classical Republicanism and the American Revolution* (Chapel Hill: University of North Carolina Press, 1992), p. 367.

8. J. G. A. Pocock, ed., *The Political Works of James Harrington* (Cambridge: Cambridge University Press, 1977), pp. 459, 607; Conkin, *Self-Evident Truths,* p. 147; Algernon Sidney, *Discourses concerning Government* (1751; reprint, London: Gregg International Publishers, 1968), pp. 130, 139–140, 434.

9. Gordon S. Wood, *The Creation of the American Rebublic, 1776–1787* (Chapel Hill: University of North Carolina Press, 1969), pp. 201–202, 211.

10. Ibid., pp. 203, 208, 213–214, 232–233.

11. Ibid., pp. 201, 213, 215, 436; Douglas L. Wilson, ed., *Jefferson's Literary*

Commonplace Book (Princeton: Princeton University Press, 1989), p. 11. For reference to Jefferson's early support for Montesquieu see Joyce Appleby, *Liberalism and Republicanism in the Historical Imagination* (Cambridge, Mass.: Harvard University Press, 1992), p. 295. For Jefferson's complaints concerning the governor's lack of power see Bernard Bailyn, *The Ideological Origins of the American Revolution,* 2d ed. (Cambridge, Mass.: Harvard University Press, 1992), p. 293.

12. Robert J. Taylor, ed., *The Papers of John Adams,* "An Essay on Man's Lust for Power," August 29, 1763, vol. 1, p. 83; "Thoughts on Government," 1776, vol. 4, p. 88; L. H. Butterfield, ed., *The Diary and Autobiography of John Adams* (Cambridge, Mass.: Harvard University Press, 1961), Diary, Spring 1772, vol. 2, p. 58; Wood, *Creation of the American Republic,* p. 434; Charles Francis Adams, ed., *The Life and Works of John Adams* (Boston: Little, Brown, 1850–1856), Adams to Thomas Jefferson, October 28, 1787, vol. 8, p. 458; Adams to Benjamin Hichborn, January 27, 1787, vol. 9, p. 551; Adams to Philip Mazzei, June 12, 1787, ibid., p. 553; Adams to Richard Price, May 20, 1789, ibid., pp. 558–559; Adams to John Trumbull, January 23, 1791, ibid., pp. 572–573; Adams to Samuel Perley, June 19, 1809, ibid., pp. 623–624.

13. John Adams, *A Defence of the Constitutions of Government of the United States of America* (1787–88; reprint, New York: Da Capo Press, 1971), vol. 1, pp. xxi, 169–182, 209, 325. For another Adams statement regarding the debt of Machiavelli and Montesquieu to the ancients see Richard M. Gummere, "The Classical Politics of John Adams," *Boston Public Library Quarterly* 9 (October 1957):172.

14. Garry Wills, *Explaining America* (New York: Penguin Books, 1981), p. 100.

15. Adams, *A Defence,* vol. 1, pp. i–iii, xii–xiii.

16. Ibid., pp. iv–vii, 139–141, 183, 210.

17. Ibid., pp. xii, 104.

18. Ibid., pp. 101–102, 217–225, 335–338.

19. Ibid., pp. 212–215.

20. Ibid., pp. 253–258.

21. Ibid., pp. 145–146, 262–285.

22. Ibid., pp. 281, 285.

23. Ibid., pp. 363; vol. 3, pp. 505–506; Gilbert Chinard, *Honest John Adams* (Boston: Little, Brown, 1933), p. 209.

24. Max Farrand, ed., *The Records of the Federal Convention of 1787,* 3d ed. (New Haven: Yale University Press, 1966), vol. 1, pp. 422–423, 431; Robert A. Rutland et al., eds., *The Papers of James Madison* (Chicago: University of Chicago Press, 1962–1977; Charlottesville: University Press of Virginia, 1977–), "Report on Books," January 23, 1783, vol. 6, pp. 76–77.

25. Alexander Hamilton, John Jay, and James Madison, *The Federalist: A*

Commentary on the Constitution of the United States (New York: Random House, 1941), No. 63, pp. 410–411, 415; Rutland et al., *Papers of James Madison,* Additional Memoranda on Confederacies, November 30, 1787, vol. 10, p. 274; Wood, *Creation of the American Republic,* pp. 410, 473, 559.

26. Hamilton, Jay, and Madison, *The Federalist,* Nos. 10, 14, 39, 47, and 63, pp. 58–59, 80, 243–244, 313, 413.

27. Farrand, *Records of the Federal Convention,* vol. 1, pp. 299–300, 308, 424, 432; Wood, *Creation of the American Republic,* pp. 557–558.

28. Hamilton, Jay, and Madison, *The Federalist,* No. 9, pp. 48–49.

29. Farrand, *Records of the Federal Convention,* vol. 2, p. 299; Herbert W. Benario, "The Classics in Southern Higher Education," *Southern Humanities Review* 11 (1977):16; Wood, *Creation of the American Republic,* p. 554; Gordon S. Wood, *The Radicalism of the American Revolution* (New York: Alfred A. Knopf, 1992), p. 292; Paul Leicester Ford, ed., *Pamphlets on the Constitution of the United States: Published during Its Discussion by the People* (1888; reprint, New York: Burt Franklin, 1971), pp. 34, 43, 57–58, 65, 189–190.

30. Jonathan Elliot, ed., *Debates in the Several State Conventions on the Adoption of the Federal Constitution* (1888; reprint, New York: Burt Franklin, 1968), vol. 2, pp. 434, 474, 523–524; Robert Green McCloskey, ed., *The Works of James Wilson* (Cambridge, Mass.: Harvard University Press, 1967), "Of Government," vol. 1, p. 303.

31. Herbert J. Storing, ed., *The Complete Antifederalist* (Chicago: University of Chicago Press, 1981), vol. 2, pp. 138–139.

32. Farrand, *Records of the Federal Convention,* vol. 1, p. 402; Elliot, *Debates in the Several State Conventions,* vol. 3, p. 218; vol. 4, pp. 326–329.

33. Storing, *The Complete Antifederalist,* vol. 2, pp. 139, 269, 380; vol. 3, pp. 58, 89, 118; vol. 4, p. 152; vol. 6, p. 103. For Henry's statement see Elliot, *Debates in the Several State Conventions,* vol. 3, p. 46. For the statement by "A Columbian Patriot" see Ford, *Pamphlets on the Constitution,* p. 4.

34. Storing, *The Complete Antifederalist,* vol. 2, p. 238; vol. 5, p. 17; Bailyn, *Ideological Origins of the American Revolution,* p. 293; Farrand, *Records of the Federal Convention,* vol. 1, pp. 48–49; Kate M. Rowland, *The Life of George Mason* (New York: G. P. Putnam's Sons, 1892), vol. 2, p. 390.

35. Elliot, *Debates in the Several State Conventions,* vol. 3, p. 421; Storing, *The Complete Antifederalist,* vol. 5, pp. 89–90. For use of the same argument by "The Federal Farmer" and "Brutus" see vol. 2, pp. 273, 380.

36. Adams, *A Defence,* vol. 1, pp. vi, 99, 181–182, 322–324; vol. 3, p. 505.

37. Wood, *Creation of the American Republic,* pp. 60–63, 218–222, 491, 579, 607.

38. Paul A. Rahe, *Republics, Ancient and Modern: Classical Republicanism and the American Revolution* (Chapel Hill: University of North Carolina Press, 1992), p. 323.

39. Ibid., p. 63.

40. Wood, *Radicalism of the American Revolution,* pp. 90–91; Rahe, *Republics,* p. 603.

41. Adams, *Works of John Adams,* "Introduction to Discourses," vol. 1, p. 454; Zoltan Haraszti, *John Adams and the Prophets of Progress* (Cambridge, Mass.: Harvard University Press, 1952), pp. 55–60; Douglass Adair and John A. Schutz, eds., *Spur of Fame: Dialogues of John Adams and Benjamin Rush, 1805–1813* (San Marino, Calif.: Huntington Library, 1966), Adams to Rush, April 11, 1805, p. 27; December 27, 1810, p. 175.

42. Lester J. Cappon, ed., *The Adams-Jefferson Letters: The Complete Correspondence between Thomas Jefferson and Abigail and John Adams* (Chapel Hill: University of North Carolina Press, 1959), John Adams to Thomas Jefferson, August 14, 1813, vol. 2, p. 365; September 2, 1813, ibid., p. 372.

43. Adams, *A Defence of the U.S. Constitutions,* vol. 1, pp. 359–360; vol. 3, p. 328; Cappon, *Adams-Jefferson Letters,* John Adams to Jefferson, September 15, 1813, vol. 2, p. 377; July 16, 1814, ibid., p. 437.

44. John Taylor, *An Inquiry into the Principles and Policies of the Government of the United States* (New Haven: Yale University Press, 1950), pp. 41, 47, 50–51.

45. Ibid., pp. 56, 79.

46. Adams, *Works of John Adams,* Adams to Richard Cranch, January 15, 1787, vol. 1, p. 432; Adams to Philip Mazzei, June 12, 1787, vol. 9, p. 553; Adams to Samuel Perley, June 19, 1809, ibid., p. 622; Adams to John Taylor, April 15, 1814, vol. 6, pp. 482–483; Adams to Charles Holt, September 4, 1820, vol. 10, p. 391; Adrienne Koch and William Peden, eds., *The Selected Writings of John and John Quincy Adams* (New York: Alfred A. Knopf, 1946), John Adams to John Taylor, April 15, 1814, p. 172. Adams suspected early that the author of the *Arator* was also the author of the *Inquiry,* saying: "They must spring from the same brain as Minerva from the head of Jove; or rather, as Venus from the froth of the sea." See Cappon, *Adams-Jefferson Letters,* John Adams to Jefferson, November 12, 1813, vol. 2, p. 394.

47. Cappon, *Adams-Jefferson Letters,* John Adams to Jefferson, July 13, 1813, vol. 2, p. 356.

48. Taylor, *An Inquiry,* p. 48.

49. Adams, *Works of John Adams,* Autobiography, 1802, vol. 3, p. 23; Adams to Charles Holt, September 4, 1820, vol. 10, p. 392; Adams to John Taylor, April 15, 1814, vol. 6, pp. 471–474; Koch and Peden, *Selected Writings of John and John Quincy Adams,* John Adams to John Taylor, April 15, 1814, pp. 175–176. For more boasts see Adair and Schutz, *Spur of Fame,* John Adams to Benjamin Rush, March 23, 1809, p. 139.

50. Hamilton, Jay, and Madison, *The Federalist,* No. 10, pp. 58–59. Madison makes a similar argument in No. 51.

51. Rahe, *Republics,* p. 584; Douglass Adair, *Fame and the Founding Fathers*

(New York: W. W. Norton, 1974), pp. 75–106. Madison seems to have learned this political lesson from religious history as well. He was fond of quoting Voltaire's contention that while the existence of one sect in England would have led to slavery, and two sects to civil war, the existence of many sects had led to toleration and peace. See Irving Brant, *James Madison* (New York: Bobbs-Merrill, 1941–1961), vol. 1, p. 68.

52. Rutland et al., *Papers of James Madison,* Madison to Thomas Jefferson, June 6, 1787, vol. 10, pp. 29–30; May 12, 1791, vol. 14, pp. 22–23; "For the *American Daily Advertiser,*" October 20, 1792, ibid., p. 388. That Madison was still concerned with the problem of majority tyranny in the winter of 1791–92 is shown by the list of "Checks devised in Democracies marking self-distrust" which may be found in his notes for the *National Gazette* essays. Dominated by the Athenian experience, the list includes the Areopagus, ostracism, an age requirement of fifty for the first speakers in the assembly, and the requirement of a character examination before orators could engage in public life. See Notes for the *National Gazette,* December 19, 1791–March 3, 1792, vol. 14, p. 166.

53. Ibid., p. 162; "For the *National Gazette,*" December 19, 1791, ibid., p. 170; January 28, 1792, ibid., p. 201.

54. Ibid., "For the *National Gazette,*" January 23, 1792, p. 198.

55. Marvin Meyers, ed., *The Mind of the Founder: Sources of the Political Thought of James Madison* (New York: Bobbs-Merrill, 1973), p. 507.

56. Richard K. Matthews, *The Radical Politics of Thomas Jefferson: A Revisionist View* (Lawrence: University Press of Kansas, 1984), p. 77; Appleby, *Liberalism and Republicanism in the Historical Imagination,* p. 295; Albert Ellery Bergh and Andrew A. Lipscomb, eds., *The Writings of Thomas Jefferson* (Washington, D.C.: Thomas Jefferson Memorial Association, 1903), Jefferson to Isaac Tiffany, August 26, 1816, vol. 15, p. 66; Julian P. Boyd, ed., *The Papers of Thomas Jefferson* (Princeton: Princeton University Press, 1950–), Jefferson to John Adams, September 28, 1787, vol. 12, p. 189; Richard M. Gummere, *The American Colonial Mind and the Classical Tradition: Essays in Comparative Culture* (Cambridge, Mass.: Harvard University Press, 1963), p. 174. Of course, Madison had already been reading Polybius and was glad to share his conclusion that the fall of the Achaean League pointed to the need for a stronger federal government. See Boyd, *Papers of Thomas Jefferson,* James Madison to Jefferson, October 24, 1787, vol. 12, p. 274.

57. A. Whitney Griswold, "Jefferson's Agrarian Democracy," in Henry C. Dethloff, ed., *Thomas Jefferson and American Democracy* (Lexington, Mass.: D. C. Heath, 1971), p. 40; Dorothea Wender, ed. and trans., *Roman Poetry from the Republic to the Silver Age* (Carbondale: Southern Illinois University Press, 1980), pp. 59–60.

58. Rahe, *Republics,* p. 414.

59. Griswold, "Jefferson's Agrarian Democracy," pp. 40–42. For Harrington's

statement see Rahe, *Republics,* pp. 414. For a full discussion of classical economics, both in Europe and in America, see Paul K. Conkin, *Prophets of Prosperity: America's First Political Economists* (Bloomington: Indiana University Press, 1980).

60. Douglas L. Wilson, "The American Agricola: Jefferson's Agrarianism and the Classical Tradition," *South Atlantic Quarterly* 80 (Summer 1981):347–354; Karl Lehmann, *Thomas Jefferson: American Humanist* (Chicago: University of Chicago Press, 1964), p. 181; Gilbert Chinard, ed., *The Literary Bible of Thomas Jefferson: His Commonplace Book of Philosophers and Poets* (1928; reprint, New York: Greenwood Press, 1969), p. 32; Cappon, *Adams-Jefferson Letters,* Jefferson to John Adams, July 9, 1819, vol. 2, p. 483.

61. Matthews, *Radical Politics of Thomas Jefferson,* p. 43; Griswold, "Jefferson's Agrarian Democracy," pp. 46–47.

62. Bergh and Lipscomb, *Writings of Thomas Jefferson,* Jefferson to John Langdon, March 5, 1810, vol. 12, p. 375; Jefferson to William Duane, November 13, 1810, ibid., p. 433; Jefferson to Francis C. Gray, March 4, 1815, vol. 14, p. 271; Jefferson to John Wayles Eppes, September 11, 1813, vol. 13, p. 361; Jefferson to Albert Gallatin, October 16, 1815, vol. 14, p. 365; Griswold, "Jefferson's Agrarian Democracy," pp. 49–50.

63. M. E. Bradford, "That Other Republic: Romanitas in Southern Literature," *Southern Humanities Review* 11 (1977):7–8. For Taylor's use of the biblical theme see Griswold, "Jefferson's Agrarian Democracy," p. 58.

64. Matthews, *Radical Politics of Thomas Jefferson,* pp. 109–110; Wood, *Creation of the American Republic,* p. 503.

65. Wood, *Radicalism of the American Revolution,* pp. 210–212, 265.

66. Ibid., pp. 288, 291; Rahe, *Republics,* p. 252.

67. Adair and Schutz, *Spur of Fame,* John Adams to Benjamin Rush, September 9, 1806, pp. 66–67; Gummere, "The Classical Politics of John Adams," p. 179.

68. Harold C. Syrett, *The Papers of Alexander Hamilton* (New York: Columbia University Press, 1961–1979), "Philo Camillus No. II," August 7, 1795, vol. 19, p. 98. Hamilton's statement concerned American neutrality in the Anglo-French conflict.

VI. Philosophy

1. Maryanne Cline Horowitz, "The Stoic Synthesis of the Idea of Natural Law in Man: Four Themes," *Journal of the History of Ideas* 35 (January–March 1974):4, 7–9, 11–12.

2. Ibid., pp. 6, 9–10, 12–15.

3. Anton C. Pegis, ed. and trans., *Basic Writings of Saint Thomas Aquinas,* 2 vols. (New York: Random House, 1945), vol. 2, pp. 774–775, 778–779, 781.

4. John Dillenberger, ed., *Martin Luther: Selections from His Writings* (Garden City, N.Y.: Doubleday, 1961), pp. 400–402; John Calvin, *Institutes of the Chris-*

tian Religion, trans. Henry Beveridge, 2 vols. (Grand Rapids: William B. Eard-man, 1970), vol. 1, p. 233; Paul K. Conkin, *Self-Evident Truths* (Bloomington: University of Indiana Press, 1974), p. 85.

5. Conkin, *Self-Evident Truths,* p. 80.

6. Thomas Hobbes, *Leviathan, Parts I and II* (New York: Bobbs-Merrill, 1958), pp. 120, 131; Conkin, *Self-Evident Truths,* pp. 88–89.

7. Conkin, *Self-Evident Truths,* pp. 92, 95, 100. For Locke's statements con-cerning natural law see Paul A. Rahe, *Republics, Ancient and Modern: Classical Republicanism and the American Revolution* (Chapel Hill: University of North Car-olina Press, 1992), p. 509. For Montesquieu's statements see Charles Secondat de Montesquieu, *The Spirit of the Laws,* trans. Thomas Nugent (New York: Co-lonial Press, 1899), vol. 1, pp. 1, 3.

8. L. H. Butterfield, ed., *The Diary and Autobiography of John Adams* (Cam-bridge, Mass.: Harvard University Press, 1961), Diary, January 1759, vol. 1, p. 73; Richard M. Gummere, *The American Colonial Mind and the Classical Tra-dition: Essays in Comparative Culture* (Cambridge, Mass.: Harvard University Press, 1963), pp. 110, 115; Albert Ellery Bergh and Andrew A. Lipscomb, eds., *The Writings of Thomas Jefferson* (Washington, D.C.: Thomas Jefferson Memorial Association, 1903), Jefferson to Henry Lee, May 8, 1825, vol. 16, pp. 118–119. See Chapter VII concerning Rush and Paine.

9. Rahe, *Republics,* p. 564; Robert Green McCloskey, ed., *The Works of James Wilson* (Cambridge, Mass.: Harvard University Press, 1967), "The Law of Nature," vol. 1, pp. 128, 139.

10. Ibid., "The Law of Nature," vol. 1, pp. 132–133, 145–146; "The Law of Nations," ibid., pp. 164–165; "Man as Member of Society," ibid., p. 237.

11. Ibid., "Man as Member of Society," vol. 1, p. 245; "Of the Natural Rights of Individuals," vol. 2, p. 609n.

12. For Jefferson's conception of the "moral sense" see Julian P. Boyd, ed., *The Papers of Thomas Jefferson* (Princeton: Princeton University Press, 1950–), Jefferson to Peter Carr, August 10, 1787, vol. 12, p. 15; Lester J. Cappon, ed., *The Adams-Jefferson Letters: The Complete Correspondence between Thomas Jefferson and Abigail and John Adams* (Chapel Hill: University of North Carolina Press, 1959), Jefferson to John Adams, October 14, 1816, vol. 2, p. 492. For his praise of the Quakers see Jefferson to John Adams, August 22, 1813, ibid., p. 368; Bergh and Lipscomb, *Writings of Thomas Jefferson,* Jefferson to Benjamin Water-house, June 26, 1822, vol. 15, p. 385. On the teaching of ethics at the University of Virginia see Saul K. Padover, ed., *The Complete Jefferson: Containing His Major Writings, Published and Unpublished, except His Letters* (New York: Duell, Sloan, and Pearce, 1943), p. 1104. For Adams' letter on "the human Understanding" see Cappon, *Adams-Jefferson Letters,* John Adams to Jefferson, September 14, 1813, vol. 2, p. 374. For his praise of Cicero's ethical and metaphysical writings see Butterfield, *Diary and Autobiography of John Adams,* Diary, August 7, 1796, vol. 3, p. 239; August 13, 1796, ibid., p. 240.

13. Marie Kimball, *Jefferson: The Road to Glory, 1743–1776* (New York: Coward-McCann, 1943), p. 115.

14. Charles Page Smith, *James Wilson: Founding Father, 1742–1798* (Chapel Hill: University of North Carolina Press, 1956), pp. 330–333.

15. Henry Steele Commager, "The American Enlightenment and the Ancient World: A Study in Paradox," *Proceedings of the Massachusetts Historical Society* 83 (Winter 1971):8.

16. Gordon S. Wood, *The Creation of the American Republic, 1776–1787* (Chapel Hill: University of North Carolina Press, 1969), pp. 63–64.

17. Peter Stein, "The Attraction of the Civil Law in Post-Revolutionary America," *Virginia Law Review* 52 (1966):404–405, 407; Peter Shaw, *The Character of John Adams* (Chapel Hill: University of North Carolina Press, 1976), p. 31; Joseph Towne Wheeler, "Reading Interests of the Professional Classes in Colonial Maryland, 1700–1776," *Maryland Historical Magazine* 36 (September 1941):283.

18. Richard J. Hoffman, "Classics in the Courts of the United States, 1790–1800," *American Journal of Legal History* 22 (January 1978):57, 62, 68–69, 71–73.

19. Stein, "The Attraction of the Civil Law," pp. 408–411, 419–420.

20. Milton E. Flower, *John Dickinson: Conservative Revolutionary* (Charlottesville: University Press of Virginia, 1983), p. 271.

21. Silvio A. Bedini, *Thomas Jefferson: Statesman of Science* (New York: Macmillan, 1990), p. 45; Douglas L. Wilson, ed., *Jefferson's Literary Commonplace Book* (Princeton: Princeton University Press, 1989), pp. 17, 59, 61, 67–68, 71, 82, 84, 107; Richard Beale Davis, *Intellectual Life in Jefferson's Virginia, 1790–1830* (Chapel Hill: University of North Carolina Press, 1964), p. 118. The other books on Jefferson's reading table when he died were two French political pamphlets and Coray's edition of Aristotle's *Politics*.

22. Cappon, *Adams-Jefferson Letters,* John Adams to Jefferson, May 3, 1816, vol. 2, p. 471; Charles Francis Adams, ed., *The Life and Works of John Adams* (Boston: Little, Brown, 1850–1856), Adams to Samuel Miller, July 8, 1820, vol. 10, p. 390; Stephen Botein, "Cicero as a Role Model for Early American Lawyers: A Case Study in Classical 'Influence,'" *Classical Journal* 73 (Spring 1978):318–319; Henry C. Montgomery, "Washington the Stoic," *Classical Journal* 31 (March 1936):371–373.

23. Montgomery, "Washington the Stoic," pp. 371–372; James Thomas Flexner, *George Washington* (Boston: Little, Brown, 1965–1969), vol. 1, p. 241.

24. Wilson Smith, ed., *Theories of Education in Early America, 1655–1819* (New York: Bobbs-Merrill, 1973), "Charles Chauncy on Liberal Learning," 1655, p. 5; "An Essay on the Memory of My Venerable Master: Ezekiel Cheever, 1708," pp. 32–38. For reference to Cheever's seventy years of school attendance see Sheldon D. Cohen, *A History of Colonial Education, 1607–1776* (New York: John Wiley and Sons, 1974), p. 60. For Montesquieu's statement see Howard

Mumford Jones, *O Strange New World: American Culture, the Formative Years* (New York: Viking Press, 1952), p. 256. For Samuel Adams' statement see Gummere, *American Colonial Mind,* p. 115.

25. Forrest McDonald, *Novus Ordo Seclorum* (Lawrence: University Press of Kansas, 1985), p. 198; Boyd, *Papers of Thomas Jefferson,* Jefferson to Peter Carr, August 10, 1787, vol. 12, p. 16; Robert A. Rutland et al., eds., *The Papers of James Madison* (Chicago: University of Chicago Press, 1962–1977; Charlottesville: University Press of Virginia, 1977–), Commonplace Book, 1759–1772, vol. 1, p. 17; Shaw, *The Character of John Adams,* p. 35.

26. L. Jesse Lemisch, ed., *Benjamin Franklin: The Autobiography and Other Writings* (New York: Penguin Books, 1961), p. 95. For Adams' defense of Cicero see Chapter III.

27. Bergh and Lipscomb, *Writings of Thomas Jefferson,* Jefferson to Peter Carr, June 22, 1792, vol. 8, p. 384; Jefferson to Thomas Cooper, October 7, 1814, vol. 14, p. 200; Jefferson to Benjamin Rush, April 21, 1803, vol. 10, pp. 381–384; Jefferson to William Short, October 31, 1819, vol. 15, p. 220. For another statement that "moderns" (Christians) were further advanced than the ancients in ethics see Jefferson to John Brazier, August 24, 1819, ibid., p. 209.

28. John Stuart Mill, *Utilitarianism, Liberty, and Representative Government* (New York: Dutton, 1951), p. 7; Dickinson W. Adams, ed., *Jefferson's Extracts from the Gospels* (Princeton: Princeton University Press, 1983), Jefferson to Charles Thomson, January 9, 1816, p. 365; Bergh and Lipscomb, *Writings of Thomas Jefferson,* Jefferson to William Short, October 31, 1819, vol. 15, pp. 219, 223–224. For more statements of an Epicurean nature see Wilson, *Jefferson's Literary Commonplace Book,* pp. 75, 83–84, 146.

29. Wilson, *Jefferson's Literary Commonplace Book,* vol. 1, pp. 56–57; Bergh and Lipscomb, *Writings of Thomas Jefferson,* Jefferson to Maria Cosway, October 12, 1786, vol. 10, p. 448. Jefferson received the doctrines of Epicurus from Lucretius, Diogenes Laertius, and Pierre Gassendi. For reference to the presence of Lucretius' *De rerum natura* in Jefferson's library see Paul MacKendrick, "This Rich Source of Delight: The Classics and the Founding Fathers," *Classical Journal* 72 (Winter 1976):101. In an 1816 letter Jefferson praised the third-century Greek historian Diogenes Laertius, whose famous *History of Philosophy* included a discussion of the life and opinions of Epicurus. See Adams, *Jefferson's Extracts from the Gospels,* Jefferson to Francis Van der Kamp, April 25, 1816, p. 369. In the same year Jefferson also praised Gassendi's *Syntagma Epicuri Philosophiae,* a seventeenth-century volume advancing a Christian version of Epicureanism. See Bergh and Lipscomb, *Writings of Thomas Jefferson,* Jefferson to Charles Thomson, January 9, 1816, vol. 15, pp. 33.

30. Boyd, *Papers of Thomas Jefferson,* Jefferson to Robert Skipwith, August 3, 1771, vol. 1, p. 80; Jefferson to Peter Carr, August 19, 1785, vol. 8, p. 407; Bergh and Lipscomb, *Writings of Thomas Jefferson,* Jefferson to William Short,

October 31, 1819, vol. 15, pp. 219–220. For more of Jefferson's criticism of "the calumnies of Stoics and the caricatures of Cicero" see Adams, *Jefferson's Extracts from the Gospels,* Jefferson to Charles Thomson, January 9, 1816, p. 365.

31. Bergh and Lipscomb, *Writings of Thomas Jefferson,* Jefferson to Miles King, September 26, 1814, vol. 14, p. 197; Jefferson to John Adams, August 22, 1813, vol. 13, p. 349; Jefferson to Benjamin Waterhouse, June 26, 1822, vol. 15, p. 385; William Peden, ed., *Notes on the State of Virginia* (Chapel Hill: University of North Carolina Press, 1955), p. 159; Cappon, *Adams-Jefferson Letters,* Jefferson to John Adams, August 15, 1820, vol. 2, p. 569; April 8, 1816, ibid., p. 468; April 11, 1823, ibid., p. 592.

32. Bergh and Lipscomb, *Writings of Thomas Jefferson,* Jefferson to Joseph Priestley, April 9, 1803, vol. 10, p. 374; Jefferson to Benjamin Rush, April 21, 1803, ibid., p. 383; Jefferson to William Short, October 31, 1819, vol. 15, p. 220; Jefferson to John Brazier, August 24, 1819, ibid., p. 210; Jefferson to William Short, October 31, 1819, ibid., p. 220; Boyd, *Papers of Thomas Jefferson,* Jefferson to Robert Skipwith, August 3, 1771, vol. 1, p. 80; Cappon, *Adams-Jefferson Letters,* Jefferson to John Adams, July 5, 1814, vol. 2, p. 433.

33. Bergh and Lipscomb, *Writings of Thomas Jefferson,* Jefferson to Benjamin Waterhouse, June 26, 1822, vol. 15, p. 385; Jefferson to Benjamin Rush, April 21, 1803, vol. 10, p. 384; Jefferson to William Short, August 4, 1820, vol. 15, p. 257; Cappon, *Adams-Jefferson Letters,* Jefferson to John Adams, April 11, 1823, vol. 2, p. 594.

34. Cappon, *Adams-Jefferson Letters,* Jefferson to John Adams, July 5, 1814, vol. 2, pp. 432–433; Bergh and Lipscomb, *Writings of Thomas Jefferson,* Jefferson to William Canby, September 18, 1813, vol. 13, p. 378; Jefferson to Benjamin Rush, September 23, 1800, vol. 10, p. 175; Jefferson to Joseph Priestley, March 21, 1801, ibid., p. 228; Jefferson to Benjamin Waterhouse, June 26, 1822, vol. 15, p. 385. For other letters criticizing Plato and Platonists see Jefferson to Charles Thompson, January 9, 1816, vol. 14, pp. 385–386; Jefferson to William Short, October 31, 1819, vol. 15, pp. 219–220; August 4, 1820, ibid., p. 258. Though expressing admiration for the Pythagoreans, who had influenced both Plato and the Stoics, Adams joined Jefferson in condemning the mysticism of the Athenian philosopher. See Cappon, *Adams-Jefferson Letters,* John Adams to Jefferson, September 22, 1813, vol. 2, pp. 378–379; December 25, 1813, ibid., pp. 410–412; March 2, 1816, ibid., pp. 465–466; July 16, 1814, ibid., p. 437; John Adams, *A Defence of the Constitutions of Government of the United States of America* (1787–88; reprint, New York: Da Capo Press, 1971), vol. 1, pp. 198, 365; Adrienne Koch and William Peden, eds., *The Selected Writings of John and John Quincy Adams* (New York: Alfred A. Knopf, 1946), John Adams to Benjamin Waterhouse, February 26, 1817, p. 200.

35. Boyd, *Papers of Thomas Jefferson,* A Bill for the Establishment of Religious Freedom, 1779, vol. 2, p. 545; Cappon, *Adams-Jefferson Letters,* Jefferson to John

Adams, April 11, 1823, vol. 2, p. 591; Bergh and Lipscomb, *Writings of Thomas Jefferson,* Jefferson to Benjamin Waterhouse, June 26, 1822, vol. 15, pp. 384–385. In 1813 Adams penned a caricature of Calvin as unfair as Jefferson's. See Cappon, *Adams-Jefferson Letters,* John Adams to Jefferson, September 14, 1813, vol. 2, p. 374.

36. Cappon, *Adams-Jefferson Letters,* Jefferson to John Adams, August 15, 1820, vol. 2, pp. 568–569; October 12, 1813, ibid., p. 385; April 11, 1823, ibid., p. 594; Bergh and Lipscomb, *Writings of Thomas Jefferson,* Jefferson to Augustus B. Woodward, March 24, 1824, vol. 16, p. 18; Jefferson to Benjamin Rush, April 21, 1803, vol. 10, p. 380.

37. Cappon, *Adams-Jefferson Letters,* Jefferson to John Adams, October 12, 1813, vol. 2, p. 384; Bergh and Lipscomb, *Writings of Thomas Jefferson,* Jefferson to William Short, August 4, 1820, vol. 15, pp. 257–260; October 31, 1819, ibid., p. 220.

38. Boyd, *Papers of Thomas Jefferson,* Jefferson to Peter Carr, August 17, 1785, vol. 8, p. 407.

39. Ibid., Jefferson to Maria Cosway, October 12, 1786, vol. 10, pp. 449–451.

40. Ibid., p. 451; Zoltan Haraszti, *John Adams and the Prophets of Progress* (Cambridge, Mass.: Harvard University Press, 1952), p. 302; Lemisch, *Benjamin Franklin,* Franklin to Ezra Stiles, March 9, 1790, p. 337. Franklin added concerning disbelief in God: "I do not perceive that the Supreme takes it amiss, by distinguishing the Unbelievers in his Government of the World with any peculiar Marks of his Displeasure." See pp. 337–338.

41. Joyce Appleby, *Liberalism and Republicanism in the Historical Imagination* (Cambridge, Mass.: Harvard University Press, 1992), p. 337; Rahe, *Republics,* p. 336. Virgil's famous fourth Eclogue predicts the coming of a great millennium, a "new order of the ages," with the appearance, presumably, of the offspring of Marc Antony and Octavia, sister of Octavian (soon to be Augustus). While Augustine later associated this prediction with the birth of Christ, the designers of the Great Seal associated it with the birth of the United States.

VII. The Myth of Classical Decline

1. Meyer Reinhold, *Classica Americana: The Greek and Roman Heritage in the United States* (Detroit: Wayne State University Press, 1984), pp. 59–108, 125–136. Reinhold acknowledges that the traditionalists routed the educational reformers and that "from 1776 to 1830 American literature remained derivative and imitative, dependent on British and classical models." See pp. 135, 179. So, why was the early national period a "silver age," in contrast to the "golden age" of the Revolutionary and constitutional periods?

2. John Hardin Best, ed., *Benjamin Franklin on Education* (New York: Teachers College of Columbia University, 1962), "Silence Dogood No. 4," May 14, 1722, p. 36.

3. Ibid., "On the Need for an Academy," August 24, 1749, pp. 135n12, 138n13, 146.

4. Ibid., "Observations Relative to the Intentions of the Original Founders of the Philadelphia Academy," 1789, pp. 173–174; J. A. Leo Le May, ed., *The Writings of Benjamin Franklin* (New York: Library of America, 1987), Benjamin Franklin to David Hume, September 27, 1760, pp. 776–777; Thomas Woody, ed., *Educational Views of Benjamin Franklin* (New York: McGraw-Hill, 1931), Franklin to Richard Jackson, September 13, 1781, pp. 110–111; L. Jesse Lemisch, ed., *Benjamin Franklin: The Autobiography and Other Writings* (New York: Penguin Books, 1961), pp. 111–112.

5. Reinhold, *Classica Americana,* pp. 128–131; Dagobert Runes, ed., *The Selected Writings of Benjamin Rush* (New York: The Philosophical Library, 1947), "Plan for a Federal University," 1788, pp. 103–105.

6. Reinhold, *Classica Americana,* pp. 73–74; Nathan G. Goodman, *Benjamin Rush: Physician and Citizen, 1746–1813* (Philadelphia: University of Pennsylvania Press, 1934), pp. 316–317.

7. For Rush's analogy of the Spanish greatcoat see Daniel Boorstin, *The Lost World of Thomas Jefferson* (New York: Henry Holt, 1948), p. 220. For reference to the *American Museum* article and the Rittenhouse eulogy see Reinhold, *Classica Americana,* pp. 131–133. For all else see L. H. Butterfield, ed., *The Letters of Benjamin Rush* (Princeton: Princeton University Press, 1951), Rush to John Adams, June 15, 1789, vol. 1, p. 516; July 21, 1789, ibid., p. 525; February 12, 1790, ibid., pp. 531–532; Rush to James Muir, August 24, 1791, ibid., p. 604.

8. Butterfield, *Letters of Benjamin Rush,* Rush to Ashbell Green, May 22, 1807, vol. 2, p. 947; Rush to John Adams, October 2, 1810, ibid., p. 1067; George W. Corner, ed., *The Autobiography of Benjamin Rush: His "Travels through Life" Together with His Commonplace Book for 1789–1813* (Princeton: Princeton University Press, 1948), Commonplace Book, 1809, pp. 346–347.

9. Runes, *Selected Writings of Benjamin Rush,* "The Progress of Medicine," 1801, pp. 227–228; "Medicine among the Indians of North America," 1774, p. 277; Butterfield, *Letters of Benjamin Rush,* p. 884n4.

10. Moncure Daniel Conway, ed., *The Writings of Thomas Paine,* 4 vols. (New York: AMS Press, 1967), *The Age of Reason,* 1794, vol. 4, pp. 56–58.

11. Lemisch, *Benjamin Franklin,* pp. 22–23, 26, 30–31; Reinhold, *Classica Americana,* p. 252; Leonard W. Labaree, ed., *The Papers of Benjamin Franklin* (New Haven: Yale University Press, 1959–), "A Man of Sense," February 11, 1734, vol. 2, pp. 15–19.

12. Le May, *Writings of Benjamin Franklin,* Franklin to Madame Helvetius, December 7, 1778, p. 924; Lemisch, *Benjamin Franklin,* p. 111; Richard M. Gummere, *The American Colonial Mind and the Classical Tradition: Essays in Comparative Culture* (Cambridge, Mass.: Harvard University Press, 1963), p. 126; Labaree, *Papers of Benjamin Franklin,* "On Civil War," August 26, 1768, vol. 15,

pp. 191–193; "An Open Letter to Lord Buckinghamshire," March 9, 1774, vol. 21, p. 134; Franklin to James Bowdoin, February 25, 1775, ibid., p. 507; Franklin to Don Gabriel Antonio de Bourbon, December 12, 1775, vol. 22, p. 298; Best, *Benjamin Franklin on Education,* Franklin to Sarah Bache, January 26, 1784, p. 90.

13. Runes, *Selected Writings of Benjamin Rush,* p. vii; Corner, *Autobiography of Benjamin Rush,* Autobiography, 1800, pp. 31, 36, 42; Commonplace Book, 1792–1813, pp. 333–334. In his autobiography Rush spoke favorably of Samuel Davies, president of Princeton, and his "reputation for classical literature, philosophy, and oratory." Davies' "mode of teaching inspired me with a love of knowledge," Rush wrote. In particular, Davies encouraged Rush to keep a commonplace book of classical passages. See pp. 35–36. For reference to Staughton's eulogy see Reinhold, *Classica Americana,* p. 153. For Rush's praise of Hippocrates and his comparison of Miller with Tacitus see Butterfield, *Letters of Benjamin Rush,* Rush to Ebenezer Hazard, June 27, 1765, vol. 1, p. 17; Rush to Samuel Miller, April 13, 1813, vol. 2, p. 1193.

14. Runes, *Selected Writings of Benjamin Rush,* "Lectures on Animal Life II," 1799, p. 158; "On Manners," 1769, pp. 375, 378; Richard M. Gummere, *Seven Wise Men of Colonial America* (Cambridge, Mass.: Harvard University Press, 1967), p. 69; Butterfield, *Letters of Benjamin Rush,* Rush to Ebenezer Hazard, May 21, 1765, vol. 1, p. 14; Douglass Adair and John A. Schutz, eds. *The Spur of Fame: Dialogues of John Adams and Benjamin Rush, 1805–1813* (San Marino, Calif.: Huntington Library, 1966), Rush to Adams, October 16, 1809, p. 156.

15. Butterfield, *Letters of Benjamin Rush,* Benjamin Rush to Ebenezer Hazard, May 21, 1765, vol. 1, pp. 14–15; July 2, 1766, vol. 1, p. 24; Benjamin Rush to Unidentified Correspondent, December 29, 1766, vol. 1, pp. 31–32; Benjamin Rush to Bayard Smith, April 30, 1767, vol. 1, p. 42; Benjamin Rush to John Witherspoon, December 29, 1767, vol. 1, p. 48. For other quotes from Virgil and Lucretius in the 1760s see Benjamin Rush to Ebenezer Hazard, September 27, 1762, vol. 1, p. 6; April 21, 1768, vol. 1, p. 56; Benjamin Rush to John Morgan, January 20, 1768, vol. 1, p. 51.

16. Ibid., Rush to Walter Minto, April 30, 1792, vol. 1, p. 616; Rush to John Adams, April 5, 1808, vol. 2, p. 964; Rush to James Rush, August 17, 1809, ibid., p. 1016; Rush to John Adams, July 18, 1812, ibid., p. 1154; Rush to Thomas Jefferson, March 15, 1813, ibid., p. 1189. For the 1808 and 1812 quotations of Sallust, the 1809 quotation of Horace, and the 1813 quotation of Virgil regarding "deterioration" see Adair and Schutz, *Spur of Fame,* Benjamin Rush to John Adams, June 13, 1808, p. 109; September 6, 1809, p. 154; July 18, 1812, p. 233. For the quotation of Tacitus see Corner, *Autobiography of Benjamin Rush,* Commonplace Book, 1792–1813, p. 333.

17. William van der Wyde, ed., *The Life and Works of Thomas Paine* (New Rochelle, N.Y.: Thomas Paine National Historical Association, 1925–1927),

vol. 1, p. 4; Gummere, *Seven Wise Men*, pp. 91, 93; Conway, *Writings of Thomas Paine, The Age of Reason*, 1794, vol. 4, p. 92.

18. For Franklin's announcement and quotation of Ovid in the *Courant* see Gummere, *American Colonial Mind*, pp. 16, 127. For some of his opening Latin quotes see Best, *Benjamin Franklin on Education*, Silence Dogood No. 4, May 14, 1722, p. 34; "The Busy-Body No. 3," February 18, 1728, p. 56. For others, for his use of Theophilus and Philomath, and for his medal proposal see Le May, *Writings of Benjamin Franklin*, Silence Dogood Essays, 1722, pp. 10, 14, 17, 29, 39; "Upon the Talents Requisite in an Almanack-Writer," September 27, 1737, p. 274; "Letters from Theophilus Relating to the Divine Prescience," March 1741, p. 291; Franklin to Robert R. Livingston, March 4, 1782, p. 1042. For Franklin's use of Americanus, Benevolus, and Fabius see Labaree, *Papers of Benjamin Franklin*, "On Obstructions in the Thames," August 22, 1766, vol. 13, p. 383; "On the Propriety of Taxing America," April 9–11, 1767, vol. 14, p. 116; "An Open Letter to Lord Buckinghamshire," March 9, 1774, vol. 21, p. 134. For information on Franklin's medal see Winfried Schleiner, "The Infant Hercules: Franklin's Design for a Medal Commemorating American Liberty," *Eighteenth Century Studies* 10 (Winter 1976–77):235–244. On Franklin's proposal to have Paine painted in a toga see Henry Steele Commager, "The American Enlightenment and the Ancient World: A Study in Paradox," *Proceedings of the Massachusetts Historical Society* 83 (Winter 1971):10.

19. Runes, *Selected Writings of Benjamin Rush*, "On Manners," 1769, p. 376; Butterfield, *Letters of Benjamin Rush*, Rush to John Dunlap with a Speech Which Ought to Be Spoken to Congress on the Subject of Inflation, July 3, 1779, vol. 1, p. 229; "To the Editor of *The Pennsylvania Journal* on the United States Navy," July 4, 1782, ibid., p. 277.

20. Gummere, *Seven Wise Men*, p. 83; Van der Wyde, *Life and Works of Thomas Paine*, "Cupid and Hymen," 1775, vol. 2, pp. 49–54; "Reflections on Titles," May 1775, ibid., p. 67; Conway, *Writings of Thomas Paine*, "Useful and Entertaining Hints," February 1775, vol. 1, p. 25; "Dialogue," 1776, ibid., p. 161.

21. Le May, *Writings of Benjamin Franklin*, "Silence Dogood No. 8," July 9, 1722, p. 25; "On Lying Shopkeepers," November 19, 1730, pp. 159–160; *Poor Richard*, 1740, p. 1217; *Poor Richard*, 1741, p. 1219; Best, *Benjamin Franklin on Education*, "The Busy-Body No. 3," February 18, 1728, pp. 56–57; "On the Need for an Academy," 1749, pp. 126, 132n8; Labaree, *Papers of Benjamin Franklin, Poor Richard Improved*, 1749, vol. 3, p. 337.

22. Le May, *Writings of Benjamin Franklin*, "On the Education of Youth," 1751, p. 328; Labaree, *Papers of Benjamin Franklin*, "Appeal for the Hospital," August 8, 1751, vol. 4, p. 150; *Poor Richard Improved*, 1756, vol. 6, p. 330; "A Letter From Father Abraham to His Beloved Son," August 1758, vol. 8, p. 125; "The Interest of Britain Considered," 1760, vol. 9, pp. 92–93; "A Narrative of the Late Massacres in Lancaster County," 1764, vol. 11, pp. 57–58.

23. Labaree, *Papers of Benjamin Franklin,* Franklin to Jonathan Shipley, August 19, 1771, vol. 18, p. 210; Franklin to Peter P. Burdett, November 3, 1773, vol. 20, p. 459. See also Lemisch, *Benjamin Franklin,* pp. 95, 97.

24. Le May, *Writings of Benjamin Franklin, Silence Dogood* No. 8, July 9, 1722, pp. 25–26; "Reply to Coffee-House Orators," April 9, 1767, p. 590. See also Labaree, *Papers of Benjamin Franklin,* "Plain Truth," 1747, vol. 3, pp. 202–204; "Papers from the Election Campaign," 1764, vol. 11, pp. 372–373; "The Colonist's Advocate I," January 4, 1770, vol. 17, p. 8; "The Colonist's Advocate V," January 25, 1770, ibid., p. 34; Best, *Benjamin Franklin on Education,* To the Printer of the London Chronicle, August 17, 1768, p. 73; Forrest McDonald, *Novus Ordo Seclorum* (Lawrence: University Press of Kansas, 1985), p. 108. Franklin may have gotten the analogy between British measures and the Carthaginian corn law from Dickinson's *Letters from a Pennsylvania Farmer.* See Paul Leicester Ford, ed., *The Political Writings of John Dickinson, 1764–1774* (1895; reprint, New York: Da Capo Press, 1970), p. 321.

25. Labaree, *Papers of Benjamin Franklin,* Franklin to Joseph Galloway, February 25, 1775, vol. 21, p. 509. For the reference to the Hessians see Gummere, *American Colonial Mind,* p. 130.

26. Goodman, *Benjamin Rush,* p. 316; Reinhold, *Classica Americana,* pp. 131, 158; Butterfield, *Letters of Benjamin Rush,* Rush to John Adams, July 21, 1789, vol. 1, p. 525; Rush to Ashbel Green, May 22, 1807, vol. 2, pp. 946–947; Rush to Thomas Jefferson, January 2, 1811, ibid., p. 1075; Runes, *Selected Writings of Benjamin Rush,* "Lectures on Animal Life III," 1799, p. 179; Corner, *Autobiography of Benjamin Rush,* Commonplace Book, 1809, p. 345; Adair and Schutz, *Spur of Fame,* Benjamin Rush to John Adams, January 10, 1811, p. 176.

27. Butterfield, *Letters of Benjamin Rush,* "To His Fellow Countrymen: On Patriotism," October 20, 1773, vol. 1, p. 83; Runes, *Selected Writings of Benjamin Rush,* "Medicine among the Indians of North America," 1774, pp. 258–259, 285–289, 299–300. For Rush's praise of Hippocrates' method see Boorstin, *Lost World of Thomas Jefferson,* pp. 129–130.

28. Butterfield, *Letters of Benjamin Rush,* Rush to Mrs. Rush, June 1, 1776, vol. 1, pp. 101–102; July 23, 1776, ibid., p. 105; "To the Officers in the Army of the United American States," April 22, 1777, ibid., p. 145; Rush to William Duer, December 8, 1777, ibid., p. 173.

29. Ibid., Rush to John Adams, July 21, 1789, vol. 1, p. 523; April 13, 1790, ibid., p. 544; Runes, *Selected Writings of Benjamin Rush,* "Of the Mode of Education Proper in a Republic," 1798, pp. 87, 91; "On the Different Species of Mania," p. 214; Corner, *Autobiography of Benjamin Rush,* p. 108; Adair and Schutz, *Spur of Fame,* Benjamin Rush to John Adams, March 2, 1809, p. 133; February 12, 1812, p. 210.

30. Gummere, *Seven Wise Men,* p. 67; Butterfield, *Letters of Benjamin Rush,* Rush to John Adams, January 22, 1778, vol. 1, p. 191; Rush to John Dunlap with a Speech Which Ought to Be Spoken to Congress on the Subject of

Inflation, July 3, 1779, ibid., p. 235; Corner, *Autobiography of Benjamin Rush,* Commonplace Book, 1789–1791, p. 199.

31. Adair and Schutz, *Spur of Fame,* Benjamin Rush to John Adams, December 21, 1810, p. 172; Butterfield, *Letters of Benjamin Rush,* vol. 1, p. xviii.

32. Gummere, *Seven Wise Men,* p. 86; Van der Wyde, *Life and Works of Thomas Paine,* "The American Crisis," 1776, vol. 3, pp. 34–35; *The Age of Reason,* 1794, vol. 8, p. 163.

33. Gummere, *Seven Wise Men,* pp. 85–86, 94; Conway, *Writings of Thomas Paine,* "The Forester's Letters," April 3, 1776, vol. 1, p. 128; *The Rights of Man,* 1792, vol. 2, p. 424.

34. Conway, *Writings of Thomas Paine,* "New Anecdotes of Alexander the Great," 1775, vol. 1, pp. 26–28; *The American Crisis,* December 19, 1776, ibid., pp. 188, 248; Gummere, *Seven Wise Men,* p. 88; A. Owen Aldridge, "Thomas Paine and the Classics," *Eighteenth Century Studies* 1 (Summer 1968):376–377.

35. Best, *Benjamin Franklin on Education,* "On the Need for an Academy," August 24, 1749, pp. 136n12–138n13.

36. Conway, *Writings of Thomas Paine, The Age of Reason,* 1794, vol. 4, p. 56.

37. Runes, *Selected Writings of Benjamin Rush,* "Of the Mode of Education Proper in a Republic," 1798, p. 93; Butterfield, *Letters of Benjamin Rush,* Rush to John Adams, October 2, 1810, vol. 2, p. 1067.

38. Labaree, *Papers of Benjamin Franklin,* Franklin to William Brownrigg, November 7, 1773, vol. 20, pp. 464–466; Best, *Benjamin Franklin on Education,* "On the Need for an Academy," 1749, pp. 150–152.

39. Runes, *Selected Writings of Benjamin Rush,* "Observations on the Government of Pennsylvania," 1777, pp. 59, 66, 71; Butterfield, *Letters of Benjamin Rush,* Rush to David Ramsay, Spring 1788, vol. 1, p. 454; Adair and Schutz, *Spur of Fame,* Benjamin Rush to John Adams, September 8, 1810, p. 166.

40. Gummere, *Seven Wise Men,* pp. 74–75; Runes, *Selected Writings of Benjamin Rush,* "The Influence of Physical Causes upon the Moral Faculty," 1786, pp. 181–182.

41. Conway, *Writings of Thomas Paine,* "Answer to the Bishop of Llandaff," 1796–1800, vol. 4, pp. 284–285; "Examination of Prophecies," 1804, ibid., pp. 410–411.

42. Labaree, *Papers of Benjamin Franklin,* Preface to Cato's *Moral Distichs,* December 18, 1735, vol. 2, p. 130; Preface to Logan's *Cato Major,* 1744, ibid., pp. 404–405.

43. Best, *Benjamin Franklin on Education,* "On the Need for an Academy," August 24, 1749, pp. 139n13, 141, 143–146, 148n25.

44. Butterfield, *Letters of Benjamin Rush,* "A Plan for a Federal University," October 29, 1788, vol. 1, p. 493; Rush to John Adams, February 24, 1790, ibid., p. 535; October 2, 1810, vol. 2, p. 1067; Runes, *Selected Writings of Benjamin Rush,* "Of the Mode of Education Proper in a Republic," 1798, p. 94; Reinhold, *Classica Americana,* p. 35.

45. Conway, *Writings of Thomas Paine, The Age of Reason,* 1794, vol. 4, p. 56; Aldridge, "Thomas Paine and the Classics," pp. 372, 376.

46. Best, *Benjamin Franklin on Education,* "Idea of the English School," 1751, pp. 168, 170; "Observations Relative to the Intentions of the Original Founders of the Academy of Philadelphia," 1789, p. 172; Woody, *Educational Views of Benjamin Franklin,* "Observations on the Founders of the Philadelphia Academy," 1789, pp. 204–222; Reinhold, *Classica Americana,* p. 60.

47. Butterfield, *Letters of Benjamin Rush,* Rush to John Adams, June 2, 1789, vol. 1, p. 518n1; Adair and Schutz, *Spur of Fame,* John Adams to Benjamin Rush, September 6, 1810; p. 168; October 15, 1810, p. 171; Lester J. Cappon, ed., *The Adams-Jefferson Letters: The Complete Correspondence between Thomas Jefferson and Abigail and John Adams* (Chapel Hill: University of North Carolina Press, 1959), John Adams to Jefferson, July 16, 1814, vol. 2, p. 438; Albert Ellery Bergh and Andrew A. Lipscomb, eds., *The Writings of Thomas Jefferson* (Washington, D.C.: Thomas Jefferson Memorial Association, 1903), Jefferson to Unidentified Correspondent, 1825, vol. 16, p. 124. Jefferson had made precisely the same argument in 1785 and 1786. See Julian P. Boyd, ed., *The Papers of Thomas Jefferson* (Princeton: Princeton University Press, 1950–), Jefferson to Peter Carr, August 19, 1785, vol. 8, pp. 407–408; Jefferson to Thomas Mann Randolph, August 27, 1786, vol. 10, pp. 305–309. For Quincy's statement see Linda K. Kerber, *Federalists in Dissent: Imagery and Ideology in Jeffersonian America* (Ithaca: Cornell University Press, 1970), p. 105.

48. Reinhold, *Classica Americana,* p. 131; Butterfield, *Letters of Benjamin Rush,* Rush to James Muir, August 24, 1791, vol. 1, pp. 605–606; Rush to Richard Rush, May 17, 1792, ibid., p. 619; Adair and Schutz, *Spur of Fame,* Benjamin Rush to John Adams, February 4, 1811, p. 178; Adams to Rush, February 13, 1811, pp. 178–179.

49. Jean S. Straub, "Teaching in the Friends' Latin School of Philadelphia in the Eighteenth Century," *Pennsylvania Magazine of History and Biography* 91 (October 1967): 453; Mark Morford, "Early American School Editions of Ovid," *Classical Journal* 78 (Winter 1982–3):152–153.

50. Reinhold, *Classica Americana,* pp. 122–124, 135; Frederick Rudolph, ed., *Essays on Education in the Early Republic* (Cambridge, Mass.: Harvard University Press, 1965), "On the Education of Youth in America, 1790," pp. 45–48, 59n–60n, 67, 74; Philip Marson, *Breeder of Democracy* (Cambridge, Mass.: Schlenkman, 1970), p. 13. Even William and Mary, which did not require courses in Greek and Latin after 1792, required competence in the languages for graduation. The assumption was that anyone entering college already had a thorough knowledge of Greek and Latin. The exit test merely ensured that students retained their knowledge. See Richard Beale Davis, *Intellectual Life in Jefferson's Virginia, 1790–1830* (Chapel Hill: University of North Carolina Press, 1964), p. 52.

51. William Peden, ed., *Notes on the State of Virginia* (Chapel Hill: University

of North Carolina Press, 1955), pp. 128–129; Cappon, *Adams-Jefferson Letters,* Jefferson to John Adams, December 10, 1819, vol. 2, pp. 549–550; January 22, 1821, ibid., p. 569. In 1781 British troops had forced the House of Burgesses to flee and had nearly captured Jefferson, then governor of Virginia. Patrick Henry was so unhappy with the situation that he led the movement, which narrowly failed, for a temporary wartime dictatorship.

52. Harold C. Syrett, ed., *The Papers of Alexander Hamilton* (New York: Columbia University Press, 1961–1979), "Continentalist," July 4, 1782, vol. 3, p. 103; "New York Assembly: Remarks on an Act Acknowledging the Independence of Vermont," March 28, 1787, vol. 4, p. 140; "Defense No. XX," October 23–24, 1795, vol. 19, pp. 335–336; "Opinion on the Constitutionality of an Act to Establish a Bank," February 23, 1791, vol. 8, pp. 76, 101.

53. Jonathan Elliot, ed., *Debates in the Several State Conventions on the Adoption of the Federal Constitution* (1888; reprint, New York: Burt Franklin, 1968), vol. 2, pp. 68–69, 422; Max Farrand, ed., *The Records of the Federal Convention of 1787,* 3d ed. (New Haven: Yale University Press, 1966), vol. 1, pp. 143, 343.

54. Stephen Botein, "Cicero as a Role Model for Early American Lawyers: A Case Study in Classical 'Influence,'" *Classical Journal* 73 (Spring 1978):317; Robert Green McCloskey, ed., *The Works of James Wilson* (Cambridge, Mass.: Harvard University Press, 1967), Miscellaneous Papers, Oration Delivered on the Fourth of July, 1788, vol. 2, pp. 773–774; "On the Study of Law," 1790, vol. 1, pp. 69–71; Aldridge, "Thomas Paine and the Classics," p. 376.

55. Edwin A. Miles, "The Young American Nation and the Classical World," *Journal of the History of Ideas* 35 (April–June 1974):263.

56. Charles Francis Adams, ed., The *Life and Works of John Adams,* 10 vols. (Boston: Little, Brown, 1850–1856), "Discourses on Davila," 1790, vol. 6, pp. 478–479; Adams to Thomas McKean, July 30, 1815, vol. 10, pp. 171–172; Cappon, *Adams-Jefferson Letters,* John Adams to Jefferson, July 9, 1813, vol. 2, p. 351; October 4, 1813, ibid., p. 382; December 25, 1813, ibid., pp. 411–412; July 16, 1814, ibid., p. 438; Jefferson to John Adams, May 5, 1817, ibid., p. 513; Butterfield, *Letters of Benjamin Rush,* Rush to John Adams, February 24, 1790, vol. 1, p. 534; John Taylor, *An Inquiry into the Principles and Policies of the Government of the United States* (New Haven: Yale University Press, 1950), pp. 354, 356–357.

57. Bergh and Lipscomb, *Writings of Thomas Jefferson,* Jefferson to Isaac Tiffany, August 26, 1816, vol. 15, pp. 65–66; Jefferson to Du Pont de Nemours, April 24, 1816, vol. 14, p. 448; Jefferson to A. Coray, October 31, 1823, vol. 15, pp. 481–482; Cappon, *Adams-Jefferson Letters,* Jefferson to Abigail Adams, September 25, 1785, vol. 1, pp. 69–70; Jefferson to John Adams, October 28, 1813, vol. 2, pp. 388–389.

58. McCloskey, *Works of James Wilson,* "On Law and Obligation," vol. 1, p. 107; "Of the Nature of Crimes and the Necessity and Proportion of Punish-

ments," vol. 2, p. 631; L. H. Butterfield, ed., *The Adams Family Correspondence* (Cambridge, Mass.: Harvard University Press, 1963–1973), John Adams to John Quincy Adams, February 12, 1781, vol. 4, p. 80; Robert J. Taylor, ed., *The Papers of John Adams* (Cambridge, Mass.: Harvard University Press, 1977–), "A Dissertation on the Canon and the Feudal Law," October 21, 1765, vol. 1, p. 126; Peden, *Notes on the State of Virginia,* p. 148.

Conclusion

1. Robert J. Taylor, ed., *The Papers of John Adams* (Cambridge, Mass.: Harvard University Press, 1977–), "Letters of Novanglus," January 23, 1775, vol. 2, p. 230.

2. Max Farrand, ed., *The Records of the Federal Convention of 1787,* 3d ed. (New Haven: Yale University Press, 1966), vol. 1, pp. 451–452; Jonathan Elliot, ed., *Debates in the Several State Conventions on the Adoption of the Federal Constitution* (1888; reprint, New York: Burt Franklin, 1969), vol. 2, p. 69; vol. 4, p. 192. Franklin declared: "We indeed seem to feel our want of political wisdom, since we have been running about in search of it. We have gone back to the ancient history for models of Government, and examined the different forms of these Republics which, having been formed with the seeds of their own dissolution, now no longer exist." But, Franklin continued, "We have not hitherto once thought of humbly applying to the Father of lights to illuminate our understanding." He then proposed a daily prayer at the convention.

3. Herbert J. Storing, ed., *The Complete Antifederalist* (Chicago: University of Chicago Press, 1981), vol. 4, p. 159; Alexander Hamilton, John Jay, and James Madison, *The Federalist: A Commentary on the Constitution of the United States* (New York: Random House, 1941), No. 9, p. 50. For the Antifederalist arguments regarding the size of republics see Chapter IV.

4. Gordon S. Wood, *The Creation of the American Republic* (Chapel Hill: University of North Carolina Press, 1969), pp. 513, 558–560, 562–563, 569, 606; Wood, *Radicalism of the American Revolution* (New York: Alfred A. Knopf, 1992), p. 230.

5. Wood, *Radicalism of the American Revolution,* pp. 581–582. But Wood demonstrates that Adams was, indeed, out of the mainstream on the question of popular sovereignty.

6. Howard Mumford Jones, *Revolution and Romanticism* (Cambridge, Mass.: Harvard University Press, 1974), pp. 127–128, 342–344.

7. For reference to the hope that war would increase American virtue and to the founders' disgruntlement late in life see Wood, *Radicalism of the American Revolution,* pp. 248, 327, 365–369.

8. Joyce O. Appleby, *Capitalism and a New Social Order: The Republican Vision of the 1790s* (New York: New York University Press, 1984), p. 46; Appleby, "Commercial Farming and the 'Agrarian Myth' in the Early Republic," *Journal*

of American History 68 (March 1982):833–849; Richard K. Matthews, *The Radical Politics of Thomas Jefferson* (Lawrence: University Press of Kansas, 1984), p. 47. For a full discussion of economics in the period see Paul K. Conkin, *Prophets of Prosperity* (Bloomington: Indiana University Press, 1980).

9. John T. Agresto, "Liberty, Virtue, and Republicanism, 1776–1787," *Review of Politics* 39 (October 1977):504.

10. Paul A. Rahe, *Republics, Ancient and Modern: Classical Republicanism and the American Revolution* (Chapel Hill: University of North Carolina Press, 1992), p. 29; Wood, *Radicalism of the American Revolution,* pp. 365, 369.

11. Edwin A. Miles, "The Young American Nation and the Classical World," *Journal of the History of Ideas* 35 (April–June 1974):270.

12. For Madison's failure to mention the Greek confederacies when attacking nullification in the 1830s see Marvin Meyers, ed., *The Mind of the Founder: Sources of the Political Thought of James Madison* (New York: Bobbs-Merrill, 1973), pp. 533–534, 548–549. Having read Madison's 1830 article in the *North American Review,* John Marshall exulted: "Madison is himself again." See p. 532. On *nomoi patrioi* and *mos maiorum* see Rahe, *Republics,* p. 604.

13. Thomas Dew, *Review of the Debate in the Virginia Legislature of 1831 and 1832* (Richmond, 1832); George Fitzhugh, *Sociology for the South* (New York: Burt Franklin, 1965); idem, *Cannibals All!* (Richmond: A. Morris, 1857); Neal Gillespie, *The Collapse of Orthodoxy: The Intellectual Ordeal of George Frederick Holmes* (Charlottesville: University Press of Virginia, 1972); J. Drew Harrington, "Classical Antiquity and the Proslavery Argument," *Slavery and Abolition* 10 (May 1989):60–72.

14. Henry Steele Commager, "Leadership in Eighteenth-Century America and Today," *Daedalus* 90 (1961):653–656.

15. Herbert W. Benario, "The Classics in Southern Higher Education," *Southern Humanities Review* 11 (1977):16; M. E. Bradford, "'A Better Guide than Reason': The Politics of John Dickinson," *Modern Age* 21 (Winter 1977):47; Douglass Adair, *Fame and the Founding Fathers* (New York: W. W. Norton, 1974), p. 110; Howard Mumford Jones, *O Strange New World: American Culture, the Formative Years* (New York: Viking Press, 1952), pp. 339–340.

16. Edward M. Burns, "The Philosophy of History of the Founding Fathers," *The Historian* 16 (Spring 1954):142; David M. Kennedy, "Bells, Whistles, and Basics in American History Textbooks," *Organization of American Historians' Newsletter* 18 (May 1990):11. McDonald made the statement on March 24, 1990, at the Organization of American Historians Convention in Washington, D.C. He was one of the commentators for the session "The Founders and the Classics."

Index